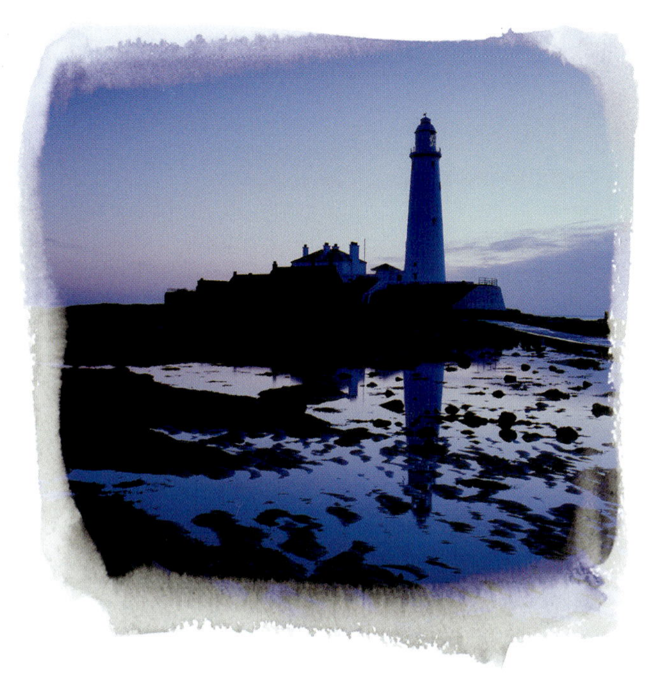

Photographing
WATER
IN THE LANDSCAPE

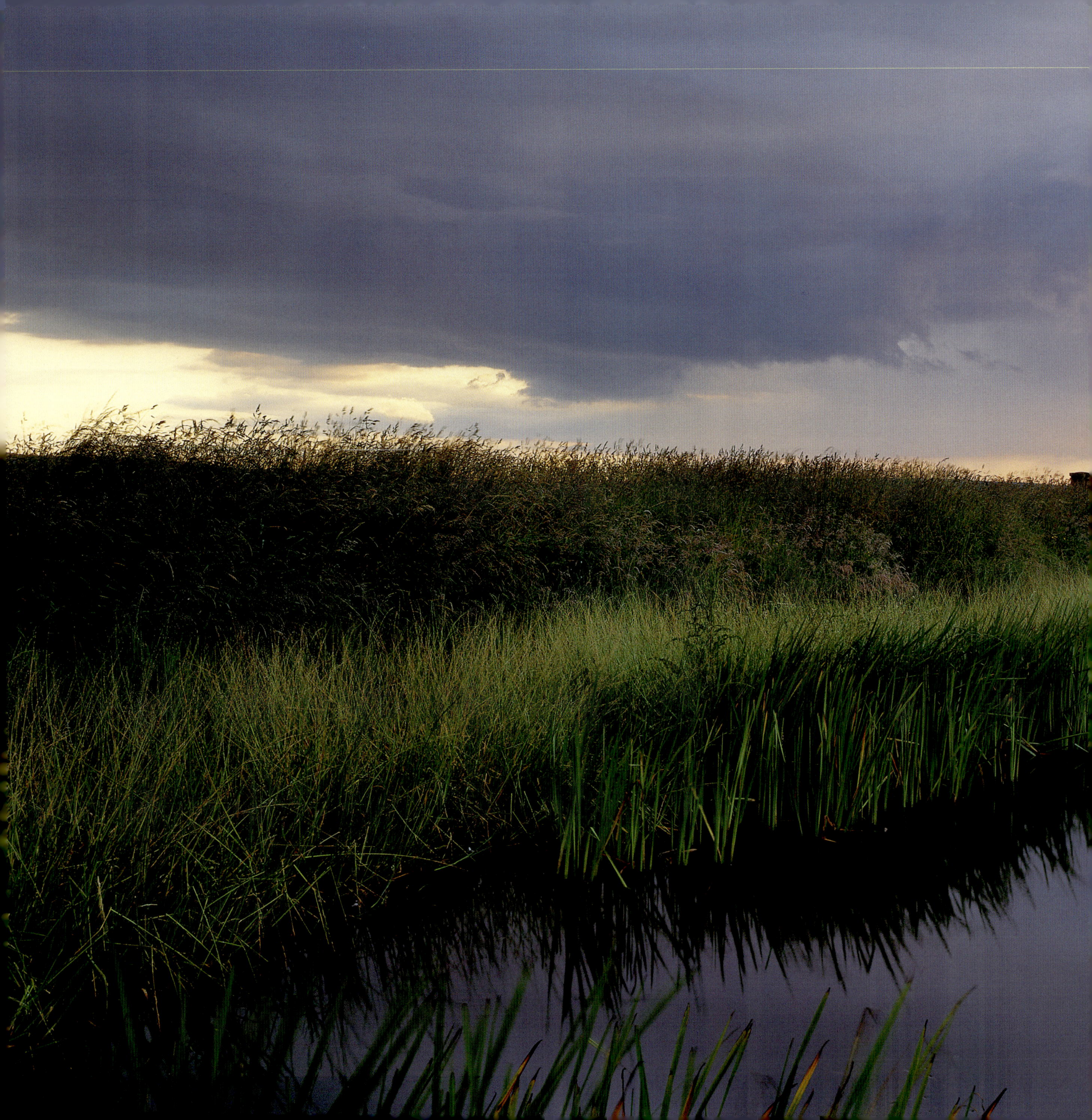

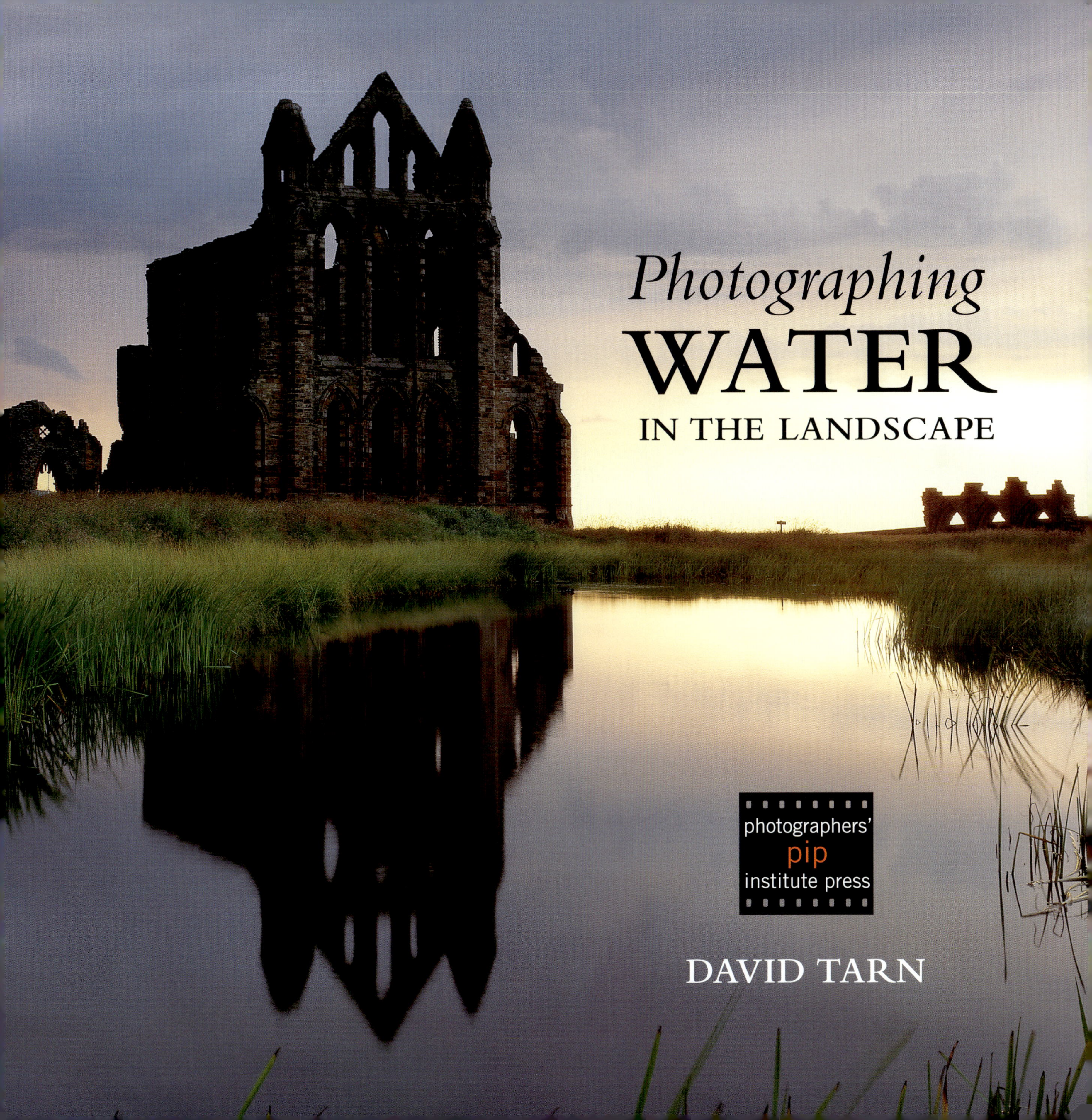

Photographing
WATER
IN THE LANDSCAPE

photographers'
pip
institute press

DAVID TARN

First published 2004 by

Photographers' Institute Press / PIP

an imprint of GMC Publications Ltd.
Castle Place, 166 High Street, Lewes, East Sussex BN7 1XU

ISBN 1 86108 396 3

Publisher: Paul Richardson
Art Director: Ian Smith
Production Manager: Stuart Poole
Managing Editor: Gerrie Purcell
Commissioning Editor: April McCroskie
Project Editor: Dominique Page
Photography Books Editor: James Beattie
Art Editor: Gilda Pacitti

Set in Bembo and News Gothic
Colour origination by Icon Reproduction
Printed and bound by Kyodo Printing Co. Ltd. Singapore

To the memory of
Jim McCourt, because
nobody ever forgets a
good teacher, also my
wife Christine and
our children Dominic
and Sara with
gratitude and pride.

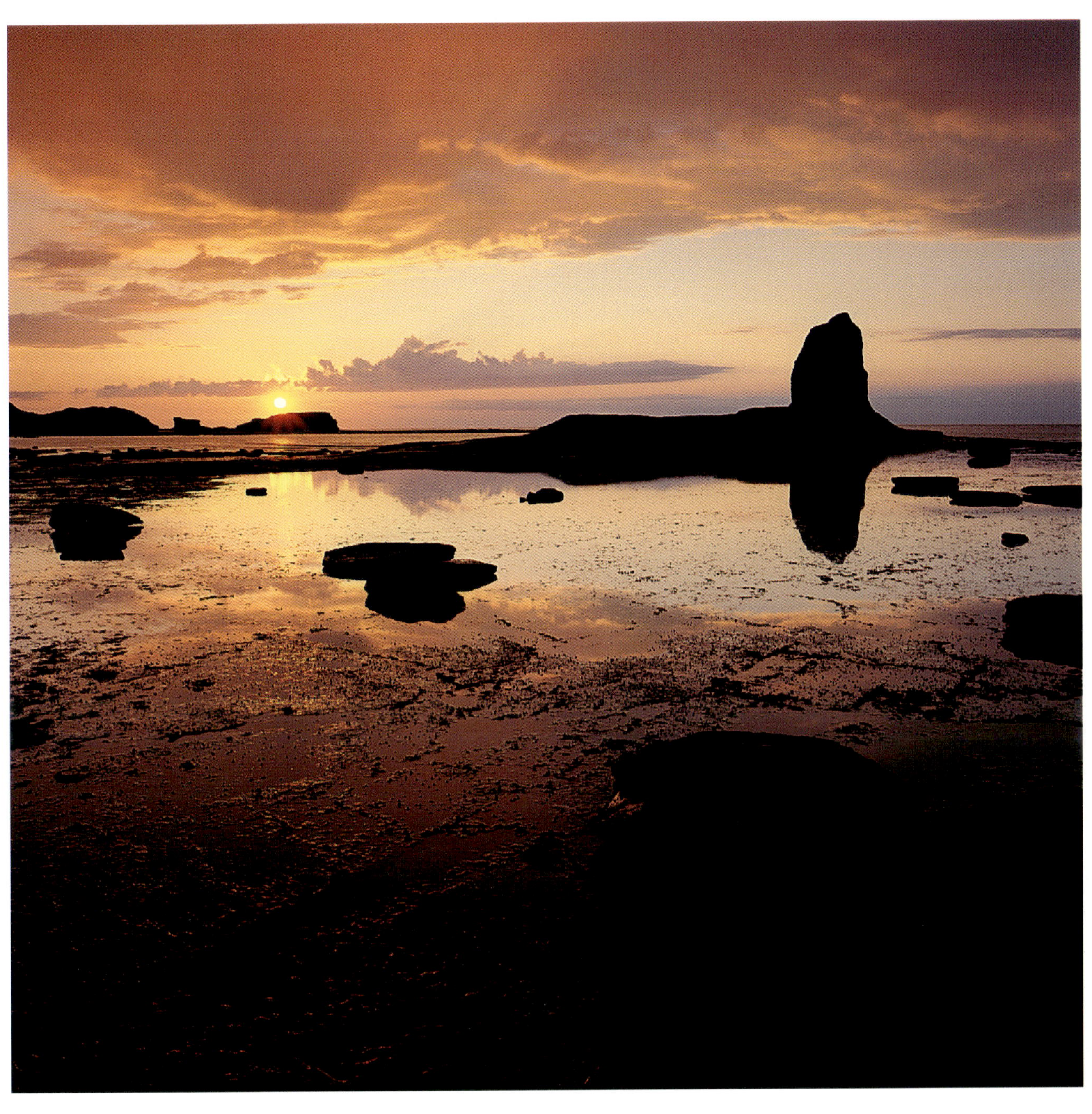

How absurd to call this planet earth when it is so clearly ocean.

ARTHUR C. CLARK

Contents

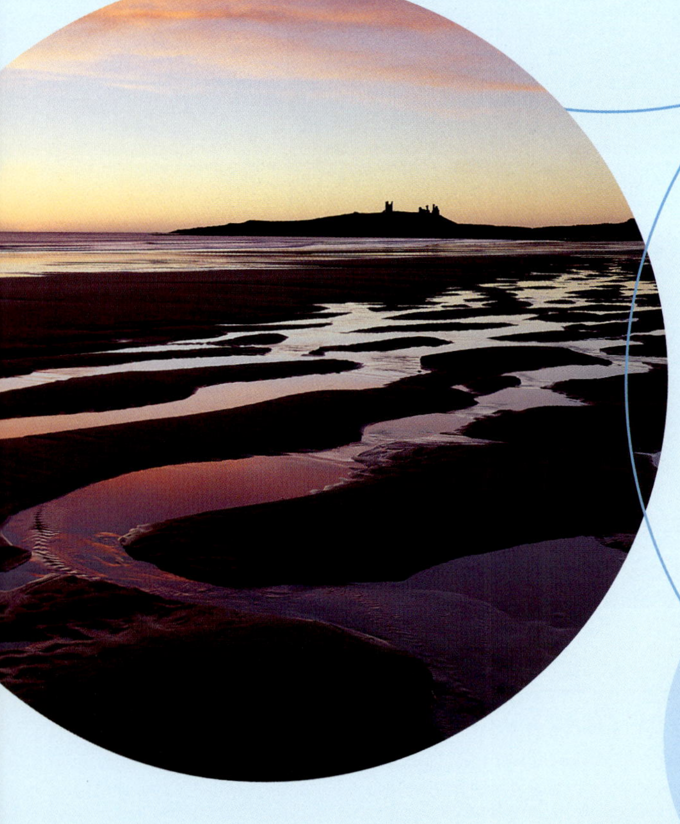

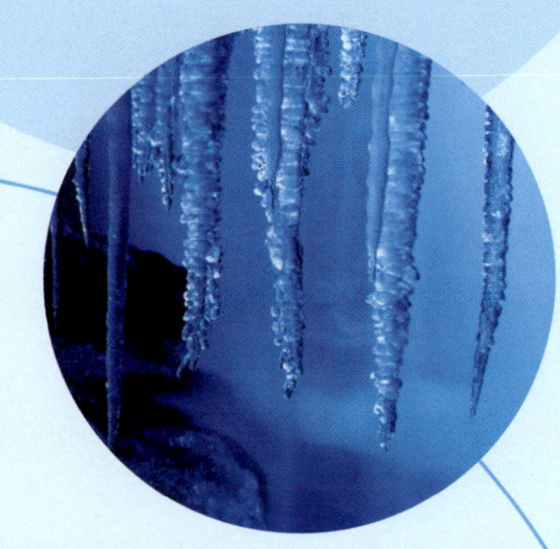

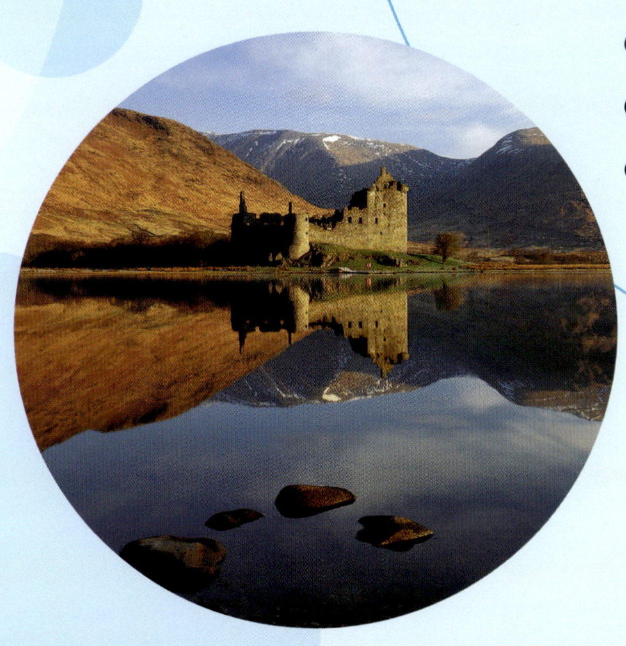

Introduction

*I*n landscape photography, as in many artistic endeavours, a subtle change can mean the difference between success and failure. A slight variation in light can lift a scene from the mundane to the extraordinary, and back again. Altering the angle of view just a fraction can dramatically improve the whole balance of a scene. Using a filter can add extra punch to the sky and make a world of difference to the final image. By contrast, just one stray element within the frame can spoil what would otherwise have been a great photograph: a distant parked car, someone out walking in a brightly coloured coat, an aeroplane trail in the sky, even a blade of tall grass.

In my opinion, water is one of those subtle elements that can really make a photograph. And this is perhaps the best indication of just how powerful a subject water can be for the landscape photographer: the realization of how very little water it takes to transform a scene into something worth photographing. A thin film of water left on a beach or foreshore rocks by the retreating tide can act like a giant reflector. Any colours in the morning or evening sky can be mirrored perfectly in just a millimetre of water on the land. The dewdrops on a spider's web or on the morning grass, the sparkle of sunshine from the surface of a distant lake.

Even in photographs where water may appear to be totally absent, its influence can often be clearly seen. The patterns left in sand by the tide are an obvious example, but every cloud in the sky is just water vapour and the green of summer grass would be brown without water. Since water is such an integral part of life on earth it is in fact impossible to take any landscape photograph that has not been affected by it in some way.

Urban landscapes are often best photographed in the crossover light of evening while there is still light in the sky and the streetlights are coming on. The whole effect can be enhanced greatly by a drop of rain to make the pavements and roads wet. The water reflects all the colours present in the scene, which doubles their impact.

Part of the beauty of these scenes is the fact that they may be short-lived: the wet beach dries in a short time; the rainwater on the pavements drains away to nothing; the dew on the grass evaporates; snow and ice melt, and then an exceptional scene becomes ordinary again.

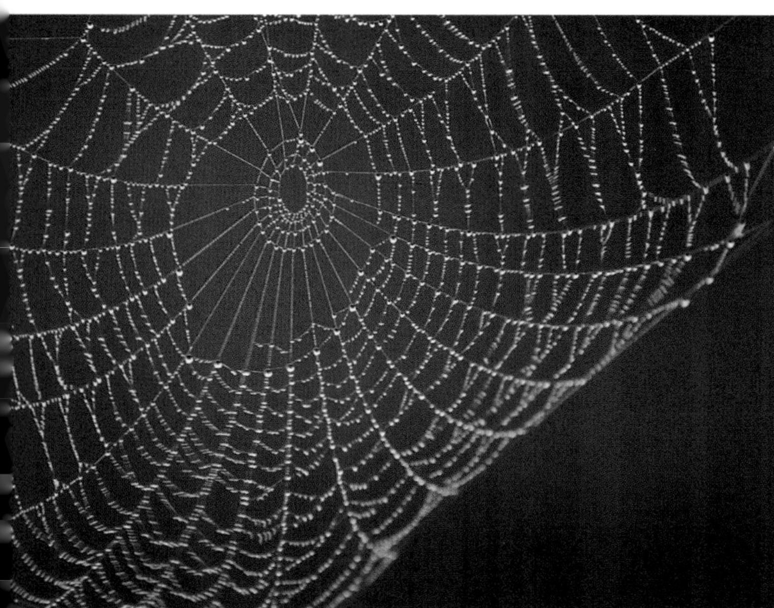

Cobweb and Dew
Without the drops of dew on this spider's web would we even see the web? Of course we would, if we looked really carefully, but it wouldn't make as good a photograph. This spider's web might well be a thing of beauty in its own right, but it is still the small droplets of water that draw our attention to it. The jewels of water that are suspended there make this a pleasing image.

Nikon FM2 with 500mm f/8 mirror lens, 1/60sec at f/8

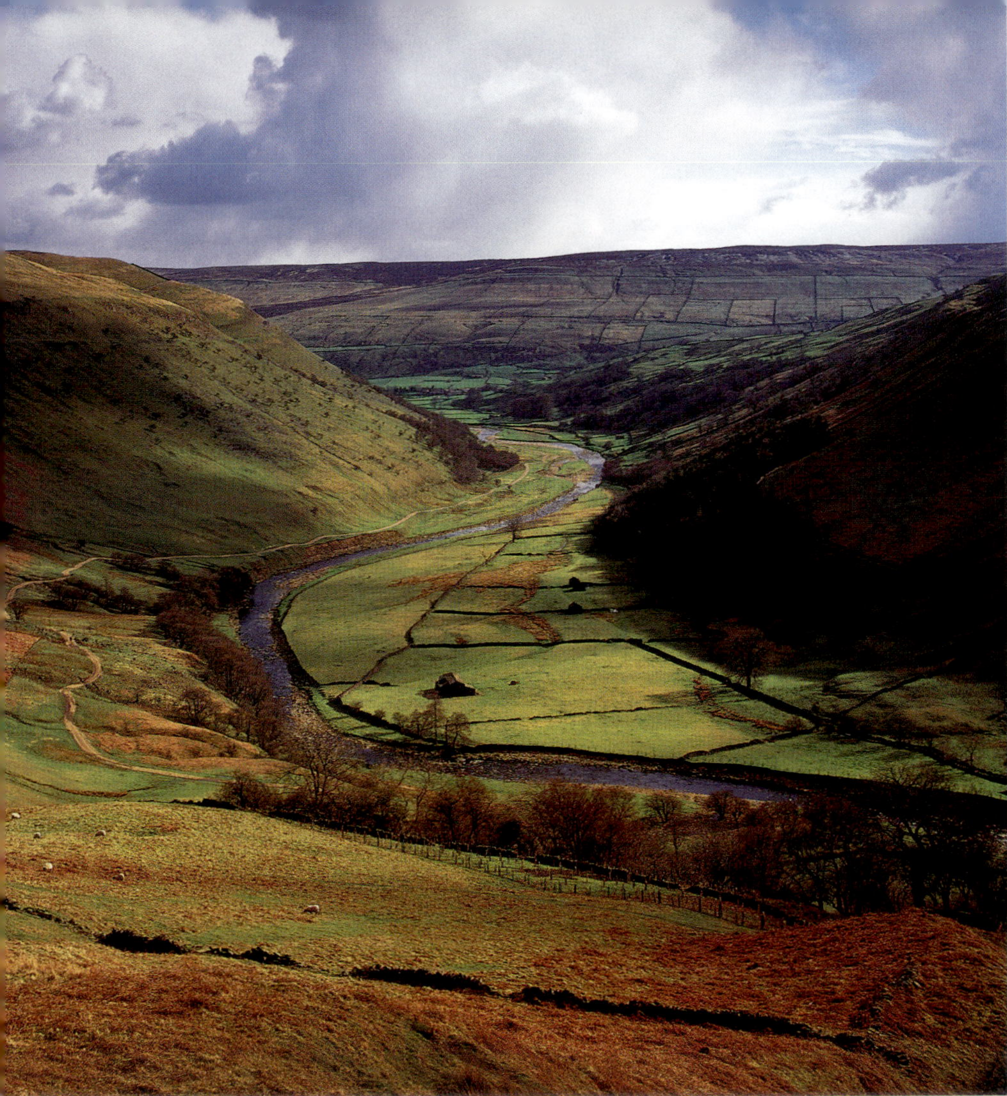

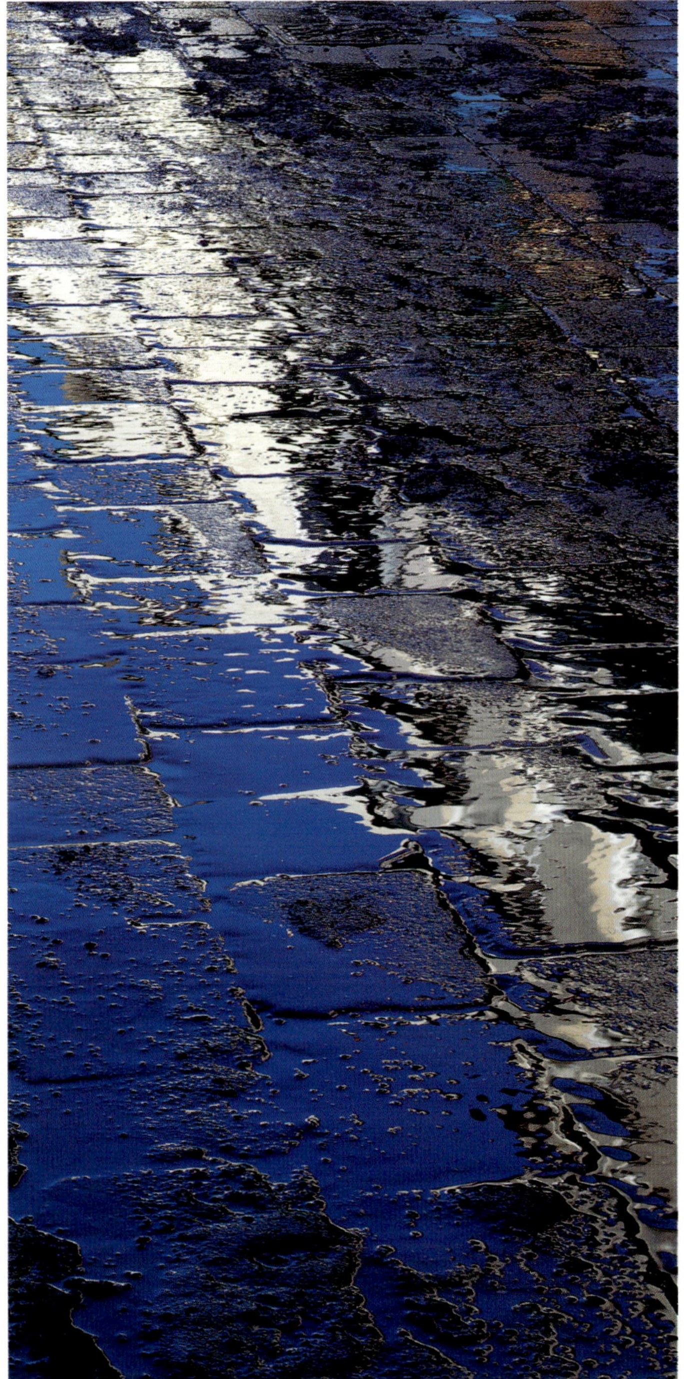

above **Swaledale, Yorkshire**

This is a traditional landscape scene taken in good, strong, late afternoon light on the edge of a weather front. By the time I was zipping shut my camera bag the scene was invisible behind a wall of rain and cloud. The river running through the valley is central to the composition; it may take up just a tiny fraction of the picture space, but it is essential just the same.

Mamiya 645sv with 55–110mm lens, 1/15sec at f/22, Coral No. 1 and 0.6 ND grad filters

right **Finkle Street, Richmond**

A totally clear blue sky is rarely what a photographer will be looking for. The reflection of a solid blue sky in this wet pavement caught my eye. The white and other hints of colour all come from the shop fronts. Though this is a pedestrian way I had to move a few times while setting up to let delivery vans pass. The picture took a while to capture, and raised a few comments.

Ebony 45s with 240mm lens, 1 second at f/22, using forward tilt for greater depth of field

Perhaps the greatest thing a photographer can do is to find a transitory moment of beauty and create a permanent record of it. With the exception of light, I can think of nothing else that has so much effect on the landscape as water.

If you are using water as a theme to inspire your photography, there are almost no limits to what you can photograph within the bounds of the theme. Subtlety is central to my own style of photography. I seek the peaceful, tranquil and gentle in nature. My aim is to find pictures that are relaxing to look at and gentle on the eye. A little water can go a long way towards that goal.

facing page **Thomason's Foss**
This is a very popular subject: fallen autumn leaves, rocks and water. The contrast of textures and colours has obvious appeal. There can be a temptation to add more leaves to a scene like this, but you can almost always tell when this has been done. On this occasion I didn't need to add any leaves, but if you do, take a tip: don't do it carefully or deliberately; just throw a few leaves into the area and let them land where they will.

Ebony 45s with 150mm lens, 15 seconds at f/22, polarizing and Coral No. 1 filters

right
Ten Peaks Moraine Lake, Canada
This scene is depicted on the reverse of a Canadian $20 bill and is one of the iconic views of the Rockies. The glacial lake looks a deep shade of turquoise because of silt, known as rock flour. It is spectacular in itself, but it does make the reflection a little less distinct – you can't have everything.

Pentax 67 with 45mm lens, 1 second at f/22, polarizing filter

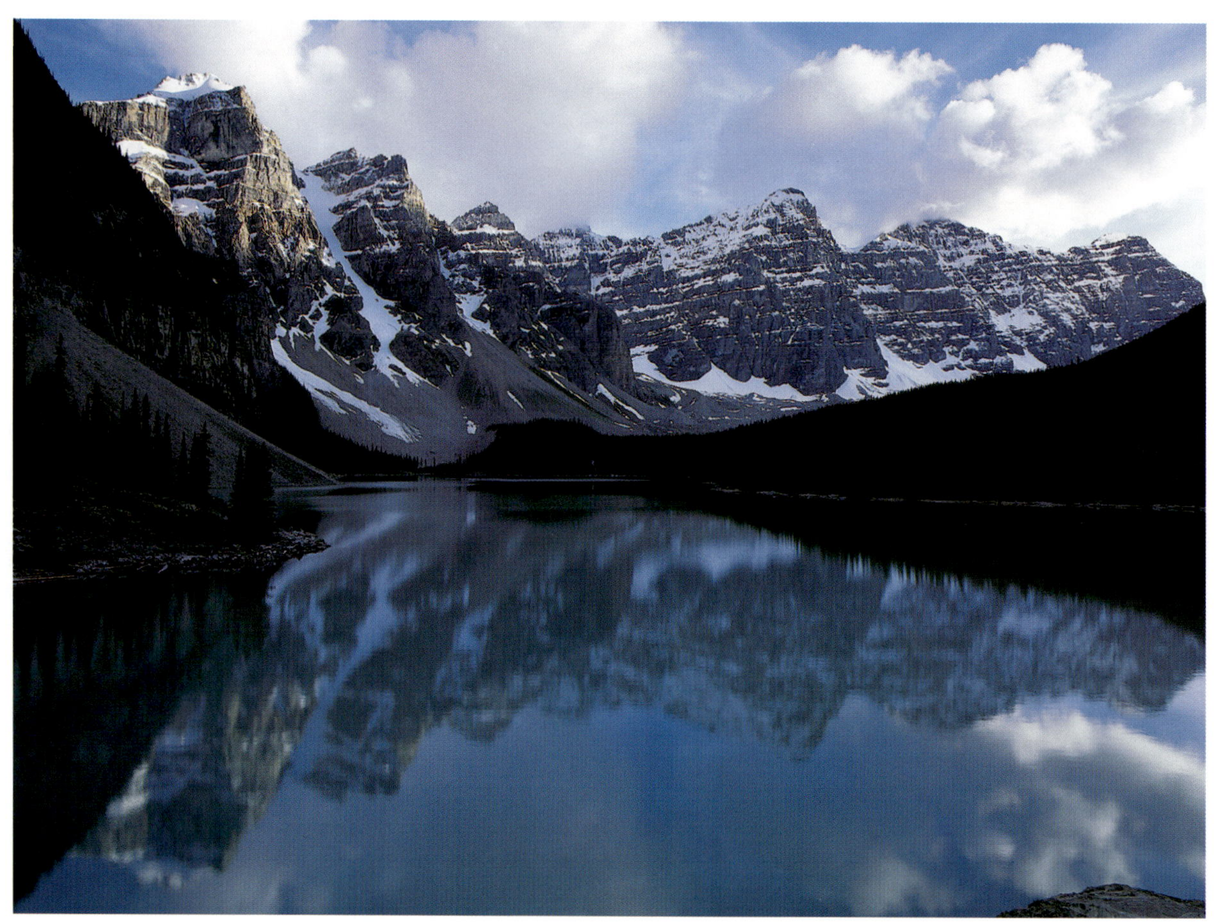

 PHOTOGRAPHING WATER IN THE LANDSCAPE

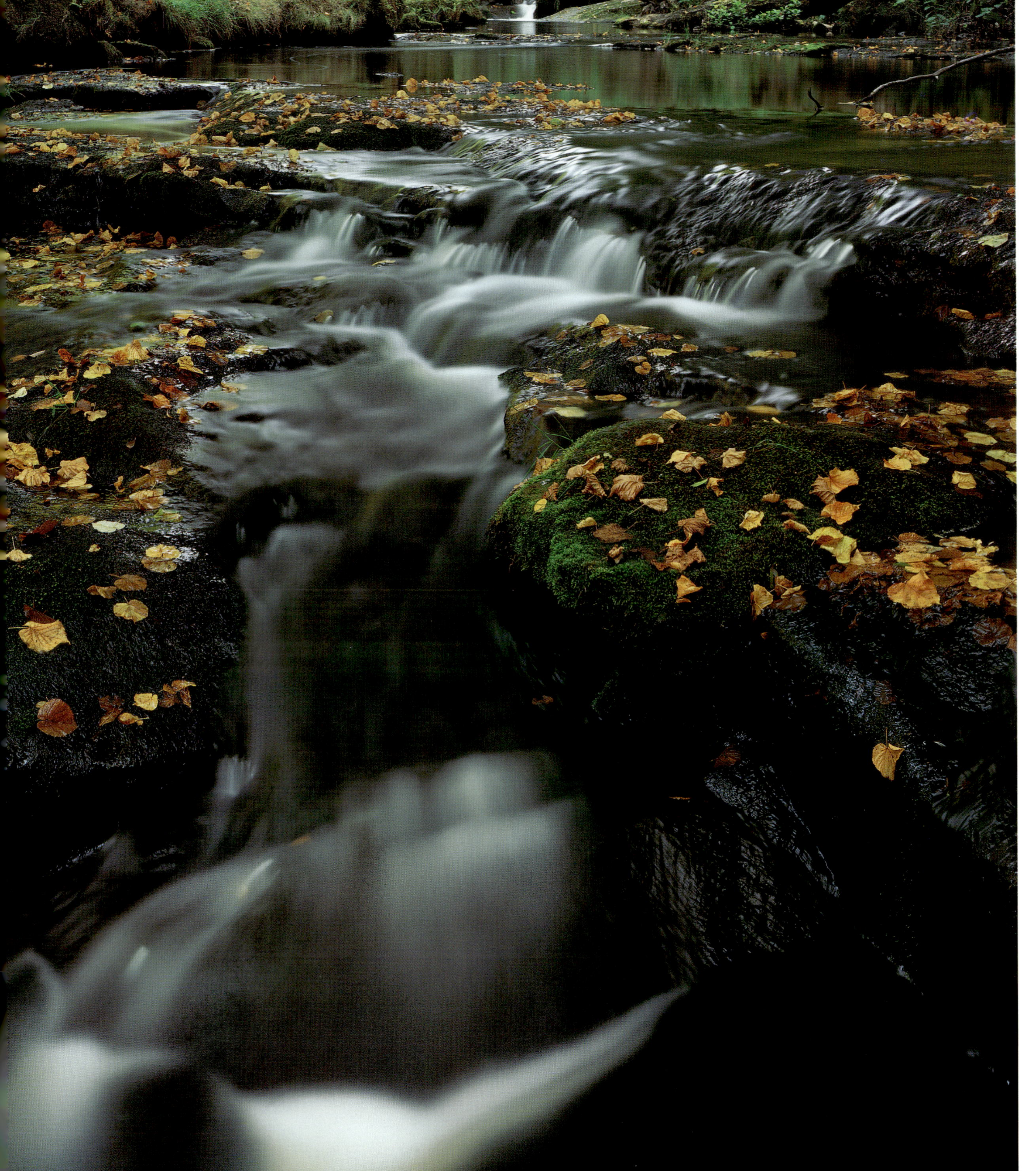

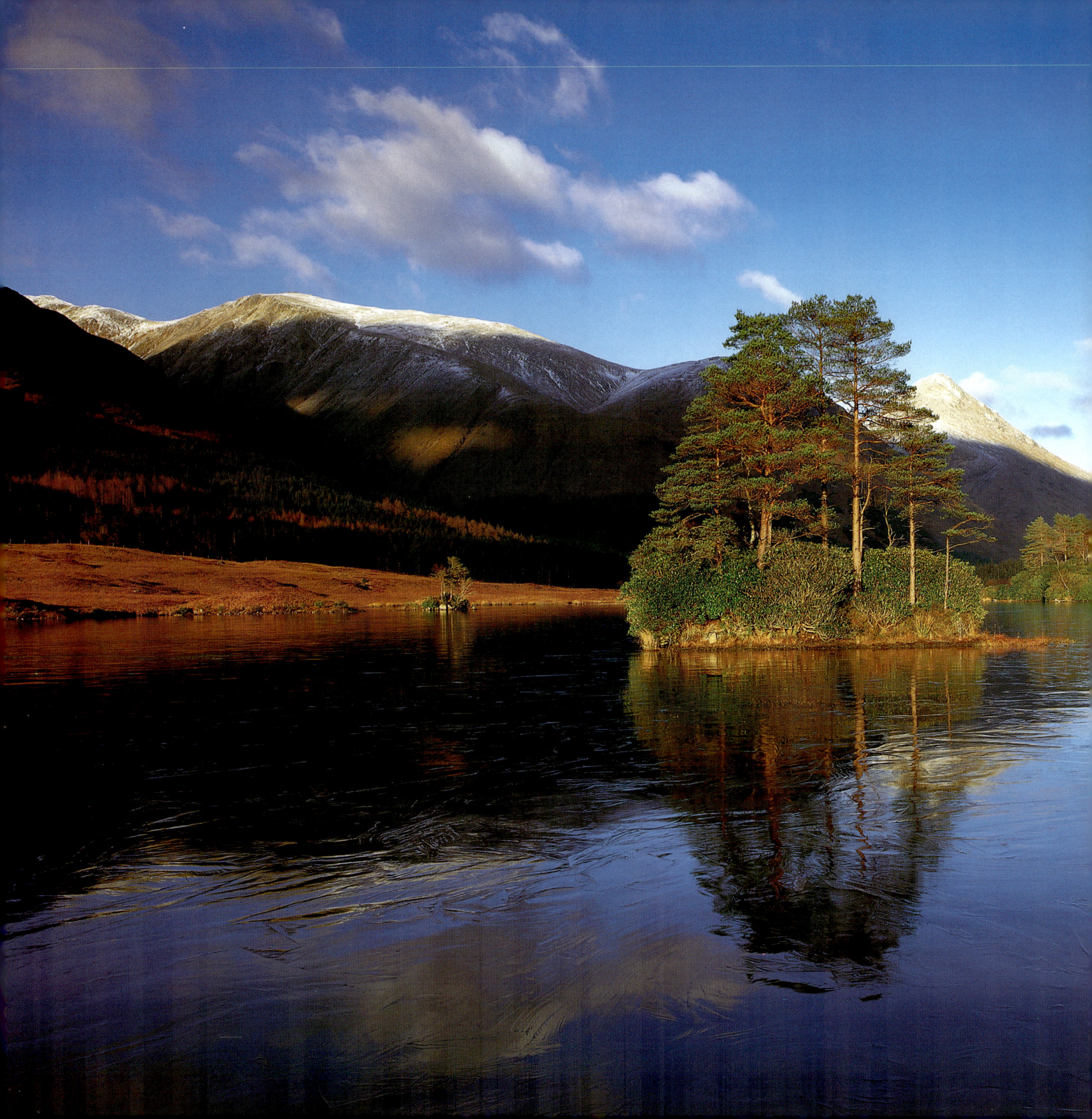

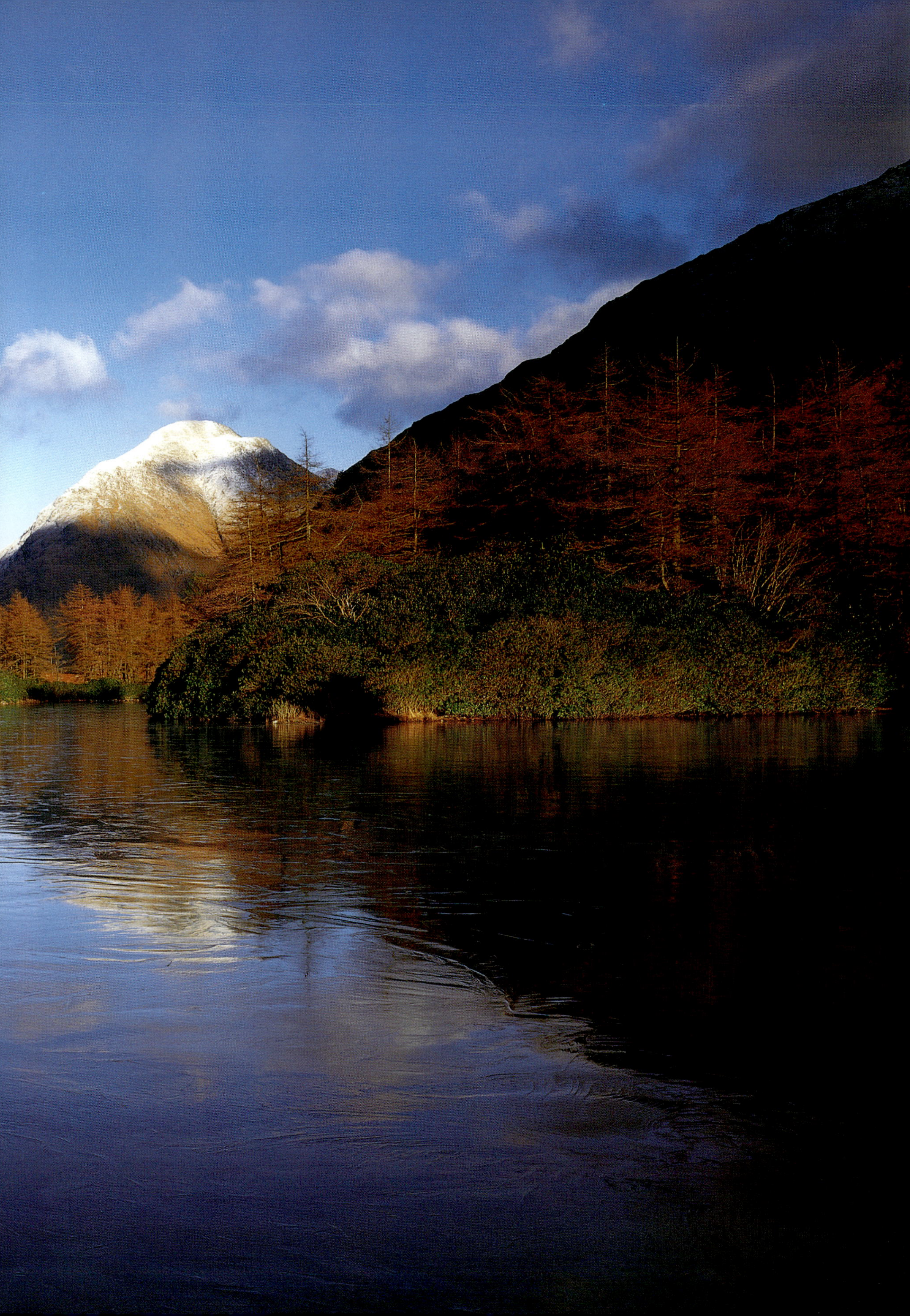

Glen Etive, Scotland

Reflections are always a welcome sight for the landscape photographer. They are the perfect illustration of peace and quiet. The slightest breeze over the surface of the water can disturb the reflection and it will be gone. However, that was not the case here, as the water in the foreground was frozen. The patterns in the ice bring interest right to the front of the frame.

Ebony 45s with 58mm lens, 6x12 rollfilm back, centre-spot, Coral No. 1 and 0.6 ND soft-grad filters

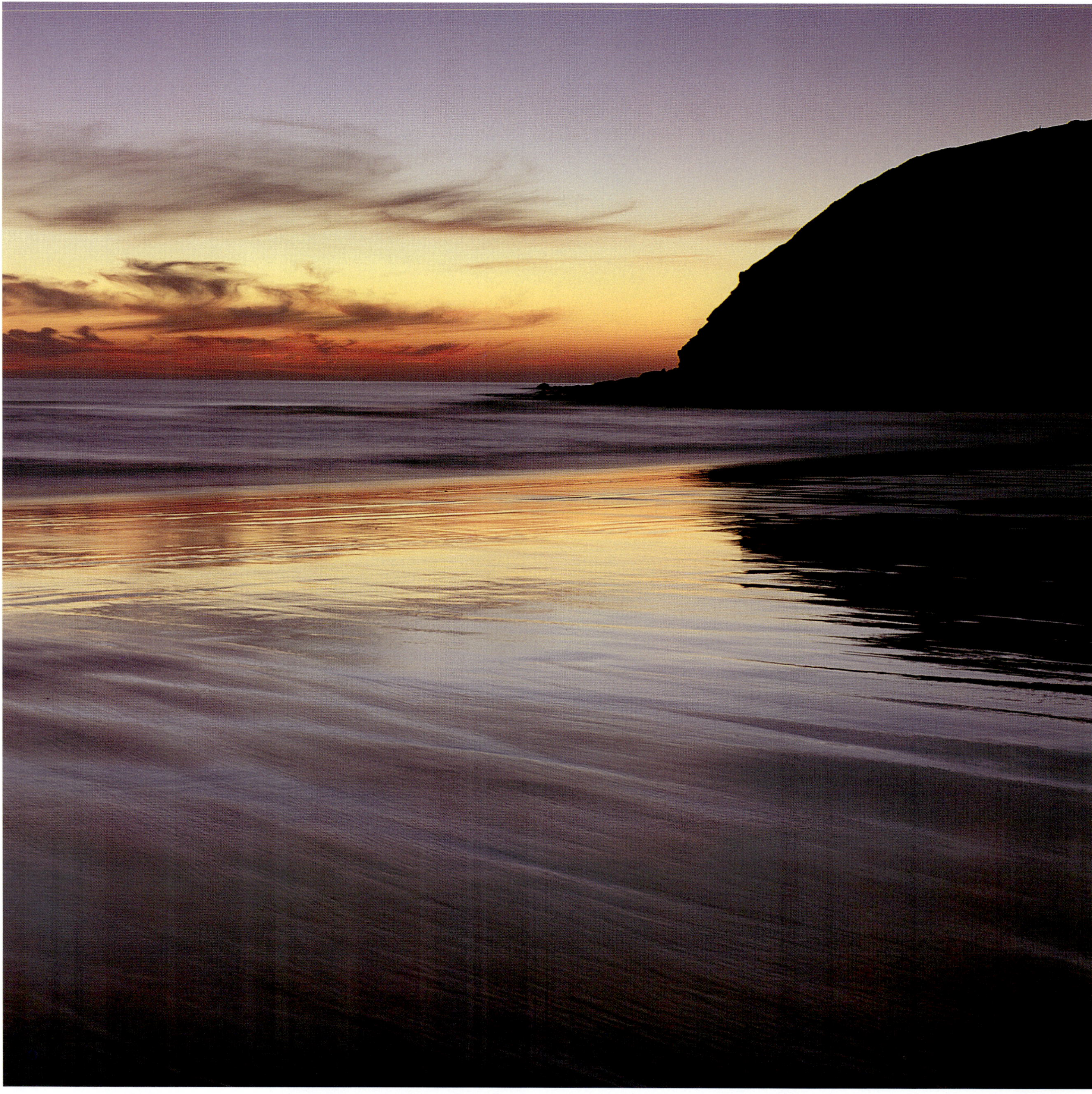

Essential Equipment

There are some popularly held myths about equipment that should be dispelled. One of the most common is that the latest and most expensive equipment will improve your photography: it won't. However, buying the right equipment can. Photography is a subject with many specialist areas, and it is important that you use the equipment that is best suited to your chosen area.

The right camera, the right lenses, film and accessories will contribute positively to the standard of your photographs. The wrong equipment will only hinder your efforts. Choosing the best equipment for you is a personal thing, and experience is your best guide.

I cannot tell you which camera will be the best one for you; I have had enough difficulty deciding which camera is right for me. I have swapped, traded and changed the equipment I use many times over the years. And while I am currently settled with the outfit I use, I cannot be sure that the relationship will last for the rest of my career. Even as a dedicated traditional photographer, I cannot ignore the relentless and rapid progress of digital technology, which offers greater control and flexibility than traditional cameras. While from a personal and perhaps artistic standpoint I still find no other form of photograph as satisfying as an original large-format transparency, I have to accept that from a practical, professional viewpoint, digital photography already offers comparable quality for most printed media.

Choosing a Camera

For landscape photography in general, and especially for photographing water, what you really need is a camera that gives you as much control as possible over exposure and focus. There are two main exposure variables with any camera: the shutter speed and the aperture. With some very simple-to-use cameras, the photographer has no access to these – the camera's in-built program determines the 'correct' exposure and sets both accordingly. These cameras do not give you the essential freedom to be in full control of how the final image will appear, how much of it will be sharp, and how much any movement will be either frozen or allowed to blur within the picture.

If you want to take successful landscapes and waterscapes you need to have complete control of the aperture and the shutter speed of your camera.

Focus on... Getting to Know your Camera

You need to form a relationship with your camera, get to know its every quirk, and find a way of working together so that it intrudes as little as possible into your thinking and seeing. While there is no substitute for experience in the field, try to familiarize yourself with new equipment before you have to depend upon it. Once you have done all of that, you may decide you want a change, need a new challenge, require some fresh inspiration. If this happens, don't fight it. No equipment guarantees successful photographs, but the right equipment will help.

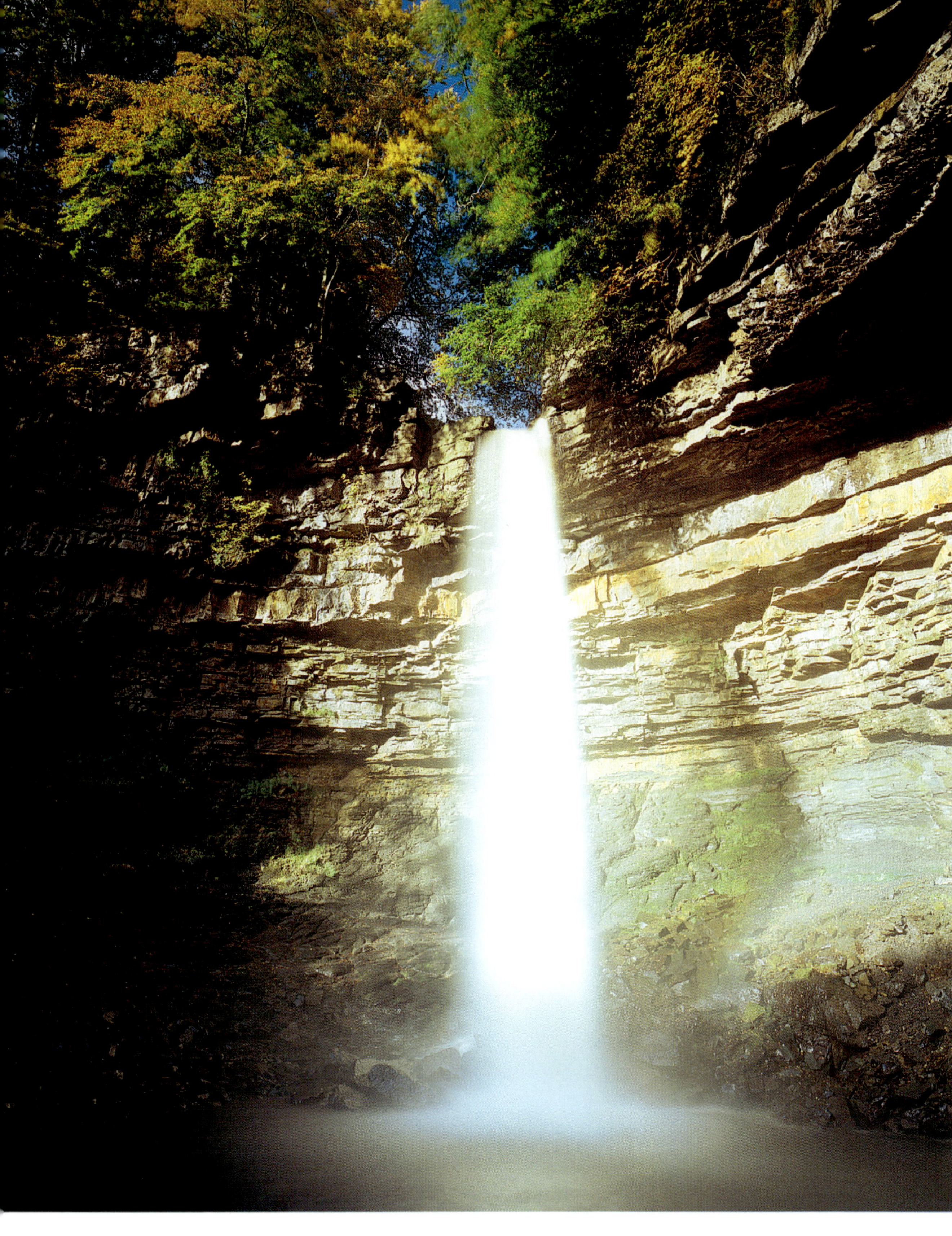

Hardraw Force Waterfall

This image is clearly the result of using the appropriate equipment combined with a particular photographic technique. Motion blur like this can only be achieved by using a tripod and keeping the shutter open much longer than normal (this picture was recorded over 20 seconds). The other piece of kit needed for this effect was a neutral-density filter to reduce the amount of light reaching the film (these are explained more fully in Chapter Two, *Techniques*, see pages 47–75).

Ebony 45s with 90mm lens, Velvia 50, 20 seconds at f/32, 0.9 ND grad and polarizing filters

Direct-View Compact Cameras

The main advantage these cameras have is their reduced size and weight. They are so small and light that you could almost carry one with you all the time, which you certainly would not want to do with an SLR or anything heavier.

With a few exceptions, compact cameras are usually fully automatic and therefore not ideal for landscape photography where you need control over the camera's settings. Most compact cameras will not accept filters or allow you to change lenses.

Rangefinder Cameras

These come in many formats, from 35mm models, such as the classic Leica M-series, through the medium-format Mamiya 6 and 7, right up to the panoramic Fuji GX617. 35mm rangefinder cameras look very much like compact cameras but offer full manual control. You can also use filters with them and normally change lenses. Not being able to see directly through the lens with a rangefinder means the use of graduated filters involves a bit of judgement and guesswork. It is difficult at first to precisely position the demarcation line of a graduated filter so that it meets the horizon. Using a soft-graduated filter and a bit of experience with the camera will solve this most of the time.

Rangefinder cameras take their name from the viewfinder system that they use. There are two main types of rangefinder: coincidence and split-image. A coincidence rangefinder superimposes two images in the viewfinder and when the image is correctly focused these two will appear as one. Split-image viewfinders display two separate halves of the same image which become aligned when the image is in focus.

35mm SLR Cameras

There are many advantages to using a 35mm SLR for landscape and water photography. A system of mirrors and prisms directs light from the lens to the viewfinder, allowing you to view the scene as the camera does. Compared to larger-format cameras, 35mm SLRs are very portable and versatile, and there is more choice of lenses than for any other format. 35mm SLRs are also quicker and easier to use than larger formats.

One advantage of most modern 35mm SLRs is that exposure readings are taken through-the-lens (TTL metering). This means that the camera automatically takes into account any filters that you use and negates the need to buy a separate handheld lightmeter. Many 35mm SLRs also provide fast autofocus and built-in motor drives. While this is very useful for wildlife and sports photography, it is not really necessary for landscape photography. As a landscape photographer you will usually have more than enough time to focus the camera yourself and while the light can change quickly, you will never need several frames per second to capture its changes. Most 35mm SLRs allow you to switch between autofocus and manual-focus modes, so you can still retain full manual control over the photographic process.

As modern technology progresses 35mm SLRs have fallen in price, giving you more technology for your money. All this technology is often unnecessary and the one thing I prize above the features many modern cameras offer is sturdy reliability. The fewer features a camera offers, the less there is to go wrong and the easier it is to repair, with the added advantage that manual cameras drain fewer batteries during daily use.

SEE ALSO:

Camera Comparison Chart *p 24–5*

Second-hand Equipment *p 45*

Medium- and Large-Format Cameras

Medium- and large-format cameras are the basic tools of photography for landscape work. They offer a clarity you simply don't get with smaller formats: every fine detail is evident on a large-format transparency. These cameras slow you down, too, as they offer less automation than 35mm cameras – and landscape is a subject that is rarely hindered by a slow and deliberate approach.

Medium-Format Cameras

'Medium format' describes a camera that uses 120 or 220 rollfilm. There are several types of camera that do this, producing pictures in a number of different formats. Rollfilm comes on a paper-backed spool rather than in the cassettes familiar to 35mm users. The format of the camera you use determines how many frames you can shoot on one roll. When using 120 rollfilm a 6x4.5 camera will give you fifteen frames, a 6x6 twelve,

a 6x7 ten, a 6x9 eight, and a 6x12 just six. Using 220 film doubles the number of frames for any format but it is less readily available.

Many medium-format cameras are modular: the film holder, body, lens and the viewing prism are all separate parts that connect to make the whole camera. This makes them versatile. You can choose to have metering or not, you can carry more than one back and therefore more than one film stock at a time and, for some models, you can even add a digital back instead of film, budget permitting.

below Some popular film frame sizes, from 35mm to 5x4. Note how the film format affects the shape of your photograph. A 6x7 frame gives you more than four times as much film area as 35mm, while 5x4 is fourteen times larger.

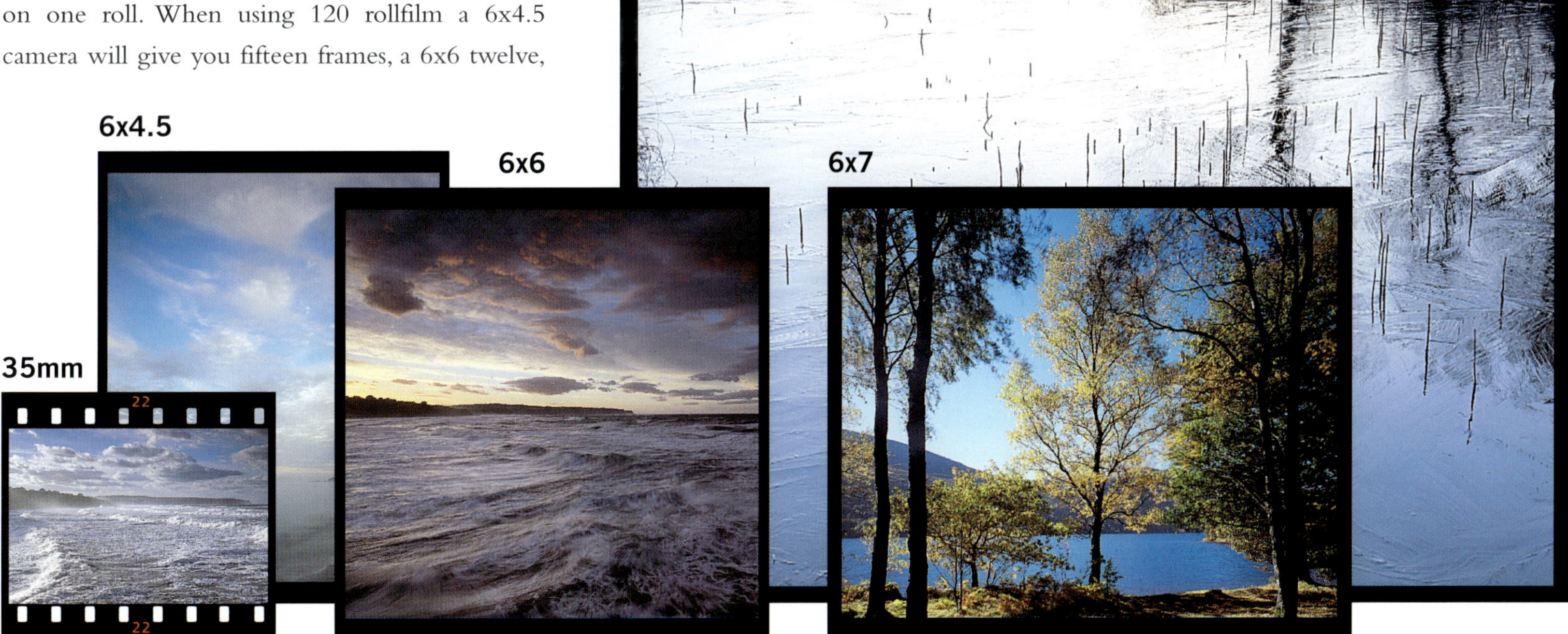

It is worth thinking about how the format you choose will affect your composition. 6x4.5 and 6x9 are a similar rectangle to the familiar 35mm and therefore an easy transition. 6x6 is of course a square, so you don't have to think about the picture as either a vertical or horizontal. 6x6 cameras also tend to be lighter and smaller than 6x7 cameras.

Most medium-format cameras use a single-lens reflex design which offers the same metering and composition advantages as a 35mm SLR. There are some that use rangefinder-style viewfinders, such as the Mamiya 7 and the Fuji GW690. These have the great advantage of being small and lightweight, which is great for travel. But the disadvantage is not seeing exactly what you are taking directly through the lens. It is then best to avoid placing elements that are critical to the composition right at the edge of the frame.

Large-Format Cameras

The advance of new technology slows to an imperceptible crawl when you reach large-format cameras. The pioneers of photography would still recognize a modern 5x4 camera, where the only real advances in the last hundred years have been in the materials used and lens technology.

Large-format cameras may seem intimidating, but they are actually very simple. Using them will even teach you about photography: every rule that you read that seems to make no sense becomes obvious when using a large-format camera.

For example, the relationship between subject distance and depth of field is much more apparent in 5x4 format where everything is magnified 14 times larger than 35mm. Closing down the aperture (depth-of-field preview) shows far greater detail than a 35mm SLR's dimmed viewfinder.

technique CHANGING THE BACK ON A LARGE-FORMAT CAMERA

One of the great advantages of the large-format camera is its versatility. It can be adapted to take individual sheets of traditional cut film, Quickload film (see page 28), rollfilm, or you can add a polaroid back in order to use instant film. Switching the back on a large-format camera is quick and easy. Catches slide to release the focusing screen (put it down somewhere safe), while the same catches slide back into place to secure the new back.

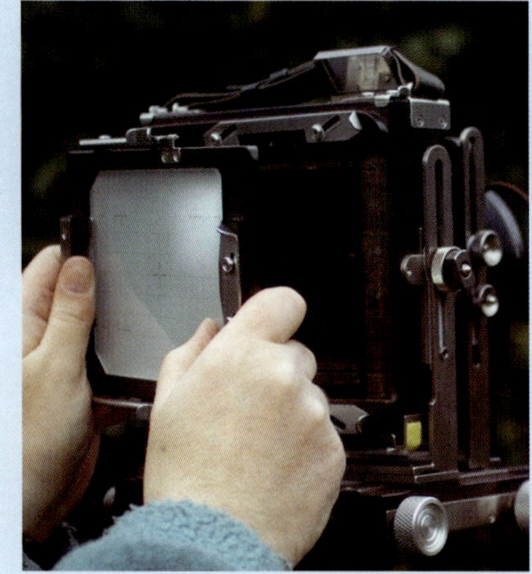
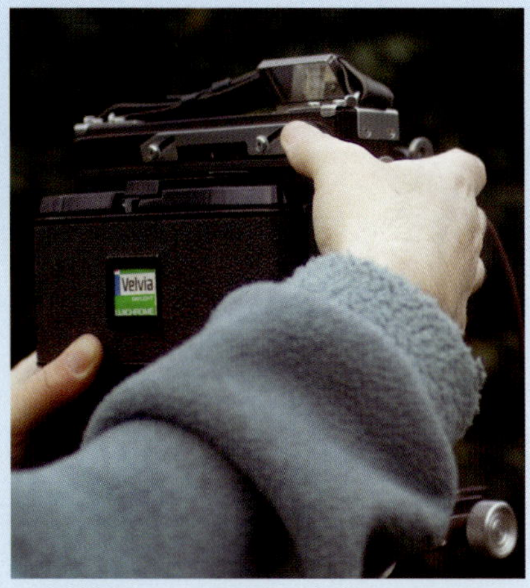

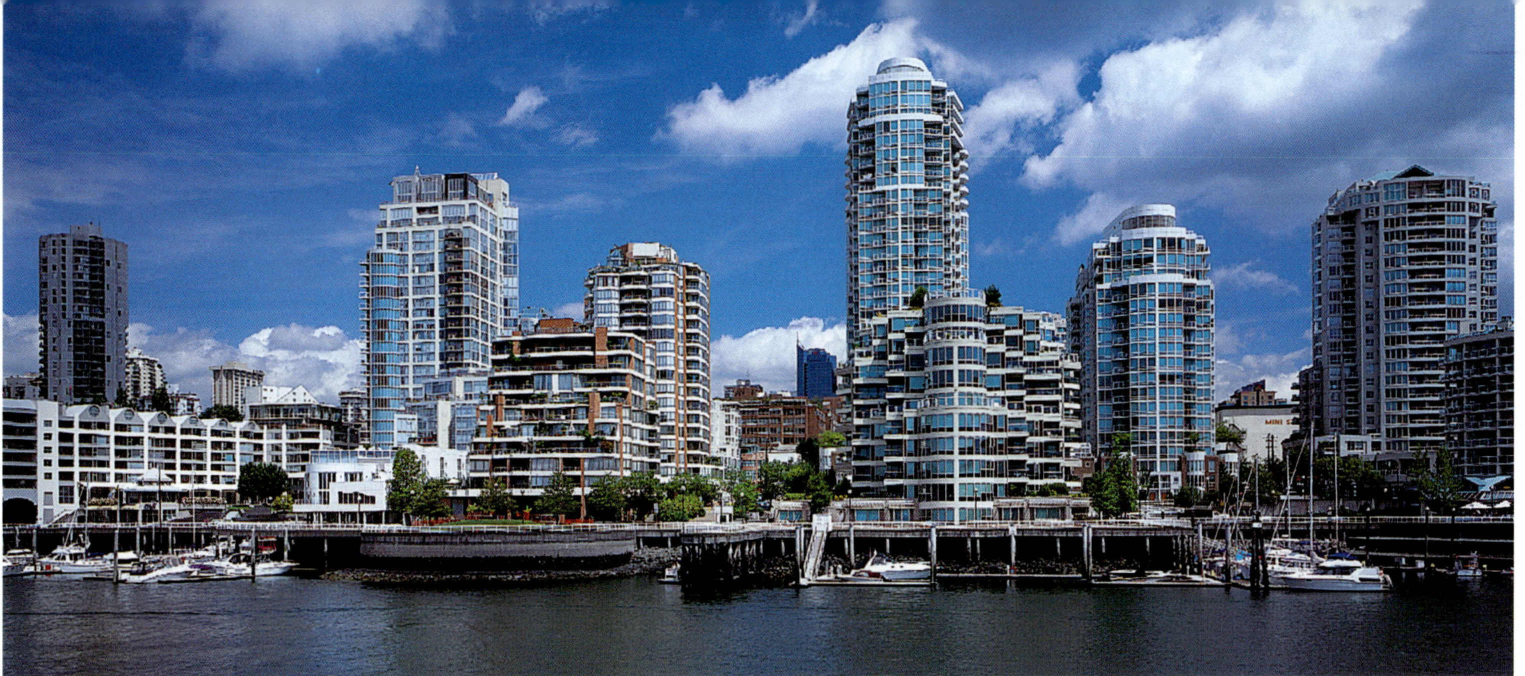

Vancouver Waterfront

For this scene the panoramic composition was the only one that worked. More sky and/or more empty water in the foreground would only detract from the scene, as would losing any of the buildings from either end.

Ebony 45s with 90mm lens, 1/15sec at f/22

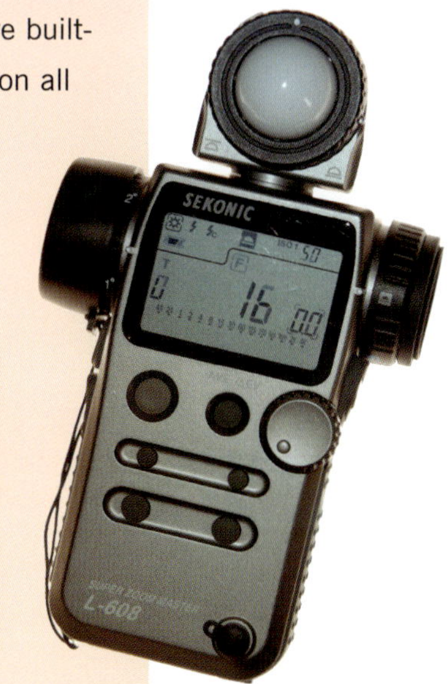

HANDHELD METERS

Large-format cameras do not have built-in meters, nor are they standard on all medium-format cameras, so you will need another method of metering. Handheld meters can take both incident and reflective light readings. Incident readings measure the light falling onto the subject (rather than the light reflecting back from it, as in a reflective reading), giving you a value based on midtone grey.

Panoramic-Format Cameras

In addition to the traditional square and rectangular formats available to photographers, there are a number of panoramic options to consider. These are specialist cameras that produce an image format at least twice as wide as it is high, 6x12 and 6x17 being the two most favoured ones. The format has become popular commercially, but it will only work for you if it comes naturally.

Panoramic cameras really affect the way a picture is composed. Something like the rule of thirds must truly become meaningless in a 6x17 composition that takes in most of the scene in front of you. If you normally fill your frame with foreground interest, middle distance and background, then trying to force your own style into a panoramic format will not work.

I use a 6x12 back on my 5x4 camera for some pictures. I have never been tempted to buy a 6x17 camera, since the format is a little stretched for my taste. This being the case, I doubt any pictures I took in 6x17 would be successful.

Digital Cameras

Digital photography is a wholesale departure from everything that has gone before. It is photography without the restrictions and limitations of film, and without the joy of film. There are advantages to digital capture, as well as some disadvantages.

Immediate Results

The first and most prominent advantage with digital photography is the immediate results – it is possible to see right away what you have taken. From the LCD screen on the back of the camera you can judge whether or not the shot has worked – you can see if the exposure looks right and you can check and compare a number of compositions. Since it costs nothing to take another picture, you can afford to experiment and try several versions of every shot. However, using the preview screen is heavy on batteries and should be kept to a minimum in the field. Back at home you can plug the camera into the mains and review your photos without fear of draining the batteries.

Editing digital images, apart from any obvious failures, which can simply be erased at the time, is best done after downloading them onto a computer. You should carry spare memory cards with you so that you will not run out of storage space before you can download your images and clear the cards.

Quality

A lot has been made of comparisons in quality between film and digital. Many people consider digital has met and even surpassed the quality of 35mm film but it really depends on what you want to do with the end result. If you want to get your photographs published or produce prints from your work then you will need to consider the size that your image will be enlarged to, and 'capture' a big enough digital file for the image to be reproduced at that size.

SEE ALSO:

Digital Storage *p 29*

technique ADJUSTING THE WHITE BALANCE

With a digital camera you can alter the 'white balance' (WB) so that it is set to record light correctly in different colour temperatures. In the examples below the top picture with the white balance set for overcast light is correcting for a blue cast and emphasizing the orange glow of the setting sun. On the lower picture the camera has corrected the orange cast and given a subtle blend of colours much closer to my memory of the scene.

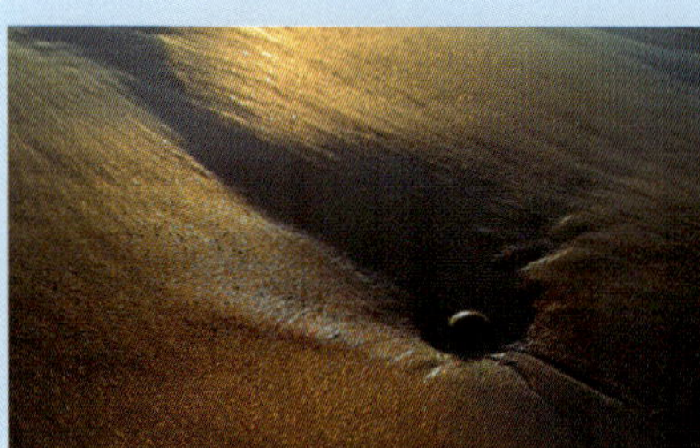

left **Sigma SD9 with 50mm lens, ISO equivalent 100, 1/90sec at f/4, WB=Overcast**

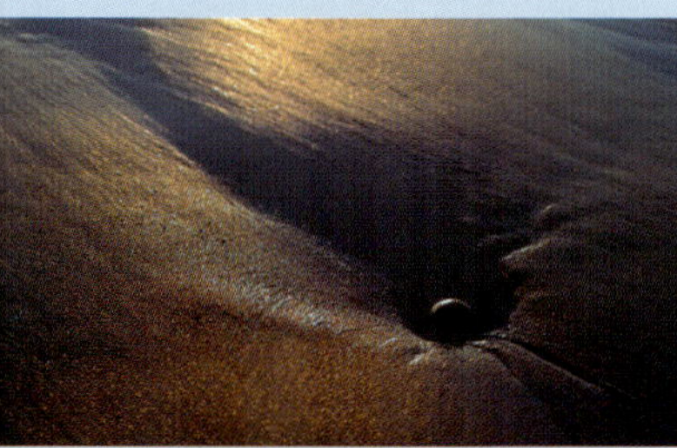

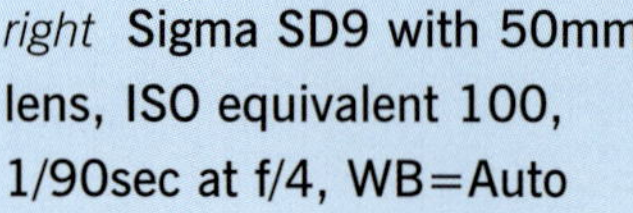

right **Sigma SD9 with 50mm lens, ISO equivalent 100, 1/90sec at f/4, WB=Auto**

The photo-sensor is basically a grid of extremely small light-sensitive cells. When light reaches these sensors (also known as pixels), an electrical signal is produced and it is from the resulting pattern that the digital image is built up. The more pixels on the sensor, the finer the image detail will be and the larger the final picture can be made. The information captured by the sensor is then passed on to a storage device. See page 29 for more on digital capture and storage.

See page 29 for more on digital capture and storage.

below **Derwentwater Dusk**

I was able to capture this gentle scene very quickly using the digital camera and a brief look at the preview screen convinced me it was worth also setting up the 5x4 camera and taking a traditional version on Velvia. I had to work very fast because these walkers were waiting for a boat that appeared to be heading for the jetty: once the boat arrived the reflection would be lost until the light faded anyway. The boat added a further element of interest.

Sigma SD9 with 15–30mm lens, 1/6sec at f/16, ISO 100, WB=Auto

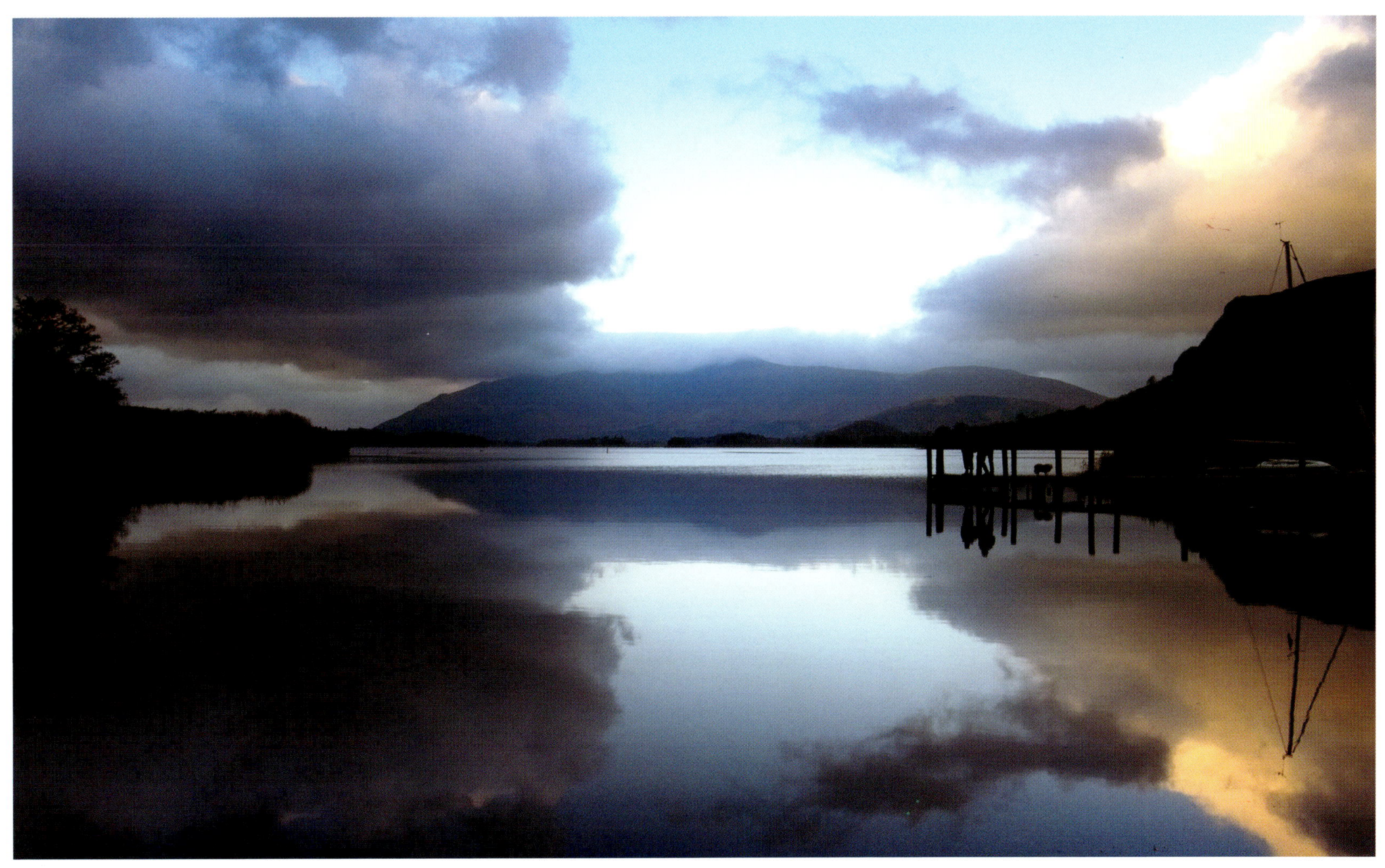

CAMERA COMPARISON CHART

Direct-View and Rangefinder Compact Cameras

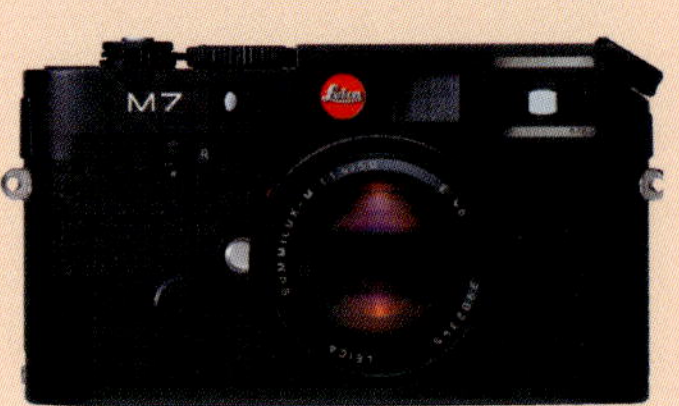

These cameras do have their limitations, but are capable of producing some good results.

Advantages

Compact cameras, whether rangefinder or direct-view systems, are light and easy to use. Some combine automation with good-quality lenses and rangefinder cameras can also provide manual flexibility.

Disadvantages

Too much automation can inhibit your creativity and you often cannot use filters. Depending on the viewfinder design, the final photograph may not be exactly the same as the scene you composed.

35mm SLRs (Single-Lens Reflex Cameras)

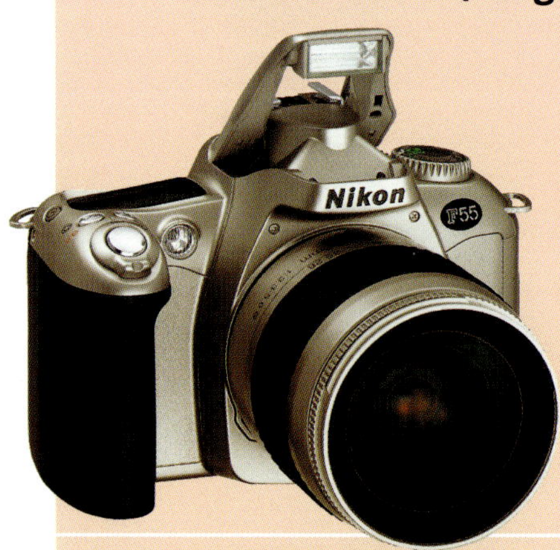

Very versatile, light, portable and still very popular.

Advantages

A well-established format, a lot of choice regarding lenses and features, great for landscape photography and most other forms of photography. Portable and light compared to larger formats. Modern SLRs include through-the-lens metering exposure systems, negating the need to buy a separate handheld meter.

Disadvantages

The relatively small format does not offer the same quality as medium- and large-format cameras. Most modern models are over-dependent on batteries and electronic automation for landscape work in harsh conditions. Professional-quality models and lenses are expensive, even compared with medium- and large-format cameras.

Digital Compact and SLR Cameras

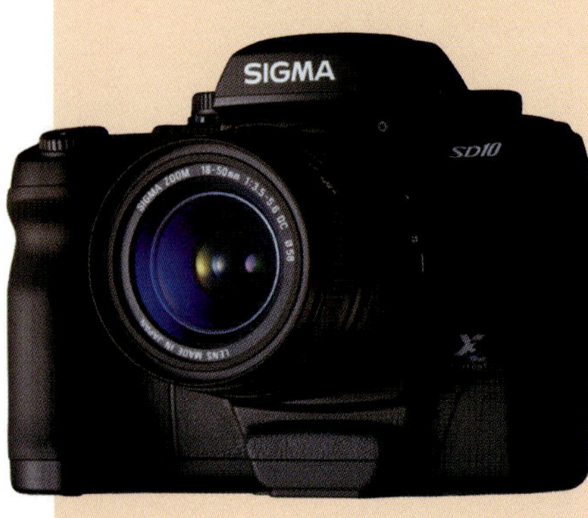

A wholesale departure from everything that has gone before – photography without film.

Advantages

You can check exposure and composition on the preview LCD screen. The actual picture-taking process is free, as there are no film or processing costs. You can also change the ISO setting and white balance for individual frames. Once downloaded onto a computer, pictures can be altered, printed and duplicated on CD.

Disadvantages

It can be expensive to get started, requiring software and storage cards, although printing can still be done by a high-street lab. Digital cameras are very battery-dependent and susceptible to weather conditions. Dirt is attracted to the sensor and leaves marks on the digital file that need to be cleaned up later.

Panoramic Cameras

These come in various formats, each being more than twice as wide as it is tall.

Advantages

Panoramic cameras are smaller, lighter and easier to use than large-format cameras. They are available in a range of formats, from the Hasselblad XPan to the Fuji GX617. They produce an interesting shape for compositions and are a commercially attractive format.

Disadvantages

Often these are large and awkward-shaped cameras to carry. Because of their specialist nature they can be expensive. They also require specific lenses, which often cost more than standard ones. This is a specialist format which has to appeal to your own photographic taste.

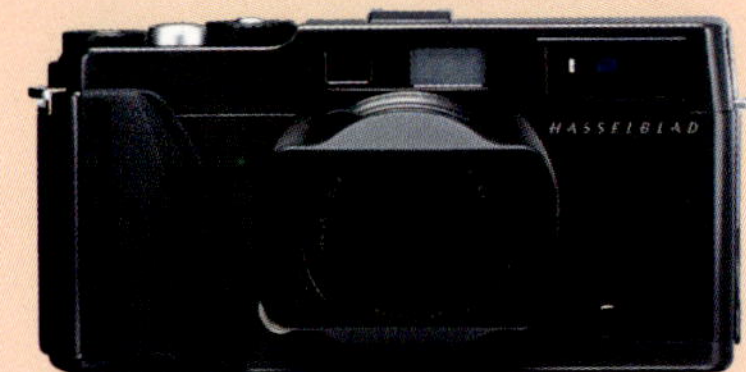

Medium-Format Cameras

'Medium format' covers a wide range of makes and models of camera in various formats and designs.

Advantages

Larger-format pictures provide greater-quality transparencies and, ultimately, enlargements. Usually they are of a robust design and well suited to the rigours of professional work in the landscape. They often give more control to the photographer because of less automation. Interchangeable film backs are available on most models.

Disadvantages

Both the cameras and lenses that go with them are larger, heavier and more expensive than standard 35mm-format equipment, although second-hand models are widely available. There is less choice regarding accessories, especially telephoto lenses.

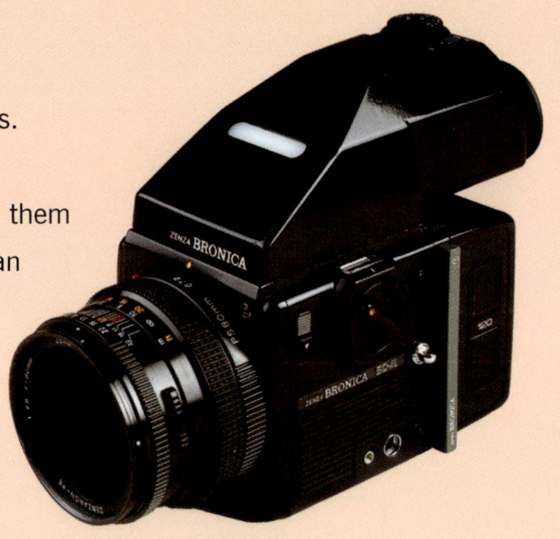

Large-Format Cameras – 5x4, 5x7 and 10x8

The ultimate in quality, simplicity and control.

Advantages

Large-format cameras offer total control over every aspect of the picture-taking process, including perspective (essential when photographing tall buildings). The quality of the large-format transparency is excellent. Even today in the digital age, a 5x4 transparency is an arresting sight on an editor's light box. It is a very commercial format.

Disadvantages

Difficult to use in a strong wind. Every technical error is magnified in the final image. Expensive to run and film is not as widely available as 35mm or rollfilm. Bulky and heavy, although not as heavy as some medium-format cameras.

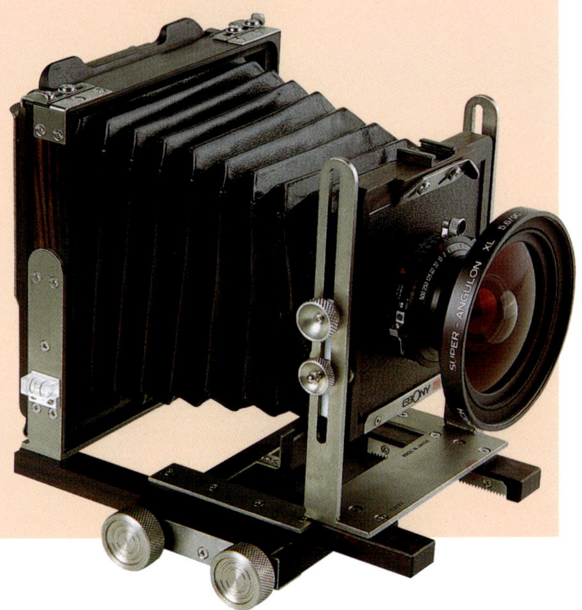

St Bees at Sunset

I always find shooting the sunset or the sunrise an exciting experience. The light can change so quickly, and I find myself wondering if the spot I have chosen to take my picture from really is the best one. Some sunsets last long enough so that you can take one view and then move on and try another. This was one such sunset.

I had never visited St Bees before and had no pre-planned view to capture, just the idea of cliff, silhouettes and reflections in wet sand. The digital camera gave me tremendous speed of operation: I could take one picture, review it, move to another spot, re-frame and shoot. With no need to bracket exposure, no need to take more than one frame for spares, and the immediate chance to review the results, I found I was capturing new images at an incredible rate compared to film. Indeed, I had to deliberately stop myself, put the digital camera away and set up the large-format camera just to take the picture on the facing page for comparison.

below These three shots are variations on a theme. Had I been working with film I would have been more careful to choose the version I thought worked best before taking any pictures. Working in digital meant that I could shoot very quickly and did not have to take three separate light readings. By seeing the images right away on the camera's preview screen I knew that the exposures were appropriate.

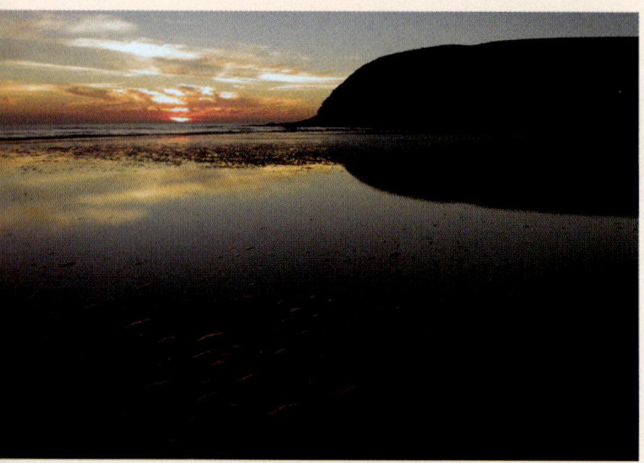

Sigma SD9 with 15mm lens,
1/15sec at f/11,
WB=Overcast

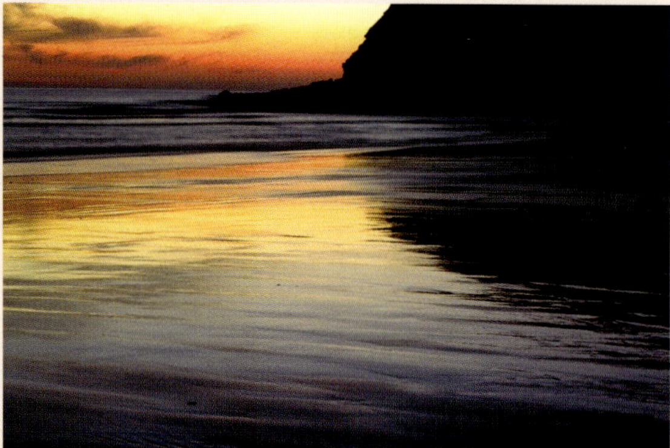

Sigma SD9 with 24mm lens,
1/15sec at f/16,
WB=Overcast

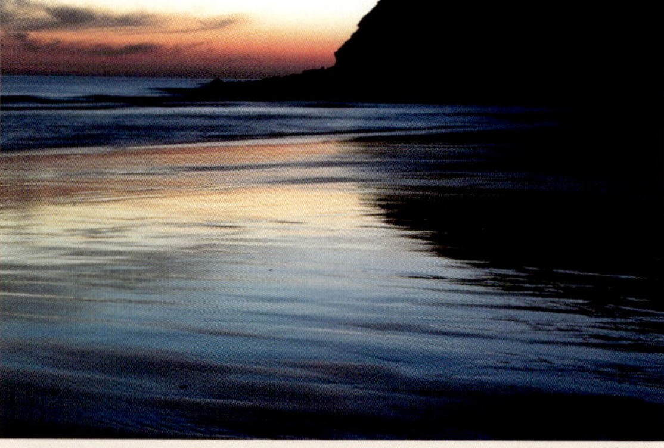

Sigma SD9 with 23mm lens,
1/15sec at f/16,
WB=Sunlight

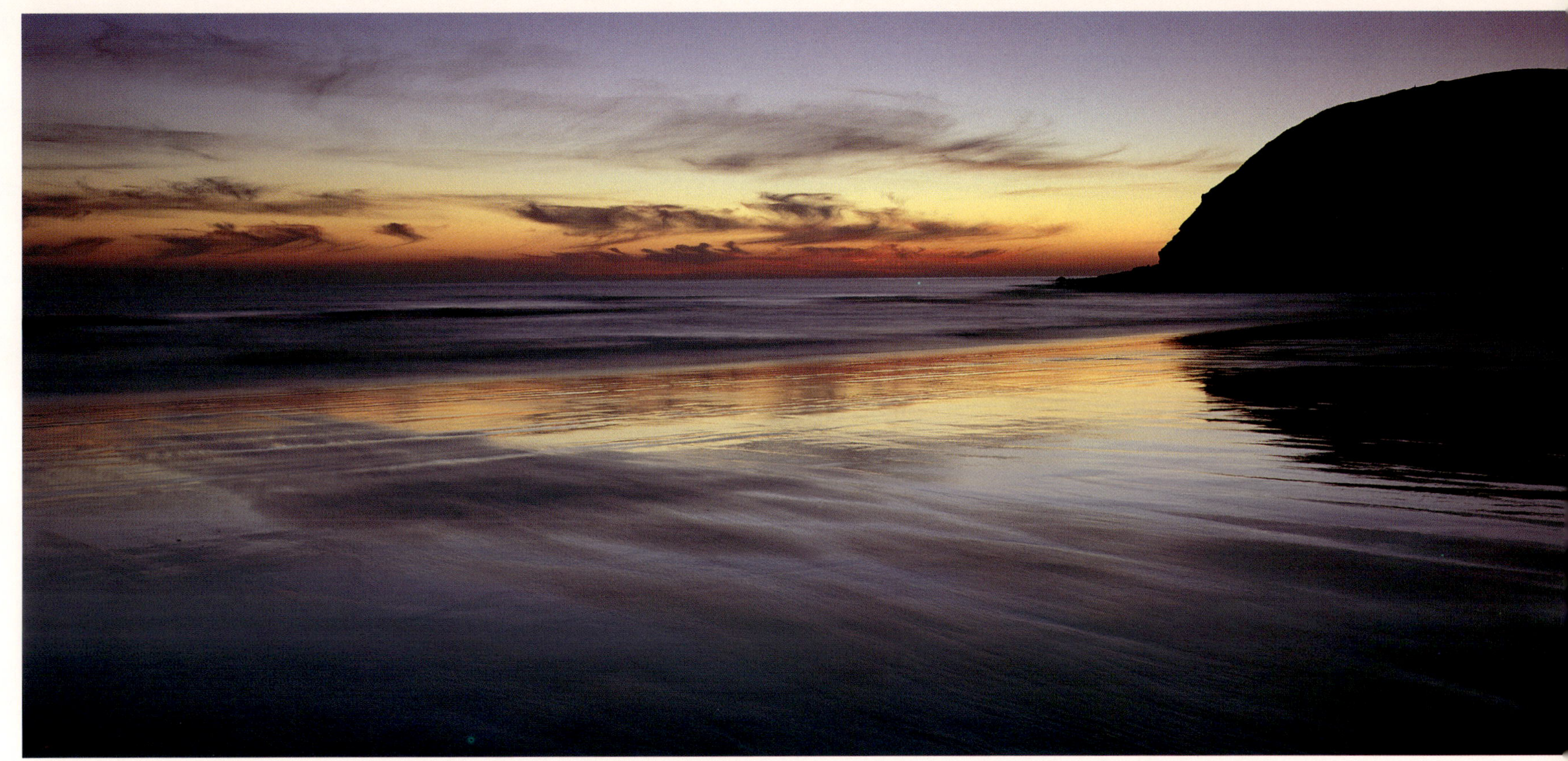

With the textures and colours in the wet sand and the silhouette of the cliffs I knew that I wanted to take some 5x4 photographs as well as capturing digital files on this evening. The panoramic format also seemed very suitable for this scene.

Ebony 45s with 90mm lens, Velvia 50, 6 seconds at f/22, 0.6ND grad filter

Film and Digital Media

Choosing and Processing Film

Perhaps the easiest of divisions to start with is between colour and black & white film. The next division is between print film and transparency. These can be either black & white or colour, although there are not many black & white transparency films around. Print film produces negatives, which are then printed as positives on photographic paper. With transparencies, the processed film is a positive, which can be projected for viewing or simply placed on a lightbox. Most professional and serious amateur photographers prefer transparency film because it gives truer, richer colours, offers greater quality and is better for reproduction in books and magazines.

Film Speed

Film comes in various speeds from slow (e.g. ISO 50) to fast (e.g. ISO 800). The speed refers to how quickly the film responds to light to form an image. The faster the better would be a natural response to learning this, but it is not that straightforward. The pay-off is that faster film has larger, and therefore more visible, grains of light-sensitive material, which you can see in the final transparency or negative, and which restricts your enlargement size. This graininess can sometimes be used to creative effect, but is generally considered to be undesirable. Slow films tend to have the smallest grain and therefore produce the sharpest pictures with the richest colours.

Slow Film
50
100
200
400
800
1600
3200
Fast Film

technique USING QUICKLOAD 5X4 SHEET FILM

Quickload is an easy way of shooting 5x4 without using darkslides. Each sheet of film is self-contained in a dark envelope, which is thinner and lighter than conventional darkslides and much less prone to dust and scratches. Quickload film has its own dedicated back, but a Polaroid 545i back will also work. Simply insert the film and envelope into the Polaroid back, take your picture, hold the release button and pull the envelope and film back out.

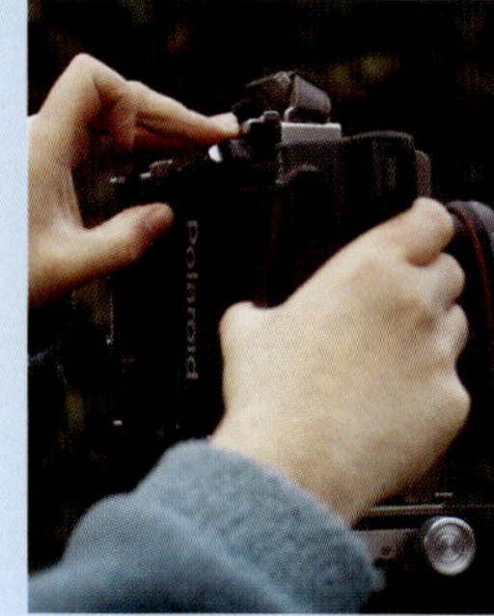
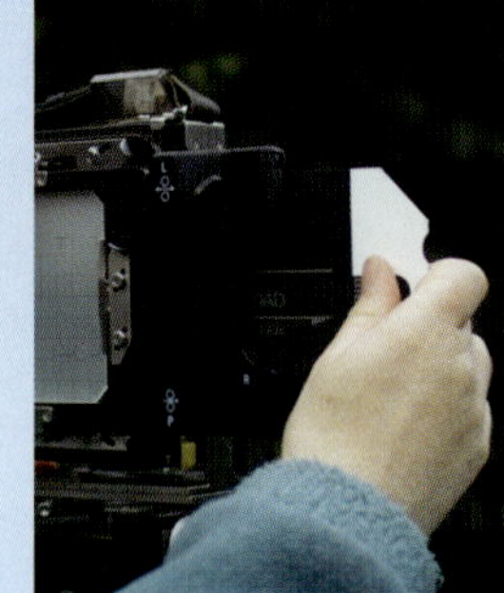
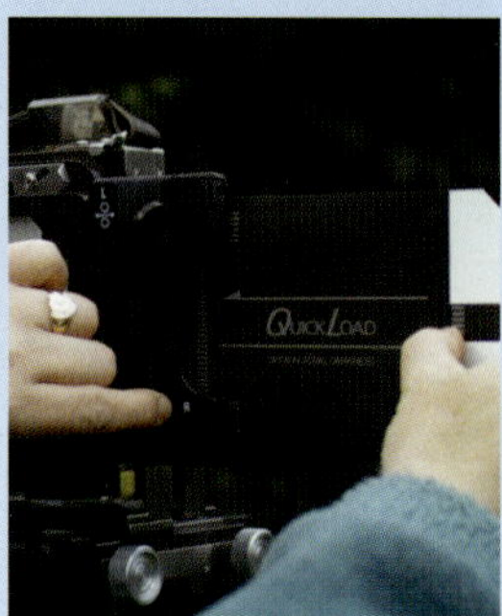

Digital Capture

The digital equivalent of film speed is sensor 'speed'. This is given in ISO equivalent numbers and so can be treated in effectively the same way. There is the same pay-off as with film: the faster you set the sensor, the more 'noise' (equivalent to graininess in film) there is apparent in the image.

The photo-sensor itself is a grid of pixels and there are a number of types of sensor available, each claiming to solve the problems inherent to digital capture in different ways. The one rule that applies to them all is that the more pixels that can be built onto the photo-sensor the finer the image detail will be and the more you can enlarge the image. If you want your photographs printed to hang on the wall or published in magazines, some of the old rules still apply – bigger is better.

This is not the end of the story, though. Once your images are downloaded onto a computer or other storage device, they can be expanded with software such as PhotoShop through a process known as interpolation. The software can add pixels, thereby increasing the size of the original file. However, the resulting image quality will not be as good as if the picture were taken at a higher resolution in the first place.

With a digital camera the file is recorded in colour, but if you want a monochrome picture then all you need to do is reduce the colour saturation until the colours are gone.

Digital Storage

Digital files take up a huge amount of storage space, although most digital cameras will give you a choice of taking pictures at different resolutions. The higher the quality, the larger the file.

BUYING DIGITAL CARDS

There are four main types of digital storage card available: SmartMedia (shown, top), CompactFlash (centre), Microdrive (bottom) and xD cards. SmartMedia, CompactFlash and xD are solid-state cards (which means that they have no moving parts). They vary in capacity, and the larger cards can store hundreds of high-quality images.

The Microdrive is actually a very small hard drive, similar to those used in PCs, and can hold a huge amount of data. However, Microdrives tend to be slightly less robust than solid-state cards and do not stand up to very rough handling.

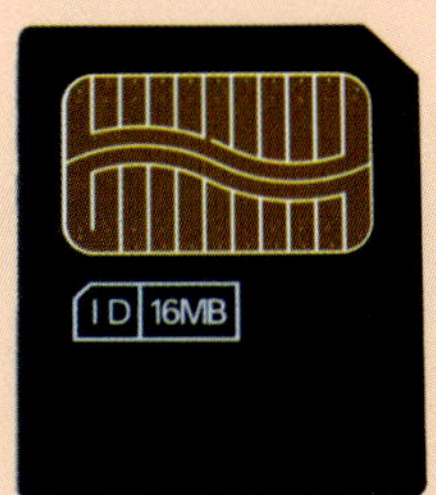

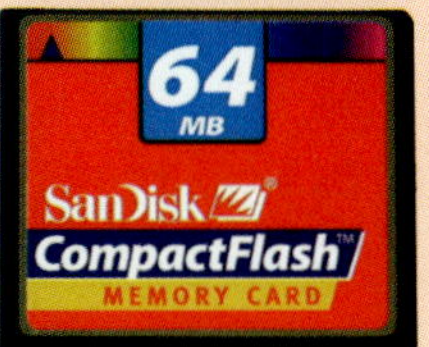

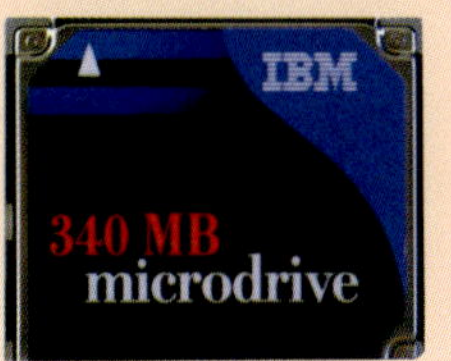

Changing Speed

A big advantage that digital has over film is that you can alter the speed of the sensor (equivalent to the ISO setting for film) for one picture then change it back for the next. You do not have to shoot a whole roll of faster or slower film, just the odd frame when conditions demand it.

Digital cameras used to have built-in storage disks and this limited the number of pictures that could be taken before they had to be downloaded to a computer. The answer to this problem was to use removable storage disks (more commonly called 'cards') that could be replaced when full, just like film (see 'Buying Digital Cards', above).

Some digital cameras use one type of storage card so that once you have chosen your camera you are tied to that storage system; however, some cameras can use a combination of cards, giving the photographer a choice of using one or indeed both systems in tandem. The price of storage cards has plummeted in recent years, but it is well worth shopping around, especially as some very good deals can be found on the Internet.

Lenses

With most digital cameras the sensor is smaller than full frame 35mm, making each lens the equivalent of a longer focal length on a film-based camera. For example, a 50mm lens on a digital camera with a standard sub-35mm sensor will give similar coverage to an 80mm lens on a film-based 35mm camera.

At its most basic, a camera is just a light–tight box. It is the lens that allows light to enter that box and affect the film to create an image. While what you need with a camera body is familiarity so that its control and use can become second nature, what you need from lenses is variety.

The first consideration is the focal lengths you want to carry. If you find that you often wish you could include more of the scene before you in your picture, then you need a lens with a shorter focal length than you are currently using and therefore a wider angle of view. Conversely, if you often wish you could crop tighter into part of a scene, then you need a lens with a longer focal length – a telephoto.

It may be good practice to make your standard lens the one you first use to view each scene. A standard lens will record on film with the natural perspective of the human eye. Any lens wider or longer than standard departs from that natural perspective. This is often a case of necessity, and sometimes a case of desire to achieve a certain effect. Both are perfectly valid reasons for using a lens that distorts perspective. It helps, though, to be fully aware of just what we are doing when taking photographs. Knowing how lenses, or any other piece of photographic equipment, work increases our control of the photography process.

Standard Lenses

A standard lens is technically described as one where the focal length is the same as the diagonal measure of the film, so that on 35mm film, a true standard lens is 43mm. Although for many years, when cameras came supplied with a 'standard' lens it was always a 50mm optic.

FOCAL LENGTH

The focal length of a lens determines how the scene before you will appear in your photograph. Lenses with longer focal lengths have narrow angles of view, meaning they include less of the scene but at a higher magnification, while the reverse is true of wideangle lenses. Long lenses also compress distance, while wideangle lenses exagerate it.

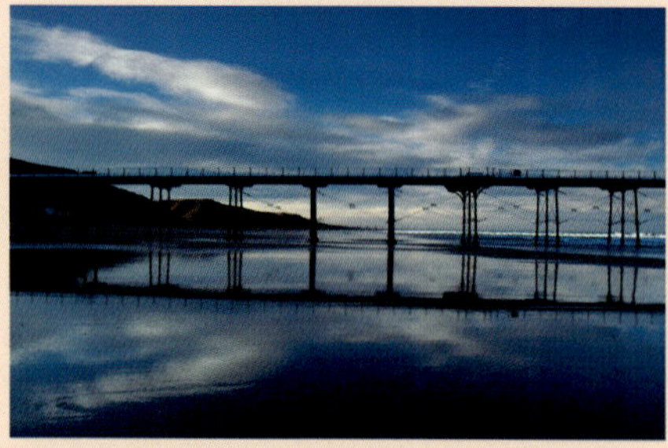

Sigma SD9 with 15mm lens, 35mm equivalent = 24mm

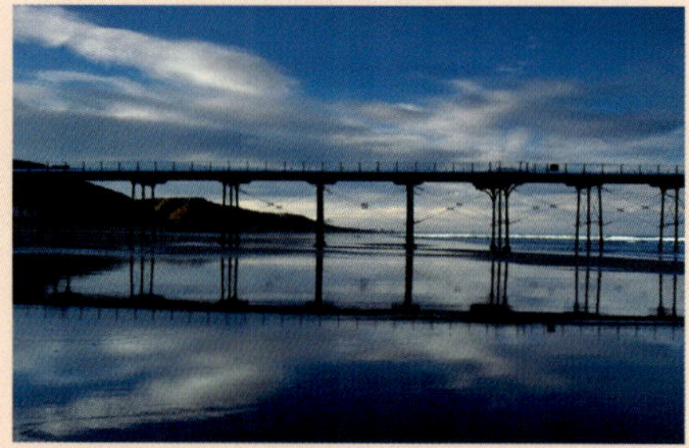

Sigma SD9 with 18mm lens, 35mm equivalent = 30mm

Zoom Lenses

Zoom lenses are very useful and versatile, offering a number of focal lengths in one compact package. The optical quality of zoom lenses these days is indistinguishable from that of prime lenses. Even some of the modern lenses with what would once have been considered an outrageous range (such as 28–300mm) perform well.

For the landscape photographer, zoom lenses are ideal. Working with 35mm SLRs you can cover all focal lengths from 17mm to 300mm in just three reasonable zoom lenses: 17–35mm, 35–70mm, and 70–300mm. This would make an ideal lightweight kit: one body and three lenses covering all those focal lengths.

The real trick to the successful use of zoom lenses is to use them at their intermediate focal lengths. If with the above kit you only ever take pictures with the lenses set at 17, 35, 70 and 300mm you are in fact using just four focal lengths while you have over 280 at your disposal.

technique **LENS CLEANING AND CARE**

Lenses don't like sand or water and especially sea water, so the landscape in general and the coastline in particular are hostile environments. However, you cannot avoid putting your lenses in harms way occasionally. Fortunate, then, that there are a whole host of products available for lens care. With lens tissues and cleaning fluids you can keep your lenses in showroom condition, if you wish. However, your lenses don't have to be pristine to produce good results. I would advise that you take reasonable rather than excessive care of your lenses. Too much or inappropriate cleaning might even damage the front element. All I ever do is gently remove particles like sand or grit with a blower brush, and wipe finger marks or water droplets away with a soft lens cloth, bought from an opticians.

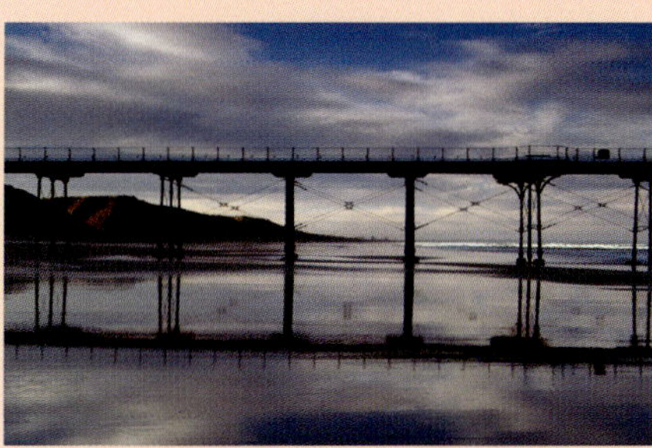

Sigma SD9 with 24mm lens, 35mm equivalent = 40mm

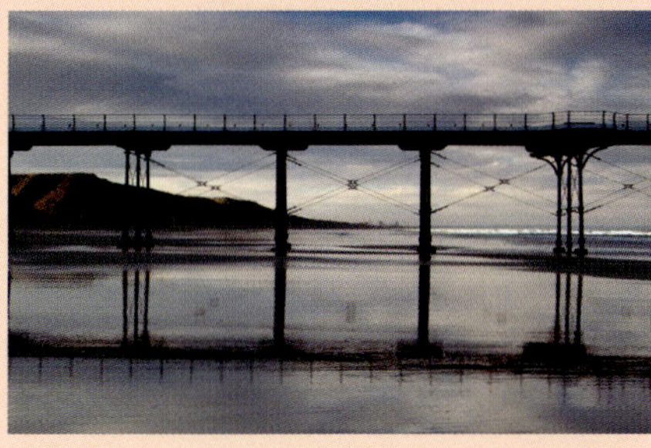

Sigma SD9 with 30mm lens, 35mm equivalent = 50mm

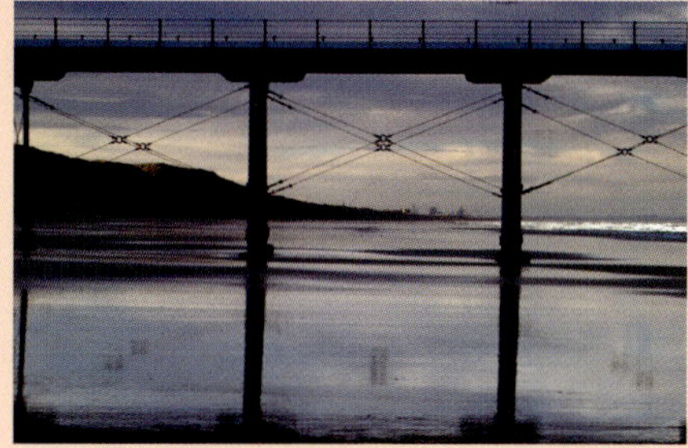

Sigma SD9 with 50mm lens, 35mm equivalent = 85mm

Prime Lenses

A prime lens is simply another term for a lens with a fixed focal length. There is a simple formula you can use to decide if your selection of prime lenses covers most situations you are likely to face. Starting with the widest lens you have, multiply its focal length by 1.4 to find the focal length of the next lens you would have in an ideal kit. Keep on doing this throughout the range, and if you have a lens close to each of the figures you come to then you should have something for most of the scenes you want to capture. For example, starting with a super-wideangle lens, say 17mm, multiplying that by 1.4 gets you to 23.8 or a 24mm wideangle lens. Multiplying 24 by 1.4 gets you to 35mm, and so on. The ideal set would then consist of 17mm, 24mm, 35mm, 50mm (standard) 70mm, etc. The use of 1.4 as the multiplying factor ensures there is sufficient difference between one lens and the next, so that you cannot easily make the same alteration just by moving your viewpoint slightly. There would be little point in owning a 17mm lens as well as a 20mm lens and a 24mm lens. Whatever scene you want to cover with a 20mm lens could very easily be covered with either one of the other two. So the extra expense of buying the third lens, and the effort of carrying it around, would be wasted. If your widest lens, then, is a 20mm, the next one in the range would be 28mm, and so on. Of course, if you are using zoom lenses then you gain all those extra, intermediate focal lengths.

Medium- and Large-Format Lenses

On a 6x7 camera, a true standard lens would be around the 90mm mark, and this is the lens I have on my Pentax 67 while it is in the bag. I therefore have to change to either a longer or shorter lens deliberately. For 5x4 cameras, the standard is 150mm, and for 6x12 cameras it is 125mm.

SEE ALSO:

The Tools for Composition p 124

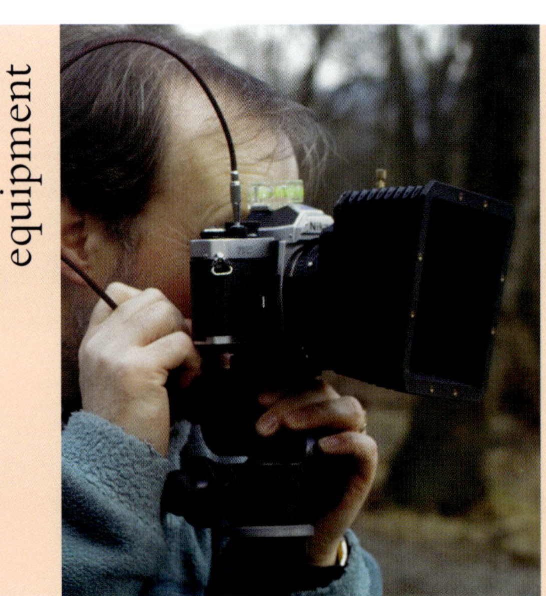

LENS HOODS

A lens hood shades the lens from direct sunlight, which can cause flare. Flare reduces contrast, can cause 'ghosts' of light to appear and generally spoils your image. Usually this is because you are pointing your camera almost directly at the sun, which means that once the lens hood is in place it is also in your picture, so check the corners of your frame for unwanted vignetting. The sun can also cause flare when it is just outside the frame, and it is then that a lens hood can do its job properly.

Moving from 35mm into the world of medium- or large-format cameras may mean saying goodbye to the convenience of zoom lenses. Although there are zoom lenses around for medium-format, and in 6x4.5 they are still a popular and reasonably priced option, at 6x7 they start to become rather large and heavy, which negates one of the very benefits they are supposed to bestow. In the world of large-format photography there is no such thing as a zoom lens.

LENS EQUIVALENTS FOR LARGER FORMATS

35mm camera	6x4.5	6x7	5x4
17mm	30mm	33mm	58mm
20mm	35mm	40mm	75mm
24mm	37mm	45mm	90mm
35mm	55mm	75mm	120mm
50mm	80mm	90mm	150mm
70mm	110mm	135mm	240mm
105mm	150mm	210mm	360mm
135mm	210mm	300mm	450mm
200mm	300mm	400mm	600mm
300mm	500mm	600mm	N/A

Note: The above lens equivalents are approximate.

below Throughout the Canadian Rockies the landscape is large. There was more than one occasion when I was there that I wished I had an even wider lens than 45mm in order to capture the scene as I wanted. It was after this trip that I bought the 58mm lens for my 5x4 camera. This was a rare chance to use a longer lens as well.

Pentax 67, 1/2sec at f/22, polarizing filter and Coral No. 1

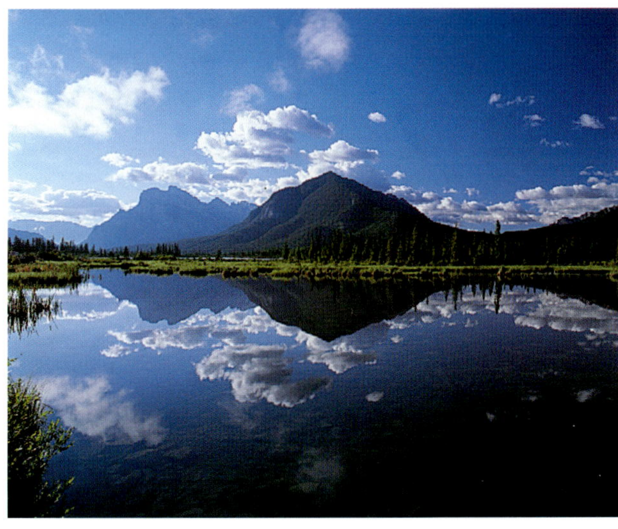

45mm on a 6x7 camera

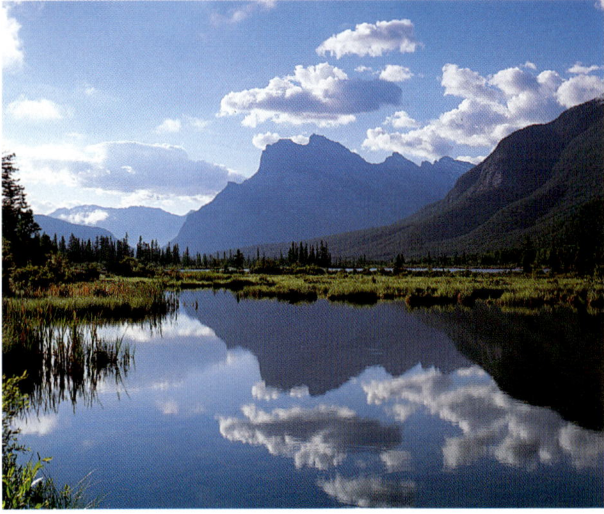

135mm on a 6x7 camera

Photographic Filters

Photographic filters can be used to produce a wide range of effects. Those most useful for photographing water separate the light we do not want from the light that we do. A warm-up filter, for example, removes cold-looking blue light and leaves a warm shade. A neutral-density filter reduces the quantity of light passing through it, allowing longer shutter speeds or wider apertures.

Many filters these days are made of optical resin, a form of plastic. Resin is lighter and cheaper than glass, but prone to scratches and slight damage. Glass filters are heavier and prone to shattering.

Basic Filter Types

There are two basic filter types: round, screw-on filters that fit directly onto the camera's lens, and square (or sometimes rectangular) filters that fit into a special holder attached to the lens.

Super-wideangle lenses can suffer from exposure 'fall off' towards the edges of the frame, especially on large-format and panoramic cameras. In order to even this out, a centre neutral-density filter has to be added. This reduces the exposure in the centre of the image, evening out the exposure across the picture. Only a round screw-in type of filter can do this, because the effect has to be right in the centre of the lens.

For the filters used in colour photography the square filter system is the best design (see 'Filter Systems', opposite). It means that all your filters will fit onto all your lenses, regardless of the size of the front element of your lens. With graduated filters, such as the coral I use for warming up the light or the graduated neutral-density filters I use to hold back light from part of the scene, you need to be able to position the demarcation line between filtered and unfiltered portions of the resin in the appropriate area. You can only do this with the square slip-into-place type of filter.

Filters for Black & White Photography

For black & white film there are filters that can help alter the tones within the scene. These are single-colour filters, such as red, green or yellow. They lighten the tone of anything the same colour and darken the tone of the complementary or opposite colour. So a red filter will turn a blue sky almost black and a red flower almost white. Looking through one of these filters helps the photographer 'see' the image in black & white as well, since they will overpower the real colour in the scene.

technique PROTECTING YOUR LENSES

Some photographers keep a round, screw-in-type UV or skylight filter (which has a very subtle effect) permanently on their lenses to protect the front element from scratches and other damage. A lens is always going to cost far more to replace than even an expensive filter.

Light Loss

All filters by their very nature reduce the total amount of light reaching the film. This is known as the 'filter factor'. If you are measuring the light with a TTL camera, the built-in meter will read the reduced light through the filter and advise accordingly. If, on the other hand, you are using a separate handheld meter, then you have to take the filter factor into account yourself and calculate the correct exposure.

To make things more confusing, some filters vary in how much light they stop. Polarizing filters, for example, can reduce the light by between 1/4 and 2 stops.

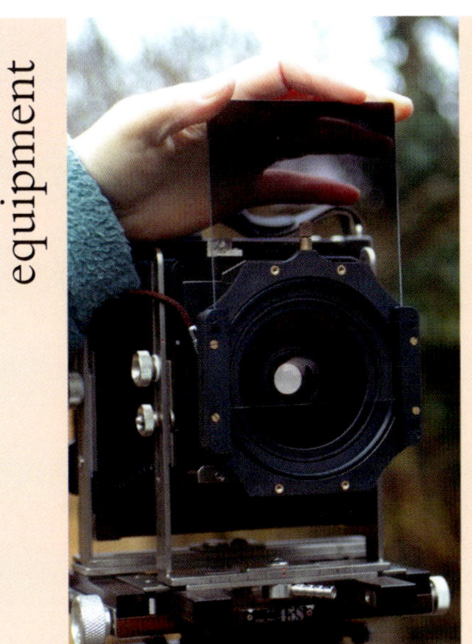

FILTER SYSTEMS

Square filters need to be used with a filter system. This consists of a filter holder and an adaptor ring that connects the holder to your lens. Professional filter holders can be assembled from individual components to accommodate up to four filters. Alternatively, you can buy a special lens hood with filter slots.

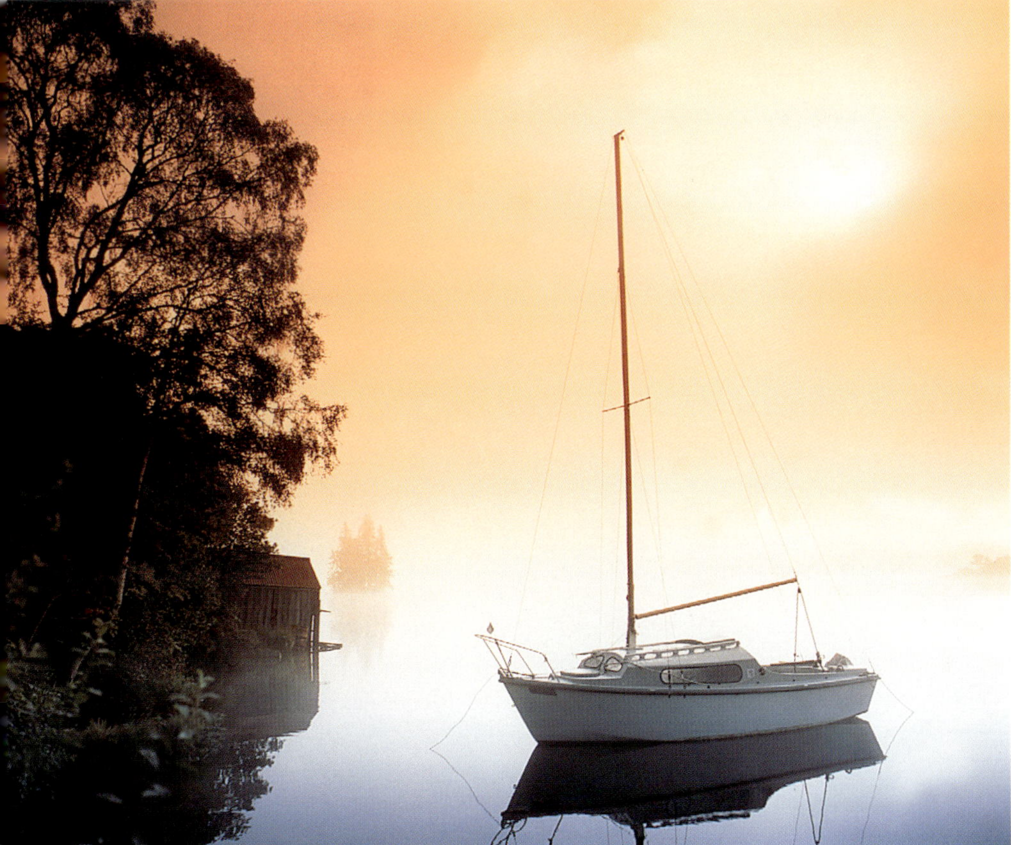

left **Boat on Loch Ness**
Two colour-graduated filters were used to create this effect. Blue was used inverted along the bottom of the picture and a tobacco was used to colour the sky. This is far from the natural approach I favour today.

below **Dusk over the Cullin, Isle of Skye**
This image was taken using a sunset filter.

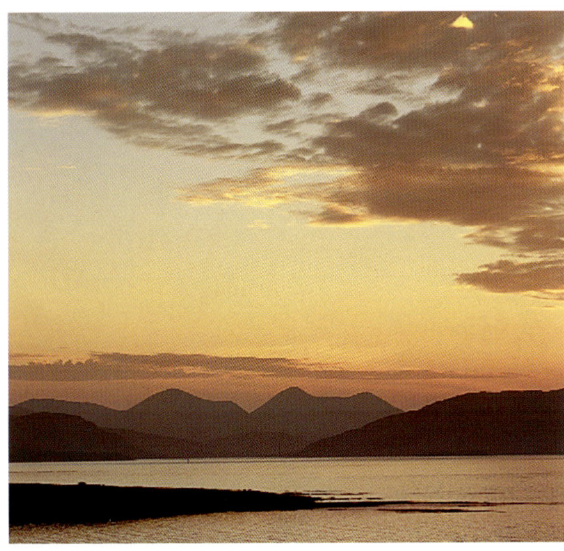

Sky-Blue Pink

Nature puts on a wonderful show every so often, and it is the landscape

photographer's job to be there and capture it for all time. Pictures like these

rely on timing and technique for their success. There are no coloured filters

used here, only neutral-density filters to balance the brighter sky with the

darker land. This enables film to 'see' the landscape as we do.

Dunstanburgh Castle, Dawn

It is a bit of a walk from the nearest convenient
car-parking spot to this location, and if you want to
catch the sunrise you have to walk here in the dark.
A head torch is therefore a real asset if you want to
take pictures like this one.

Dunstanburgh Castle on the north-east coast of
England is one of the most dramatic and inspirational
scenes I know. This picture is taken from the north
looking south towards the sunrise. While I waited for
the light the clouds were clearing and I did wonder
if all the clouds would be gone by the time the sun
reached the right spot. Just this one lingered long
enough. As well as the wonderful sky, it is the
foreground pools reflecting all that colour that really
bring this scene to life.

Pentax 67 with 55mm lens, 1 second at f/22,
0.6 ND soft-grad filter

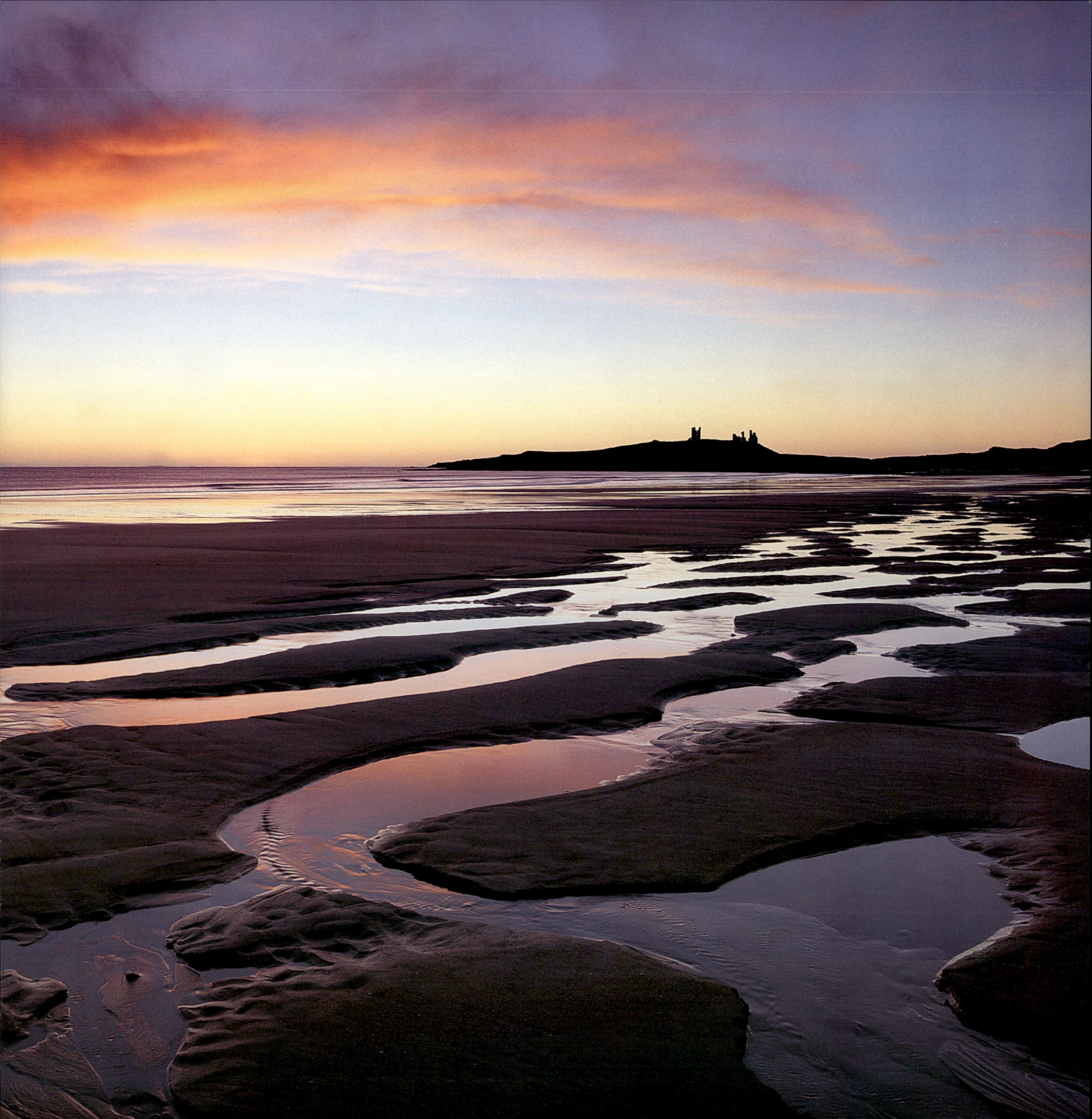

River Ure at Sunset

I needed much more than just a camera and a lens to make this picture happen:
wellington boots meant I could wade out into the river and lose some of the
foreground algae; a tripod with sealed legs meant I could set it up without causing
problems for myself later; a spirit level ensured a straight horizon; and a midge hood
meant I could take the time to carefully frame the scene without being eaten alive.
Moments like this have to be anticipated as well. You cannot chase the sunset; you
have to be there and be ready. A tripod is essential for this. With the scene found
and composed the camera can just be left in place, ready for the right light to occur.

**Pentax 67 with 55mm lens, Velvia 50, exposure details not recorded,
0.6 ND grad filter**

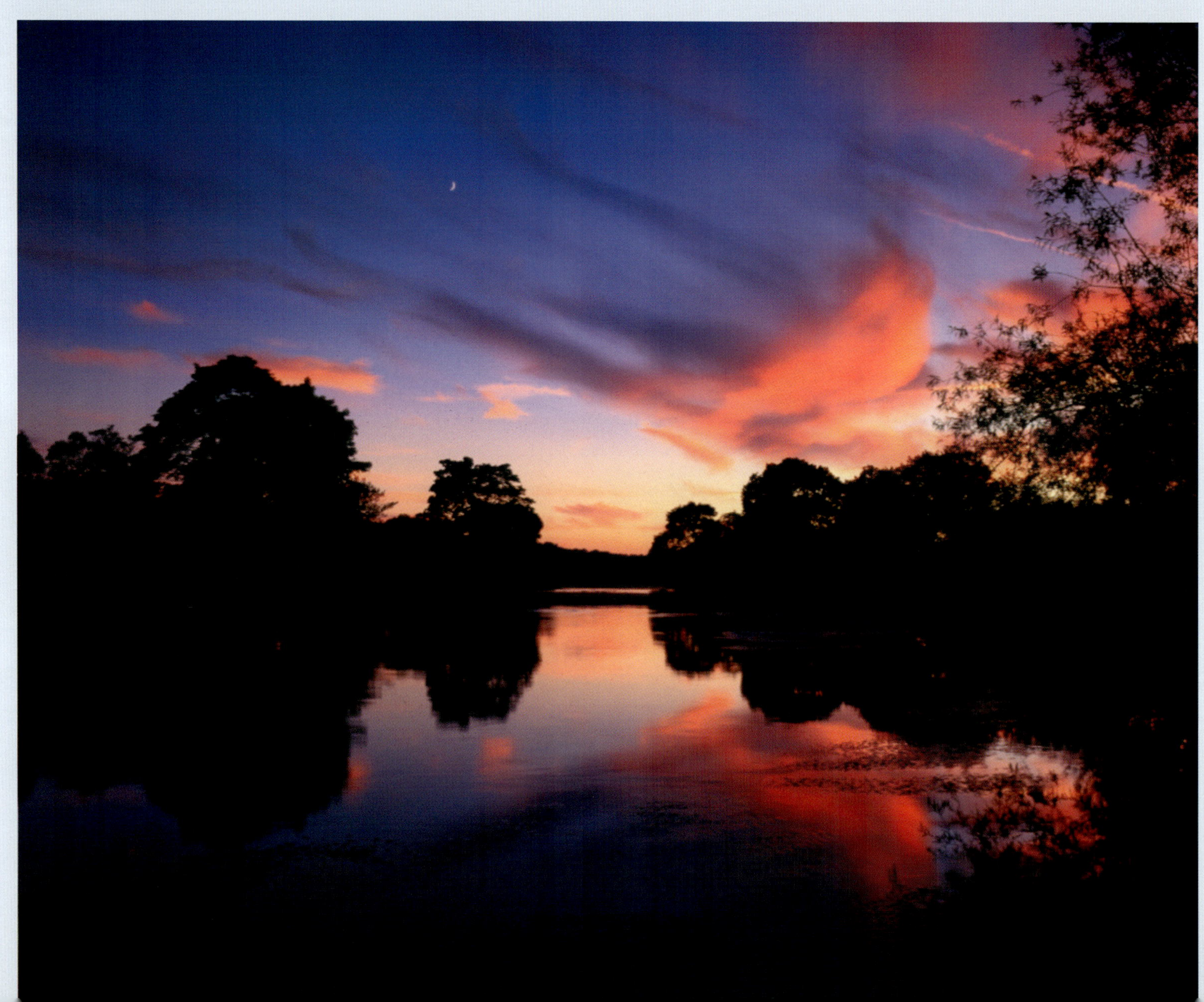

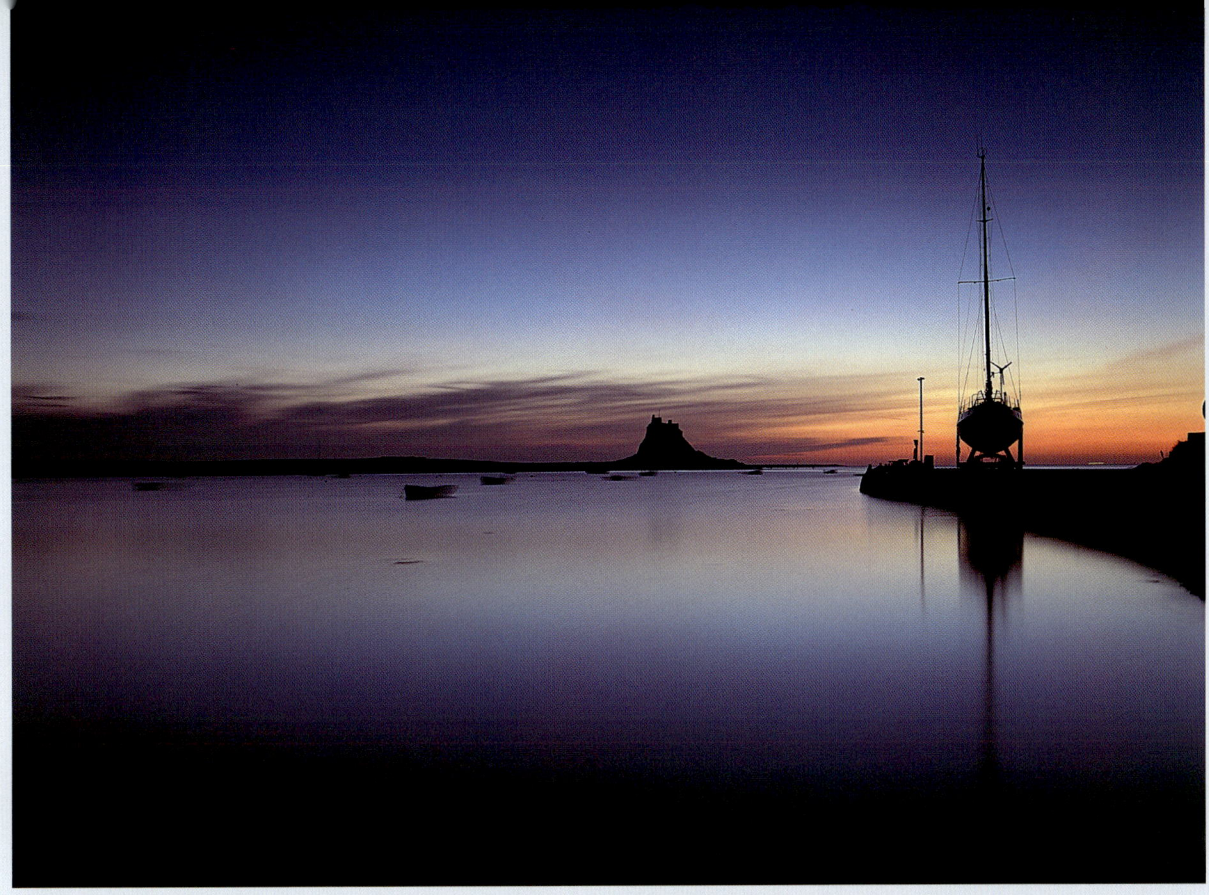

right **Saltburn Sunset**

In the late afternoon and early evening when the sky shows promise of a sunset to come, I will almost always seek a foreground that features water. Beaches at low tide are great, since the standing water left by the retreating tide is usually shallow and still enough to reflect the colour of the sky. Even wet sand can do this. Lakes and rivers can serve as well, but you have to be doubly lucky – you need the colour in the sky and you need the water to be sufficiently still to form a reflection. When it is available, then, a beach is the safer bet. Saltburn can only serve during the height of the summer when the sun sets out to sea; for much of the rest of the year the sunset is inland, and then I have other places worth considering. This was one of those occasions when the photograph looks better than my memory of the real event.

Pentax 67 with 45mm lens, 1 second at f/22, 0.6 ND grad filter

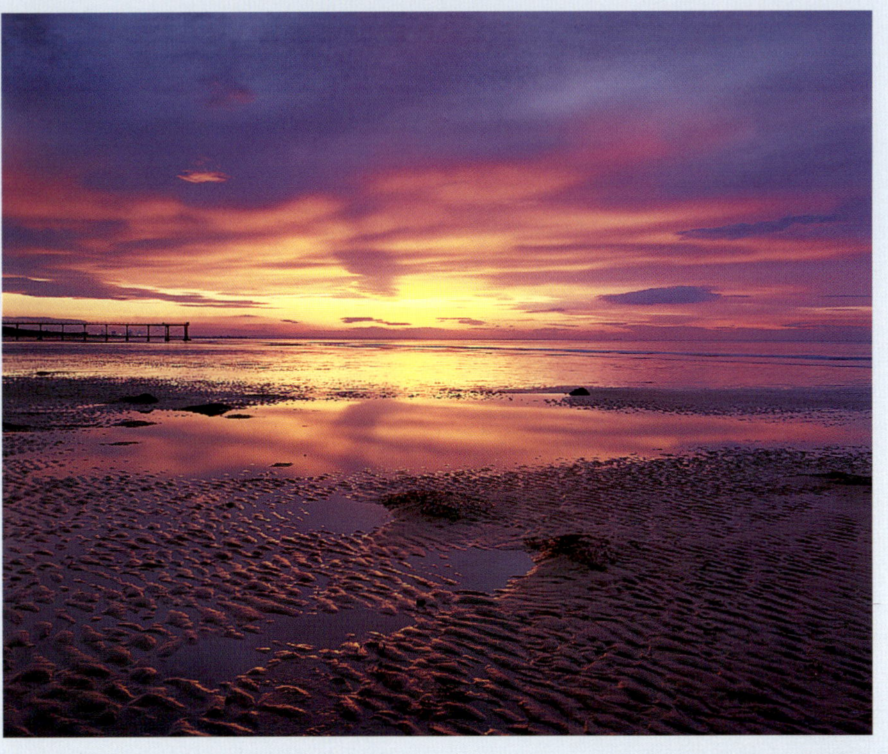

Tripods and Accessories

Your pictures will only ever be as sharp as the weakest link in the process, and if your camera is not perfectly still when the picture is taken, then that is likely to be the weakest link. Metaphorically speaking, a tripod is the sharpest lens you can buy, if you use it all of the time.

A tripod may look like a nuisance, bulky and possibly heavy (especially one like my Benbo). It may appear to be something else to slow you down and hinder the picture-taking process. Perhaps this is why I often meet photographers in the landscape who own a tripod and confess they wish they had brought it along. This, then, is one of the key pieces of advice I can impart – use a tripod all the time. Follow this advice and your photography will almost certainly improve.

A tripod sets you free to use whatever shutter-speed and aperture combination you choose. This means you can select very small apertures for great depth of field and/or use very long exposures to allow flowing water to blur. It also means you can carefully compose your picture and then wait as long as it takes for the right light to appear. It also slows you down, which can be a good thing, giving you more time to think about the picture you intend to take.

Cable Release

A cable release is a further guard against camera shake when taking pictures at slow shutter speeds. However, not all modern cameras have a cable-release socket. You can use a camera's self-timer instead, but it may not be convenient if you are waiting in quickly changing light for the sun to strike in a particular spot, or if you need to take a two-minute-long exposure at night.

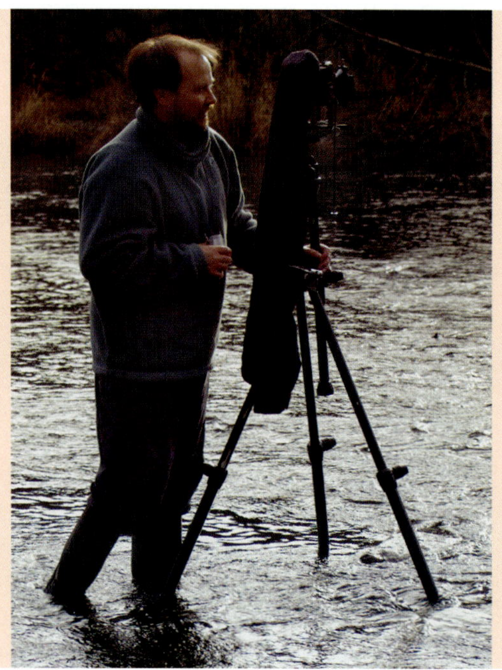

equipment

TRIPODS FOR PHOTOGRAPHING WATER

More so than any other piece of equipment, a sturdy and reliable tripod will improve your photography, so it is worth doing your research before buying one. Prices vary, but a cheap tripod is a false economy, since it will not stand up to the rigours of regular use and may not offer enough support for your camera, especially on a breezy day. For photographing water, your best bet is a tripod with sealed feet that can be immersed in the water without any part of the leg-locking mechanism getting wet. I find the Benbo tripod (pictured) perfect for photography on the beach or in water, as the mechanisms are high up so that the tripod can stand in a foot of water without suffering any ill effects. Some other tripods, where the locking mechanisms are lower down the legs, will get wet even in shallow water. They will need careful cleaning and regular greasing to keep them from sticking after much use.

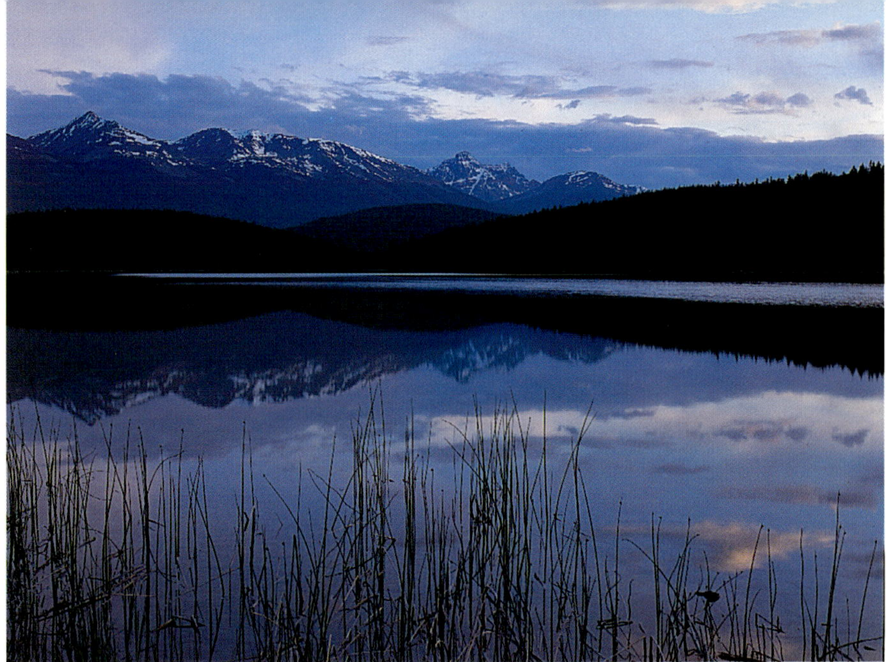

Patricia Lake, Jasper National Park, Canada

The importance of a tripod cannot be overstated. As the quantity of light fades so often the quality increases. This picture, taken in the early evening, would not have been possible without a tripod. The low level of light and the required depth of field – so that both the foreground reeds and the distant mountains appear sharp – meant a small aperture, long shutter speed and perfectly still camera were all essential. My spirit level confirmed that the horizon would be straight.

Pentax 67 with 90mm lens, Velvia 50, 1/2sec at f/22, 0.6 ND grad filter

SPIRIT LEVEL

Sometimes it really helps to have a spirit level that sits in the hotshoe of your camera and lets you know when it is perfectly straight. If you take a picture with a sloping horizon and you missed it through the viewfinder, everyone will be able to see it in the picture – especially if that sloping horizon is a distant lake shore or the sea.

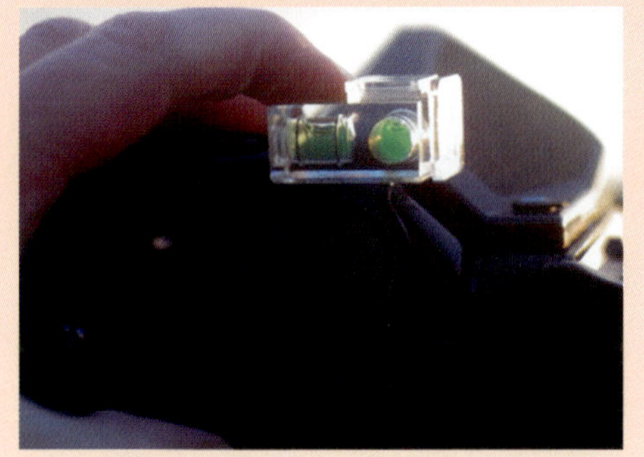

Other Essentials

There are other accessories that all photographers should carry: spare batteries, spare cable release, a set of jewellers' screwdrivers and a lens cloth. When photographing water, you may also find a midge hood beneficial. These pests gather to feast on all who venture to the wrong place at the wrong time, and that often means those who stand around by the lake shore in the early morning or evening.

Waterproof sheets to place on the ground before you put your camera bag down and waterproof bags to place over cameras to protect them from the rain are also invaluable.

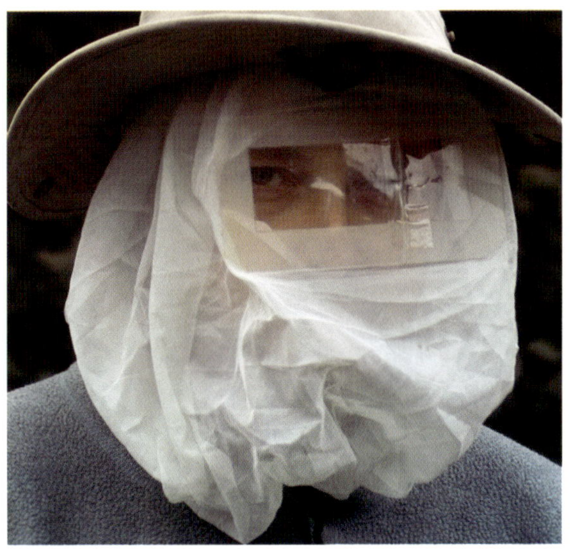

You might look slightly ridiculous with a piece of net curtain over your head, but at least with a midge hood you will be comfortable enough to get on with your photography, or wait for the right light.

STOPWATCH

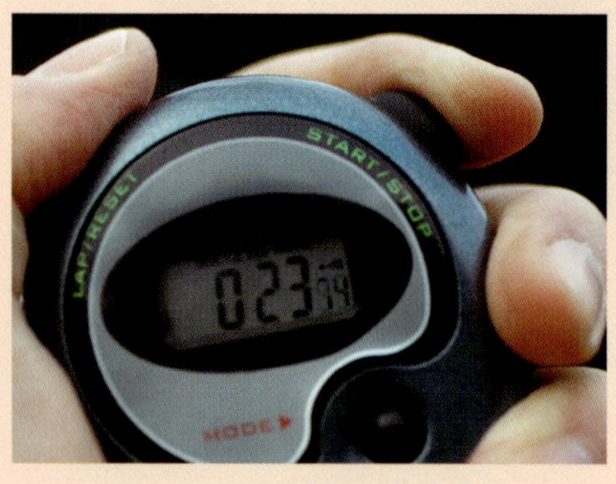

A stopwatch is another unlikely accessory in a camera bag. If you are shooting in very low light and trying to capture the blur of moving water, then a two-minute exposure is a terrific way to get a great effect with incoming tide over rocks. You can count 'one thousand, two thousand', but by the time you are getting to one hundred and twenty thousand, accuracy may have gone out of the window. On the other hand, a stopwatch does not lose count when someone comes along and asks you what you are doing.

In order to be in the right place at the right time, it may be necessary to walk to or from the viewpoint in the dark. For this, a head torch is very useful; it will illuminate the way for you while leaving your hands free to carry a tripod. I have also found that a sun-positioning compass is useful when planning where to shoot and when. Anything that makes you better prepared means that you are more likely to come home with some good photos for your efforts.

Bags

Finding the right bag for your equipment isn't something you can take for granted. It is one of the hardest pieces of equipment to select. What I decided to do was take all the equipment I wanted to carry with me to the shop and filled the bags in turn until I found one that took everything and which could be carried in reasonable comfort.

Shoulder bags are inappropriate for landscape photographers, as you need something that sits comfortably on your back and distributes the weight evenly on both shoulders and on your back. Even relatively light camera equipment carried on one shoulder can soon make you feel uncomfortable on a short walk. Prolonged use of a shoulder bag to carry camera gear, especially heavy camera gear that includes a tripod, can cause back and shoulder problems.

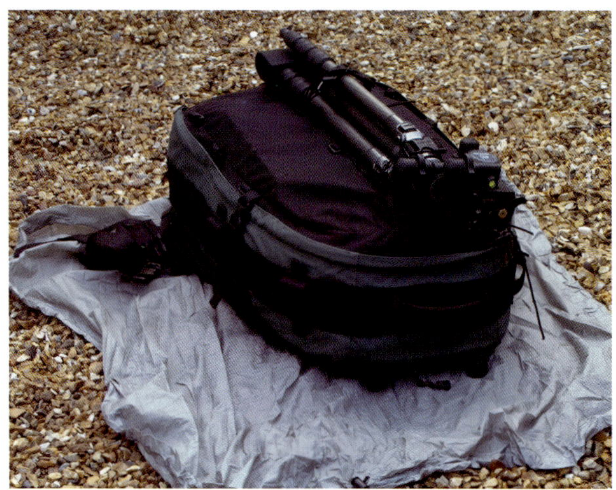

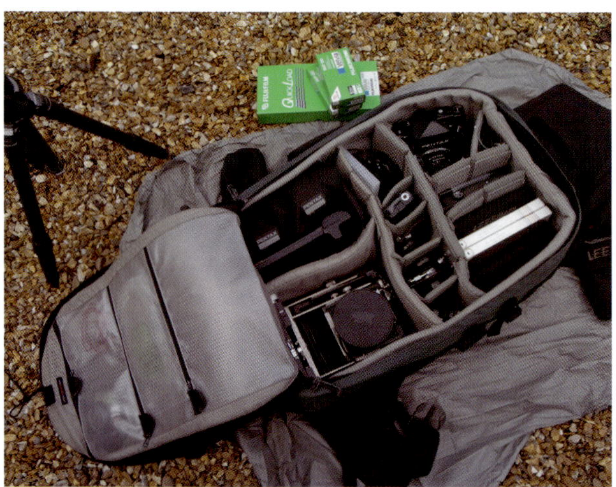

left and right
The Lowepro bags I use have variable storage sections to protect the equipment inside and an all-weather cover, which can be used, for instance, on the beach as a groundsheet for the bag. The rucksack design and padded straps make them comfortable to carry.

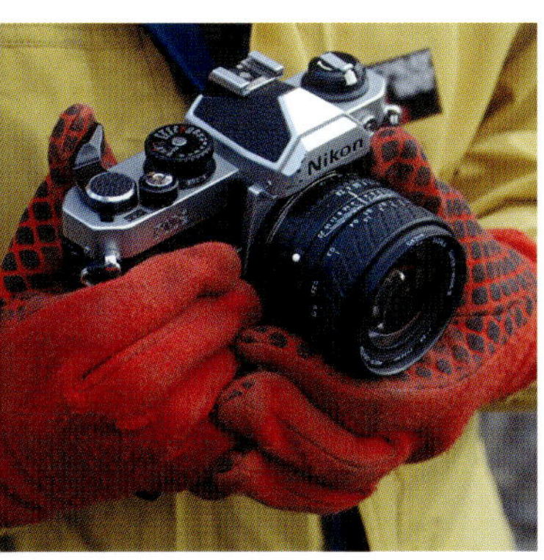

Gloves that can keep your fingers warm while you operate a camera are very useful.

Outdoor Clothing and Footwear

It is always worth doing as much as you can to keep yourself comfortable. In the summer, this means wearing a sun hat and cool, breathable material that will keep you dry. There are few things worse than your own sweat on your back when it has turned to iced water, and especially so when you have to press it onto your back with a camera bag. In winter, you need to wear layers of clothing that you can peel off as you get hot while walking and carrying a heavy load. Since the best light is often found in changeable weather, carrying a lightweight waterproof coat is also a good idea, and wear proper walking trousers that dry quickly if they get wet, rather than jeans that will stay wet and uncomfortable for the rest of the day.

Footwear

If you are going to photograph water, a pair of wellington boots is essential. You need to be able to walk anywhere without worrying about getting too wet. On a beach, as the sun goes down in winter, the last thing you want is cold, wet feet. They are great, too, if you want to walk to a point on the beach without leaving a trail of your own footprints in the sand. If you walk through the water where the tide is washing your own footprints away as you go, you then have a clean beach to photograph when you arrive at the viewpoint. Just don't look at your feet while you do this: the combination of moving water and moving feet can really affect balance.

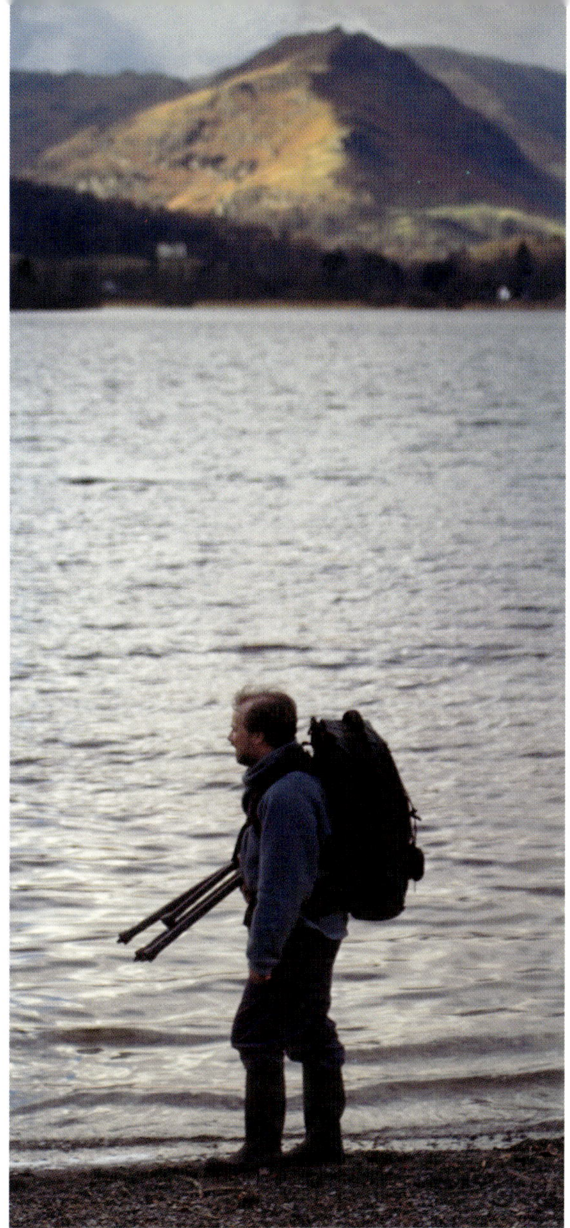

You can buy innersoles for walking boots that add a great deal of support to your footwear; putting a pair of these inside your wellingtons will make them more suitable for walking over hard rock. I once made the mistake of walking a long way to the beach in wellies without an innersole – a mistake I only made once.

RECOMMENDED EQUIPMENT SET-UPS

For Beginners

35mm SLR camera body with full manual control, cable-release socket

Or a digital SLR camera. You could even have the best of both worlds by buying a 35mm body and digital from the same maker, and use the lenses on both

Three zoom lenses: 17–30mm, 30–70mm and 70–300mm

Small backpack for carrying some spare clothes, accessories, food and water (with enough room still for the camera)

Filters: 0.6 ND grad, soft coral or straw grad for warm-up and polarizer

Sturdy tripod

Intermediate Level

As above plus:

Replace amateur-spec SLR with professional 35mm film or digital SLR with mirror lock-up facility

Additional lenses: macro for very close work

Additional filters: full set of ND grads 0.3, 0.6 and 0.9 in both soft and hard graduation

Medium-format camera and three prime lenses (unless you go for a 645 and then there are suitable zoom lenses). On 67 a wideangle lens in the 45–55mm range, a 90mm standard and a short telephoto in the the 135–200mm range

Advanced Level

As above plus:
A specialist camera of your own choice, large format or panoramic with a range of lenses to suit. By the time you are an advanced photographer you will know what type of photography you want to do, and therefore what camera equipment you need

THE AUTHOR'S KIT

Lowepro super trekker AW bag

Ebony 45s large-format camera

6x12 panoramic film back for 5x4 camera

58mm lens for 5x4 camera

90mm lens for 5x4 camera

120mm lens for 5x4 camera

150mm lens for 5x4 camera

240mm lens for 5x4 camera

Pentax 67 medium-format camera

45mm lens for Pentax camera

90mm lens for Pentax camera

135mm lens for Pentax camera

Loupe magnifying glass

Lee filters: 6 ND grads, 1 polarizing filter and 1 coral no. 1 filter

Filter rings and holders for the Lee filters

Lee lens hood

Sekonic lightmeter

Polaroid 545i back for use with the Fuji Quickload film

Stopwatch, midge hood, six cable releases, normal compass and sun-positioning compass

Two 5x4 Quickload boxes, one containing 21 sheets of Quickload film (giving seven pictures' worth at three sheets to a picture), the other containing 15 rolls of 120 film

Second-hand Equipment

Buying second-hand camera equipment can be a very sensible way to acquire the right camera for landscape photography. Most modern cameras are overqualified for landscape with autofocus, multimode metering and more bells and whistles than a ship. All you need for photographing water is a manual-control, manual-focus, sturdy and reliable camera.

Cameras

When buying second-hand equipment, just keep in mind what a camera is. The body is a light-tight box, so does it look and feel light-tight? When you close the back does it shut with a reassuring click? Does it feel tightly closed? Does the film wind on smoothly? It is likely there will be some signs of wear, but these should not be excessive. Attach and detach the lens. Does that work smoothly? You shouldn't have to force anything. If you buy from a reputable dealer you should get a short guarantee, but long enough to run a few rolls through and see that everything works. If you buy privately, buy from someone you trust. Run a film through the camera as quickly as you can to check for any obvious faults.

Lenses

When buying lenses look for clean glass, a good connection to the camera and check that the iris closes quickly. I came back from Canada with a number of grossly overexposed shots taken using a 300mm lens on the Nikon because the iris had become sticky. This can easily be fixed, but is something that should be avoided. Slight defects on the front element of a lens may be cause for a price reduction and are not always the death knell of a lens. My own equipment comes in for some heavy treatment, and there have been occasions when a small scratch might have appeared in the front element, but I have never noticed any reduction in the quality or sharpness of my photographs as a result. If there is damage, ask to try the lens out before you buy, and expect a reduced price. Make sure the lens connects properly and easily to the camera.

BUYING AND SELLING

If you are buying second-hand equipment you will probably pay more at a camera shop than if you buy from a private seller, but the equipment is likely to have been checked over and may come with a short guarantee. On the other hand, if you are selling second-hand equipment you are likely to get more for your equipment selling privately than trading it at a shop.

There is also the Internet, which has led to the development of some good deals for private buyers and sellers of second-hand goods, but be wary of buying equipment you haven't seen.

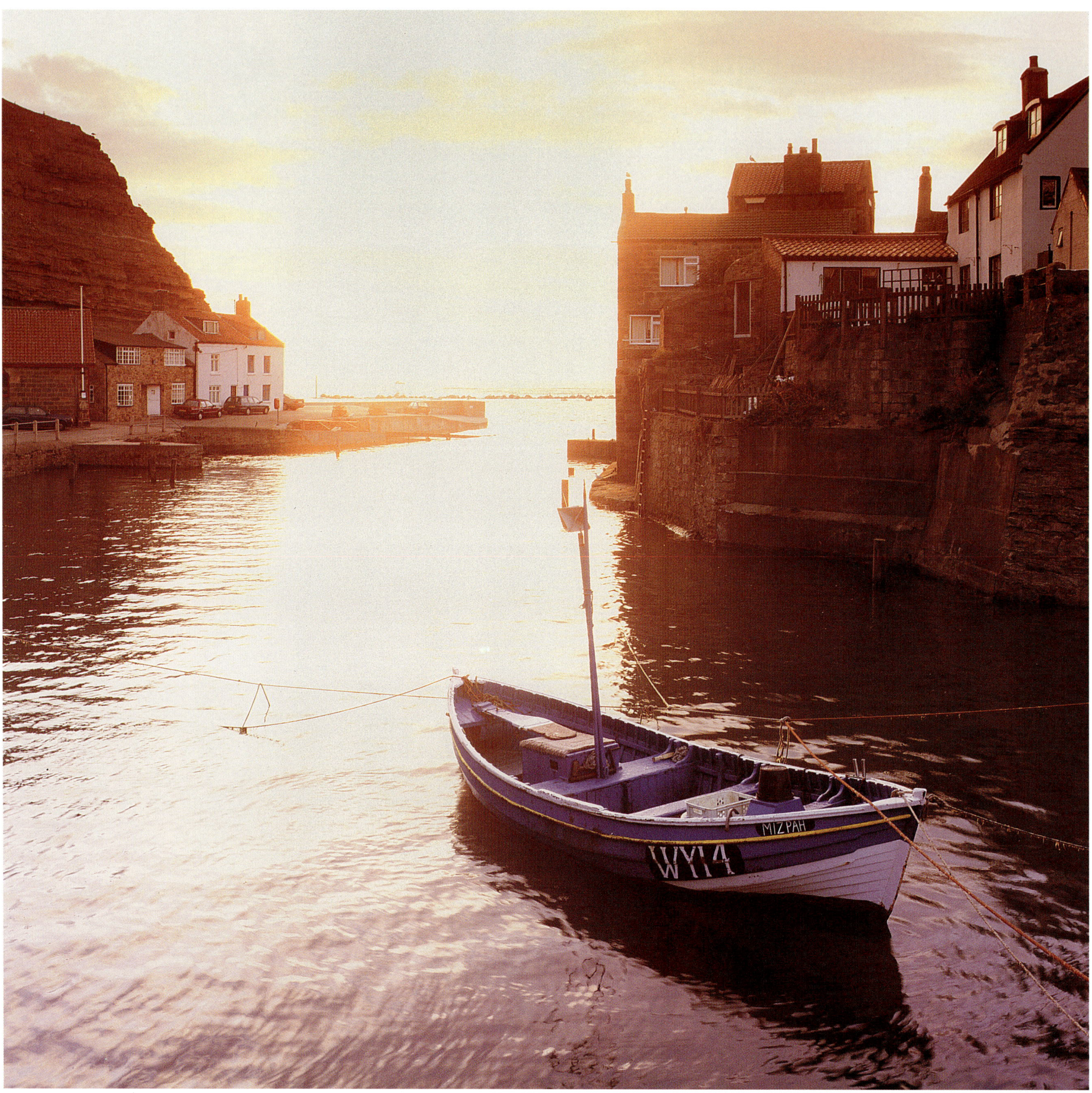

Technique

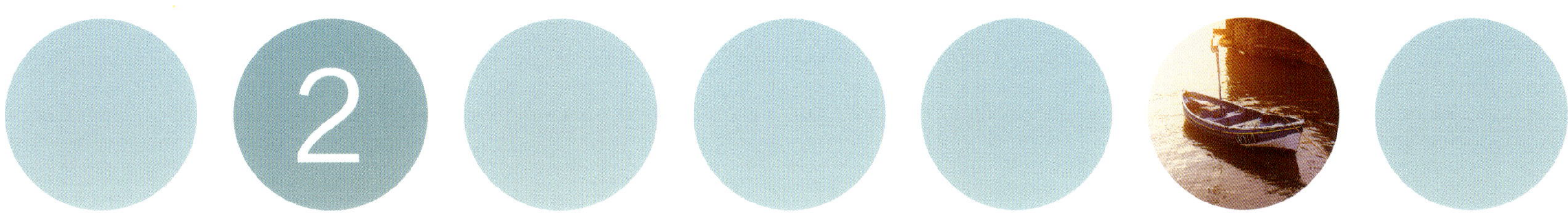

Photography is like life, the universe and everything, insomuch as nothing works in isolation. Any photograph is a combination of the photographer's taste and judgement, the light, the composition, the elements and the techniques used. A successful photograph results when all these parts combine in an appropriate way.

Technique is only a means to an end, never an end in itself. Sharp focus and correct exposure alone will not guarantee a good photograph. Lighting and composition are the more important considerations. Poor technique can spoil what would otherwise be a good picture, but the best technique cannot rescue what was always going to be a dull and uninteresting photograph. If you are ever going to succeed as a photographer, technique has to become second nature to you. Knowledge is helpful, but experience is the only route to true understanding. Your mind needs to be free to think about the more important issues of composition, light, texture and tone. If conscious thoughts of exposure, focus, shutter speeds, depth of field, the use of filters and the choice of film are all clouding your mind it will be difficult to be really creative.

The correct technique to use in any situation is as much a matter of taste as it is of science. You will always have choices: which combination of shutter speed and aperture to use for a correct exposure in any given light; how to record motion within a picture; where to place the plane of focus; how much depth of field to have; which filters, if any, to use and how to use them. All these considerations are technical in nature, yet along with the composition and lighting, they determine the aesthetic of the final image.

In Control
The more control you have over the picture-taking process, the more freedom you gain to express your vision.

Most technical matters can be over-complicated to such a degree that many people would throw up their hands in despair and give up. Personally, I like to work on the need-to-know principle. For instance, I do not understand the exact science behind photographic film or polarizing filters but I have found that it is helpful to know how they work if you are to have maximum control over your photography. Knowing how photographic equipment works in practice is far more important than being caught up in technical and scientific jargon. I will therefore explain the techniques covered here in as short and as straightforward a way as possible.

Focus on... Developing your own Technique

I have never made the investment in time and effort to learn how to cook properly. I have noticed that people who can cook do not slavishly follow a recipe; they have the confidence to alter the quantities if they see fit to do so, and even to substitute some of the ingredients. It is the same for photographers – there is no fixed recipe for a successful photograph. If you really want to be a good photographer, you need to find the confidence to ignore the 'recipes' that other photographers lay down and develop some of your own.

Determining Appropriate Exposure

Getting exposure right, especially if you are using transparency film (see 'Exposure Latitude', page 50), would seem to be very important, except that there is not always a right way to expose a picture.

Exposure can determine mood; it can be used to emphasize one part or another of the picture. It is largely a matter of opinion, yet when it is wrong it can be very obviously wrong. As a result, it is often seen as being complex. Further complication is added because the tool for determining exposure is a lightmeter. A lightmeter measures light, but it does not tell us the correct exposure to use for the subject we want to photograph. The reading a lightmeter gives is only a starting point in determining the appropriate exposure.

The Controls for Exposure

There are a total of five elements that influence exposure. The first two are the shutter speed and the aperture. The shutter on a camera opens for a variable amount of time and allows light to reach the film. That light has to pass through the aperture, which is variable in size. The longer the shutter is open, the more light that passes through to reach the film. Equally, the wider the aperture, the more light that passes through to reach the film.

The next two elements are the quantity of light and film speed (see page 28). Velvia is a slow film, officially rated at ISO 50, though many photographers rate it slower than this (ISO 32–40). Provia is rated at ISO 100 and so is officially one stop higher, or twice as fast, as Velvia. This means that in the same light you could use 1/60sec shutter

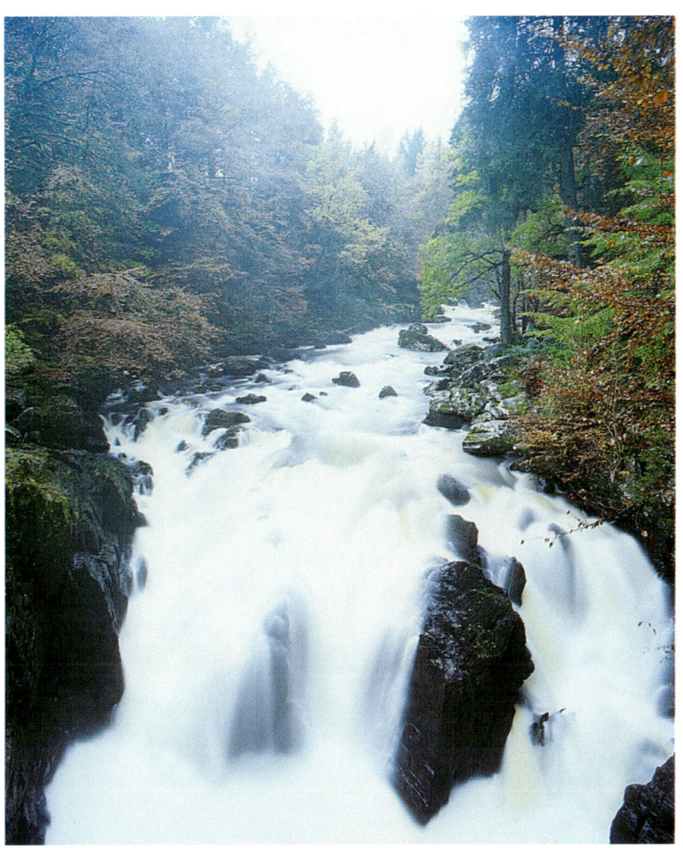

right **Waterfall, The Hermitage**
This picture is grossly overexposed, but it appears exactly as I hoped it would. It was a pretty awful day for landscape photography. I took a spotmeter reading from the trees, then used this reading to take the picture. I knew that by doing so I would be able to record the colours in the leaves but that the sky and much of the river would burn out through overexposure as a result. The final image has a dreamlike quality, rather than simply looking dull, as the day truly was.

Pentax 67 with 45mm lens, Velvia 50, 8 seconds at f/22

SEE ALSO:

Film *p 28*

Shutter speed *p 56*

Aperture *p 60*

Depth of field *p 60*

Film Speed			
50	100	200	400
0	1	2	3
Stops			

Changes in exposure are often referred to in terms of stops. A doubling of the aperture, a halving of the shutter speed or a doubling of the film speed equals a one-stop increase in exposure.

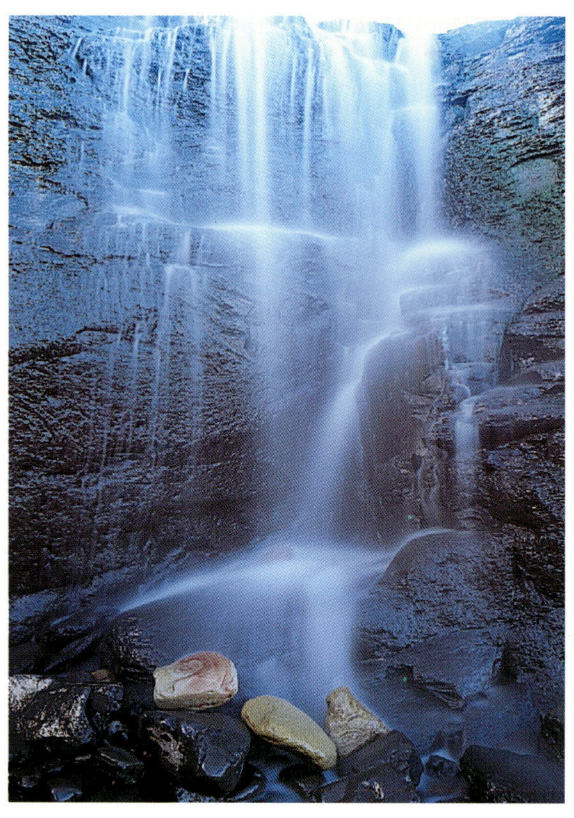

speed for Provia, whereas with Velvia you would need 1/30sec at the same aperture. Alternatively, you could leave the shutter speed alone and reduce the aperture from, say, f/11 to f/16. ISO 400 film is then three stops faster than an ISO 50 film.

The fifth element is the photographer's opinion and taste. Do you want detail in the highlights or the shadows, or do you want as much detail as possible in both? Then you need to take into account the other effects shutter speed and aperture have on the final image. For example, as you reduce the size of the aperture you increase depth of field, and if you keep the shutter open longer you increase motion blur, if there is anything moving within your picture.

Focus on... Exposure Latitude

If you are using print film, all you have to do is get in the ball park and your pictures will be acceptable. This is because any under- or overexposure can be compensated for at the printing stage. Digital cameras have a similar latitude to negative film, although they tend to be more tolerant of underexposure than overexposure. In any case, since you can see the result instantly you can usually put errors right in the field and take the picture again. Most professional and serious amateur photographers use transparency film for landscape work. When exposed correctly it is sharper and gives better colour rendition than print film ever can. It is, however, very unforgiving of exposure errors – as little as a 1/2 stop under- or overexposure can seriously spoil a shot.

Metering

If you point a lightmeter at a subject that is perfectly white and use the meter's suggested exposure settings to take your picture, the white scene will be underexposed and will record as grey. Likewise, if you photograph a subject that is totally black and follow the suggested exposure the result will be overexposed and your black subject will also record as grey. If you find a midtone grey subject your exposure will be correct. If, having taken a reading from something midtone grey in the same light, you use that reading to photograph a black or a white subject then the photo will be correctly exposed and come out as black or white respectively. This works fine, except that the world is not black and white. Many photographers suggest carrying a midtone grey card or material with you to meter off, but I doubt anyone who writes this advice ever follows it. In my experience, it is far better to meter off the land around you and learn through experience what works best in different conditions.

Lightmeters work on the assumption that if you blend all the tones in a scene together they will make midtone grey (technically this is called 18% grey but midtone describes it better). For the majority of ordinary scenes in ordinary light this is correct, and for prints it is close enough not to matter. The reason exposure is such a thorny issue is because photographers are attracted to those situations where this assumption is wrong. The most interesting subjects do not blend to a midtone grey; they are darker or brighter than this. So the meter does not give us a useable exposure

reading; we have to use it as a starting point and then apply our judgement. The other reason, of course, is that serious photographers who think about and take control of their exposure tend to use transparency film, which is less forgiving.

Metering Systems

These days, cameras come with very sophisticated metering systems. Some have the 'experience' of thousands of photographs built into their memory, so that they can recognize different lighting situations and ensure correct exposure. While in normal light these cameras cope very well and free photographers from being too concerned with exposure, in difficult conditions or situations where you want to be able to decide what mood

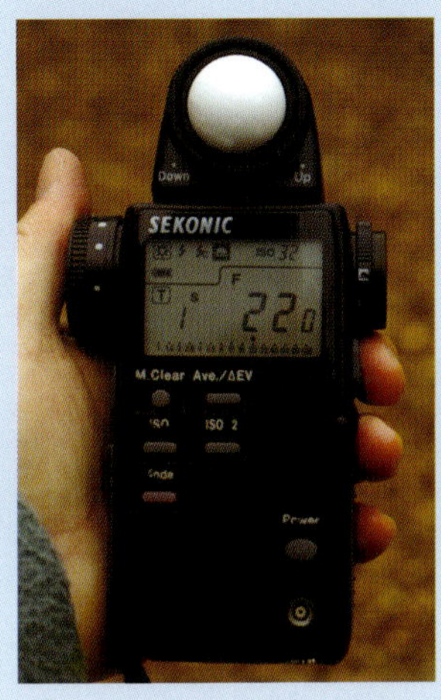

With a handheld meter you can take incident as well as reflective readings. Some photographers prefer this to TTL metering, as it takes a reading not from the light reflected from the scene but from the light falling on the scene. It therefore takes no account of the colour or tone of the subject and gives the reading for a midtone right away. You still have to use your own judgement to adjust the reading properly.

Sneak Preview

Digital cameras give us another method for determining the appropriate exposure. The immediate preview of the picture just taken can also act as a guide for exposing transparency film at the same time. With practice, I am sure this could become a very useful tool.

your picture should convey, you need to know how to take control of exposure. I am not saying these cameras will give inaccurate readings in difficult conditions, but exposure is as much a matter of opinion as it is of fact, especially in difficult lighting situations. That does not mean you should not use these very sophisticated meters as a starting point, but you may wish to make the final decision over exposure yourself. Each camera is different, and experience is your only guide. With a new camera, shoot a few test rolls and learn how its meter suggestions match your own expectations and adjust accordingly.

CALIBRATING YOUR CAMERA OR METER

To suggest accurate exposures, lightmeters need to be set correctly for the speed of the film you are using. If your exposures are consistently under- or overexposed you can adjust the film speed on your meter to compensate. For instance, I normally use Velvia 50 and with my meter set to ISO 50 my images were consistently underexposed. To correct this I reset my meter to ISO 32. When using two cameras they should suggest the same exposures for the same scene when set at the same film speed. If they don't, decide which gives the most accurate readings and alter the film speed setting on the other.

TTL Metering Patterns

There are three main meter patterns: multi-zone, centre-weighted and spot. Each measures the light reflected from the subject in your viewfinder. The spotmeter is particularly useful since you can use it to read the light reflected from a particular element within the scene or choose a midtone area from the whole scene and read from that to determine the appropriate exposure.

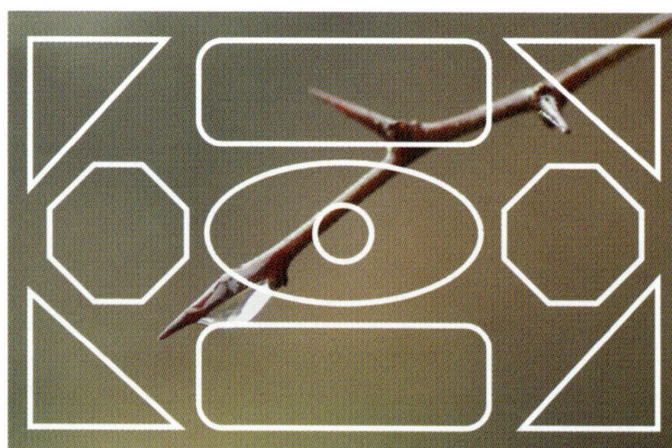

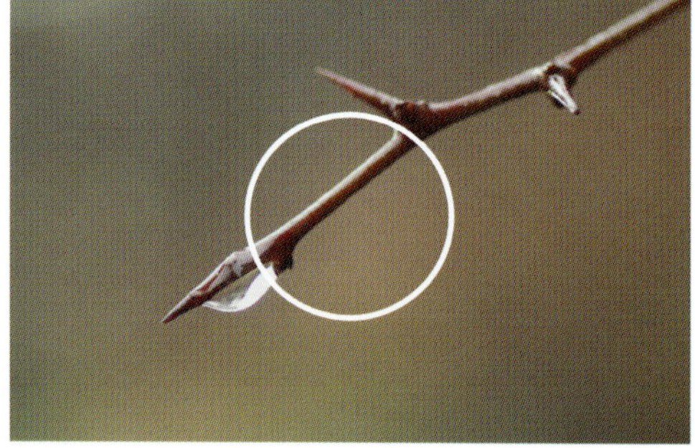

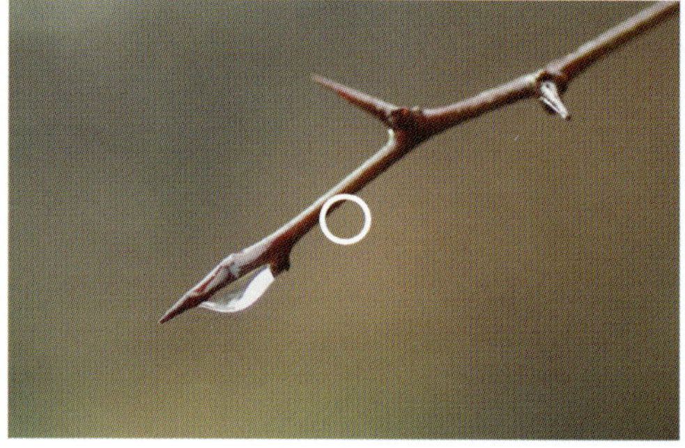

Multi-zone patterns take data from many areas of the viewfinder and calculate an exposure value based on the average of those findings, sometimes combined with the position of the subject, and sometimes in relation to a database of actual images stored in the camera's memory banks.

Centre-weighted metering weights the majority of the exposure calculation in the centre circle of the viewfinder. This is useful if the subject fills the central portion of the frame. It also takes into account some of the surrounding scene. Normally the central part of the frame is given a 75% weighting.

Spotmeters provide by far the greatest level of flexibility of any metering system. They can read light levels from very small areas of a scene. You can use a spotmeter to take exposure-level readings from specific parts of the scene, giving you complete artistic control over the final image.

If you have a film 'push processed' the lab processes it for a little longer than usual, effectively increasing the exposure you gave it in the first place. Conversely, if you 'pull process' the film, the processing time is reduced, effectively reducing the exposure you gave the film.

This can be used as a get-you-out-of-trouble measure, if you have accidentally set your camera to the wrong film speed, for example, and is especially helpful for users of medium- and large-format cameras. With a 36-exposure roll of 35mm film you would have to know that you want to push or pull it from the start, and expose all your pictures on the roll accordingly.

You can also push or pull film on purpose. If the light is failing and you feel the need for a faster film than you are carrying, you can just rate the film a stop higher, effectively underexposing it by one stop, then have the film push processed by one stop to get back to the appropriate exposure.

Pushing is generally preferable to pulling, since pushing increases colour saturation, while pulling reduces it a little.

Staithes Harbour and Boat

This photograph was accidentally two stops under-exposed so I marked the film to be pushed two stops

Fuji GSW69111 with 65mm lens, Velvia 50, 1/30sec at f/16, push processed 2 stops

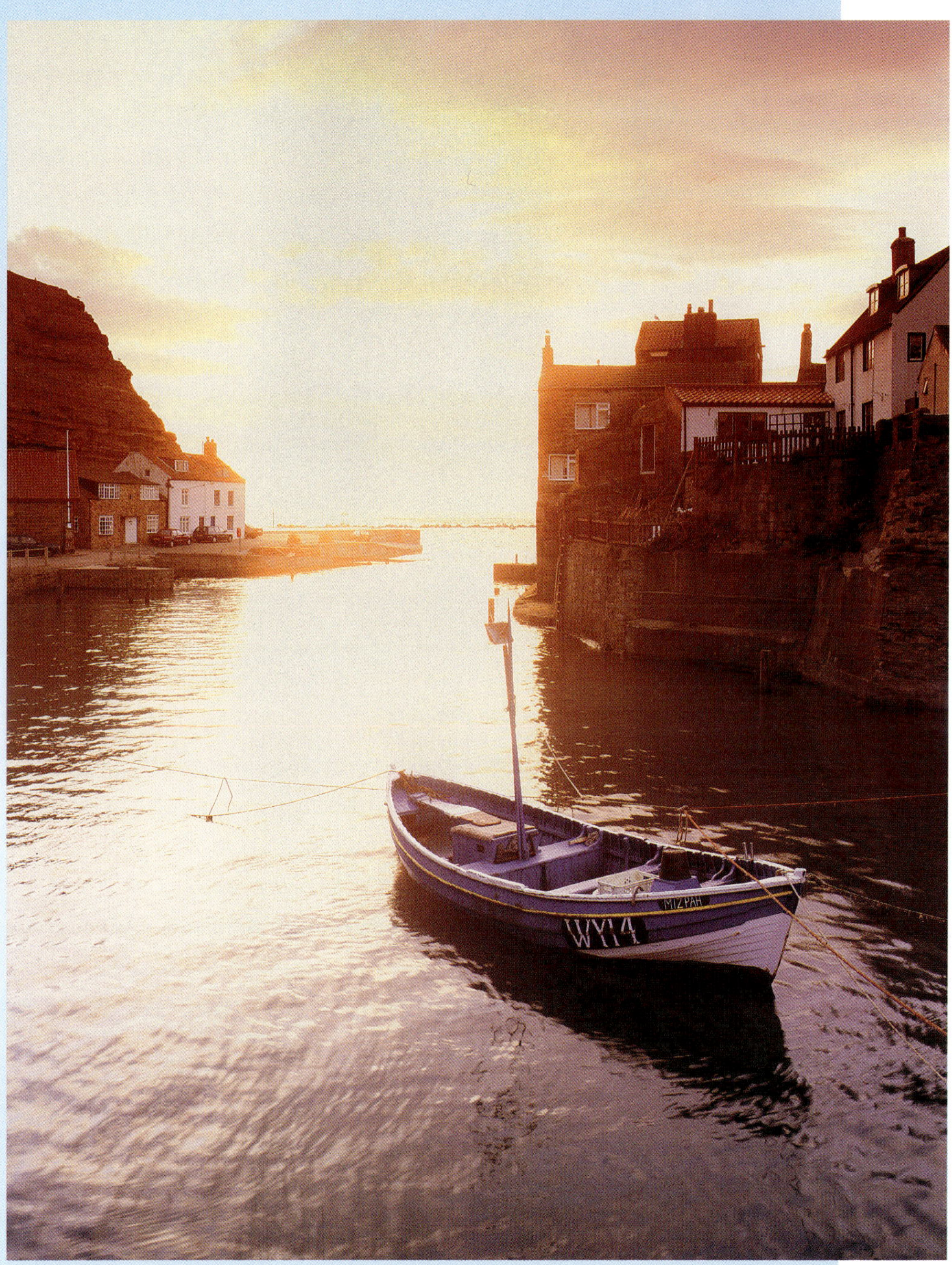

The Lakes at Dusk

Location:
Elterwater, in the
Lake District

Time of year:
August

Camera:
Ebony 45s

Lens:
120mm

Film:
Velvia 50

Filters:
0.6 ND hard grad,
0.6 ND soft grad

The wonderful Langdale Pikes are perhaps one of the best-known and most-loved scenes in the English Lake District. What's more, in the height of summer the sun sets right behind the Pikes when viewed from the tiny lake of Elterwater. Being so tiny, the lake often provides a striking reflection.

While watching the colours develop in the sky, I took three spotmeter readings from the scene. The first reading was from the midtone grey stones in the foreground – the suggested exposure was four seconds at f/22. The next reading was taken from the middle of the lake, and the suggested exposure for that was one second at f/22 – two stops more than the foreground rocks. The third reading was from the sky and this gave a suggested exposure of a quarter of a second at f/22, two stops more than the middle of the lake, and four stops more than the foreground rocks.

To balance the exposure for the whole scene I used two neutral-density filters. The first, a hard-graduated 0.6 (two stop) filter, was pushed down over the lens so that just the sky was held back two stops; the second, a soft-graduated 0.6 (also two stops) was pushed down over the sky and past that point over the middle of the lake. The foreground rocks were not affected by the filters and so the exposure for them remained four seconds at f/22. The exposure for the middle of the lake, now held back two stops by the filter, was also four seconds at f/22, and the exposure for the sky, now held back a total of four stops by the two filters combined, was four seconds at f/22.

After processing the first of the three sheets of 5x4 I used on this scene, I felt the overall mood was a little dark, so I had the next two sheets push processed by half a stop which improved the final image you see here just ever so slightly. Had I been shooting on a smaller format, I would have bracketed exposures, shooting for four, six and eight seconds, these respectively being a half and a full stop over the original four seconds suggested by the meter.

Ebony 45s with 120mm lens, Velvia 50, 4 seconds at f/22, 0.6 ND hard-grad and 0.6 ND soft-grad filters, push processed by 1/2 stop (equivalent to 6 seconds at f/22)

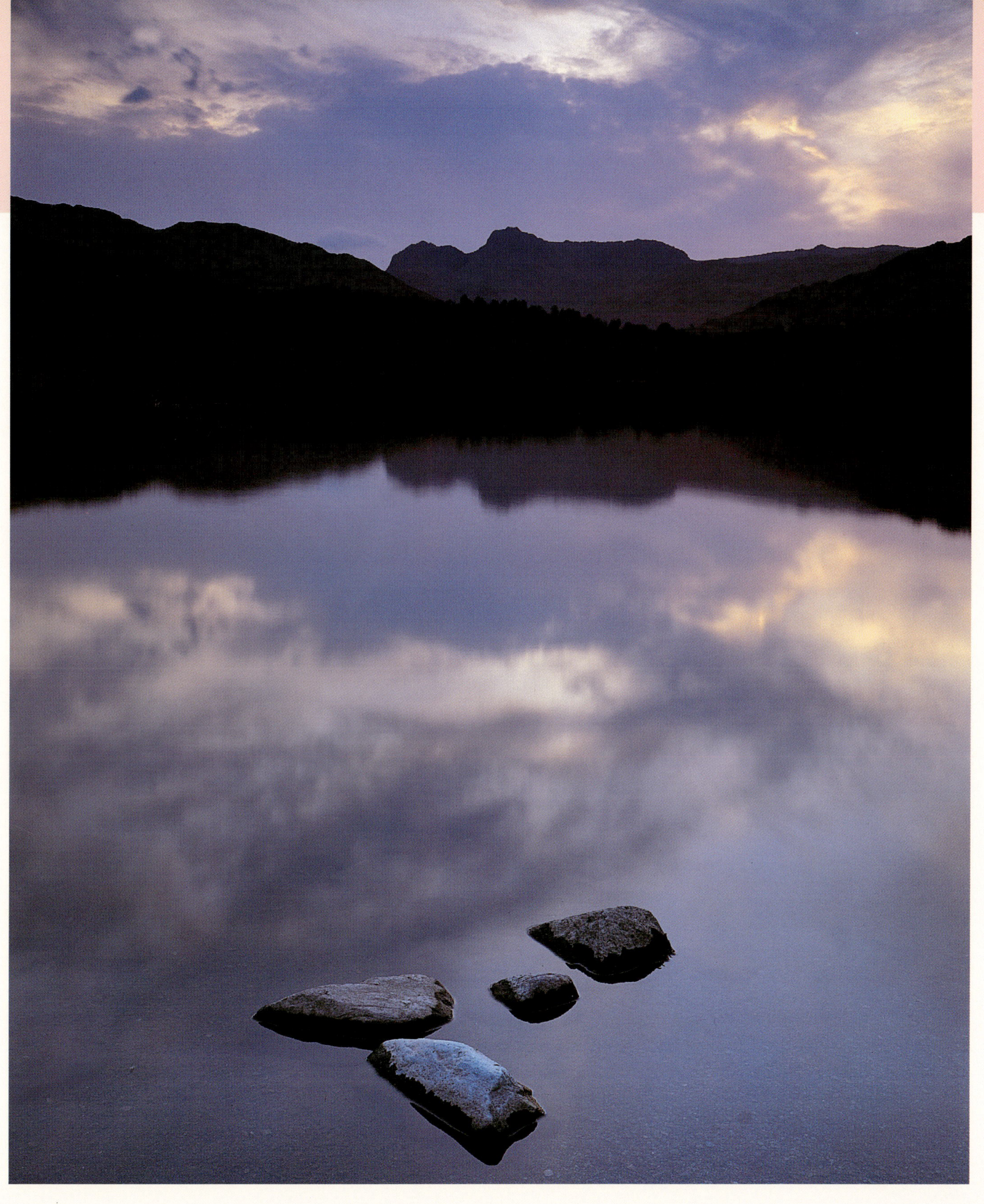

Shutter Speed

The longer the shutter is held open, the more light will reach your film. With the shutter open longer, the aperture needs to be closed down smaller so that the equivalent amount of light reaches your film (see 'Exposure Value Equivalent Combinations', below). This is called the law of reciprocity.

Typically, for landscape photography I find myself using a shutter speed of between a quarter of a second and one second. This is because I use film that is slow to react to light with a small aperture to gain greater depth of field, and often I am shooting in low light. In bright conditions I may also have a polarizing filter on the camera, which reduces the light reaching the film by up to a further two stops.

With fast shutter speeds you can use a very fast film and a wide aperture in bright conditions. This may be something that you as a photographer want, perhaps to get the muted colours of a very fast film with shallow depth of field.

EXPOSURE VALUE EQUIVALENT COMBINATIONS

Shutter speed	Aperture	ISO	Exposure value
1/250	f/4	200	11
1/125	f/4	100	11
1/500	f/4	400	11
1/250	f/2.8	100	11
1/250	f/5.6	400	11

Reciprocity Failure

An exposure of 1/60sec at f/11 is the same as 1/30sec at f/16. However, an exposure of 60 seconds at f/22 will not appear exactly the same as a scene photographed for 30 seconds at f/16, because of 'reciprocity failure'. This is simply because the properties of a film change during a long exposure. Film manufacturers publish exposure compensation and filter recommendations to correct colour casts. For Fuji Velvia 50, exposures longer than 64 seconds are not recommended. Although this has not stopped me using two-minute exposures when I have wanted to.

SEE ALSO:

Film and Digital Media *p 28*

Tripods and Accessories *p 40*

Long Exposures

If you need a shutter speed longer than the longest your camera offers, then it will probably also have the option of a bulb setting. With this you can hold the shutter open for as long as you like. It can be useful to carry a stopwatch with you to time these longer exposures. This is also when having a tripod and a cable release is vital. It is supposed to be the case that you can handhold a 35mm camera with a standard lens using a shutter speed of 1/30sec without affecting the quality of your picture, but any slower than this and you risk camera shake. This varies from person to person and from picture to picture. A longer lens is harder to keep still. If you doubt this, take a 300mm lens or longer and aim it at something small in the distance – just try to keep the small object in the centre of the viewfinder.

When you take a photograph of anything stationary, such as a traditional landscape subject, the shutter speed you choose really does not matter – so long as it is in conjunction with the film speed and light you will get an appropriate exposure. Water, though, is seldom totally static and often moves at great speed. The shutter speed you choose, then, can have a dramatic effect on the appearance of your subject. Stills photography freezes time.

Motionless or slow-moving water can be recorded as it appears, like any other photographic subject, but fast-moving water is a different matter. If you use a very fast shutter speed (something in the order of 1/125sec or faster) the water movement will be 'frozen' (pictured, top). If, on the other hand, you use a very long shutter speed of half a second or more, the water will photograph as a gentle blur (pictured, below). While neither is a record of what we actually see with our eyes, the gentle blur seems to be the popular option for most landscape photographers. This may partly be the result of also wanting good depth of field, which requires a small aperture and therefore a longer shutter speed to make the exposure. For my taste, the gentle blur of water through a scene, while not strictly accurate, is the more pleasing.

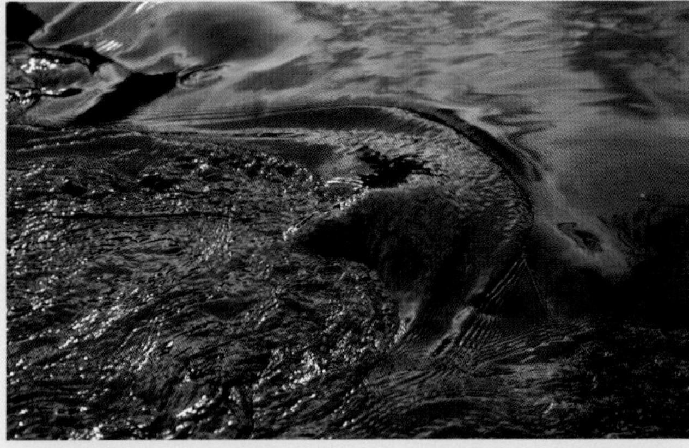

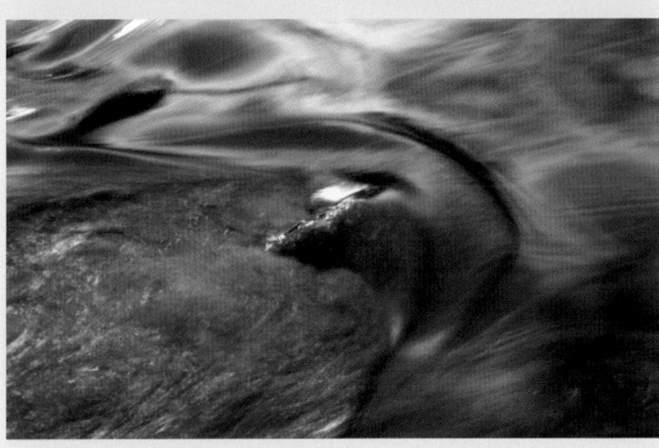

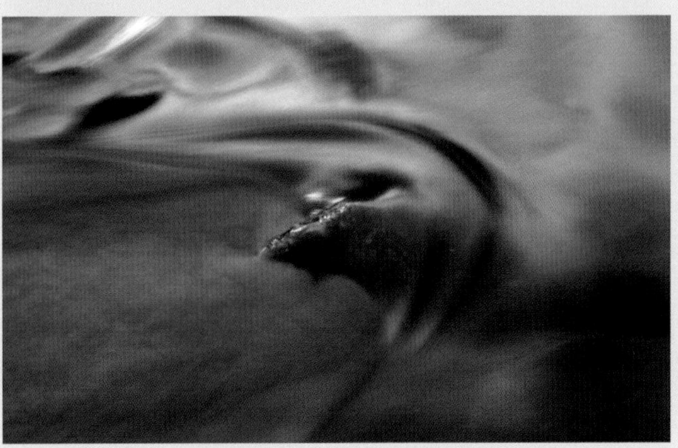

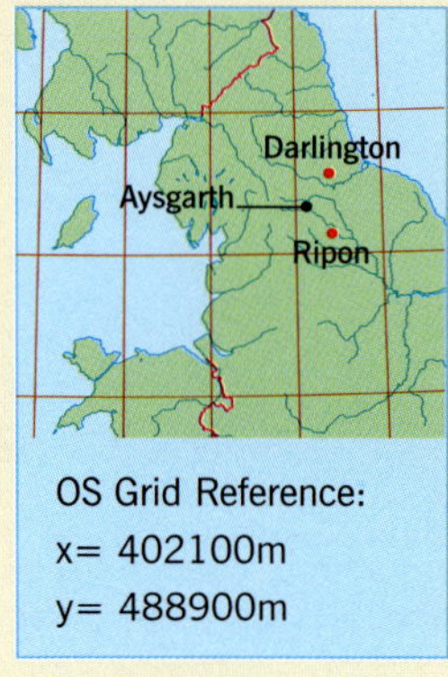

OS Grid Reference:
x= 402100m
y= 488900m

The Aysgarth Falls are a spectacular sight. Set in a wooded gorge in the heart of the Yorkshire Dales, there are three falls spread along a short stretch of the River Ure in Wensleydale. I have visited these falls many times and tried to capture the energy and sheer beauty I always find there.

Fuji GSW69111 with 65mm lens, Velvia 50, 1/8sec at f/22, polarizing filter

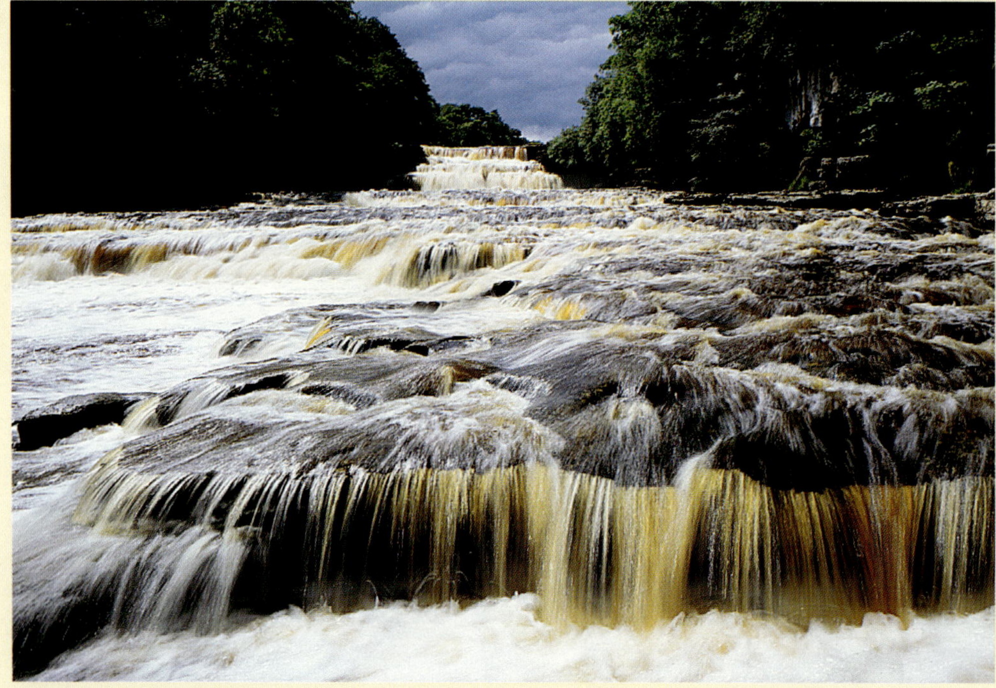

I find the upper falls the least photogenic. The middle falls look best after rain when there is a good volume of water, but the best viewpoint for them is now screened off because the land around is unstable. My usual favourite is the lower falls, where there is access to the riverbank, and they look good even with just a moderate amount of water flowing in the river.

These two photographs were taken a few years apart. The first (below left) shows the river in full spate. At the time I was not using neutral-density filters. I did use a polarizer, which took two stops off exposure. Still, the slowest shutter speed I could use was 1/8sec at my minimum aperture of f/22. The result is a very realistic image of water in motion. There is a slight blur, but nothing artificial or creative about it. Ever since I took this picture I have counted 1/8sec as the shutter speed to use for the most natural-looking photographs of water in motion.

For the second picture (right) the conditions were very different and so I took an alternative approach. While I feel both have worked well, the techniques used could not have been transposed. Had I used a neutral-density filter when I took the first picture I would have lost some of the picture's dynamism. The water would have become inappropriately smooth and gentle, the sheer power of the photograph would have been lost. On the second visit the scene never did have the same dynamism, and so the very long exposure worked.

On this occasion the sky was almost clear blue and there was much less water in the falls. I had no wish to make a repeat of the earlier picture but felt there was room for another interpretation of this scene. This time I used a neutral-density filter to cover the whole of the picture as well as the polarizing filter. This led to an exposure of 20 seconds at f/27. The water was then recorded as a milky, gentle blur.

Ebony 45s with 120mm lens, Velvia 50, 20 seconds at f/27, polarizing and 0.9 ND grad filters

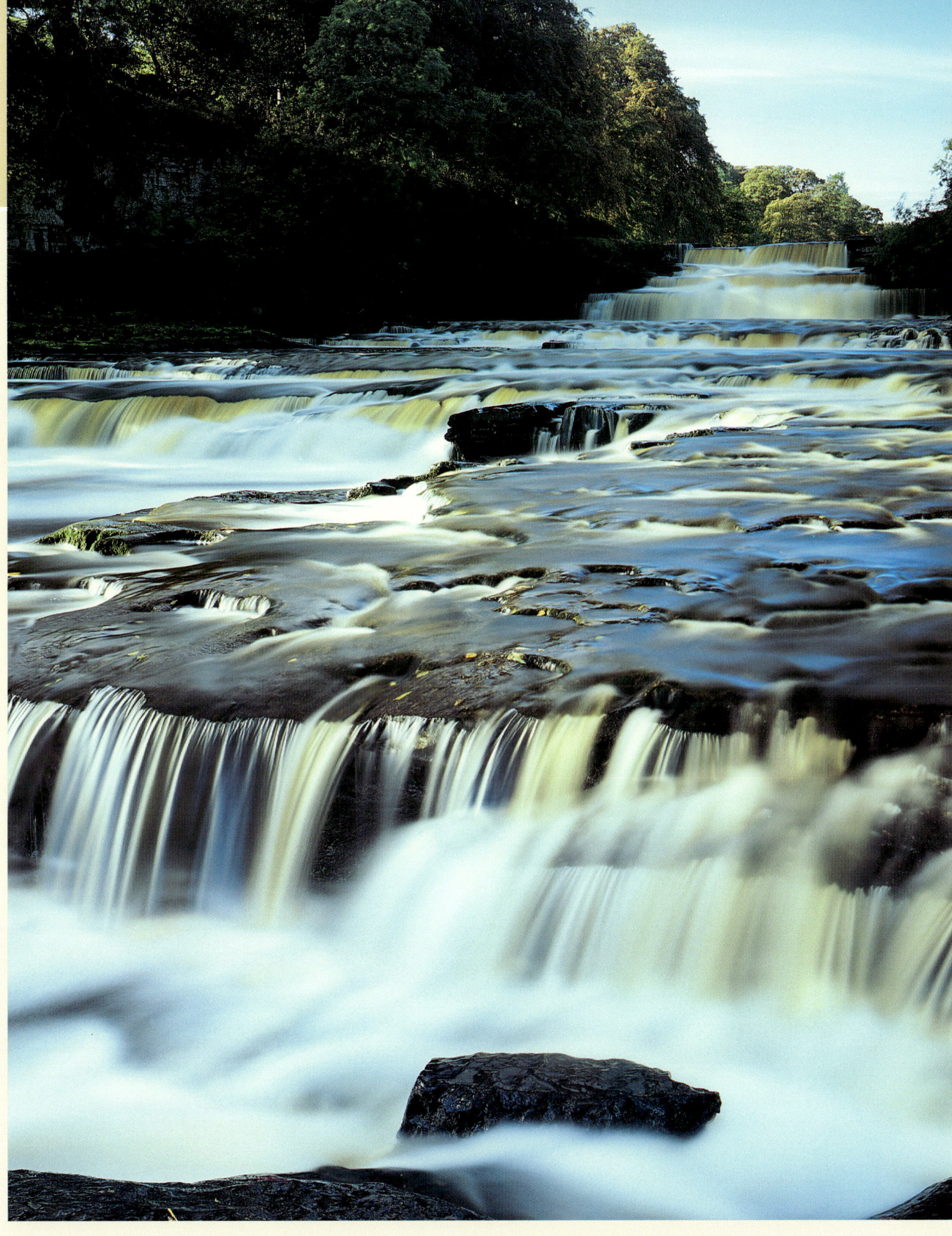

Aperture and Focus

If you squint your eyes, your vision dims. It is the same with a camera. The aperture on the lens is the opening through which light must pass to reach the film. The smaller that aperture, the less light that passes through and, as a consequence, the longer the shutter needs to be open in order to get a correct exposure. The speed of your film also needs to be considered in this equation.

Aperture is measured in f-stops, which are relative fractions of the focal length of the lens. This explains why some zoom lenses show two widest apertures, one for each end of the zoom's focal-length range. The actual aperture size does not alter, but as a fraction of the focal length it does. Being fractions, of course, the smaller the number, the larger the actual aperture, so f/4 is a much wider aperture than f/22.

Wide Aperture

f/1.4

f/2

f/2.8

f/4

f/5.6

f/8

f/11

f/16

f/22

f/32

f/45

Narrow Aperture

Creative Use of Aperture (Depth of Field)

Depth of field is the distance from the nearest point in acceptable focus to the furthest. That is, the area in front and behind the 'point of focus' (or subject) of your photograph. For the landscape photographer, perhaps 90 per cent of the time you do not care what shutter speed you are using, since the subject is not going anywhere. But you do want control over depth of field.

I tend to use the very small aperture of f/22 most of the time. It is important, though, not to lose sight of the fact that the aperture control is there, that you can use it to reduce the depth of field if you want just part of the scene you are photographing to be sharp. This may be the effect you desire if your aim is to draw attention either to or away from some foreground within a scene.

technique ALTERING THE PLANE OF FOCUS ON A LARGE-FORMAT CAMERA

With a large-format camera there is another way to gain greater depth of field. You can alter the plane of focus by tilting either the front or the rear standard. If you think of the plane of focus as a pane of glass, tilting the standards tilts the pane of glass. So rather than having a flat plane you can have a plane that touches both the foreground and background.

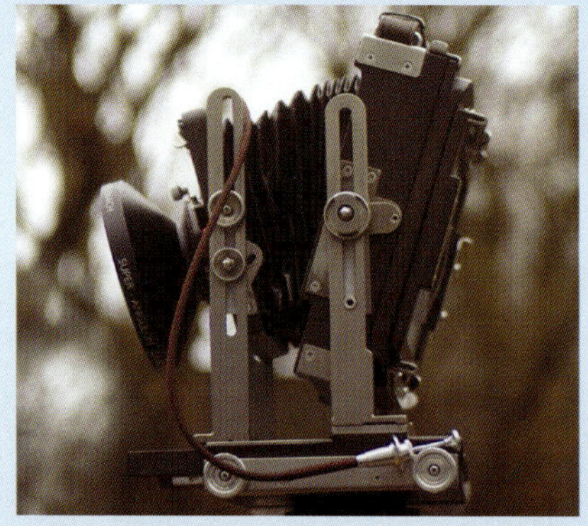
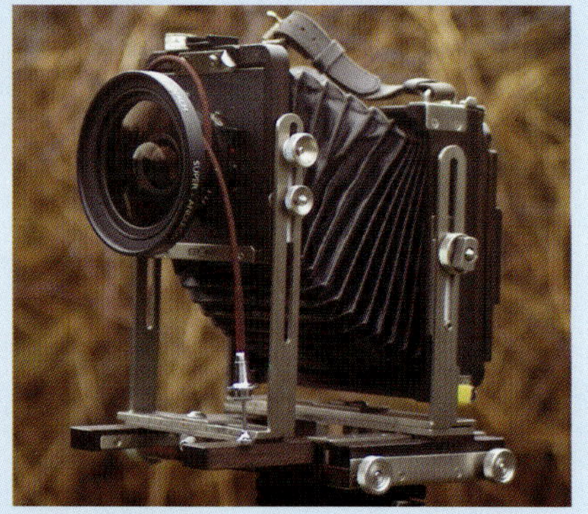

DEPTH-OF-FIELD PREVIEW

Some cameras do have a depth-of-field preview button, which is a very useful feature. Pressing the depth-of-field preview button before you take the picture stops the lens down to the aperture you will be using, allowing you to preview how much of your photograph is going to be in focus at that aperture; this will usually cause the viewfinder to dim.

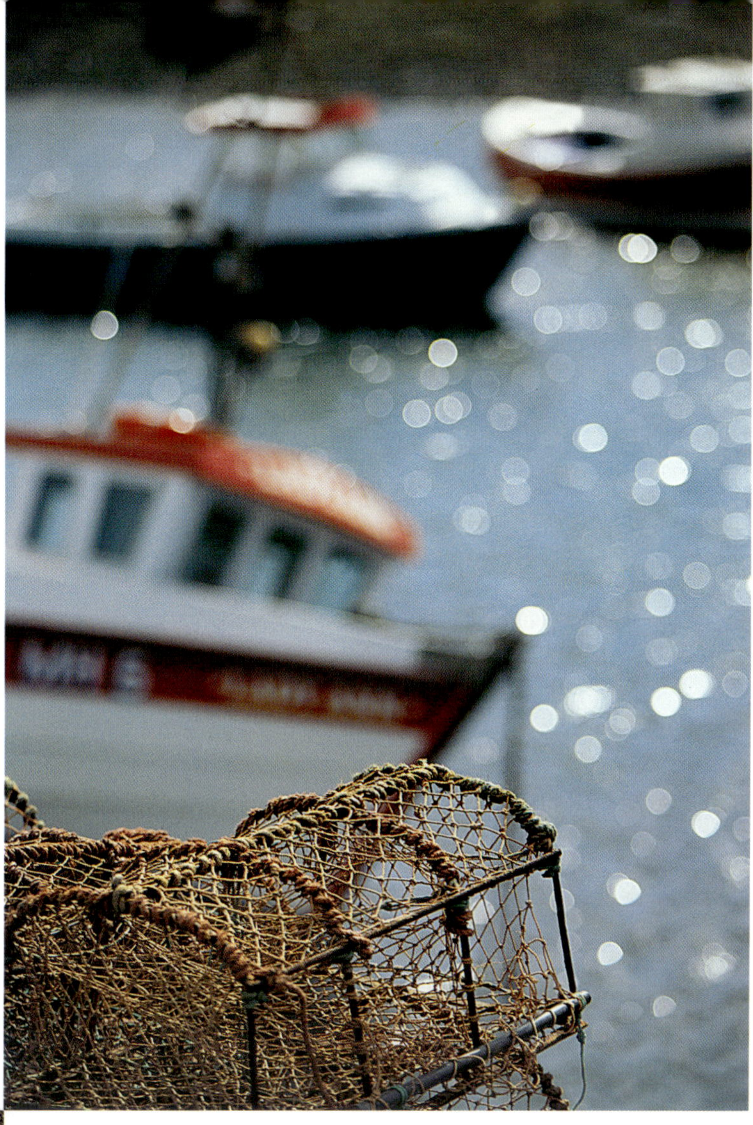

right **Lobster Pots and Harbour**

Photography is, at its core, a very realistic representation of the world. Everything can be recorded in startlingly sharp detail, and sometimes in more detail than we would wish. Opening the aperture up to its widest point and focusing on the lobster pot in the foreground has rendered the harbour in the background a gentle impression of boats on sparkling water.

Nikon FM2 with 70–300mm lens, Velvia 50, 1/250sec at f/2.8

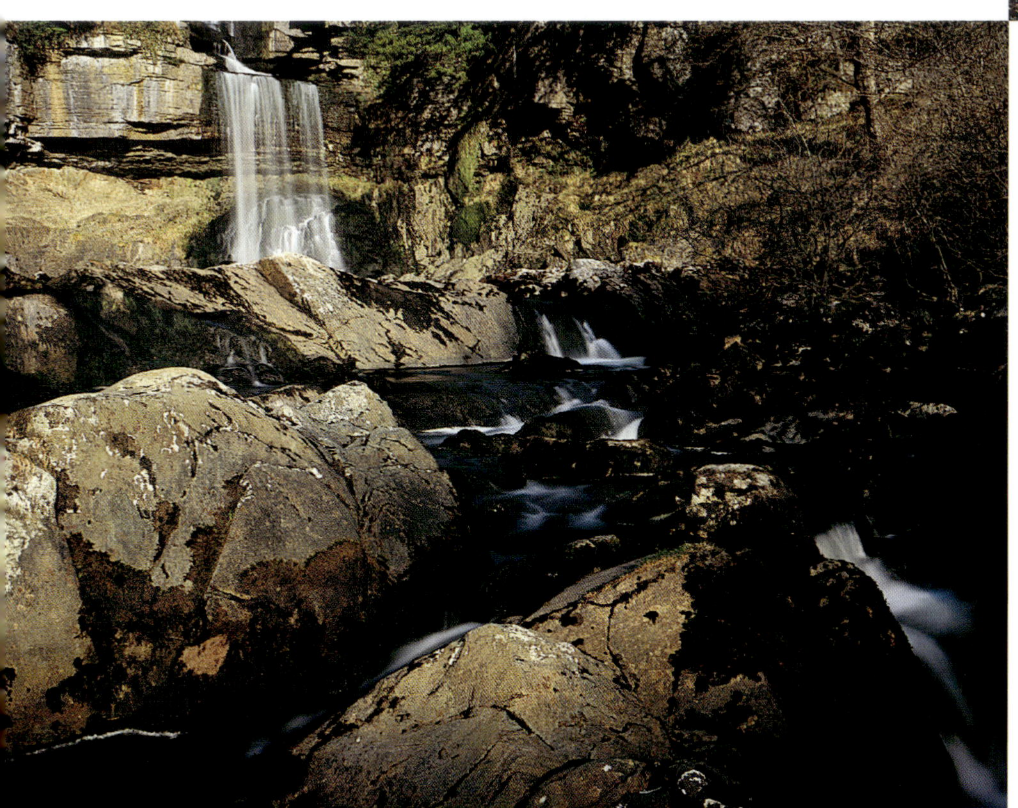

left **Thornton Force Waterfall, Yorkshire**

This is a study in texture and gentle light, the contrast between rock and water. For the picture to work, everything had to be pin-sharp from the foreground rocks to the main waterfall in the distance. Had I focused on the rocks, the waterfall would not have been sharp, even at the very small aperture of f/32. Likewise, if I focused on the waterfall, as I would normally, the foreground rocks would not be sharp. So I focused on the third line of rock, the last one before the waterfall. With the aperture closed down, I could tell that the whole picture was sharp.

Ebony 45s with 90mm lens, Velvia 50,
2 seconds at f/32, Coral No. 1 warm-up filter

Focusing

Different cameras focus in different ways, some basic and some complex. To the photographer, though, focusing the camera is the most basic of operations. You just turn the focusing ring (or extend or contract the bellows of a large–format camera) until the image looks sharp where you want it to. Most cameras rely on your own judgement as to what is in focus. However, some cameras use split or double images that are slightly unaligned until the picture is correctly focused.

Many of the modern 35mm SLR and compact cameras have autofocus, which can often be overridden. For landscape photography you do not really need autofocus and, in fact, it can be a bit distracting while the lens zips in and out of focus searching for something to settle on.

You focus a large-format camera by moving the lens closer to or further from the film by extending or contracting the bellows. The dark cloth stops light falling onto the focusing screen from behind, so that only the light projected through the lens illuminates the screen. This makes the image clearer to see and easier to focus.

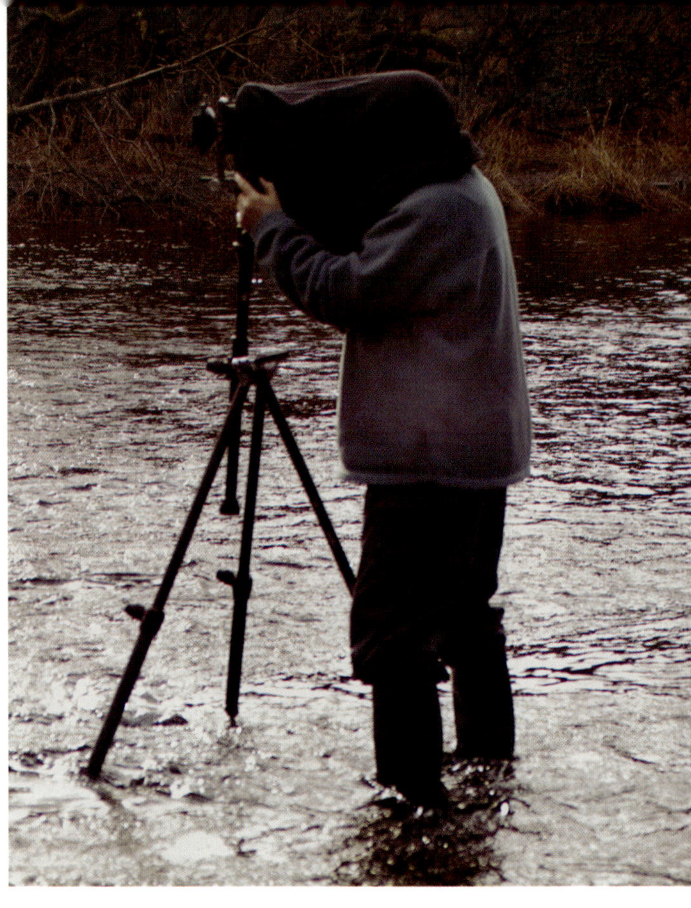

LOUPE

With a large-format camera you can only really tell whether the image is sharp by looking closely through a loupe magnifying glass held up to the ground-glass screen. I use a six times loupe so any area that is not pin-sharp shows up right away. Normally you would do this under a dark cloth (see picture above) so that you can see the image clearly.

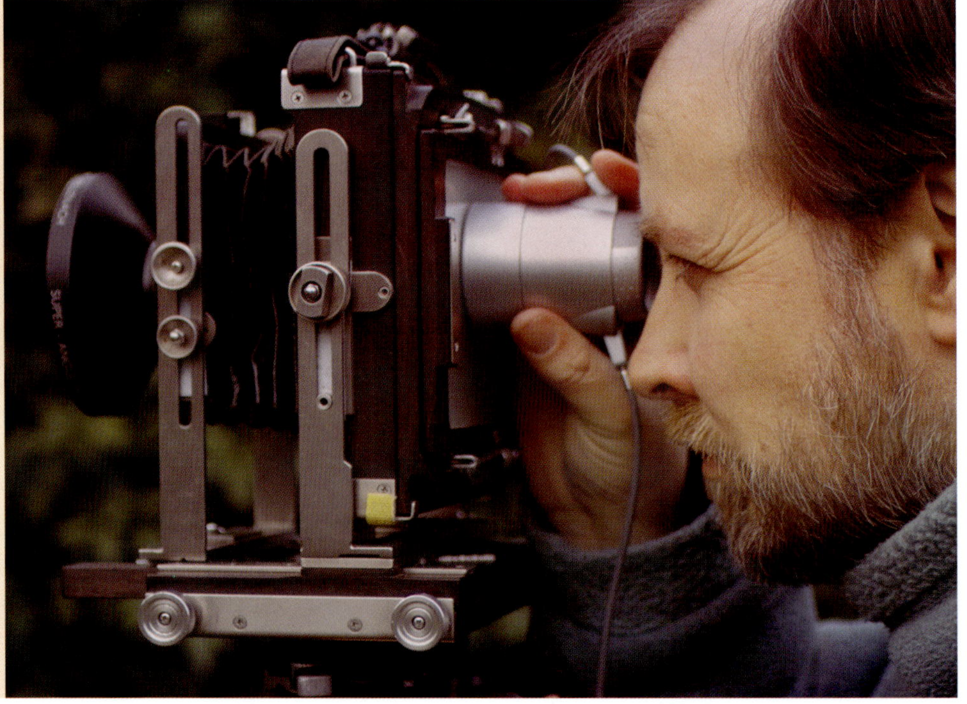

Hyperfocal Focusing Simplified

There are many standard landscape subjects where the photographer does not have to give very much thought to either focus or depth of field. With most of what I call 'grand vista' shots, focus is on infinity, aperture is closed down reasonably small, and there is nothing in the very close foreground to cause any problems with depth of field.

Hyperfocal focusing is a simple tool with a complicated name for overcoming those occasions when this is not the case. These are the times when you want to place something in the close foreground and keep both it and the distant horizon pin-sharp.

Photography is a science as well as an art, and if you choose to you can get really bogged down with the technicalities. It will not help your creativity to do this and so I have always felt it best avoided. Having said that, hyperfocal focusing is a useful tool for squeezing the maximum depth of field out of any given scene.

Since for most landscapes the point of focus is infinity – the distant horizon – depth of field extends back towards the camera. If it does not reach far enough to include the nearest object in the frame you are going to have a blur in the forefront of your picture, which may or may not be desirable. One way to avoid this is to focus on the object in the foreground, but then depth of field may not extend far enough behind that object to keep the distant horizon sharp as well. If you want both the near object and the distant horizon in acceptable focus you need to focus on a point in front of infinity but behind the foreground object, so that both fall within the depth of field.

The most effective way of doing this is to set the lens to its hyperfocal distance. You simply focus on infinity and then look to see which is the nearest point to the camera in acceptably sharp focus. You then move your focus to this point. Because depth of field always extends one-third in front of the subject and two-thirds behind, you will find that the depth of field now extends from infinity to halfway between your camera and the focal point.

When thinking about depth of field you should remember that there are three variables that will affect the way the final image appears: the aperture used, the distance to the subject and the focal length of the lens. Depth of field is shallow when the subject is close, the focal length is long, or the aperture is wide. Conversely, depth of field is at its greatest when the subject is distant, the focal length is short, or the aperture is narrow.

technique **USING DEPTH-OF-FIELD SCALES**

Many lenses have a depth-of-field scale (as shown right) and this can be used as a means of double-checking the depth of field. Simply align the infinity symbol on the depth-of-field scale with the aperture you are using; for maximum depth of field this will be the minimum aperture.

You can use complex calculations to find out the exact depth of field of a lens. However, it is far easier and more practical to judge by eye, using either depth-of-field preview or scales.

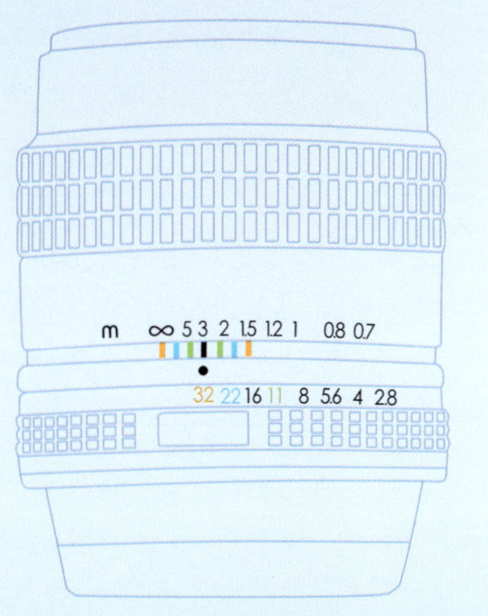

A technique many professionals use is bracketing their exposures. First, work out what you think is an appropriate exposure and take your picture, then reduce the exposure by half a stop and take the picture again, and then by a further half a stop, and so on. You can use a lot of film this way. Starting from any mid-point and bracketing in half-stop increments up to two stops under and two stops over your original exposure you will use nine frames of film. That is assuming you only take one frame at each exposure. If you take four frames at each exposure you will use a whole roll of film this way just to ensure one picture, assuming the light stays constant enough while you shoot a whole roll. Once you are certain you are in the right area with your original exposure, and you know whether under- or overexposure is the greater risk, you can reduce the number of frames you need to bracket.

When shooting 35mm I take three frames at each exposure and seldom use more than nine frames in total, bracketing a half and then a full stop in whichever direction I feel the error may be. Often I end up with nine useable images, three at each exposure and just a slight difference in the 'mood'.

Some modern cameras offer auto-bracketing functions, although you can always work manually if you want more control.

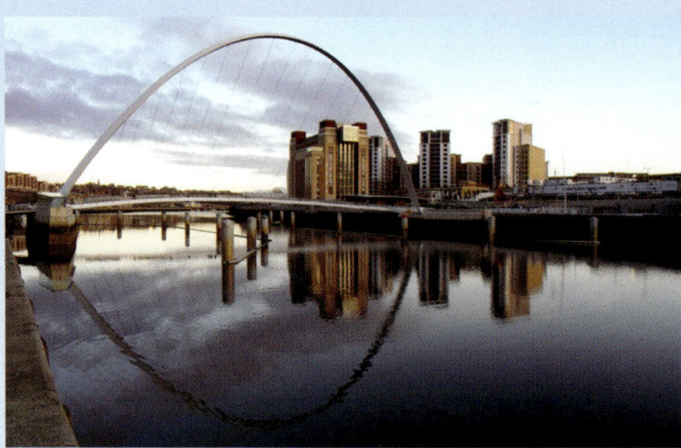

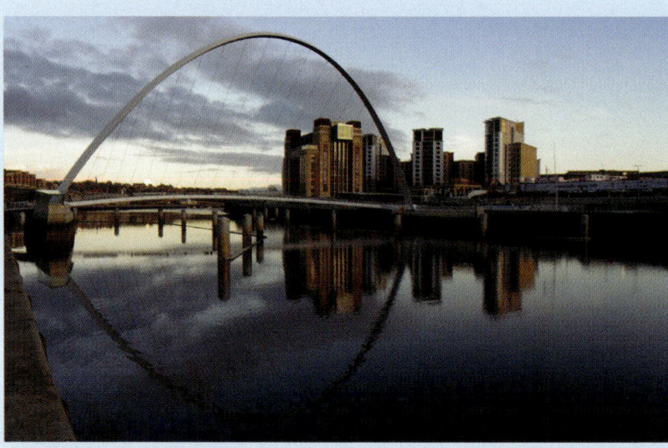

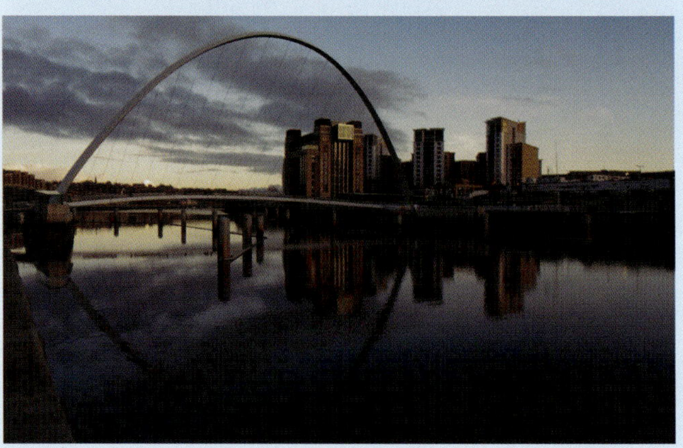

Filters for Landscape Photography

While filters can't 'magically' improve an ordinary scene on a poor-weather day, they can be used to bring a subtle something extra to an image. There are many different types of filter available, from those with delicate effects, to the horribly garish.

Filters gained a poor reputation because of overuse in the past, especially coloured graduated filters, tobacco, sunset and pink. There was something of a backlash among photographers who claimed they never used filters. This would be a mistake: filters do not have to be used to excess, they can be used with subtlety and finesse.

It is worth experimenting with different types of filter until you find something that suits your style. If you are new to photographic filters, a mixed set might be the most economical way to get started. Second-hand filters are widely available.

I only carry three types of filter with me these days: neutral-density – one, two and three stops in both soft and hard graduation; warm-up filters – also graduated so that I can warm the land but leave the sky clear from the effect; and a polarizing filter. These can all be used to gently enhance a scene or persuade film to see the world as we do.

equipment

GRADUATED FILTERS

A graduated filter allows you to darken or alter the colour of just one area of a landscape. The way in which the transition within the scene is affected depends on whether the filter has a hard or soft graduation. In other words, how quickly the filter changes from graduated to clear.

A 'stripe' graduated filter restricts the zone where the filter takes effect even further, with a clear area both above and below the colour. It is mostly used on the horizon for photographing landscapes.

All graduated filters are available in different strengths and can be moved up and down in the holder to vary the effect.

Hard-Grad Filter

The sharp graduation means the delineation of the filtered and clear parts is very precise, but it is important to place it correctly.

Soft-Grad Filter

These are easier to use than hard grads and errors of alignment are harder to notice. However, they are a less precise tool.

Stripe Filter

Stripe filters are clear at either end and filtered in the middle. They are normally used on the horizons, particularly at sunset or sunrise.

Neutral-Density Filters

Neutral-density filters are another device for controlling exposure, and are an essential part of any serious landscape photographer's kit. These filters reduce the amount of light reaching the film through the lens. They are either plain or graduated and come in various strengths, one, two and three stops being the most common, although you can buy stronger or intermediate-strength filters.

The most useful of these filters for water is the 0.6 (two stop) filter, and my favourite is the soft-graduated version, although other photographers prefer the hard-graduated version which can be placed more precisely to divide a scene.

The principal use of these filters is to balance the overall exposure in a scene where part of the picture is much brighter than the rest. Usually this

BUYING A NEUTRAL-DENSITY FILTER

It would simplify matters if all ND filters were just called No. 1, 2 and 3, etc. However, the way your filters are named depends on the manufacturer you use. Some manufacturers name their filters by the number of stops they reduce exposure by; for example an ND1 filter cuts the amount of light entering the lens by one stop. However, other manufacturers use a different system; a one-stop ND filter is a 0.3, two stops 0.6 and three stops 0.9. (See table opposite.)

One very important feature of a neutral-density filter is that it must indeed be neutral. Some makers produce what they very honestly describe as grey filters. These can, and do, cause the colours to shift as well as holding back the light. Professional filters may seem expensive, until you learn they are all handmade carefully, and then you realize just what a bargain they are.

below **Saltburn Evening**

This is exactly the type of scene that benefits from the addition of a neutral-density graduated filter. The effect is subtle, but subtlety is often at the heart of a successful photograph. Taking a spotmeter reading from the wet sand, and then one from the clouds, showed a difference of two stops. Using a two-stop neutral-density filter therefore balanced the scene. There are some photographers who prefer to use just a one-stop, or one-and-a-half-stop filter, so that the reflection still appears a little darker than the sky, making it truer to the eye. Personally, I quite like the sky to look a little stronger than it does in real life.

Ebony 45s with 90mm lens, Velvia 50, 1/2sec at f/22

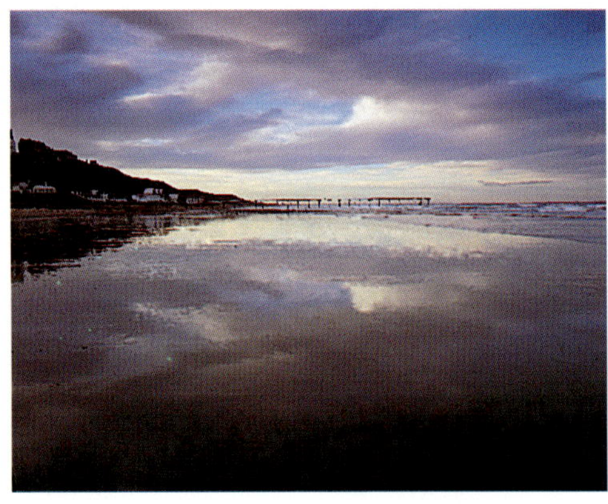

With 0.3 ND filter (too little)

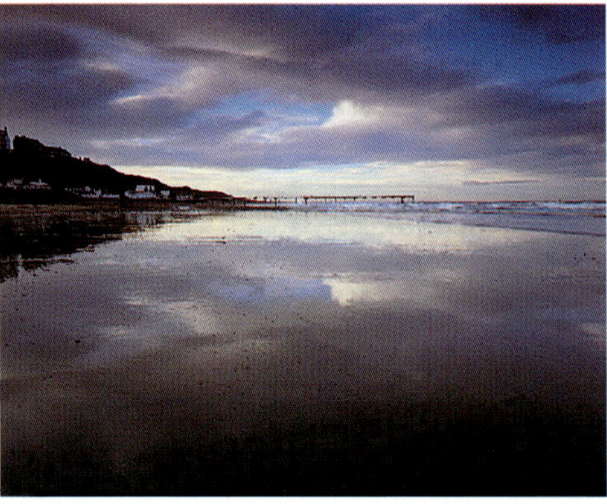

With 0.6 ND filter (correct)

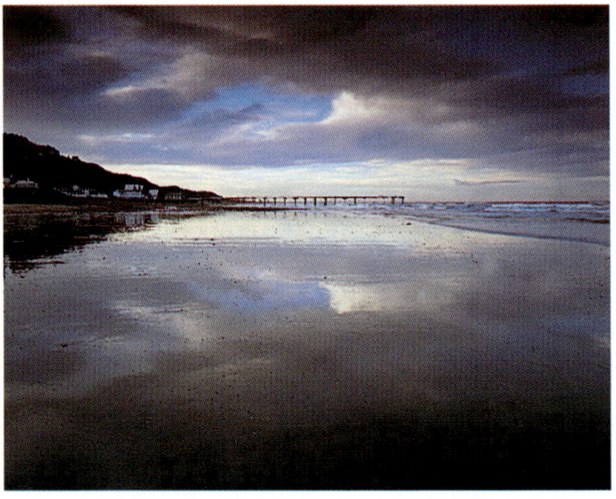

With 0.9 ND filter (too strong)

means holding back light from a much brighter sky so that film can cope with the contrast in a way closer to how we see things ourselves.

When photographing moving water, you can use plain ND filters to allow longer shutter speeds than would otherwise be the case to blur moving water. Alternatively, I use the large Lee filters, and the dark part of these filters is large enough so that you can cover the whole picture and reduce the light reaching the film for the whole of the scene, saving the need to buy a separate plain ND filter.

LIGHT LOSS WITH ND FILTERS

Filter strength	Exposure compensation
0.3 ND	1 stop
0.45 ND	$1\frac{1}{2}$ stops
0.6 ND	2 stops
0.75 ND	$2\frac{1}{2}$ stops
0.9 ND	3 stops

below **River Details**

The only difference between these two pictures is the shutter speeds I used and the neutral-density filter that made them possible. The respective shutter speeds are 1/4sec (below left) and 2 seconds (below right), both at f/22, and a 0.9 (three stop) neutral-density filter made this possible. In this light and for this composition I favour the pencil-sketch look created by the 1/4sec exposure, rather than the blur of the 2-second exposure. The effects differ depending on so many variables that I cannot simply say one shutter speed is best for photographing water in motion. The conditions of the day will always need to be taken into account, as will the photographer's personal vision and taste.

Pentax 67 with 135mm lens

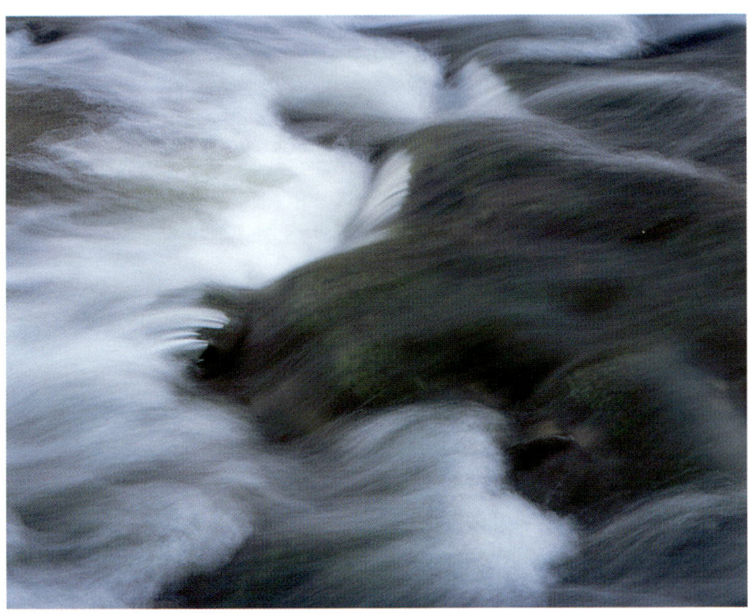
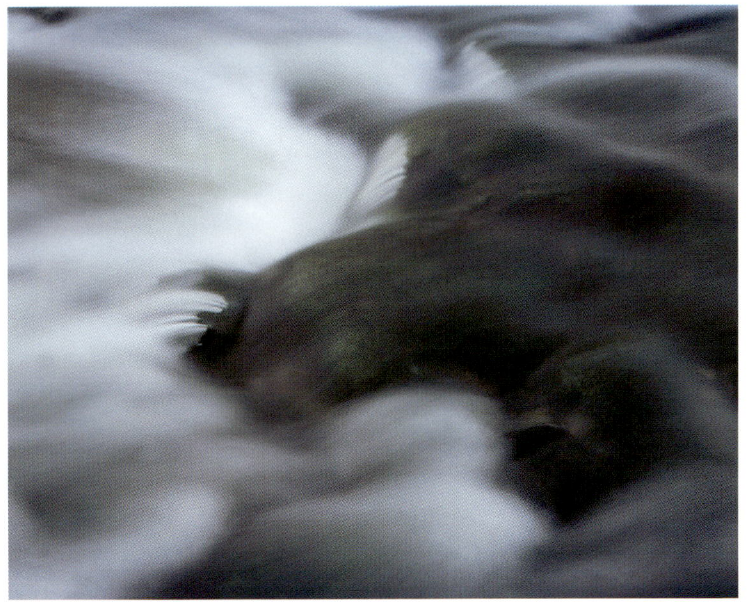

Polarizing Filters

Polarizers strengthen colour saturation and remove white reflections from foliage and from the surface of water. They turn bright blue skies deeper blue and they make the white clouds stand out in stark contrast to the sky.

Full polarization also takes two stops off exposure so that if your light reading suggests f/22 for 1/15sec, then with the polarizing filter in place that might be f/22 for 1/4sec. Polarizing filters can really give a picture punch but they can also be overdone. They can lead to a dark blue patch in the sky, fading in intensity around the patch. They do not affect the sky if the sun is directly behind you, and have the most effect when it is at 45 degrees to the angle your camera is facing.

BUYING A POLARIZER

There are two types of polarizing filter available, and this causes some confusion. They are known as either circular or linear, and their names have nothing to do with the shape of the filter. If your camera uses a semi-silvered mirror in either the metering or autofocus then you will need a circular polarizing filter rather than a linear one. If your camera doesn't need a circular polarizing filter, then you do not need to pay extra to have one, as it will not make any improvement to your pictures. Don't forget that the names do not refer to the shape of the filter; both will either be square to fit a filter holder, or the round type that screws directly onto your lens.

Ashness Bridge

These two frames show how a polarizing filter can gently enhance a scene. The picture on the right with the polarizing filter is better defined than the one on the left without. The sky is a slightly deeper shade of blue, the white clouds stand out a little better, and the greens stand out crisper against the browns of the bracken. As an additional benefit, the water in the stream is a gentle blur, thanks to the longer exposure required by losing two stops of light with the polarizing filter, rather than being almost frozen.

Both pictures: Ebony 45s with 120mm lens, Velvia 50

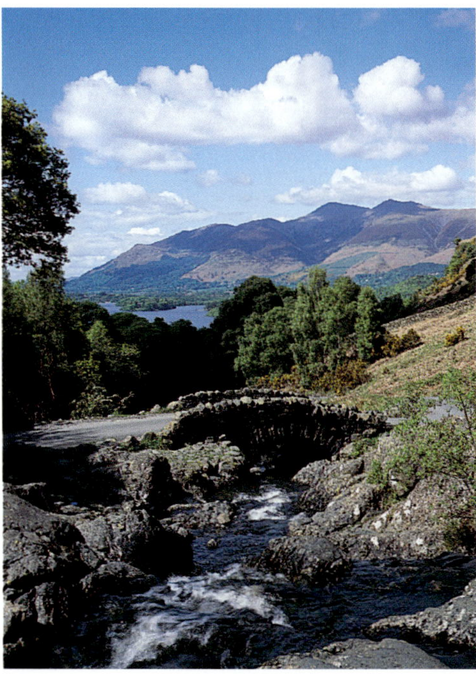

Without filter: 1/15sec at f/22

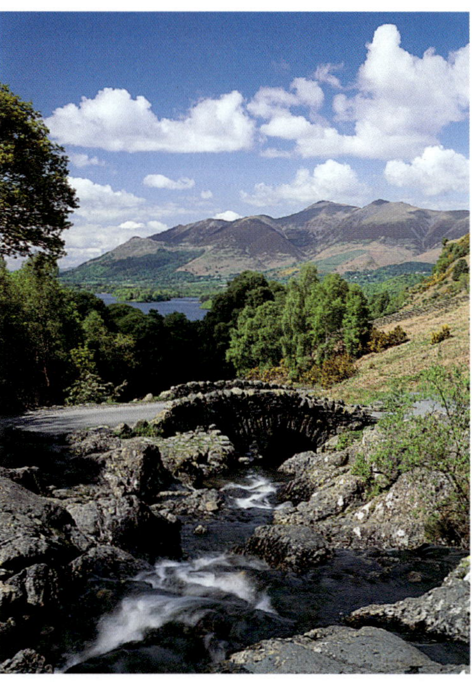

With polarizing filter: 1/2sec at f/27

Water Lilies

Polarizing filters reduce reflections, specifically glare. They take the white reflections off the surface of foliage and water leading to better colour saturation. They do not take away reflections of distant hills on the far shore of a lake. These two pictures of water lilies demonstrate this effect. The reflections on the water in the foreground of the top picture have vanished in the bottom one, while the reflections of the trees on the distant shore are still clearly visible. The greens of the lily pads are also more densely saturated in colour.

Fuji GSW69111 with 65mm lens

right Without filter: 1/8sec at f/22

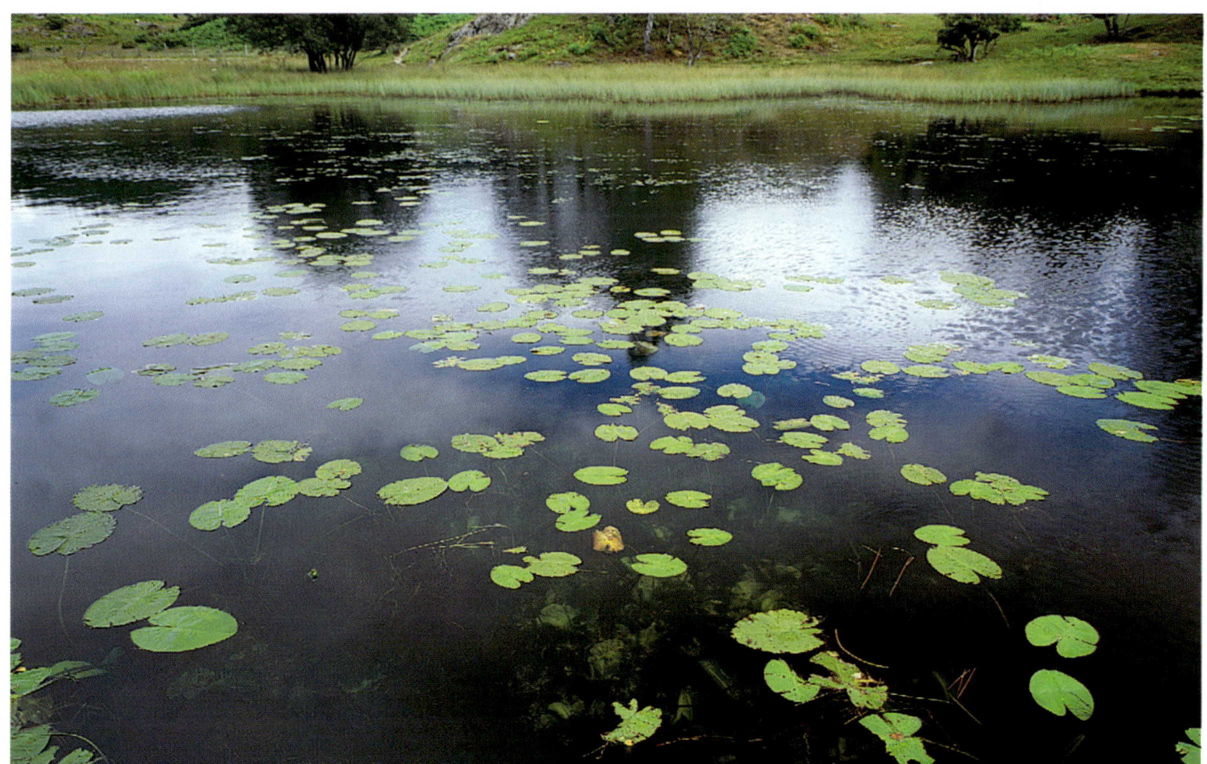

above With polarizing filter: 1/2sec at f/22

Reflected Glory

Reflections are transient, but if you plan your visits early

and late in the day when little or no wind is forecast,

then glorious reflections are reasonably predictable.

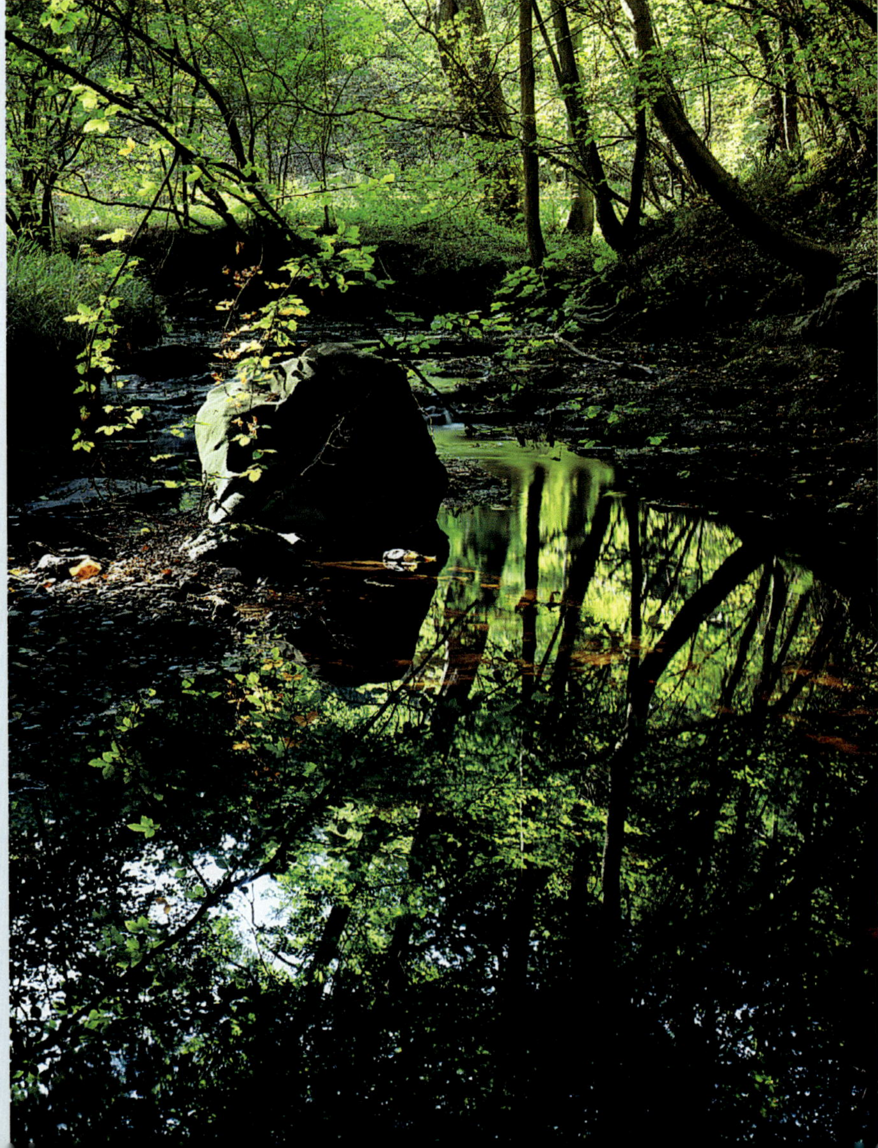

May Beck

The trick with the colour green is to catch it at the right time and in the right light. Spring and autumn are the best, with strong directional side- or backlighting. Here the dappled sunlight hits the water in parts and we see then the brown of the stream bed in the direct sun as opposed to the green where the only light is 'borrowed' from the reflected trees.

I had a number of technical concerns with this picture, not least of which was how to determine the most appropriate exposure. The contrast is enormous and I was concerned that film might not be able to cope. There was little scope, either, to use a graduated neutral-density filter. It was not a simple composition where just one part was brighter than the rest and could be filtered down, there are hot spots everywhere. In the end, I took a number of spot readings from the scene, using a 5° spot, and then applied a little dose of experience and guesswork. I got it right – the first sheet from the camera looked just fine.

**Ebony 45s with 150mm lens, Velvia 50,
8 seconds at f/22**

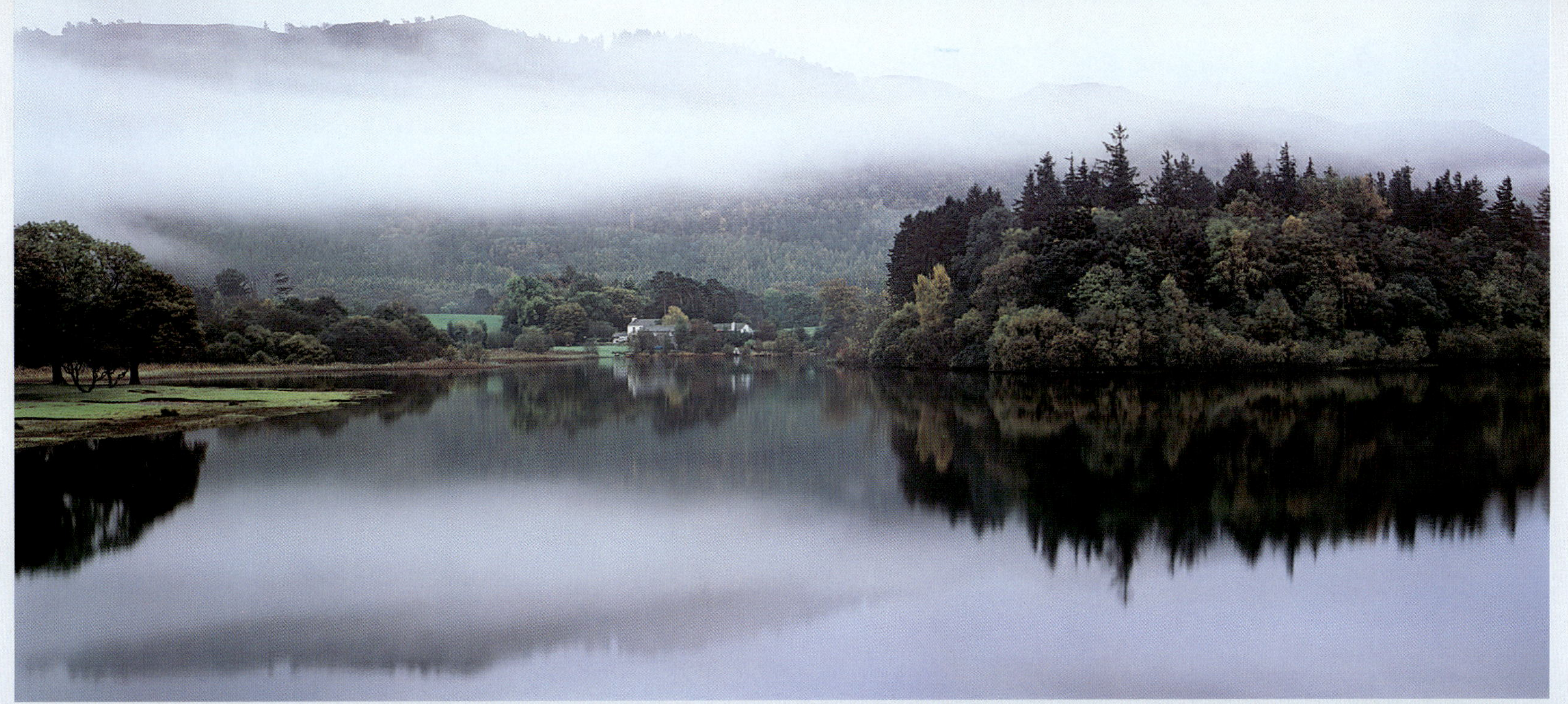

In light like this a landscape that did not include water would be unlikely to succeed, but water is a second light in the landscape and lends structure to the scene. The mood of the picture is peace and tranquillity, generated by the hanging mist (water vapour) and the reflection in the peaceful lake.

Ebony 45s with 90mm lens, 6x12 rollfilm back, Velvia 50, 1/2sec at f/22

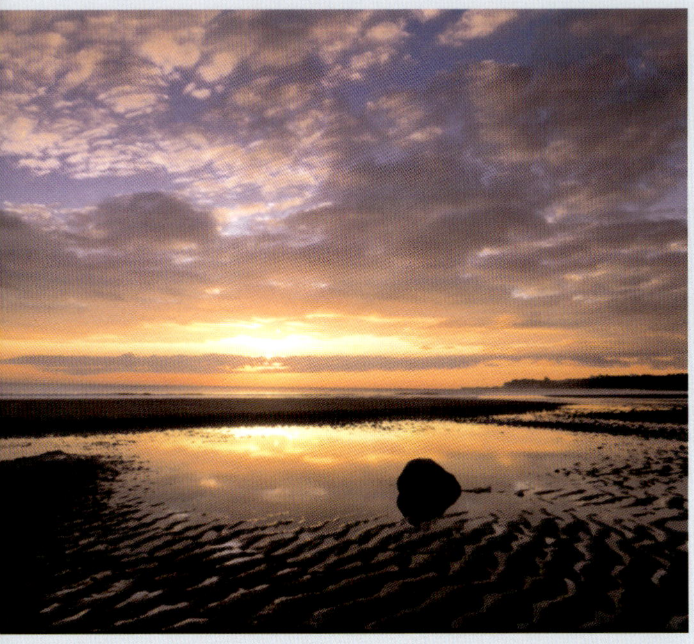

left **Whitby**

The open sea is never still enough for a perfect reflection, but pools of water on a beach often are. At low tide this pool was left behind a sandbank, and on this still morning, filled the foreground with light. This is a record of the wonderful colours of the sunrise.

Pentax 67 with 45mm lens, Velvia 50, 1/4sec at f/22, 0.6 ND grad filter

on following page
Vermilion Lakes and Mount Rundle

Banff, Alberta, Canada is a wonderful place for the landscape photographer. The scenery is breathtaking, and right on the edge of town are the Vermilion Lakes – three shallow lakes joined by a gentle, shallow river. I was only there four evenings, and on three of those the lakes were perfectly still, reflecting the mountains all around. While I was taking this image, someone asked me why. He seemed to think the light was gone. He didn't count on the second light did he?

Ebony 45s with 90mm lens, Velvia 50, f/22, 0.6 ND grad filter

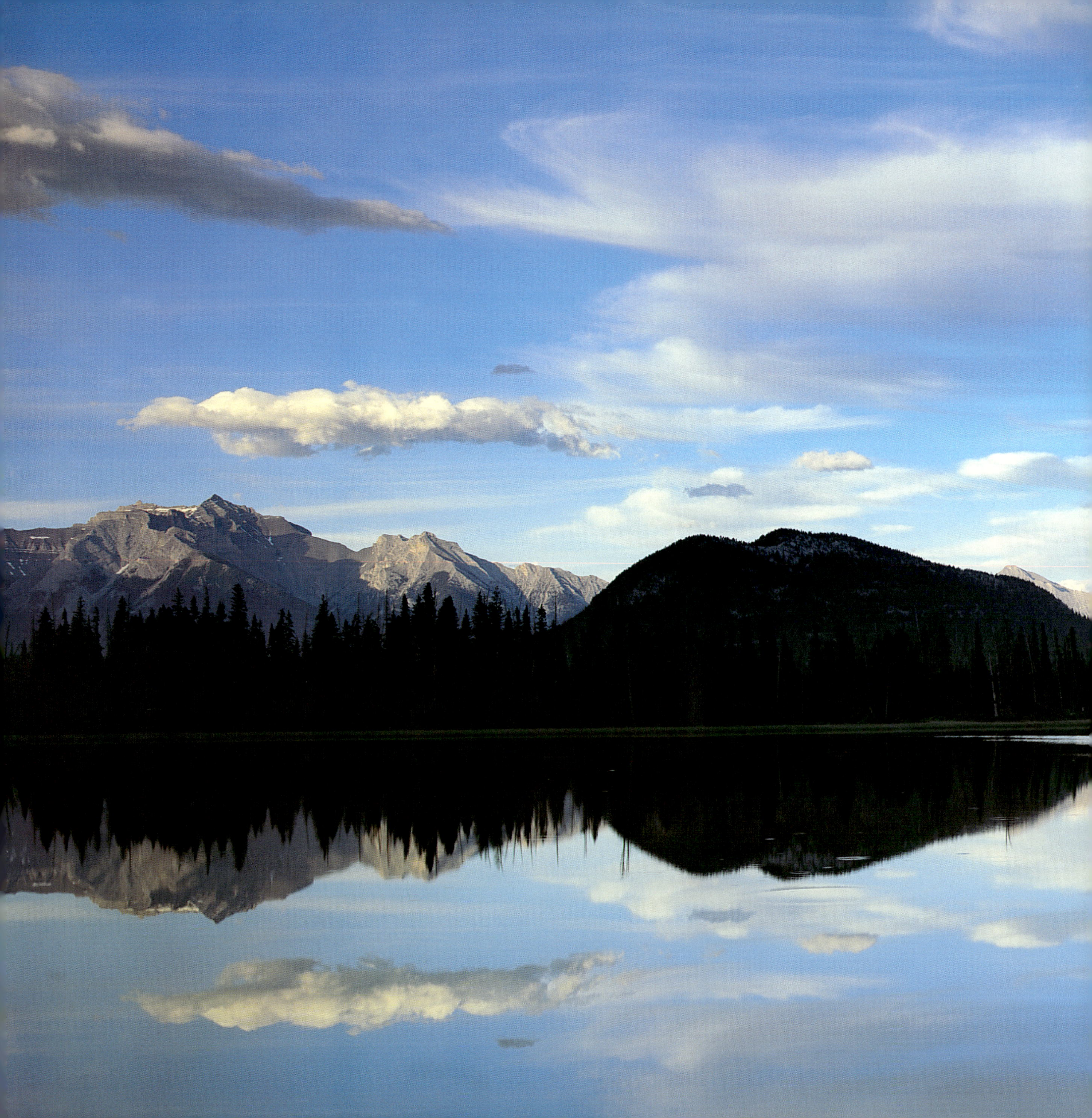

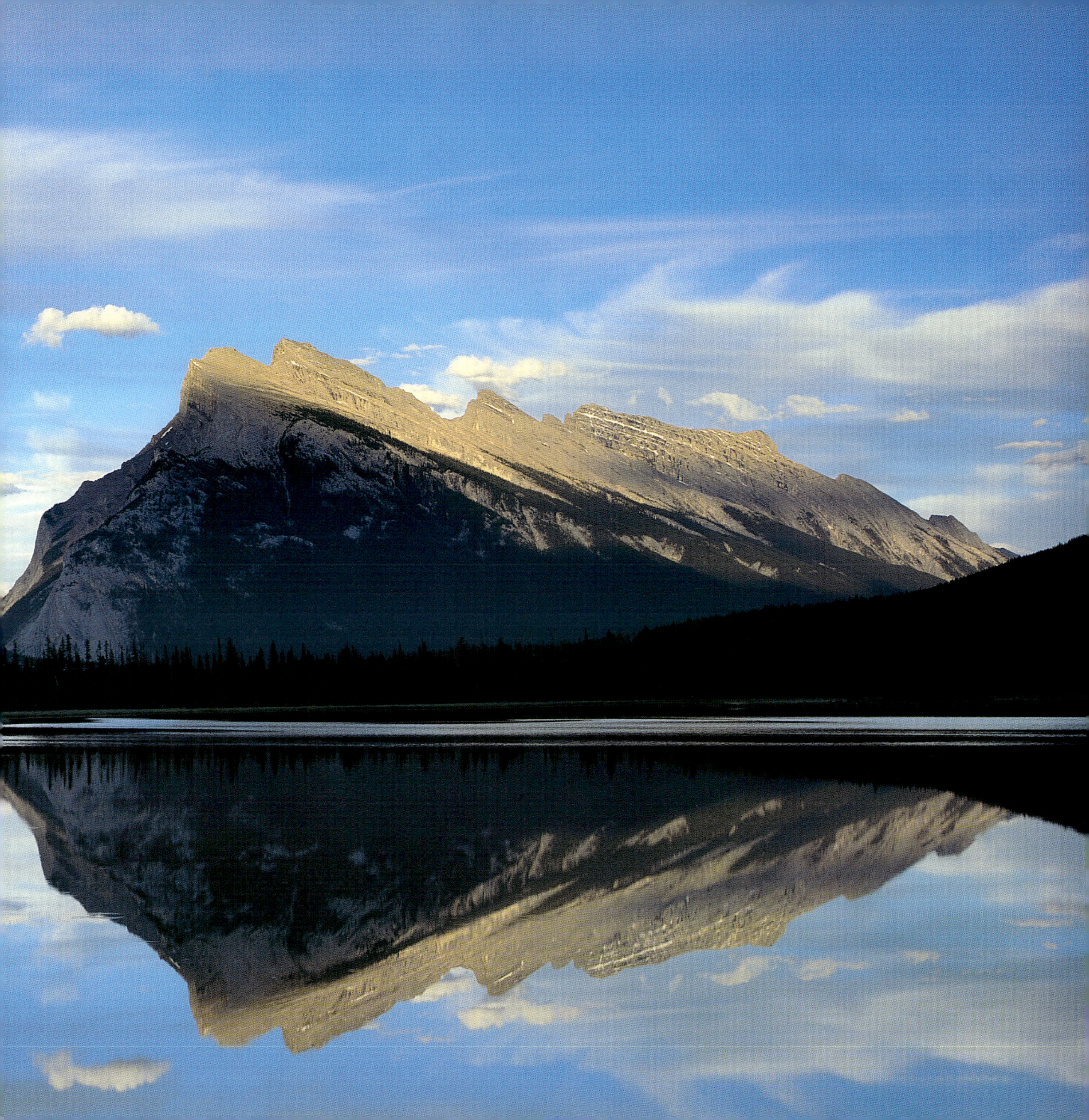

Colour-Correction Filters

There are many occasions when my photographs look even better than I expected, better than my memory of the real event. I can take little credit for this. It is the result of one inescapable fact: film does not 'see' light as we do. Most film is balanced to 'see' perfectly well in ordinary daylight. That is daylight with a blue sky, a few fluffy white clouds and sunshine. Photographs taken using daylight–balanced film in ordinary daylight should yield accurate colour photographs. Photographs taken in any other kind of daylight will 'suffer' from a colour cast unless you take steps to correct this cast with filters. There are times when it is appropriate to use these filters and correct the colour cast; equally, there are times when it is not.

WARM-UP FILTERS

Warm-up filters are essential, because in reality light is often blue and cold. Our eyes compensate for this but film does not. These filters, used properly, bring a photograph closer to the reality we perceive with our eyes than film can on its own. Most photographers use filters in the 81-series for warming. These vary in strength from a mild 81A to a much stronger 81E. Personally I do not use these, preferring coral graduated filters. My preference is based simply on the effect the 81-series filters have on blue skies. I feel they give the sky a very slight green tinge. The graduated coral filters do not have to affect the sky at all, since the line of their effective area can be placed on or below the horizon. The effect of a warming filter should be mild. I use coral no. 1 filter, the mildest, almost exclusively.

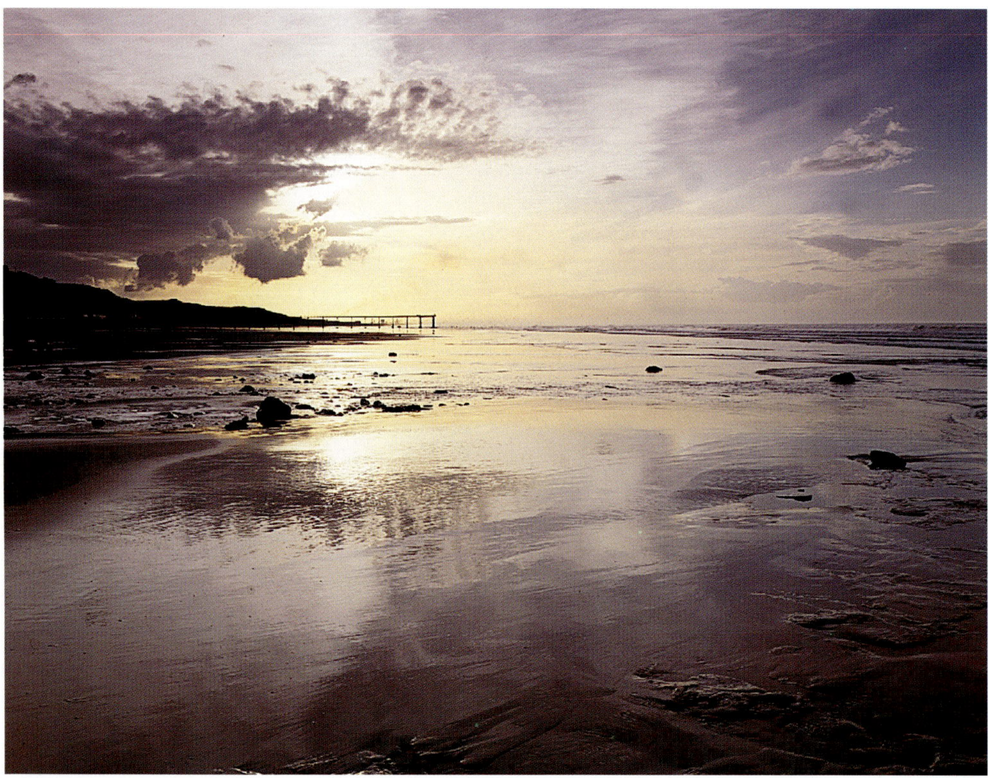

left **Saltburn by the Sea**

A wet beach in the late afternoon. These wonderful blue tones were not what I saw with the naked eye, they are a creation of unfiltered colour film. This light has a high colour temperature despite blue looking a cool colour. A pale amber filter might have 'corrected' this colour cast, and were my subject a landscape of rolling farmland and wheat fields I would no doubt have used a filter to correct the blue cast, but it suits this subject and so none was used.

Pentax 67 with 45mm lens, Velvia 50, 1/2sec at f/22, 0.6 ND grad filter

 Kelvin Scale

Light can be measured on the Kelvin scale. It's a bit like Celsius, only Kelvin can be used to measure the temperature of colour. Normal daylight measures about 5,400 degrees Kelvin (K). In open shade under a blue sky, that might reach 11,000K, leading to a strong blue colour cast. A sunset might be around 2,000K, leading to a strong orange cast. Though we think of blue as a cold colour and orange as a warm one, technically it is the other way around.

right and below
Sligachen, Isle of Skye
Both these pictures were taken using a polarizing filter but only the one below has the added benefit of an 81B warm-up filter. This filter has given the photograph the same colours I recall seeing when I was there.

Mamiya Pro SV 645 with 55–110, Velvia 50, 1/2sec at f/22

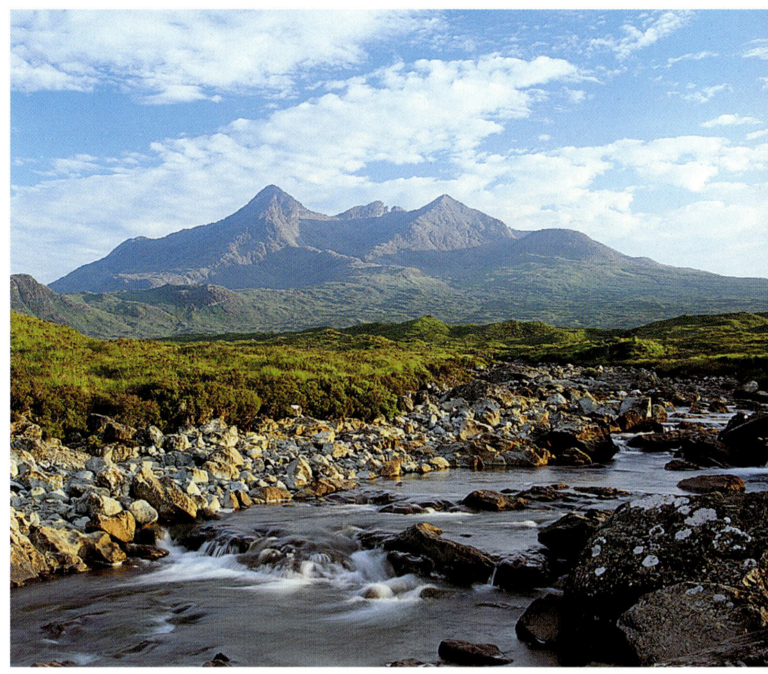

RECOMMENDED FILTERS FOR COLOUR CORRECTION

Light source	Filter	Light loss	White balance equivalent (digital cameras)
Clear blue sky	85B		Shade
Shade on a sunny day	81C	+1/3	Shade
Overcast (cloudy) day	81B	+1/3	Cloudy
Noon sunlight	81B	+1/3	Cloudy
Average daylight (4 hours before sunset and 4 hours after sunrise)	81A	+1/3	Cloudy
Early a.m / late p.m	81A	+1/3	Cloudy
1 hour before sunset	81A	+1/3	Cloudy
Sunset	None	–	Cloudy

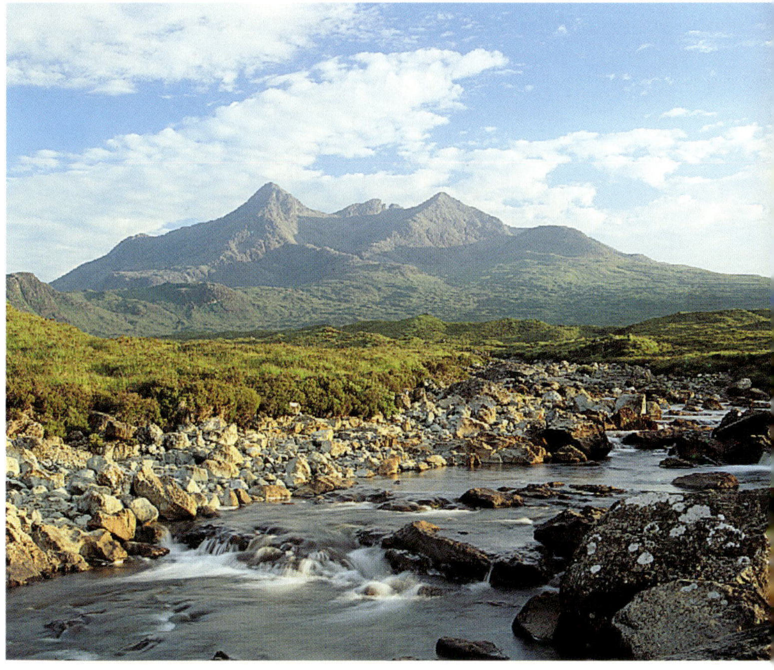

SEE ALSO: The Colour of Light at Different Times *p 110*

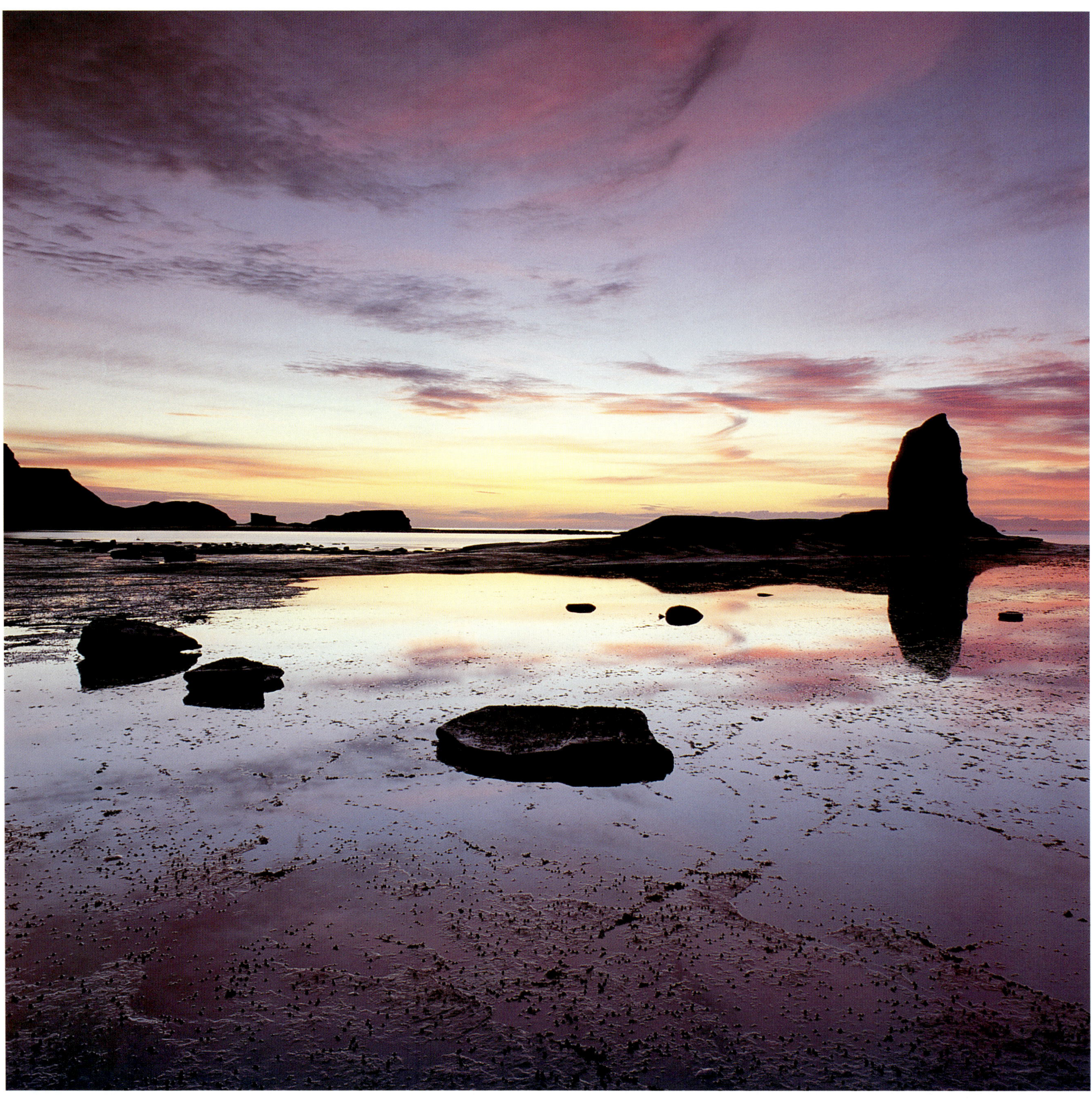

In Search of Inspiration

Where does inspiration come from and how do we nurture it? The desire to create new images and the ideas behind them are as vital to a photographer as film or pixels. You won't get very far without either one.

Much of our inspiration to take a photograph comes directly from the land. However, you need to seek out locations that you find emotive to photograph rather than trying to force yourself to take exciting pictures of places that do not interest you. It is a common misconception that a landscape photographer ought to be able to take a good photograph of any

Bruges, Belgium

Long before visiting Bruges I had seen this picture on calendars, in travel brochures, even as a jigsaw puzzle, and knew that I wanted to photograph this scene. I did not have any one picture in mind that I wanted to copy but I had clearly been inspired by other photographers who had been there. I am confident, though, that had I just happened upon this scene I would still have been moved to take my own picture.

Ebony 54 with 90mm lens, 6x12 panoramic back, Velvia 50, 1/2sec at f/22, polarizing and Coral No. 1 grad filters

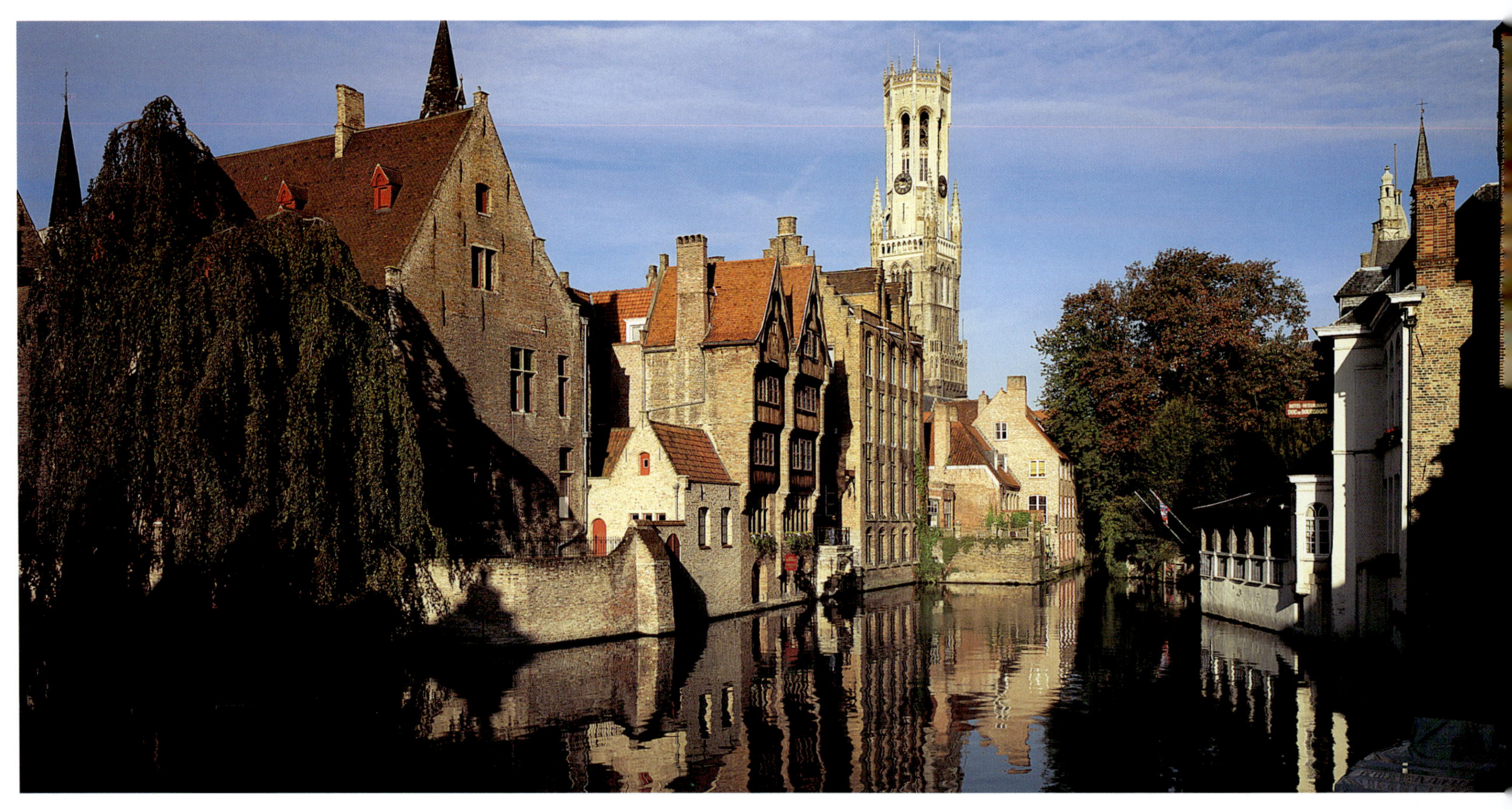

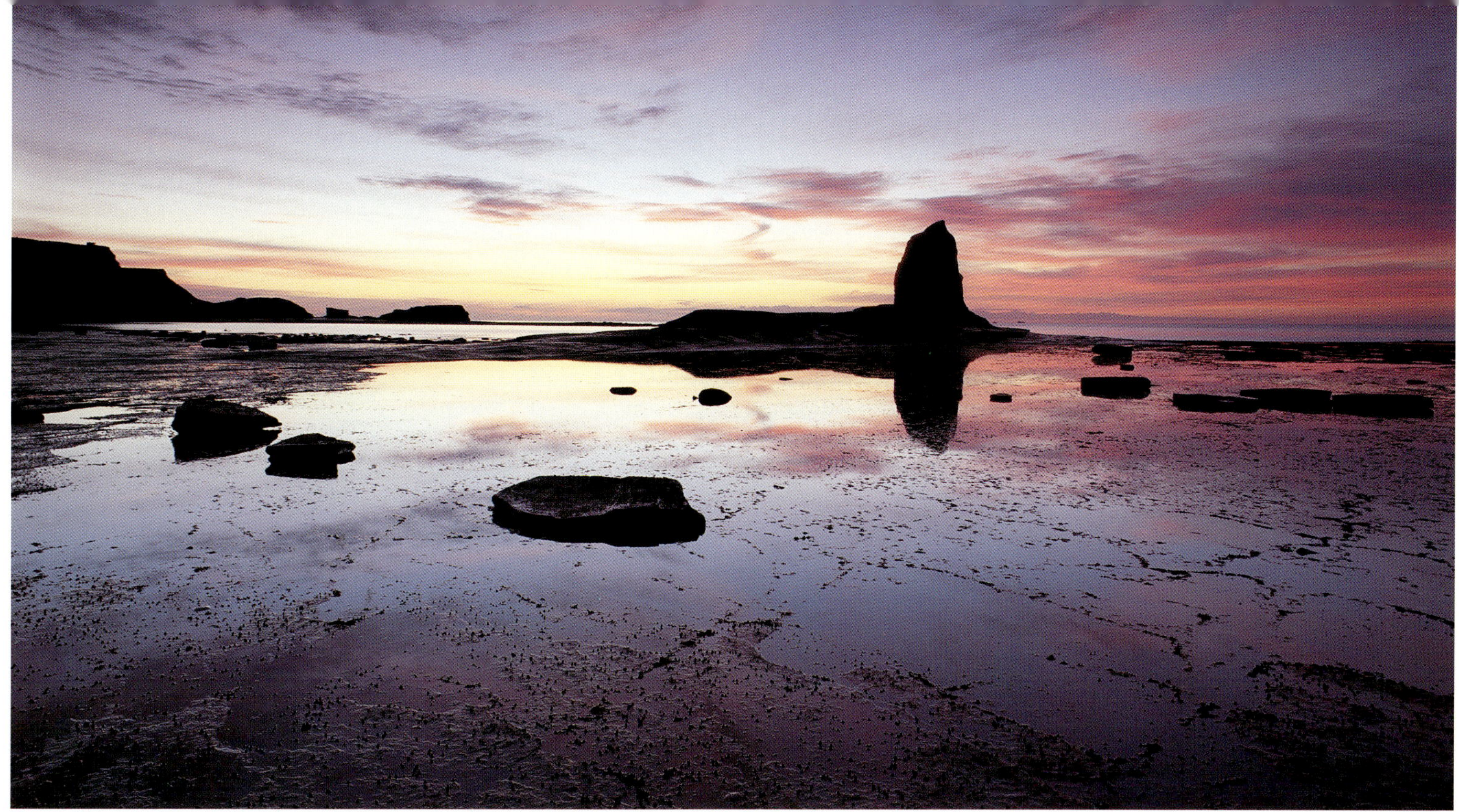

landscape. This simply isn't true. There are many places that do nothing for me. If the location does not stir your soul how on earth can you expect to take a picture of it that will? If your own emotional response to a place is negative it will be hard to be honest and take a positive image of it. Although we don't have the same degree of control over our subject as an artist or studio photographer, we can choose whether or not to respond to the land, the light and the conditions we find.

There is also another element to consider and that is our mood. Our state of mind contributes greatly to the success, or otherwise, of our efforts. There will be days when we are in tune with the land and the light, and there will be days when we we are not, and this will be clearly evident in the photographs we take. Feeling inspired will help you to respond positively to the landscape.

Black Nab, Saltwick Bay at Sunset

This was the first time I had visited Saltwick Bay for the summer sunset. I already knew that sunset and low tide would arrive more or less at the same time. Since taking this photograph I have been back to the same spot many times and have taken many more versions of this scene, each one of them different. The shallow pool in front of Black Nab is often still like this, and Saltwick Bay is close enough to home that I can tell if a good sunset is likely before I set off.

Mamiya 645 Pro SV with 55–110mm lens, Velvia 50, 6 seconds at f/22, 0.6 ND grad filter

Whitby Abbey

This small pond in front of Whitby Abbey has been
used by photographers as foreground interest since
Frank Meadow Sutcliffe's days. However, I had been
inspired to take a look at this view by a painting of the
Abbey at sunset. The artist had used a much higher
vantage point – the top of a nearby wall – and had
been able to include the headland as the sun went
down. I could see the same view, but there was no
way to set the camera up on the top of the wall to
take a similar composition. I moved in much closer
and lower, filling the foreground with the pond.
The only way I could do this was to stand in the pond.
Wellington boots and a Benbo tripod with sealed ends
meant everything stayed dry.

**Ebony 45s with 90mm lens, Velvia 50, 1 second
at f/22, Coral No. 1 and 0.3 ND grad filters**

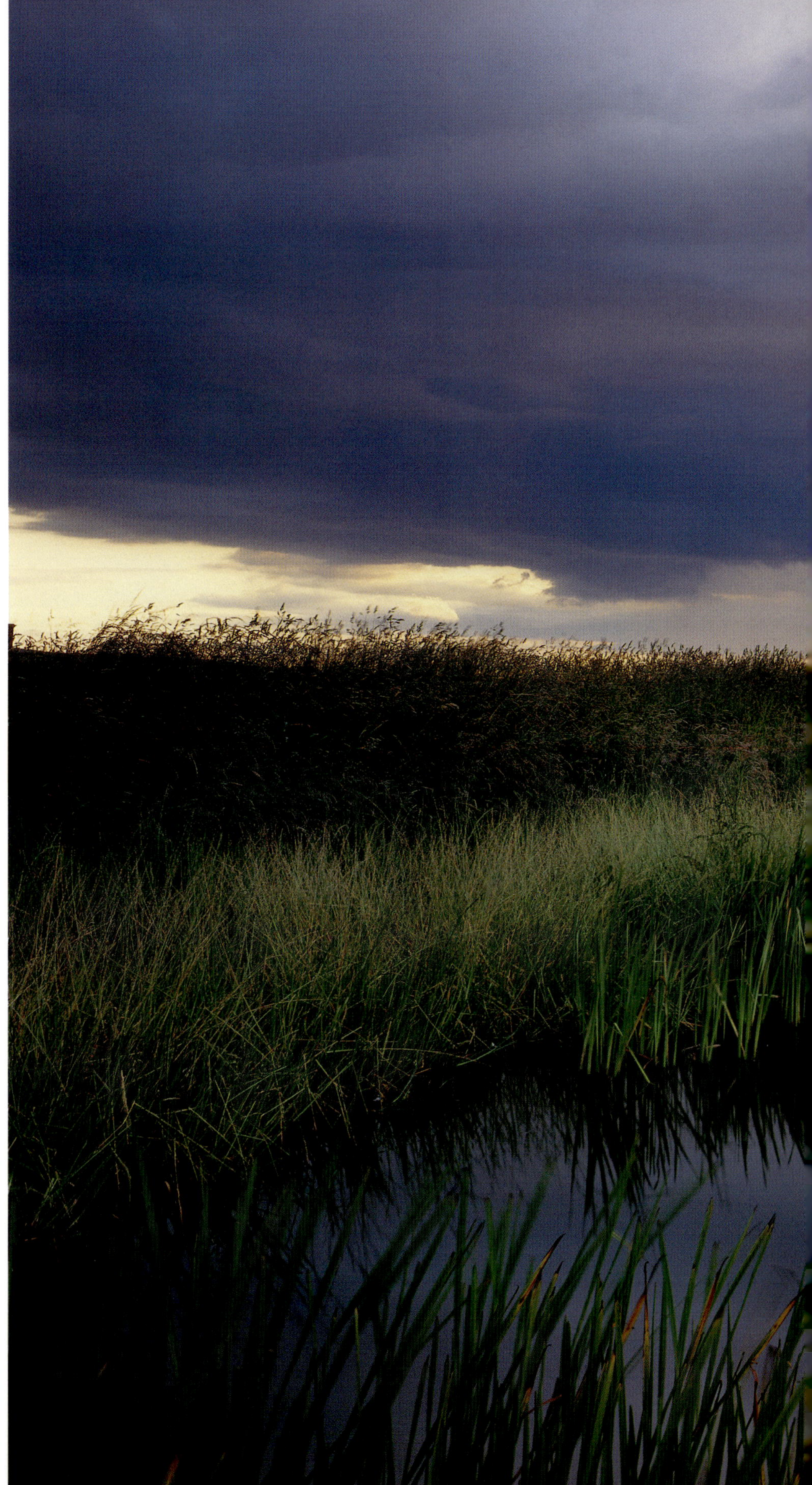

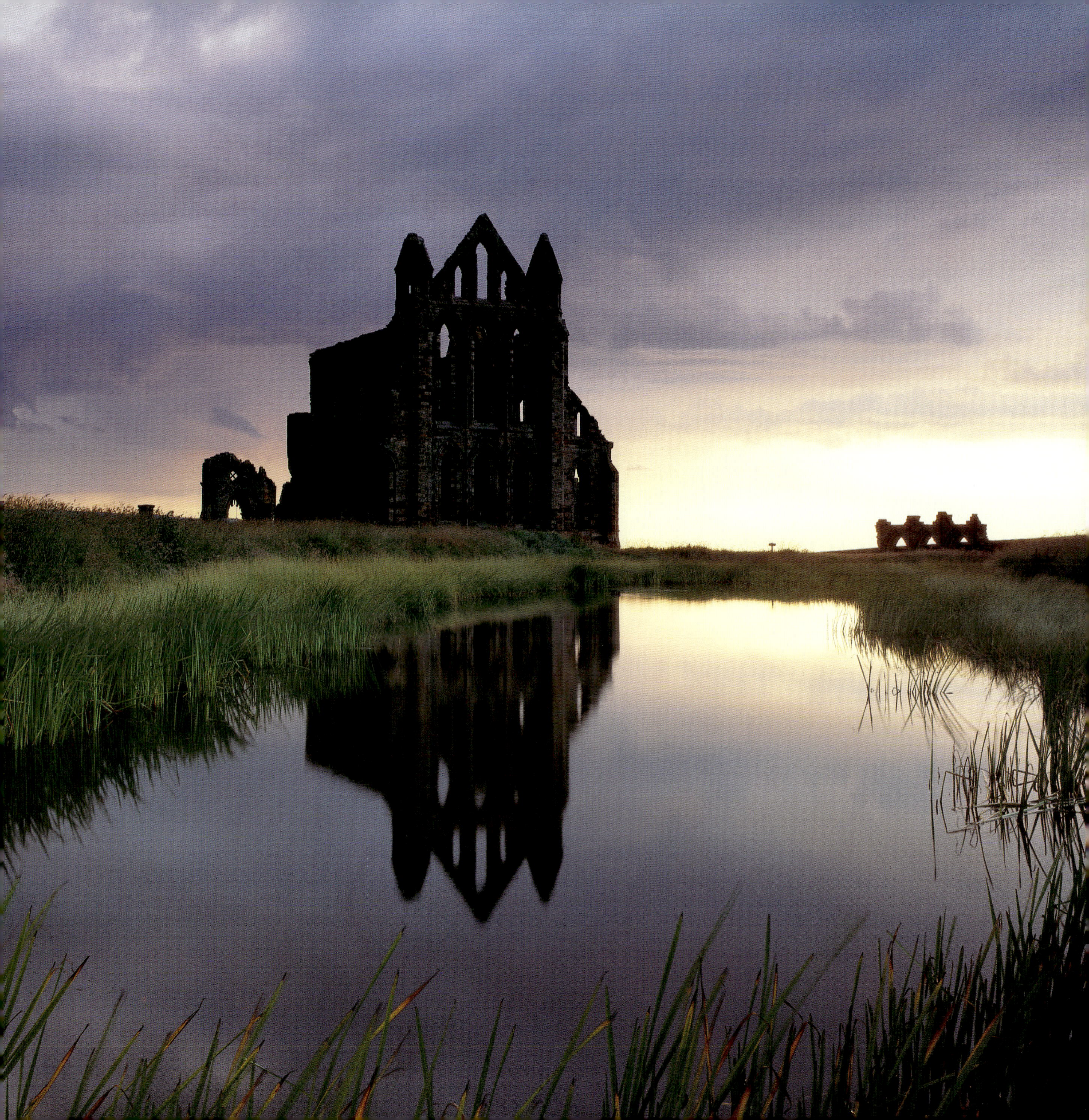

The Northumberland coast is an awesome place for landscape photography, but let's keep that to ourselves shall we? That way the combination of wonderful light and empty, tranquil beaches will not become a thing of the past.

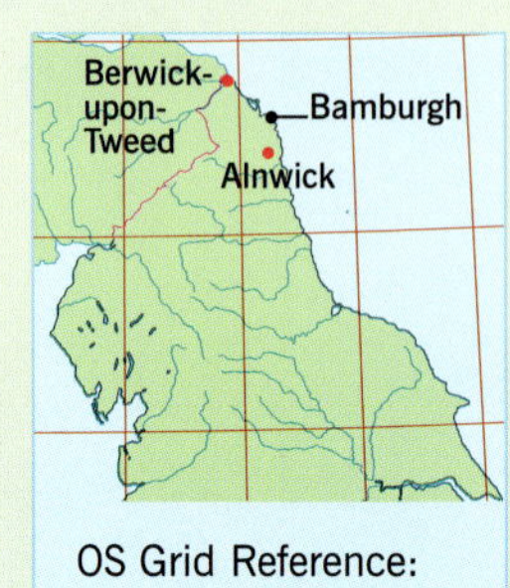

OS Grid Reference:
x= 418986m
y= 635114m

There are three classic castles along the length of the Northumberland coastline. Dunstanburgh to the south and Lindisfarne to the north are enchanting and dramatic. It is Bamburgh, though, that offers the most imposing presence.

There is more to Bamburgh than just the castle. In fact, I always feel that wherever you are, once you have photographed the obvious scenes it is time to explore the area for its other attractions. The seaweed detail (facing page) is a case in point. It was the subject to hand which best suited the weather conditions on that day – overcast and dull. The beach itself can also offer some rewarding scenes, especially looking east towards the Farne Islands. Gentle light and simple composition can combine to capture the feel of the place – peace and wide open space, quiet and solitude.

Bamburgh Castle, Dawn

Sometimes with a scene like this I will give the photograph a little more exposure than the camera suggests, depending on the mood I am trying to record. On this occasion I wanted a blacked-out silhouette, to make the castle appear as a brooding presence on the shore. I added the 0.6 neutral-density graduated filter to hold light back from the brighter sky. On an aesthetic level, the water on the beach created the whole appeal of this scene. Without the sheen and the reflection it creates, there would be no picture.

Pentax 67 with 55mm lens, Velvia 50, 1/8sec at f/22

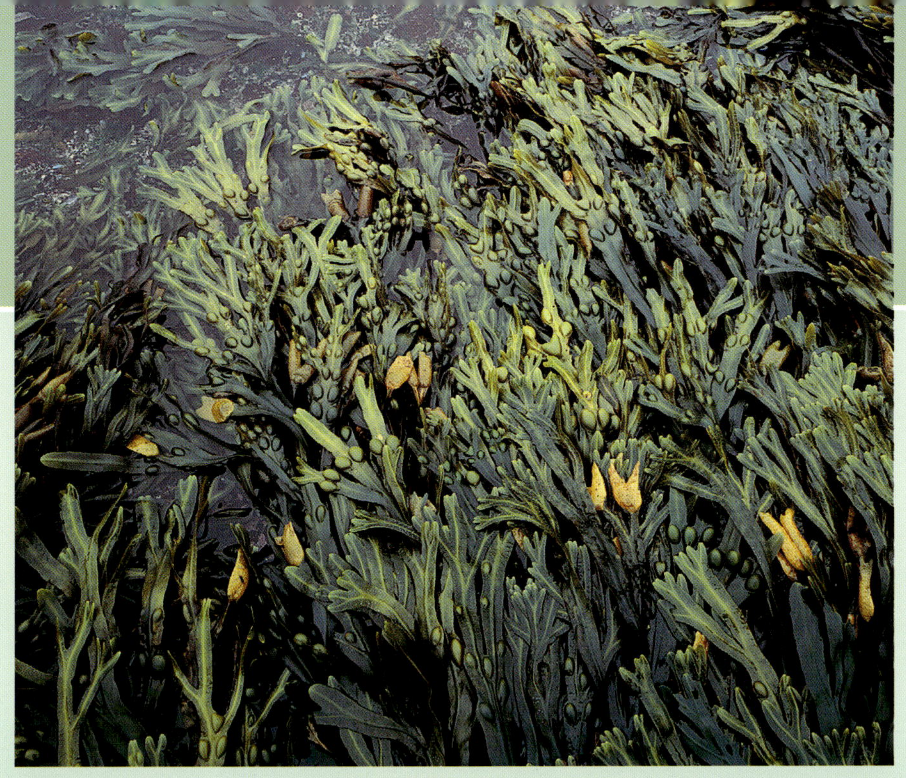

left **Seaweed on Bamburgh Beach**
On a dull day a classic view like the castle is not worth taking, but it suited this seaweed detail shot perfectly.

Cambo 54 monorail with 58mm lens, 6x9 rollfilm back; 4 seconds at f/22

below **Farne Islands**
The Islands themselves are very small within this picture, which only serves to emphasize the vastness of the sea and the expanse of sky.

Ebony 45s with 90mm lens, 10 seconds at f/22, 0.6 ND grad filter

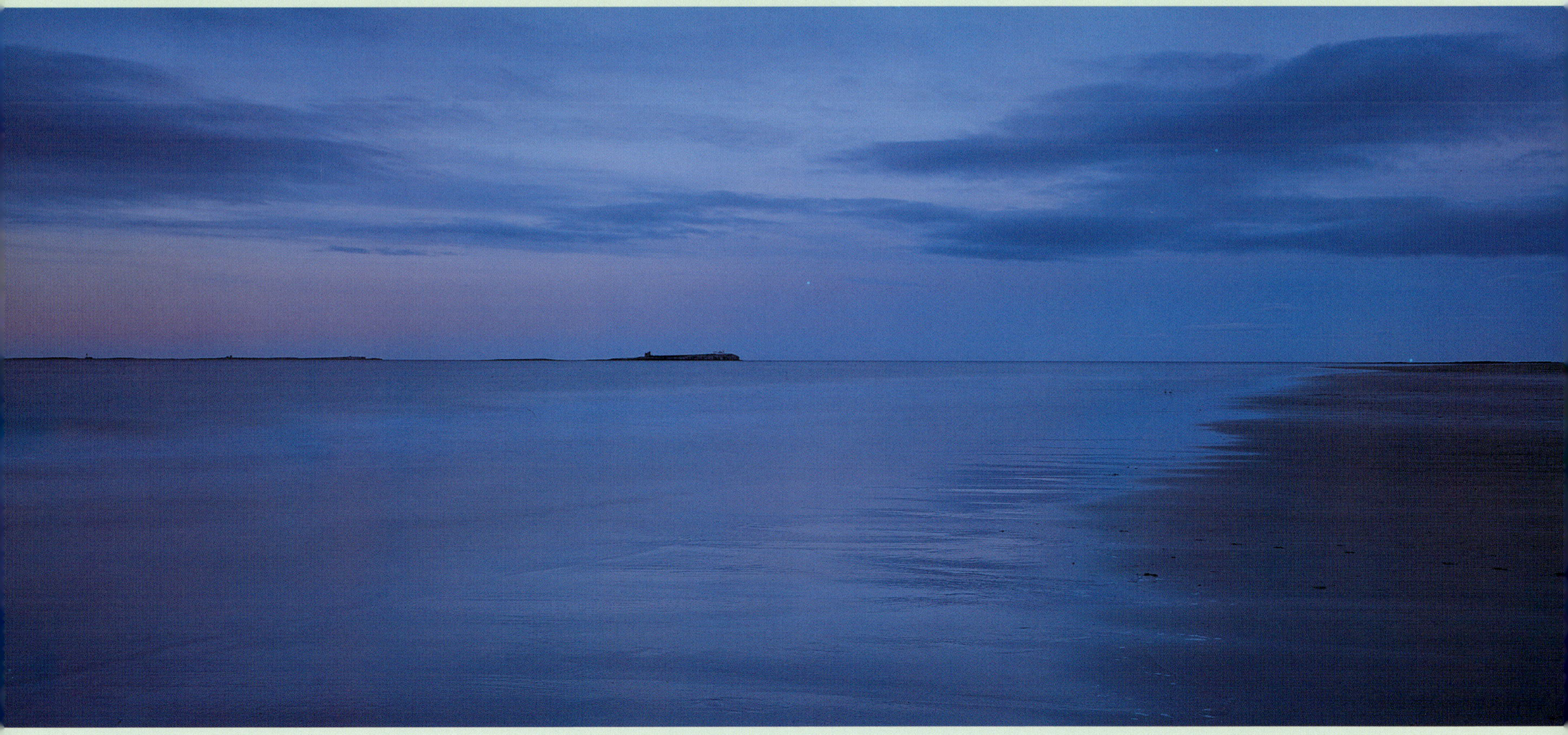

Even as a full-time landscape photographer it is impossible to be out taking pictures all the time. However, there are things that both the novice and professional photographer alike can do to remain inspired.

1 RESTRICT YOUR EQUIPMENT

Limiting yourself to one lens, rather than the usual range you carry, can be an interesting challenge and inspire some new photography. Last time I tried this I took just my 35mm camera with a 500mm mirror lens. This really limited the pictures I could take and focused my mind on the opportunities that remained. Next time I may try just my 5x4 camera and a 150mm standard lens. Anything that forces you to think a little harder about the pictures you take will stimulate creativity.

2 RESTRICT YOUR FILM

One of the harshest exercises in gaining inspiration I ever heard about was the project Jim Brandenburg set himself. He decided to take just one photograph every day for 90 days between the autumn equinox and winter solstice. There would be no second chance: if the best light came along after he had made his exposure, then it would be lost. The project he set meant he had to take no more and no less than one picture a day, whatever the conditions. The resulting book *Chased by the Light* is a masterpiece and suggests to me that such an exercise really does focus the mind.

If restrictions inspire and concentrate the mind then there are less frightening ways to do so than limiting yourself to one picture per day. The usual advice when going somewhere great for a photographic holiday is to work out how much film you will need and then double it. So try this: work out how much film you will need and halve it. It is not as restricting as one picture a day, but it will make you think hard before you take a picture, and that can only be a good thing.

3 EXPLORE A THEME

Selecting a single theme from within the wide canvas that is the landscape is a way of limiting your choices and therefore focusing the mind. Water is a wonderful theme for the landscape photographer. At the very least it is a beginning, somewhere to start your search within the landscape for subjects that can become images. Even if you end up taking pictures that contain no water, say in a woodland by the shore of a lake, the theme will have done its job and acted as inspiration leading to new photographs. While the landscape photographer discovers pictures rather than creates them, it does not hurt to have some idea of what you are looking for before you start. This is what I call inspirational planning; if you know what you are looking for you have a better chance of finding it.

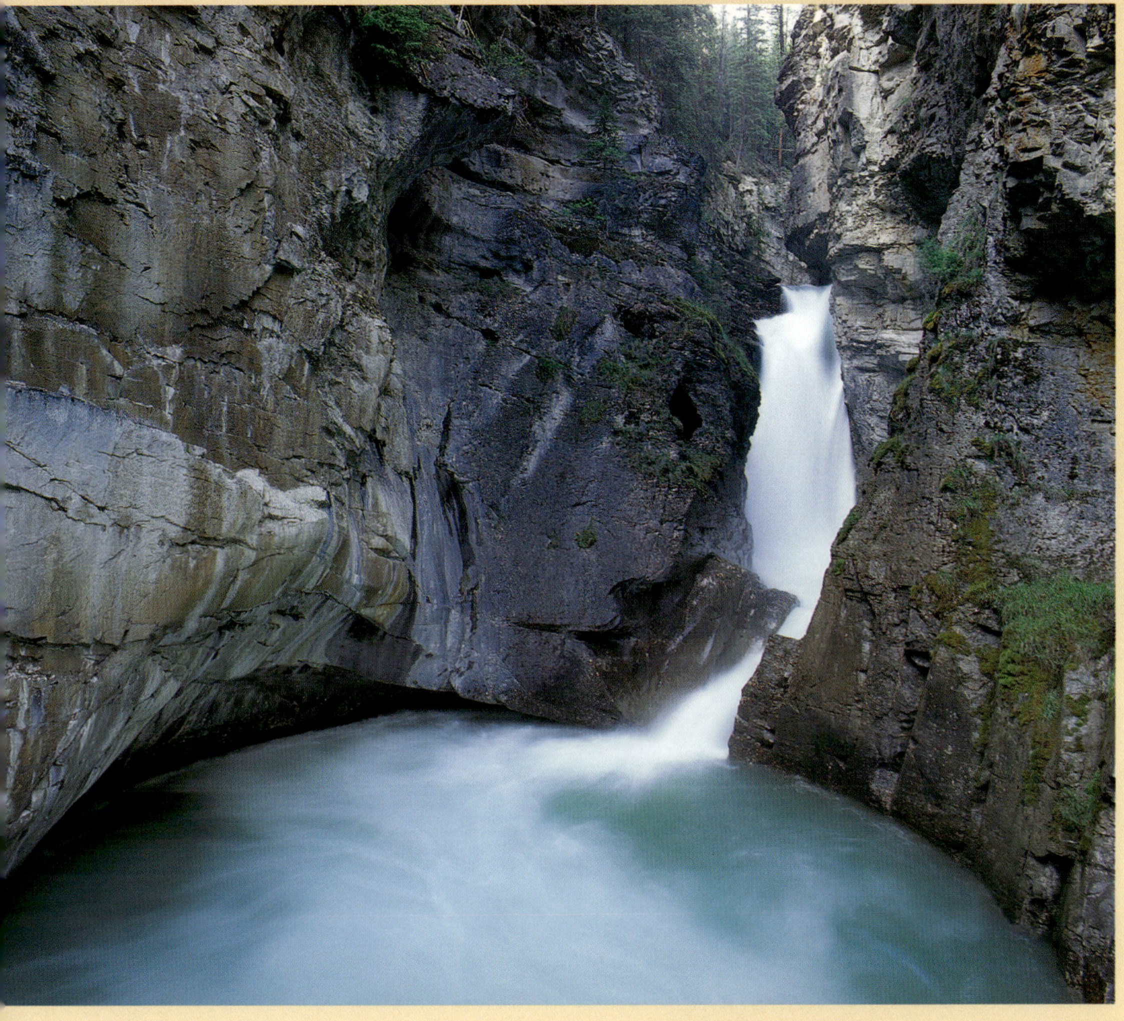

Johnston Canyon Lower Falls, Alberta, Canada

Before my trip to the Canadian Rockies I had done plenty of research and knew a lot of the scenes that I wanted to record. However, it was the discovery of areas that I had not seen photographed before that really excited me. This picture of the lower falls in Johnston Canyon came at the end of a short walk, and I had no idea what to expect when I set off.
The wonderful colours in the glacial water, the honey tones in the rock and the swirl of water in motion combine to make this photograph work.

Pentax 67 with 45mm lens, Velvia 50, 1 second at f/22

4 **RESEARCH NEW LOCATIONS**
Researching new areas you think you might like to visit is a good way to keep inspiration alive. This has the added benefit that you know more about the place when you do eventually visit. The Internet is great for this, as are guide books. By the time I arrived in the Canadian Rockies I already had a list of the places I wanted to see and photograph. I found many more while I was there, and I look forward to a return visit, armed this time with personal experience and knowledge of the area. Closer to home, it is a good idea to learn as much as you can about the places around you. Even if the weather does not look great for photography, you can always go for a walk and look for viewpoints that might be worth visiting in better weather conditions, or at another time of year. Take a camera with you on these walks, since you never can tell what the light might do, even on a day of poor weather.

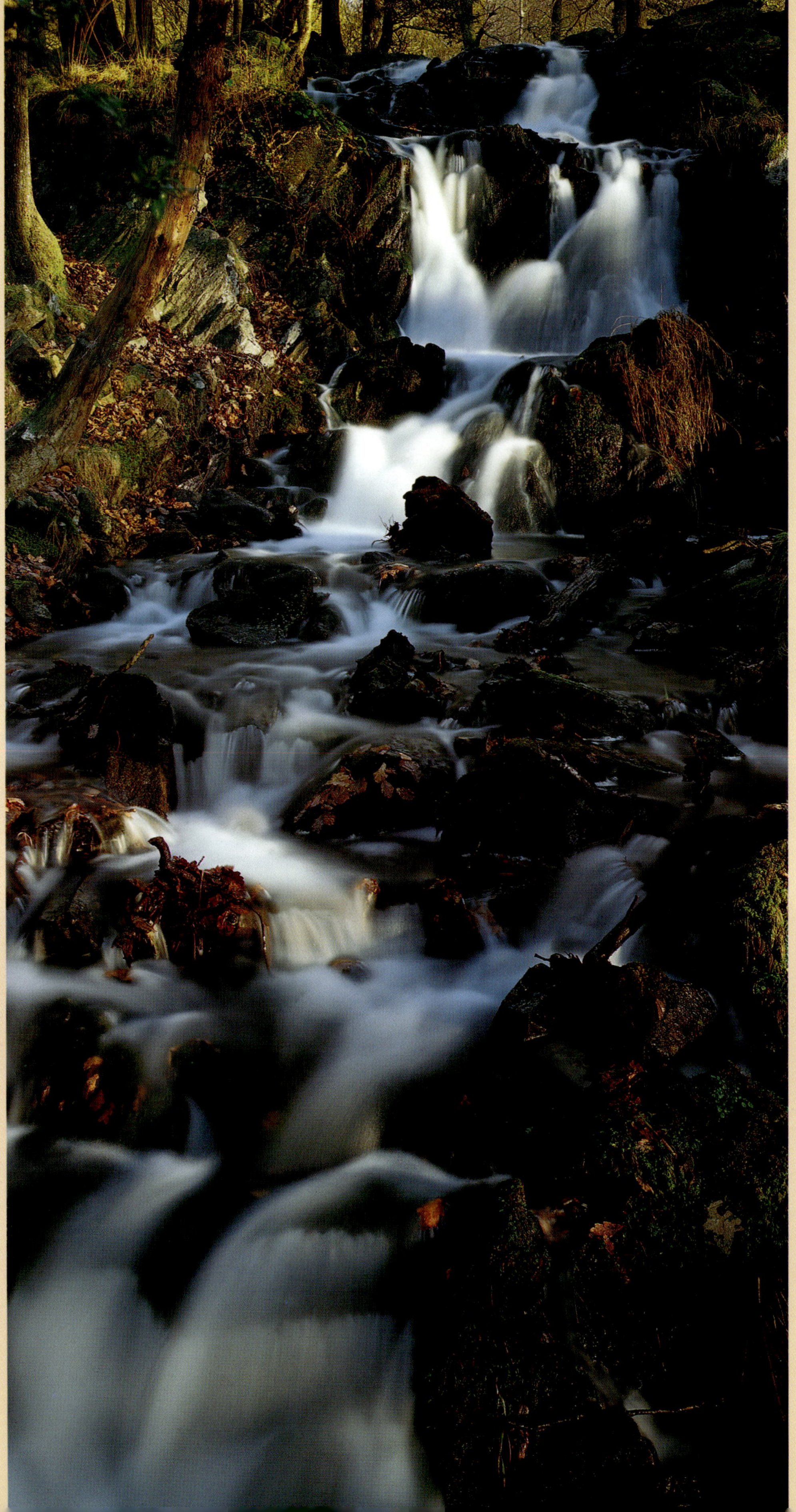

5 EXPERIMENT WITH NEW EQUIPMENT

Once you have purchased or borrowed a new camera or lens you will not be able to resist taking it out. I added a 58mm lens to my large-format camera kit, that is a super-wideangle lens (roughly equivalent to a 15mm lens on a 35mm SLR). Suddenly, with this new lens, a number of places I had already visited were worth re-visiting to see what new compositions had become possible. Sometimes this resulted in new shots using the lens and sometimes it resulted in new shots using one of the same lenses I had the last time I was at the location. However, it was the new lens that had acted as the inspiration.

Waterfall, Cumbria

Super-wideangle lenses have to be used with care. They are not suitable all of the time, but there are occasions when they make photographs possible. This whole section of the river, the rapids and the waterfall is a good example. There is no vantage point from further away that shows the extent of the falls. The only way to compose this is with a super-wideangle lens like the 58mm on a 5x4 camera.

Ebony 45s with 58mm lens, 6x12 rollfilm back, Velvia 50, 1 second at f/22

Looking to Others for Inspiration

When seeking inspiration one very obvious starting point is the work of other photographers. While it is true that nobody's work is wholly original, it is important to remain honest in our responses to the landscape. There are two ways the work of other photographers can help inspire us. The first is with regard to the places they have photographed. If someone else's photograph is exciting, one of the first things I want to know is the location; not because I want to copy their photograph, but because their photograph has shown me an exciting landscape I want to see for myself. The second way the work of other photographers can inspire is with regard to style and technique. This too is valid inspiration, though care must be taken not to allow your own way of seeing, your own unique style, to be submerged under the influence of anyone else. The first time I saw the effect of a very slow shutter speed used on moving water, I was inspired to try the technique myself. It is perfectly legitimate to copy the techniques other photographers have used without plagiarizing them. What I would not advise is to try to copy exactly the pictures other photographers have taken. Every time you get the chance to take a really good landscape photograph,

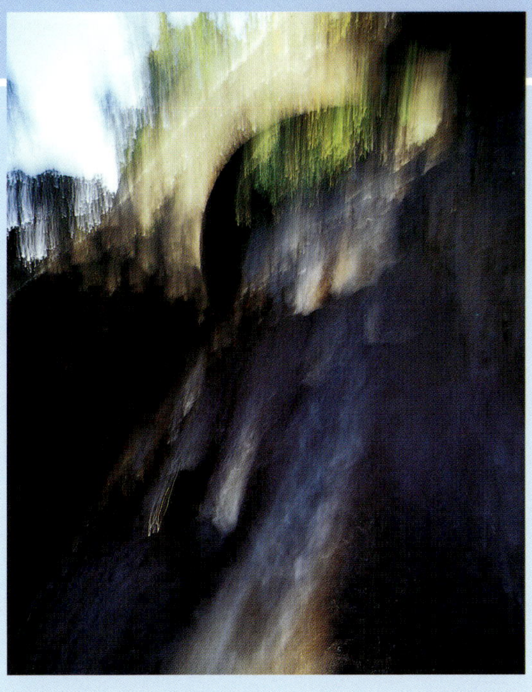

technique **BREAKING THE RULES**

A meeting with portrait photographer Annabel Williams inspired me to challenge some of the assumptions and rules I had made. This photograph is one of the results. While it is nothing like anything Annabel herself might have taken, equally it is nothing like anything I had taken before meeting her and seeing her work.

I have broken all the rules with this picture: clearly no tripod was used, the horizon is not level, the water appears to be travelling uphill and the highlights are overexposed. Does it work? It works for me. I do not like paintings that are so detailed that they could be photographs, but I love photos that look like paintings or rough pencil sketches, as this one does.

Pentax 67 with 55mm lens, Velvia 50, 1 second at f/22, panning the camera along the flowing water

it is a once in a lifetime opportunity. So if you did try to copy the work of another photographer you would most likely fail, and nothing will destroy inspiration quicker than regular failure. On the other hand, if your picture did, by chance, look like the one you wanted to copy, the resulting picture is then, at best, a reproduction. Not nearly as exciting as creating something new that is your own. We all have a personal style as photographers. This is not something you have to work for, it is inherent, and it will always be there. It is really a question of personal integrity. If you are honest in your responses to the landscape, your personal style will shine through and your photographs will be better for it. If you want to be excited by your own photographs then stay true to yourself and your own personal style.

Courses and Tours

These days many of the world's best-known photographers host tours and workshops. These may vary from a one-day course to a three-week tour of some exotic location. Which you opt for will depend on your budget and the time available. In any event, you should be able to ask questions and gain first-hand expert advice out in the field.

Perhaps the most inspirational thing you can learn on these workshops is that the professionals have no magic wand. They cannot order the sun to shine or the clouds to part. The reason their own work is so exciting is sheer determination in the face of the same challenges we all have to overcome. You may well learn that you have been doing everything right for years and now all you have to do is more of it. The expert will not be the only inspirational photographer you meet on the tour or workshop – your fellow delegates will all be like-minded photographers, and many of them will have interesting photographs to show you and advice to impart.

In the history of any art you will find that the famous artists of any age often knew each other. This is because they inspired each other, and therefore sought each other's company. Though nature photography is, for the most part, a solitary activity, I have made many friends with people, both amateur and professional, who simply want to share and exchange ideas and anecdotes. When you have waited all day for a glimmer of light that never came, it can be a comfort to know that you are not the only one. It is also great to see inspiring work first hand and to know that with persistence and determination the very best results are available to everyone.

Purpose

Few things will inspire you as much as having a purpose for your photography. It's one of the principal differences between a professional and an amateur photographer. As a professional you always have a purpose. As an amateur, then, it is worth finding reasons to take more photographs.

Trying to get your work published in any medium will spur you on, especially when you succeed. Putting on an exhibition of your work will inspire you to get out and take some great photographs to display. And giving talks at photographic societies or local schools can make you analyse your work while choosing which pictures to use to demonstrate your points. In my experience this has resulted in me feeling I can do better, so I go out and try.

As a visual artist your style will develop through exposure to as many creative influences as possible. For instance, looking at the work of painters can help you to see the landscape before you as they might. I am very much a fan of Monet and love the technique he used to create an impression of his subjects rather than a detailed study. Check out the pictures on pages 145 and 147 to see how I have composed these photographs to create a similar abstract effect.

Inspiration works in mysterious ways, and you may find that someone else's work has had an effect on you without you even being aware of it. Many years ago my brother and I visited the Tate Gallery in London to see some of Mark Rothko's work. He had seen the exhibition earlier and been impressed with it. I wasn't at all taken by Rothko's work. So it comes as something of a surprise to me to find that there are people who think this photograph of a beach in Cornwall is reminiscent of Rothko's work. It comes as even more of a surprise to admit that I can see why.

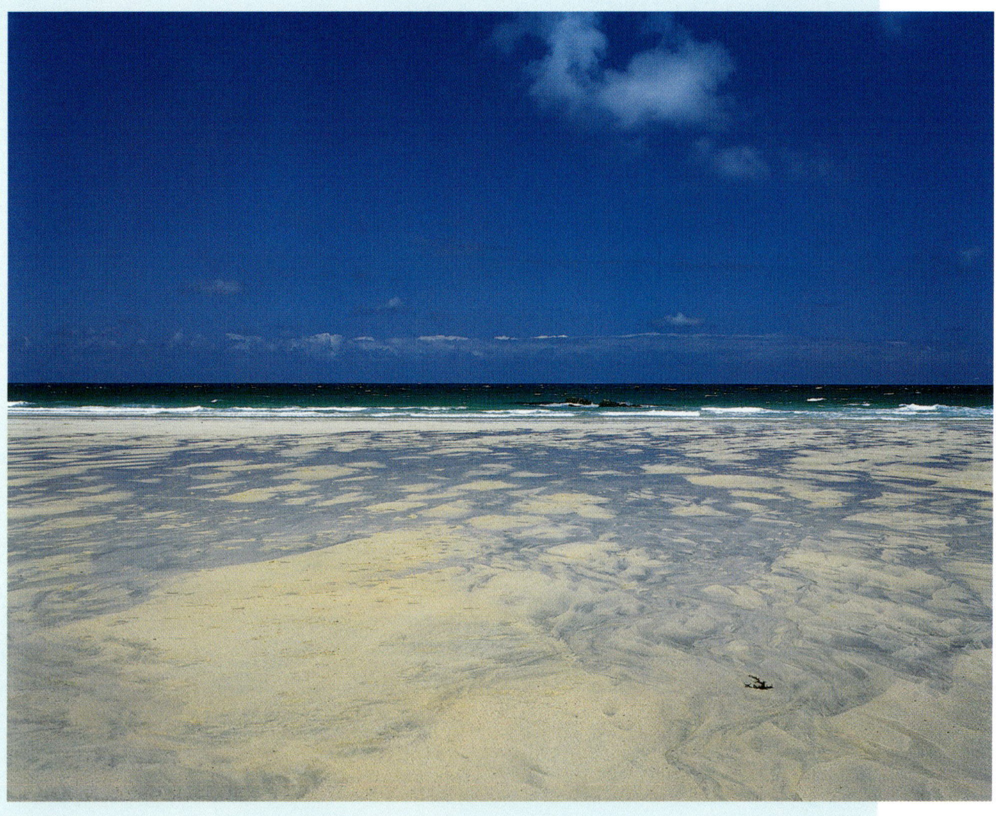

Beach

If you walk around St Ives in Cornwall you will find a lot of art galleries, and a number of them will contain minimalist paintings of just beach, sea and sky in vivid colours. I was surprised to find this beach so empty so late in the day. I had to wonder for a while 'is there enough here?' I decided that if it was enough for the painters then it was worth a try. I used a polarizing filter to emphasize the tiny rivulets of water running through the sand and following the retreating tide back into the sea.

Pentax 67 with 90mm lens, Velvia 50, 1/2sec at f/22, polarizing filter

Water Colours

Water can appear to be any colour, since it reflects the colours around it. Your pictures of water can then be pastel or bold, gentle on the eye or striking. The possibilities are infinite and limited only by the time you have to spend looking for them.

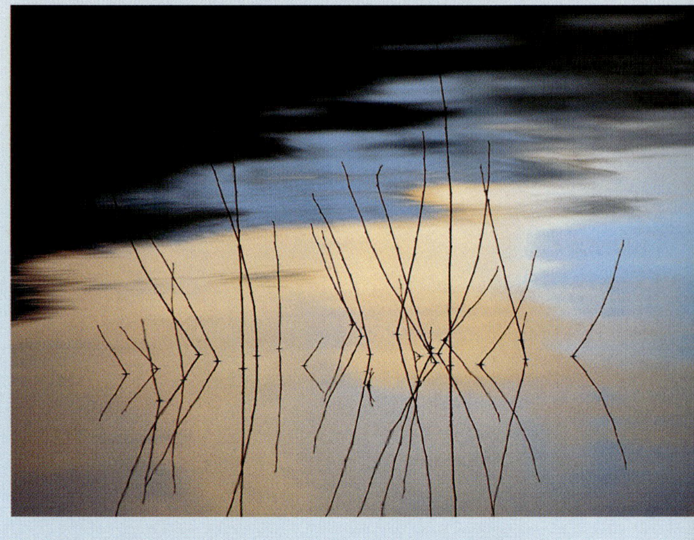

above **Thirlmere Detail at Dusk**
The pale pink sunset is still obvious in this picture, even without seeing the sky.
Nikon FM2 with 75–300mm lens, Velvia 50, exposure details not recorded

St Bees Head, Cumbria
As the sun set and the afterglow reflected in the textures of the wet beach I took this detail picture of the colour.
Ebony 45s with 150mm lens, Velvia 50, 2 seconds at f/22, 0.3 ND hard-grad filter

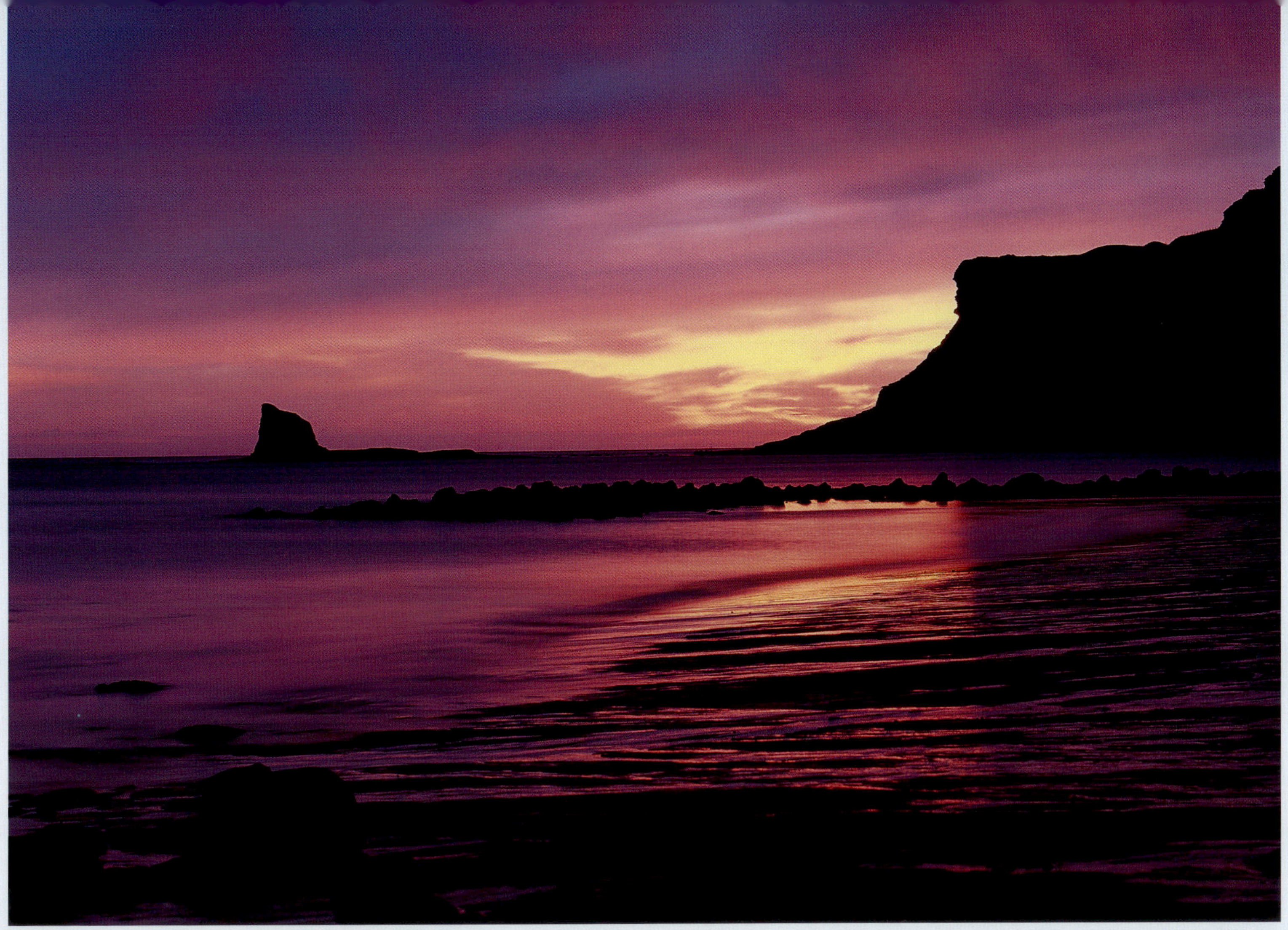

The wonderful shapes of Black Nab and the cliffs at the south of Saltwick Bay make great silhouettes. Here, a good sunrise is reflected in the sea, filling the frame with colour. A long shutter speed has blurred the movement of the tide as it ebbs and flows over the beach.

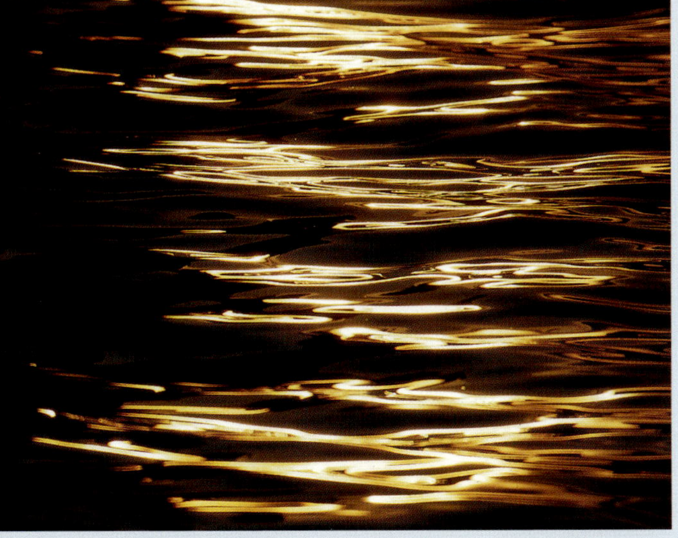

left **Golden Water**

For this picture I used a 500mm mirror lens and focused on a small section of the sea as the setting sun was close to the horizon. I selected an area where part of the sea was in the shade of the nearby cliffs. This created an edge in the line of light reflected off the waves. Exposure was difficult to determine, so I bracketed widely. In the end, the exposure that worked best was the one the camera's meter suggested.

Nikon F301 with 500mm f/8 mirror lens, Velvia 50, 1/500sec at f/8

above **Saltwick Bay, Sunrise**

The wonderful shapes of Black Nab and the cliffs at the south of Saltwick Bay make great silhouettes. Here, a good sunrise is reflected in the sea, filling the frame with colour. A long shutter speed has blurred the movement of the tide as it ebbs and flows over the beach.

Mamiya 645 Pro SV with 105–210mm lens, Velvia 50, 6 seconds at f/22, 0.6 ND grad filter

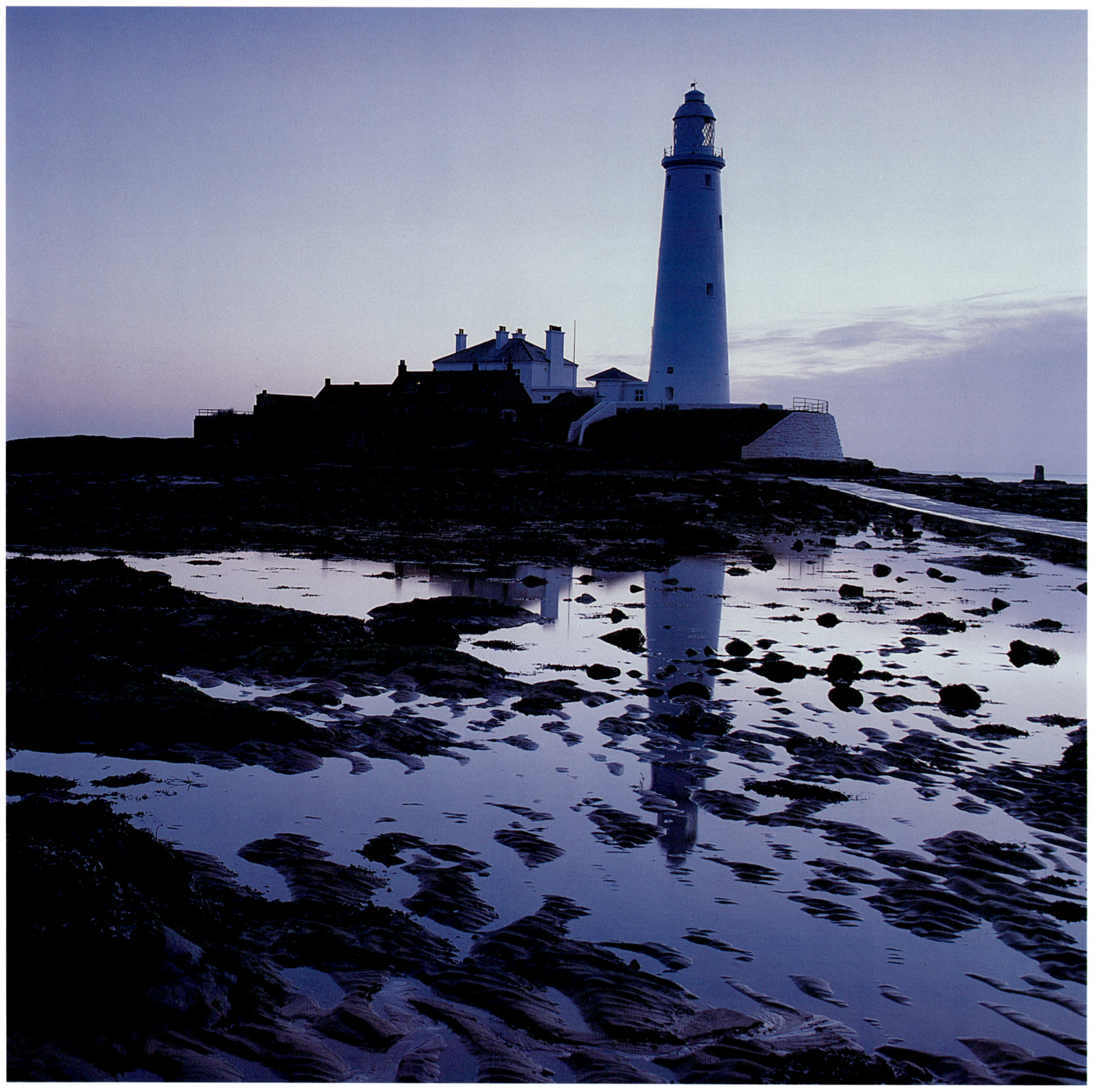

Light

Photography literally means drawing with light, so from the very name we immediately
know that light is an essential part of the process. While technically anyone can draw on
paper with a pencil, we can all see the touch of an artist. It is the same with light.

hotography is easy enough (drawing with light having been made very simple with modern technology), but we can appreciate the style of an accomplished photographer. Considered and creative use of light makes the elevation from snapshot to work of art. Film is just a material that responds to light, and it will respond to any light, whether it be good, bad or indifferent. So long as the right quantity reaches the film, and so long as that light is well focused, a technically correct photograph will result.

Beyond mere technical considerations, less attention is paid to the quantity of light and much more to the quality. As with so many things, there is a trade-off between quality and quantity: as one increases, the other decreases.

As well as the predictable times of dawn and dusk, there are other
moments when the light might be wonderful: on the edge of a weather
front, for example, on a day when broken cloud blocks and then reveals
the sun. I have sat under grey, leaden skies and waited for hours for just
a few minutes of golden light. When the clouds part and allow a thin
sliver of sunshine to caress the hills, the whole scene can come to life.
Quite often, though, the sun will not come. In the landscape our only
control is timing and choice.

Studio photographers have complete control over lighting conditions. Such control might, at times, be the envy of landscape photographers, except that it would destroy one of landscape photography's greatest joys. Capturing those wonderful moments when the light briefly transforms the land from the ordinary to the extraordinary is a joy precisely because you cannot be certain of doing it.

Capturing the Best Light

The very best light for landscape photography is transient. It might last just a few seconds and then be gone forever. Capturing the light on film during those brief moments requires planning, preparation and luck. The more you try, the more chances you will have to strike lucky. The more you practice, the more you will experience this transitory light, which will result in you becoming more skilled at predicting and recording it. Luck, then, is not something that just falls into your lap – you have to work for it.

Correct timing is vital. There are nuances to light which only experience can teach. The old adage 'if you've seen it you've missed it' is very true. When I say the best light is transitory, I mean it is fleeting. Certainly, the very best light does not last long enough for you to find a view, compose the image, set up the camera on a tripod and take your picture. This is why the very best light has to be anticipated. You have to be in place waiting for it, camera ready, mounted on a tripod, filters in place. Perhaps this is why medium- and even large-format cameras are popular with the landscape photographer. To gain extra quality you give up some convenience, but convenience will seldom help you capture the very best light.

Light and Composition

Light is one half of the overall content of any photograph. The other half being the composition. The great thing about landscape composition is that it does not change: once you have framed a good view where the land is laid out in a way that pleases the eye, you can return to it any number of times and wait for the right light. Although I ought to qualify that statement a little. While the topography does not change, many other things do. With each season the vegetation changes, water levels rise and fall in rivers and lakes and, of course, the sky is never the same twice. All of these things might alter your composition. And then there are the numerous possible man-made changes: parked cars, new buildings, scaffolding . . . the list goes on. Even light itself can affect the best way to compose a picture; the two are inextricably bound. Bands of light and shade create form on the land, form you might never see repeated. Hence, the next time you visit a location, while the topography may be the same, the best composition might have changed, even if just by a little.

The great thing about light is that it is never the same twice. While light and composition are the two halves of every photograph, it is not often that they are equal halves. Of course, the very best landscape photographs result when you have a strong composition and wonderful transitory light.

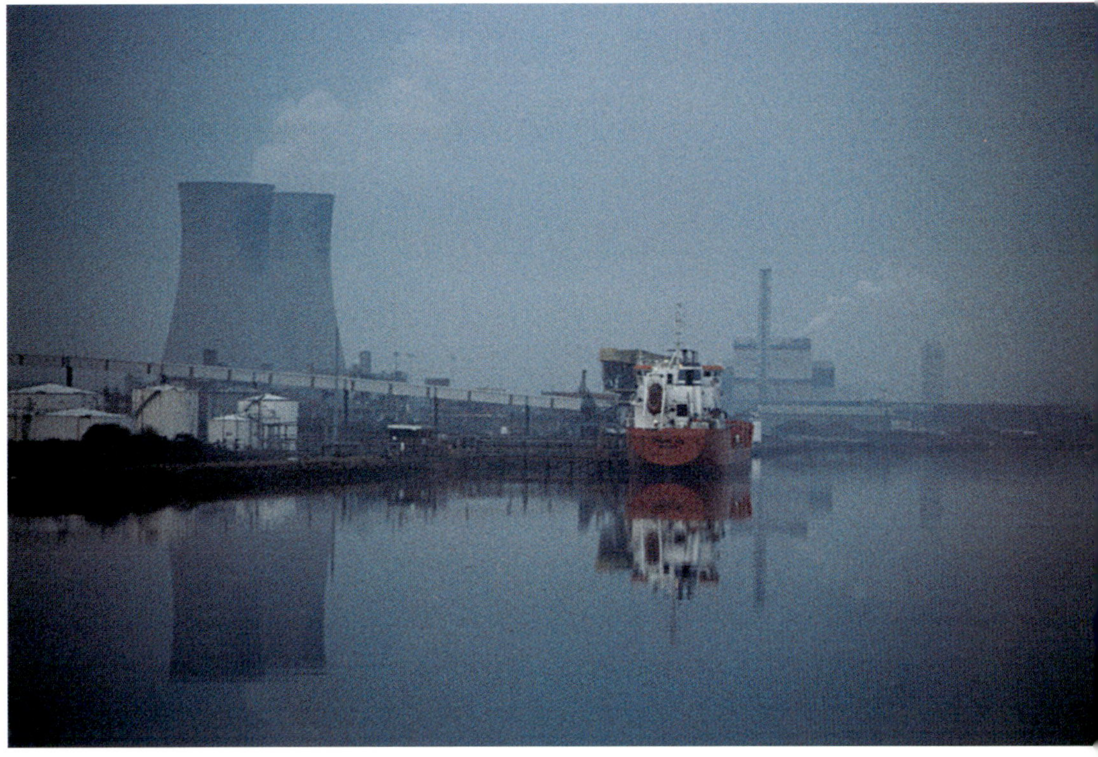

River Tees, Middlesbrough

For a landscape photographer who loves wilderness and natural beauty, I perhaps live in a strange place. Though it is surrounded by some truly inspiring scenery, Teesside is one of the largest industrial conurbations in Europe. In parts, it is plain grim. This picture was taken on the journey between home and the lab that processes my film. While the mood of it suits the subject, the light is truly appalling. Colours are muted, nothing is well defined, and there is no modelling on anything. Despite all this, it is a picture I am pleased to have taken. The red accent lifts the scene, and without it I doubt the picture would have had as much appeal. Once again, it was the presence of water and especially the reflection that turned this very unlikely day into a photographic opportunity. This is perhaps an extreme example of water acting as a 'second light', but often it is at the extremes that a point can be effectively illustrated.

Nikon FM2 with 75–300mm lens, Fuji 1600, 1/125sec at f/4.5

Photographs like these are the jewels in any photographer's portfolio. More often than not, either the light or the composition will be the stronger element within a photograph. One of them can often carry the other.

Being able to find a subject that will yield good results even when the light is poor is a great motivator for the photographer. It takes a lot of dedication and faith to go out seeking pictures on days when there seems to be no attractive light. Knowing that the best light is transitory and that luck will always be involved in catching it will not always be enough to tempt you away from home comforts. If the prospect is possibly one or two great pictures, but more likely nothing at all to show for your efforts, that might not be very appealing. Knowing that whatever happens you can get some new photographs might be just what is needed. Being out there is the only way to catch those truly wonderful golden moments.

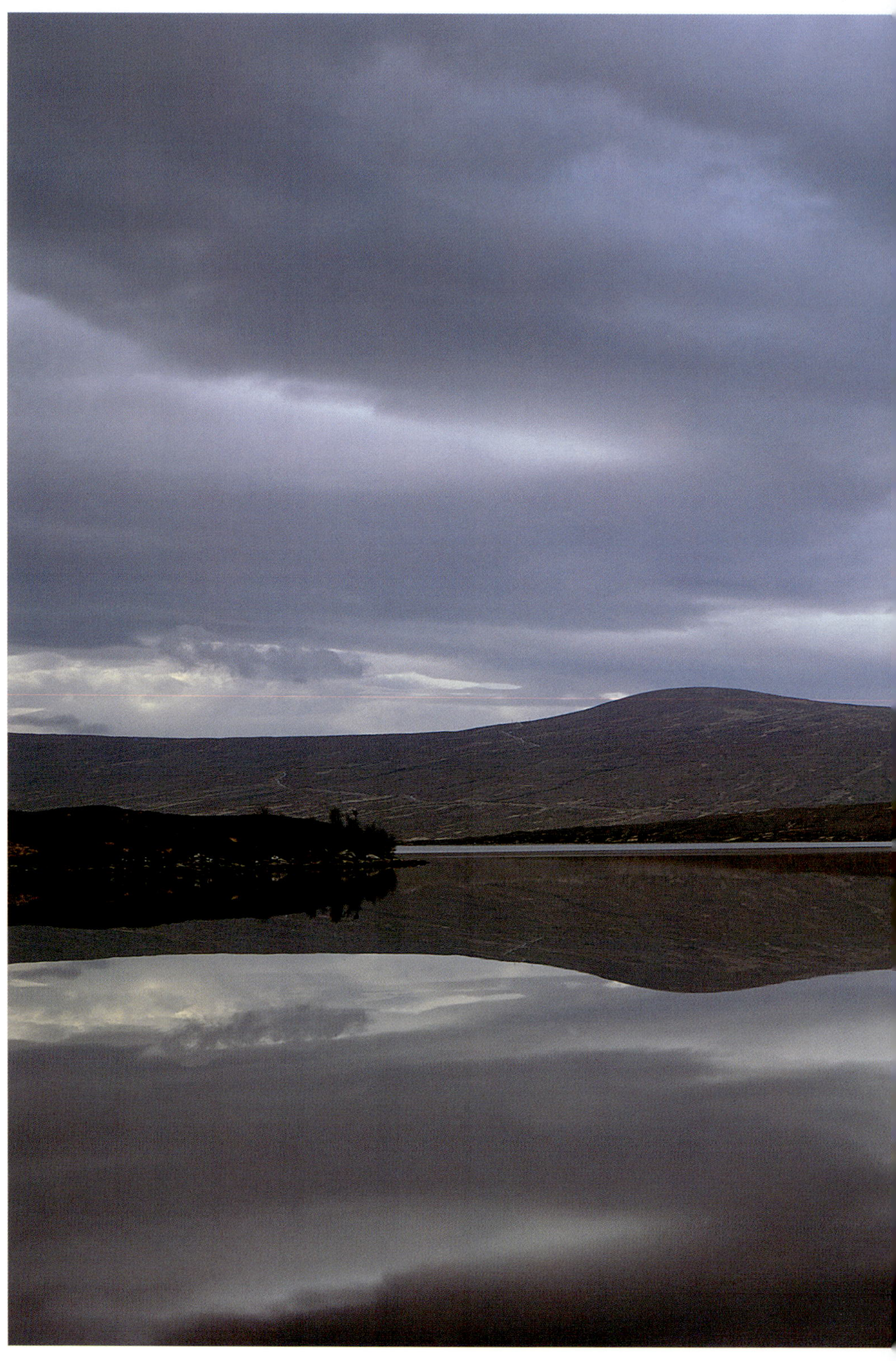

Loch Shin, Sutherland, Scotland
This is not the light landscape photographers usually seek. As I drove past Loch Shin it was the reflection and the patterns in the clouds that caught my eye. Of course, clouds are just water in another form. To that extent water is not just a second light by virtue of its reflective qualities, it also has a dramatic effect on the first light, the sun, as it shades us from it or allows it to diffuse through. On this occasion it was doing a little of both and so there is a colourful subtle pattern in the sky and reflected in the lake.

Ebony 45s with 90mm lens, 6x12 rollfilm back, Velvia 50, 1/2sec at f/22

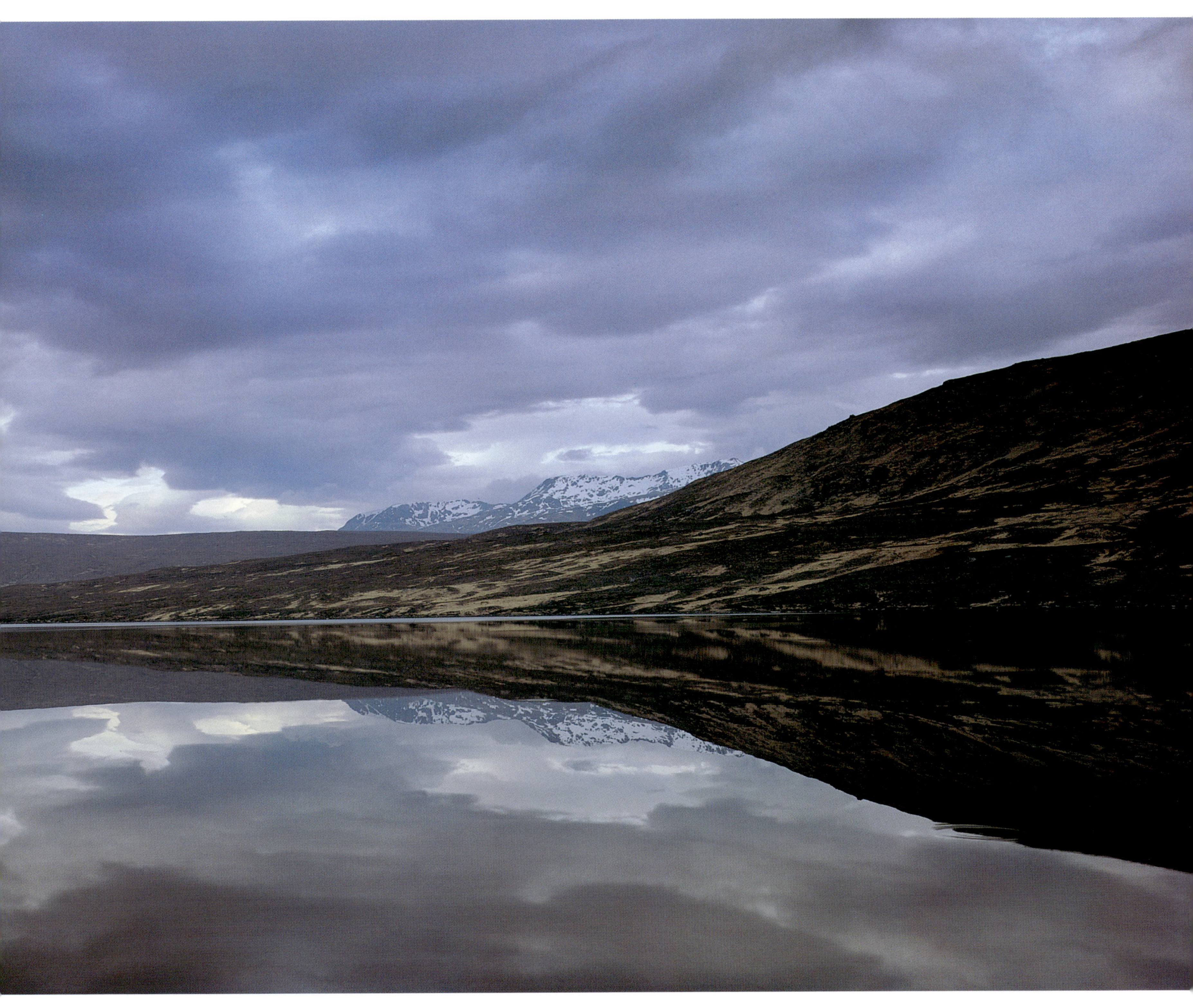

Whatever the Weather

The humble picture postcard is not held in very high regard by most serious landscape photographers because they mostly show places at the height of summer in the full blaze of sun, not technically overexposed, but over-lit. Often the best landscape photographs are taken in low light – less is more – which goes someway to explaining why dawn and dusk are the favourite times for the landscape photographer. The winter months, when the hours of sunlight are fewest and the sun

below **Dunstanburgh**
In conditions like these it is tempting to think it is easy to take a great picture but you still need to use the light to its best advantage.

Ebony 45s with 90mm lens, Velvia 50, 1/2 sec at f/27, polarizing and Coral No. 1 filters

remains low in the sky, are considered by many photographers to be the best time of the year.

When the sky is grey, sunlight is soft and diffused. This kind of light is perfect for any number of photographic subjects, portraits or flower studies for example, close details and scenes of water in motion. Waterfalls in woodlands look good in these conditions. Sometimes the very last thing you want is strong sunshine causing a great deal of contrast in a scene.

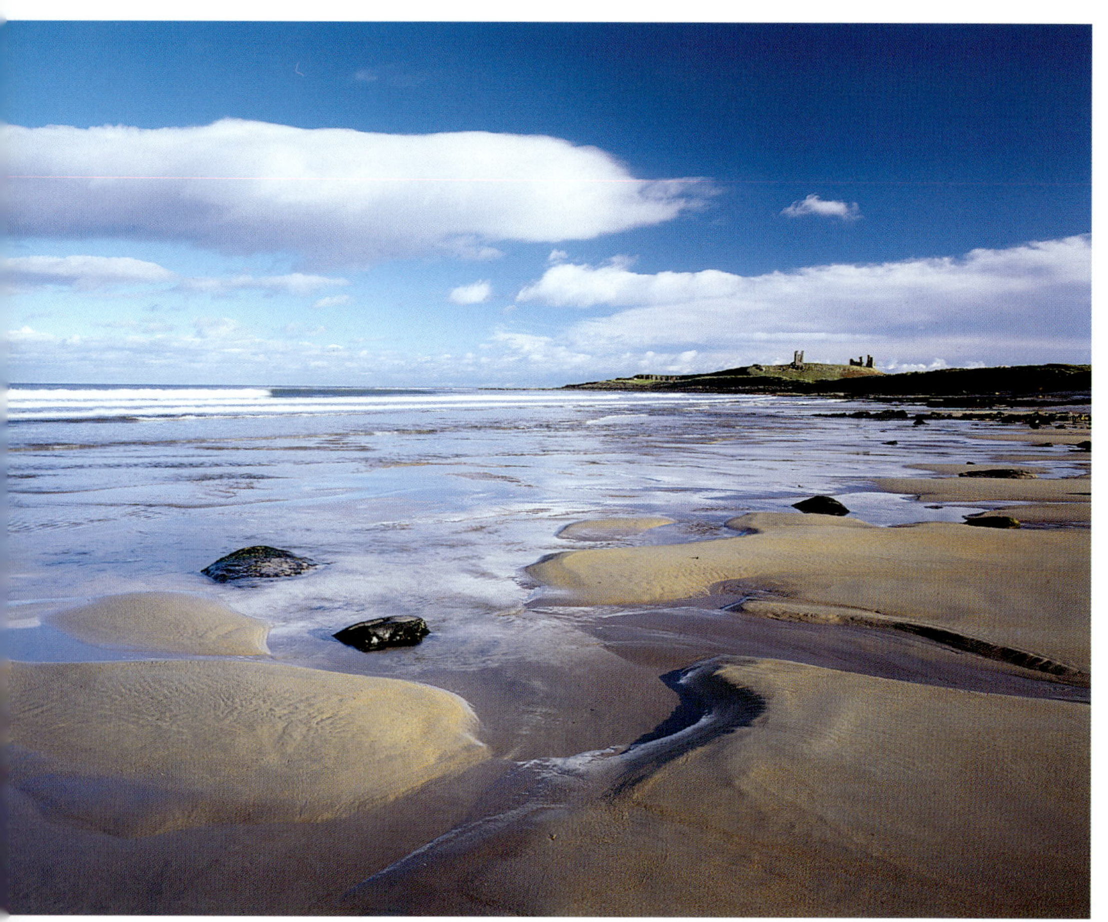

facing page **Bamburgh Castle**
It is great knowing that there is something to photograph, even on a really dull day like this one. I took this picture while I was still an amateur photographer on a day trip to Bamburgh. I knew the weather was not great but I only had the weekends for photography in those days and I wanted to get a shot. Crashing tide over rock and moody, grey skies – it all seemed to work. It is the sense of movement and the patterns formed by the sea as it tumbles off the coastal rocks that make this picture.

Mamiya RB67 with 90mm lens, Velvia 50, 1 second at f/22

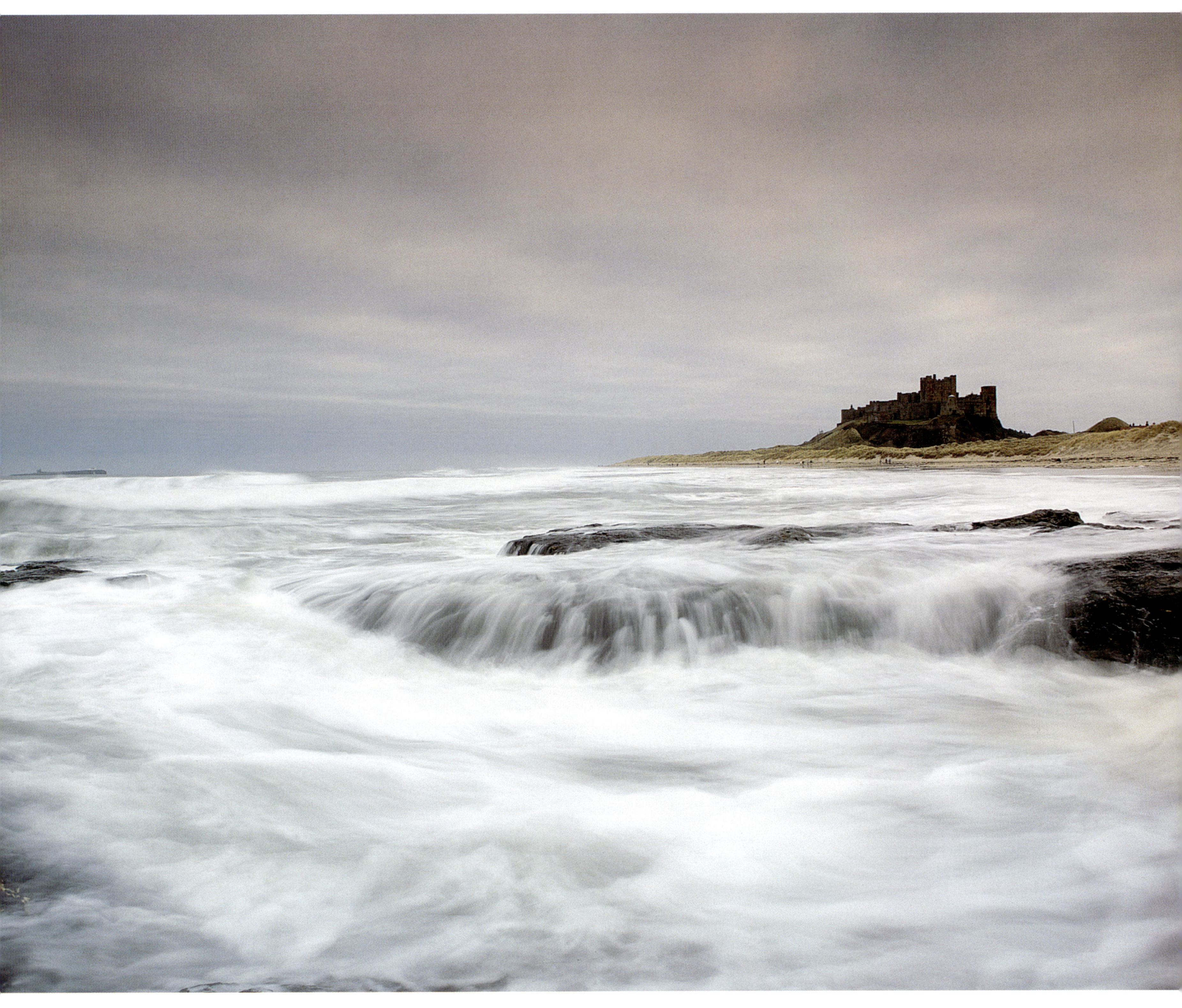

Quality and Quantity

As photographers, light is our primary tool. It is the raw material from which we create our work. A better camera will not necessarily transform your work, but better light can.

We can find better light by being a bit more adventurous – by being out at the very beginning and at the end of the day, or at the edges of a break in the weather. We also get a better effect by using light from a different direction in our photographs. Shooting directly into the light, for example, can create silhouettes with dramatic, colourful skies behind them, and low sidelighting can give wonderful texture. You do not always need the light to be behind you. Indeed, with a low sun behind you, one of the most frustrating things is to find that your own shadow is the only blot on an otherwise perfectly lit landscape.

The best light has to be anticipated – if you have seen it you have probably already missed it. Be ready: set your camera on a tripod, place the filters and anticipate the appropriate exposure.

A Second Light

In what can only be called poor light one of the few features that might lift a landscape photograph is water. On an overcast day when the light is diffused by the clouds and there is no modelling or texture on the land, you can still take a great photograph of water tumbling over rock. Late in the evening, when the land is rendered black as a silhouette and the only available light comes from the sky, that light can be reflected in still water to create an interesting image. When the sun rises or sets, water makes the perfect foreground, and a reflection can double the impact and colour of the scene. This is because water acts like a second light in the landscape. Light and water are both in a constant state of change. It is the two of these combined that make each photograph unique.

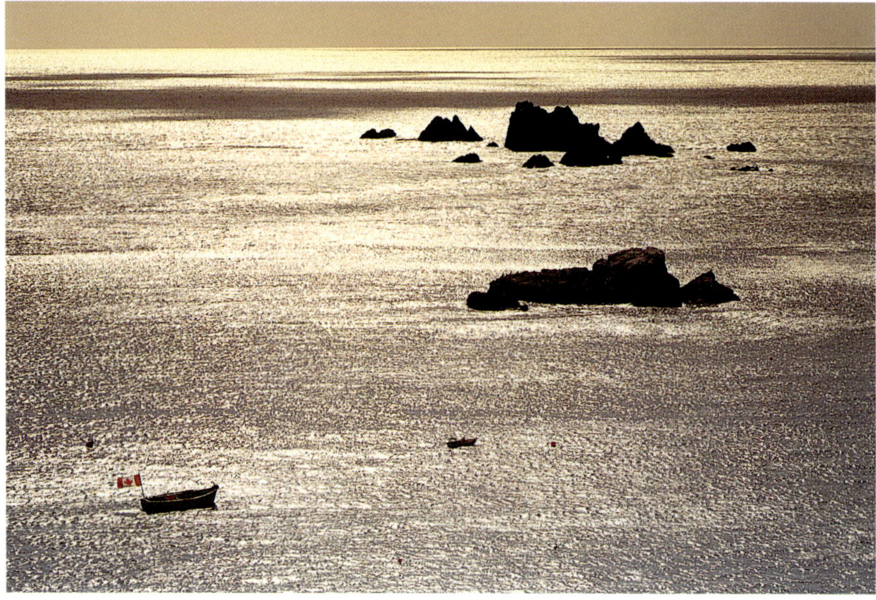

left **Sunshine on the Sea, Cornwall**
This is a photograph where composition and light are certainly not evident in equal measure. The composition is very simple. The entire success of the image is due to the light reflecting from the water.

The tiny fishing boat in the left-hand corner of the scene is sporting a Canadian flag. Given the light levels and the astonishing contrast, I am really pleased that the flag can be made out at all. The level of brightness reflected from the sea was such on this day that the correct exposure was one stop less than I had ever used before. This caused me enough concern that I also took a version for 1/15sec, but it was this one, at 1/30sec, that worked.

Horseman 45HD with 240mm lens, 6x9 rollfilm back, Velvia 50, 1/30sec at f/22, 81B filter

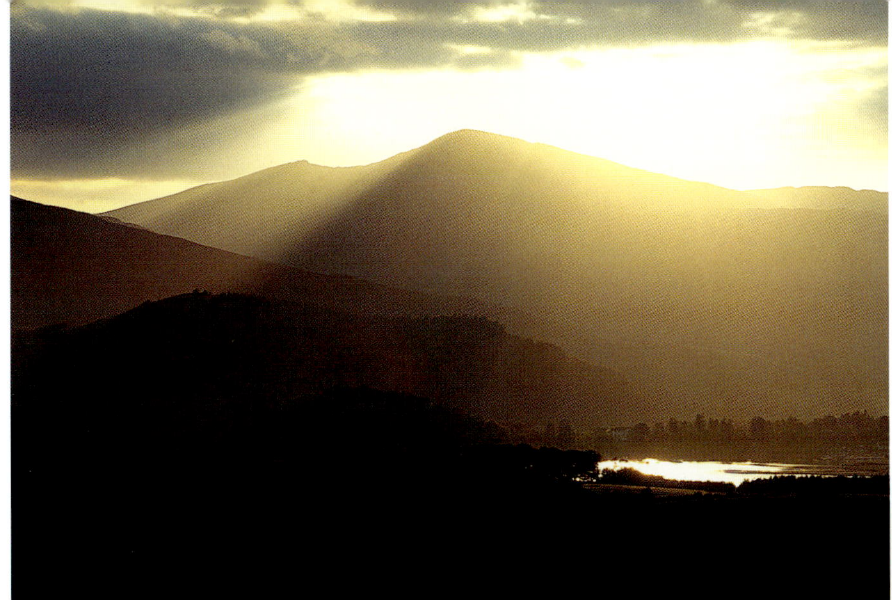

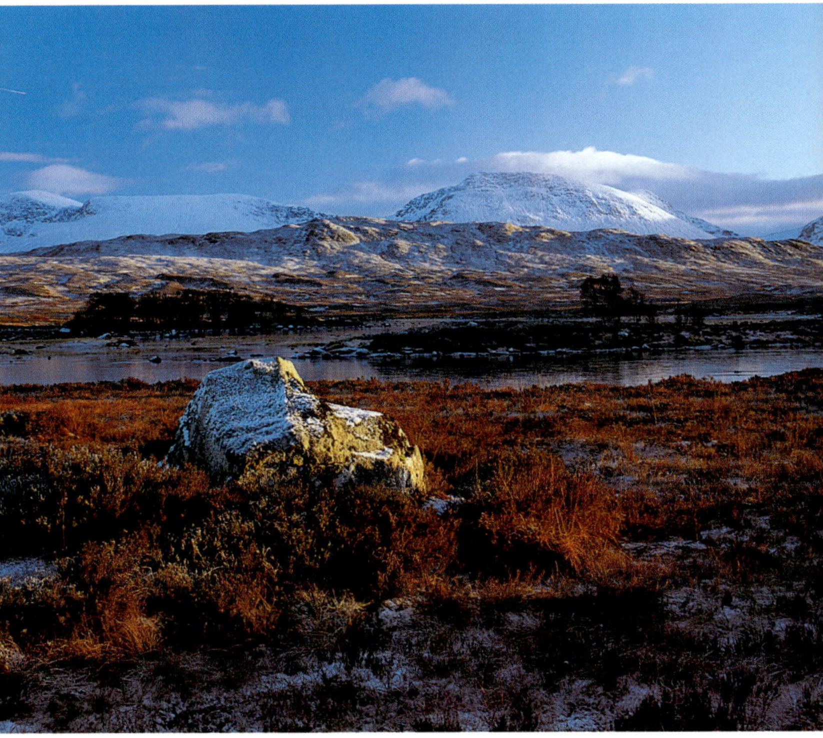

left **Dramatic Light over Derwentwater**

Raking sunlight and layers of tone inspired me to grab this shot. Though it takes up a very small part of the overall picture space, it is the glint of sunlight from the surface of the lake in the valley that balances the scene.

Mamiya 645sv with 105–210mm lens, Velvia 50, 1/8sec at f/22

right **Rannoch Moor**

A low sun in front of me and to the right cast its last rays on this scene, bringing out the texture of frost on rock and the gorgeous colours. I was not really ready for this light, and it came and went very quickly.

Pentax 67 with 90mm lens, Velvia 50, 1/2sec at f/22, Coral No. 1 and 0.6 ND filters

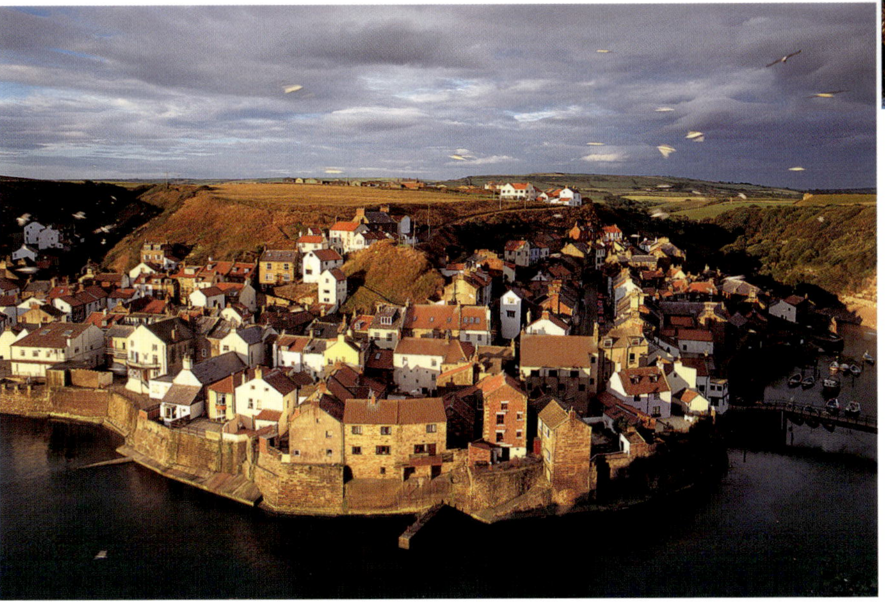

left **Staithes from Cowbar**

The fact that the sea in this photograph is in shade and therefore has recorded almost black really sets off the brightly coloured and strongly lit cottages of the fishing village. Wheeling sea birds add atmosphere to the scene, although at the time I was concerned they might spoil the shot. This wonderful light was the result of a thin sliver in the clouds, which closed shortly thereafter and remained closed for the rest of the day.

Pentax 67 with 45mm lens, Velvia 50, 1/2sec at f/22, Coral No. 1 and 0.6 ND grad filters

While you can emphasize the shape and form of a landscape with composition, the texture of an object or of a place can only really be brought out in photography with the careful use of light.

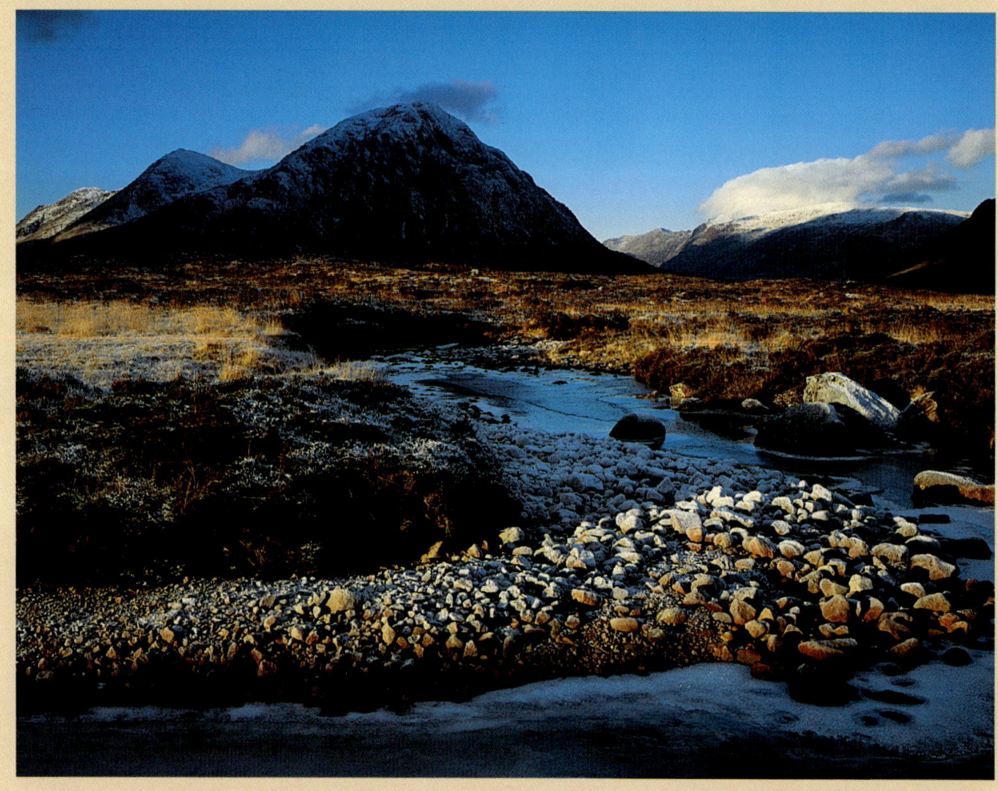

Glencoe and Buachaille Etive Mor
This portrait of the dark and brooding presence of this famous Scottish mountain, Buachaille Etive Mor, is a study in contrasting textures and light.

Ebony 45s with 120mm lens, Velvia 50, 1/2sec at f/32, Coral No. 1 and 0.6 ND grad filters

'Please do not touch.' The National Trust places this sign all around its properties. Why is that? Recently they took the opposite approach, placing some material near a door with instruction that people feel the texture. The material lasted three months before total disintegration. This is why they do not want us to touch, but why do they have to ask us not to touch? What is it that compels people to want to do so? We are a very tactile species, we like to know what things feel like, and we can feel more connected to things once we have touched them.

Photography is a purely visual medium – one of our skills as photographers is to ignore information from the other senses. The evocative sounds of a seagull cannot be recorded on film, the wonderful smell of a flower will not be reproduced, and nor will you be able to reach out and touch the rough texture of a rock.

Texture, though, can be captured on film, at least all the visual clues that will tell the viewer what that texture is likely to feel like. This is a way to make your photograph seem more real to someone who was not there.

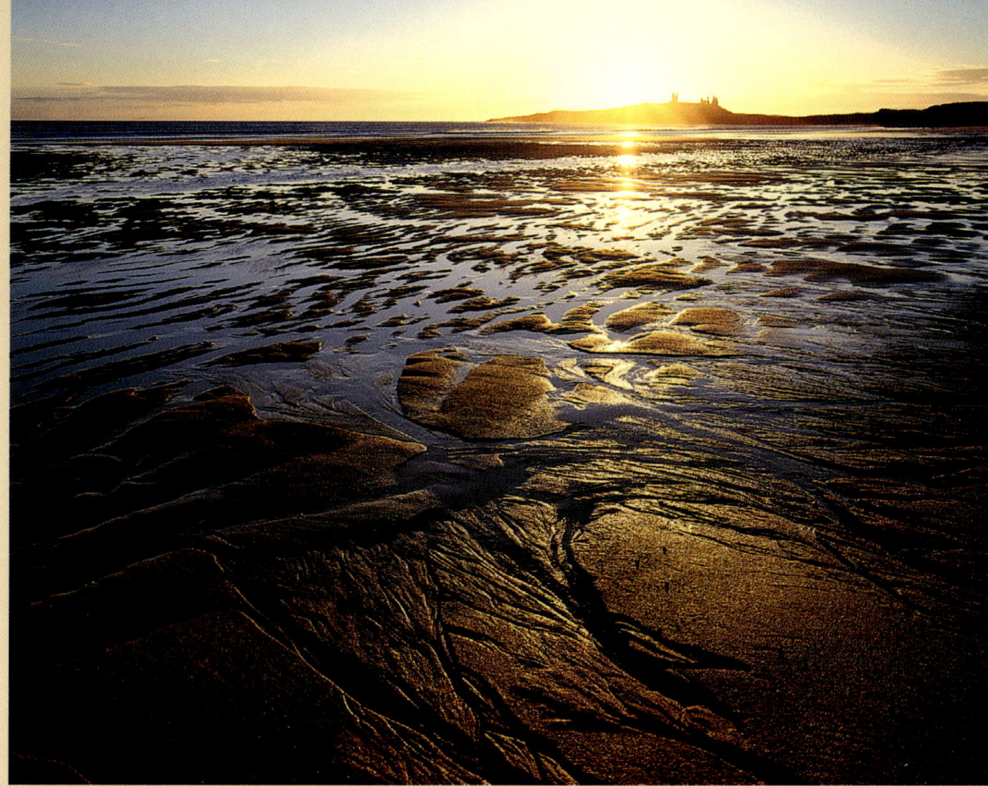

I fancy you can see every grain of sand in the foreground of this image; one of the things I love about a large-format camera is its ability to record fine detail. A very low sun means the slightest elevation of anything casts a shadow, and thus there is distinctive texture on this beach.

Ebony 45s with 90mm lens, Velvia 50, 1/15sec at f/22

3 IDEAS TO TRY

1 Choose a subject with a good textured surface and photograph it while the sun is low in the sky (either early in the morning or at sunset). Using side- or backlighting will provide some modelling on the subject.

2 Go in really close and fill your viewfinder's frame with the texture. Shooting from a low angle will help to emphasize detail.

3 Try to juxtapose two or more contrasting textures. Hard, solid rock with rough, springy moss and smooth, flowing water, for example.

right **Rough Sea, Whitby to Sandsend**

Due to the strong wind on this day and the fact that I was chasing a moving subject in the waves, I chose to try taking a picture handheld rather than setting up the camera on a tripod. The resulting image has captured the texture and colours of the rough sea. The depth of field is not wide enough to reach the distant headland, but I feel the image has recorded the scene as I remember it. However, I recommend you use a tripod all the time unless you have a good reason not to.

Pentax 67, 135mm lens, Velvia 50, 1/125sec at f/4, handheld

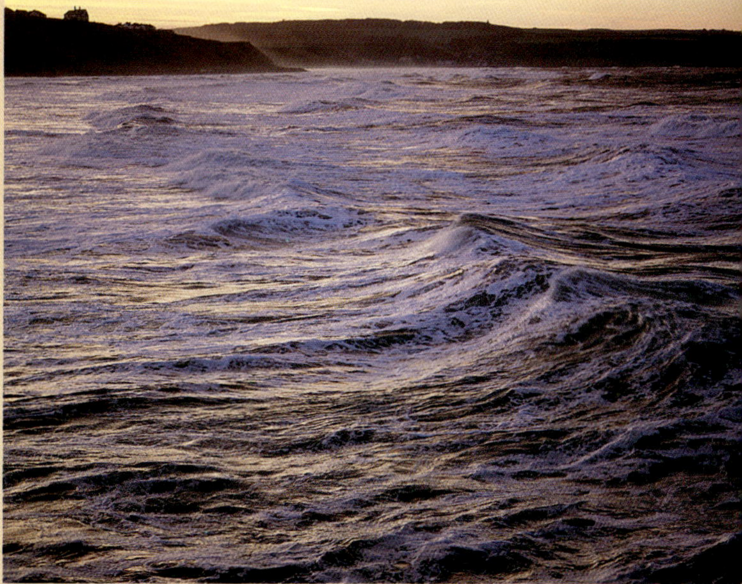

There are two essentials in the creation of a good silhouette photograph. The first is an interesting shape in the landscape and the second is a strong light behind that shape. The sky is one such light, and water can be a second light.

The normal rules of exposure do not apply when you are trying to create a silhouette. The main subject should be reduced to a blacked-out shape, or very close to it. This means that the subject should be underexposed and all detail will be contained in the light sources. When we shoot a silhouette we are exploiting the fact that film cannot handle contrast as well as the human eye does.

The key to a successful silhouette is the same as for any landscape photograph, composition and light, but, as ever, there are no hard-and-fast rules.

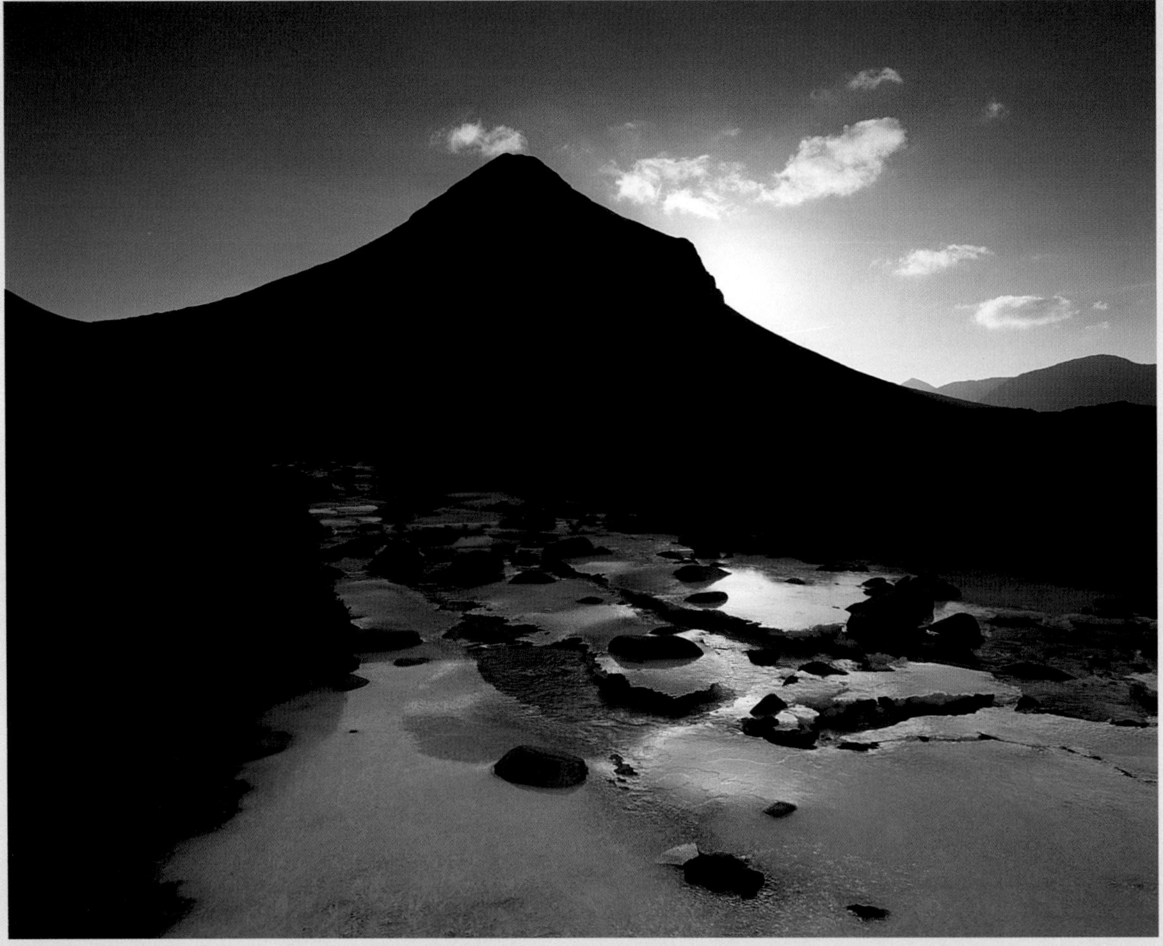

Cullin Hills, Isle of Skye
Simplicity is the key to near monochrome pictures like this. The frozen mountain stream provides the texture in this picture. Framed as it is by the brooding shapes of the surrounding mountains, it leads the eye into darkness and mystery.

Pentax 67 with 45mm lens, Velvia 50, 1/30sec at f/16

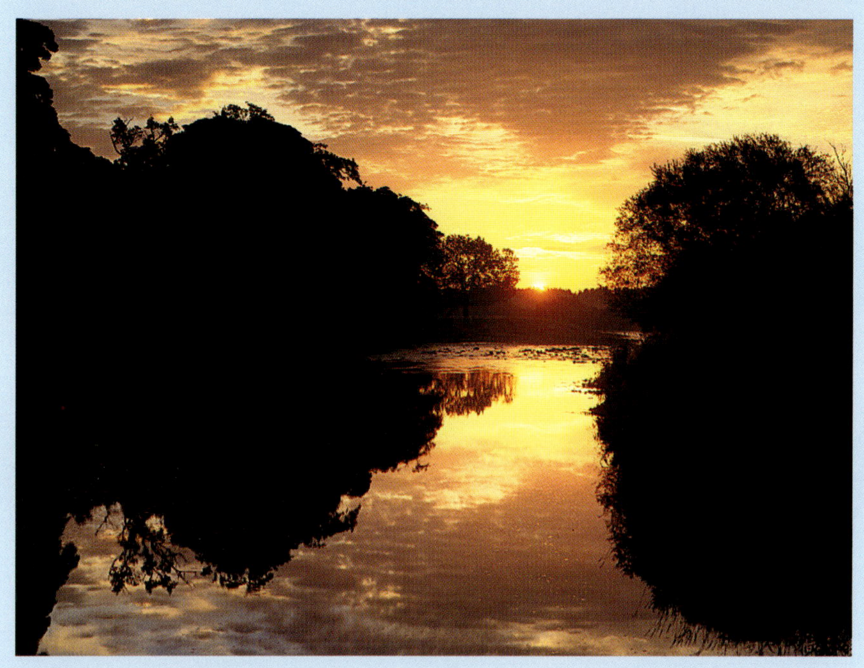

right **River Ure, Sunrise**
Sunrise and sunset offer a wonderful opportunity for silhouette pictures. The river reflects the light and colours in the sky, while the trees and surrounding land record as nothing more than shapes. I was in a race against time to take the picture before the sun climbed too high. A race you can see I only just won.

Ebony 45s with 150mm lens, 1/2sec at f/22, 0.6 ND hard-grad filter

left **Loch Tay**
The evening sky and the reflection that was forming when I saw this scene were enough to persuade me to stop the car and take a closer look. The wonderful shape of this bare tree and the island beyond made the structure of the image. It is, however, the light in the sky and the reflection in the still water that make this photograph work.

Pentax 67 with 45mm lens, Velvia 50, 1/8sec at f/22, 0.6 ND grad filter

Low Light

Our primary concern as photographers is always for the

quality rather than the quantity of light. When the level

of light is low, very often the quality is at its highest.

Blue Dusk, Eilean Donan Castle

Pictures like this have to be timed carefully. Ideally you
want some light in the sky and reflected in the water
behind the floodlit building. Once the sky is pitch-
black it is too late. Working with Velvia, I know from
experience that in conditions like this an exposure of
15 seconds at f/8 works, or one of two minutes at f/22.

For this image I wanted to take a few frames.
There were no traffic trails to record, so the 15 seconds
at f/8 option seemed like the perfect exposure.
Using two minutes I might have lost the light before
the third frame; that is how critical timing can be.

This photograph had to be taken in the summer,
since the floodlights only come on around 9p.m., and
in winter it is already pitch-black by then.

Mamiya 645sv with
55–110mm, Velvia
50,15 seconds at f/8

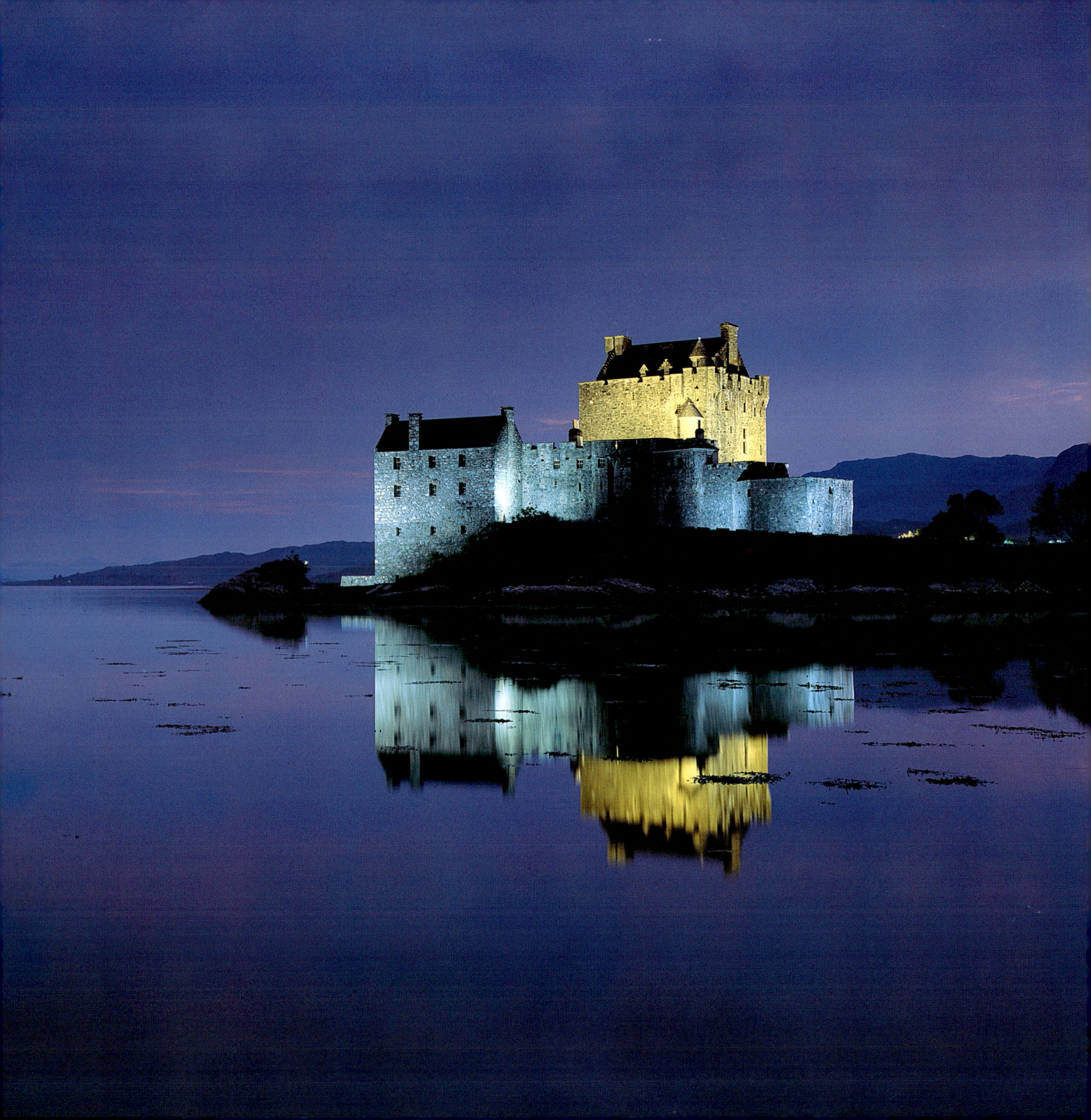

right **The Shambles at Night, York**

This wonderful street in the heart of medieval York is usually crowded with shoppers and tourists. At the end of a cold, wet day in February the place was alive with colour and sparkle, all brought about by the reflections in the wet pavements.

Ebony 45s with 90mm lens, Provia 100, 120 seconds at f/22

below **Loch Tay at Sunset**

The graphic shapes and the almost monochrome tones in this photograph work well, thanks to the reflection. Without water in the foreground this scene would have been too dark to make an interesting picture.

Ebony 45s with 240mm lens, 6x12 rollfilm back, Velvia 50, 1 second at f/22

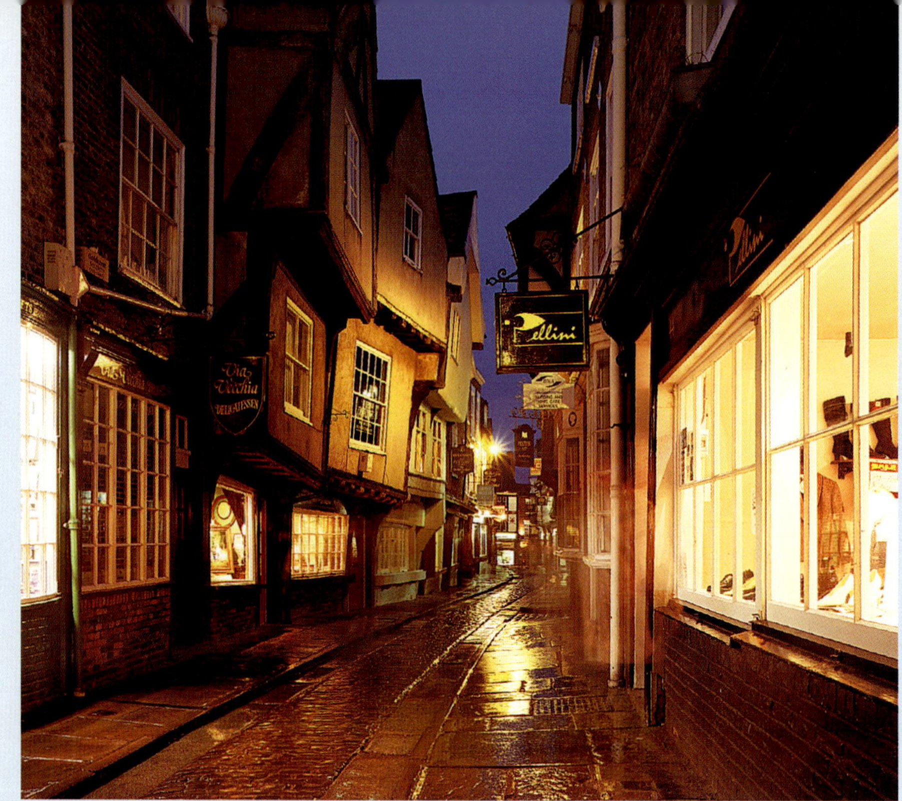

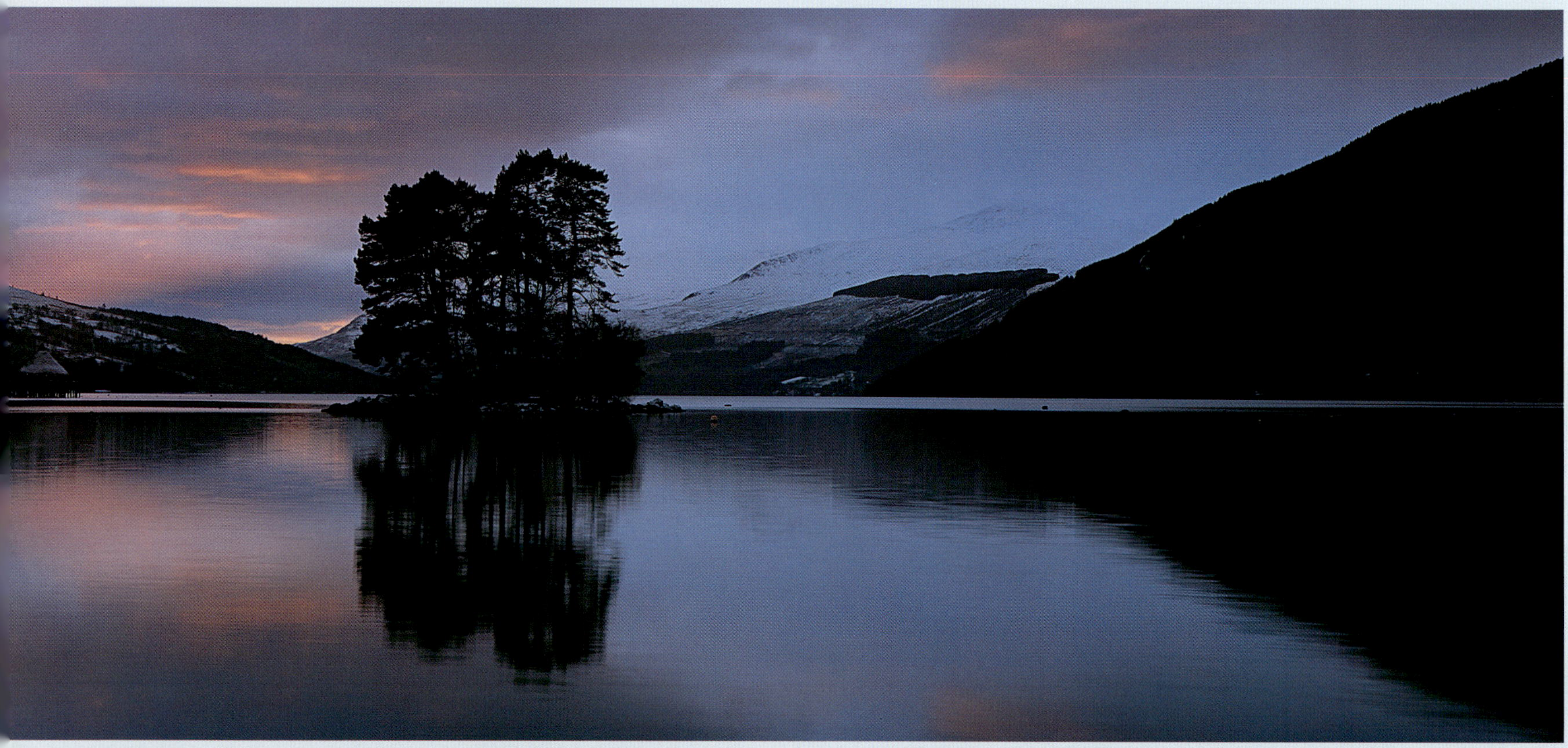

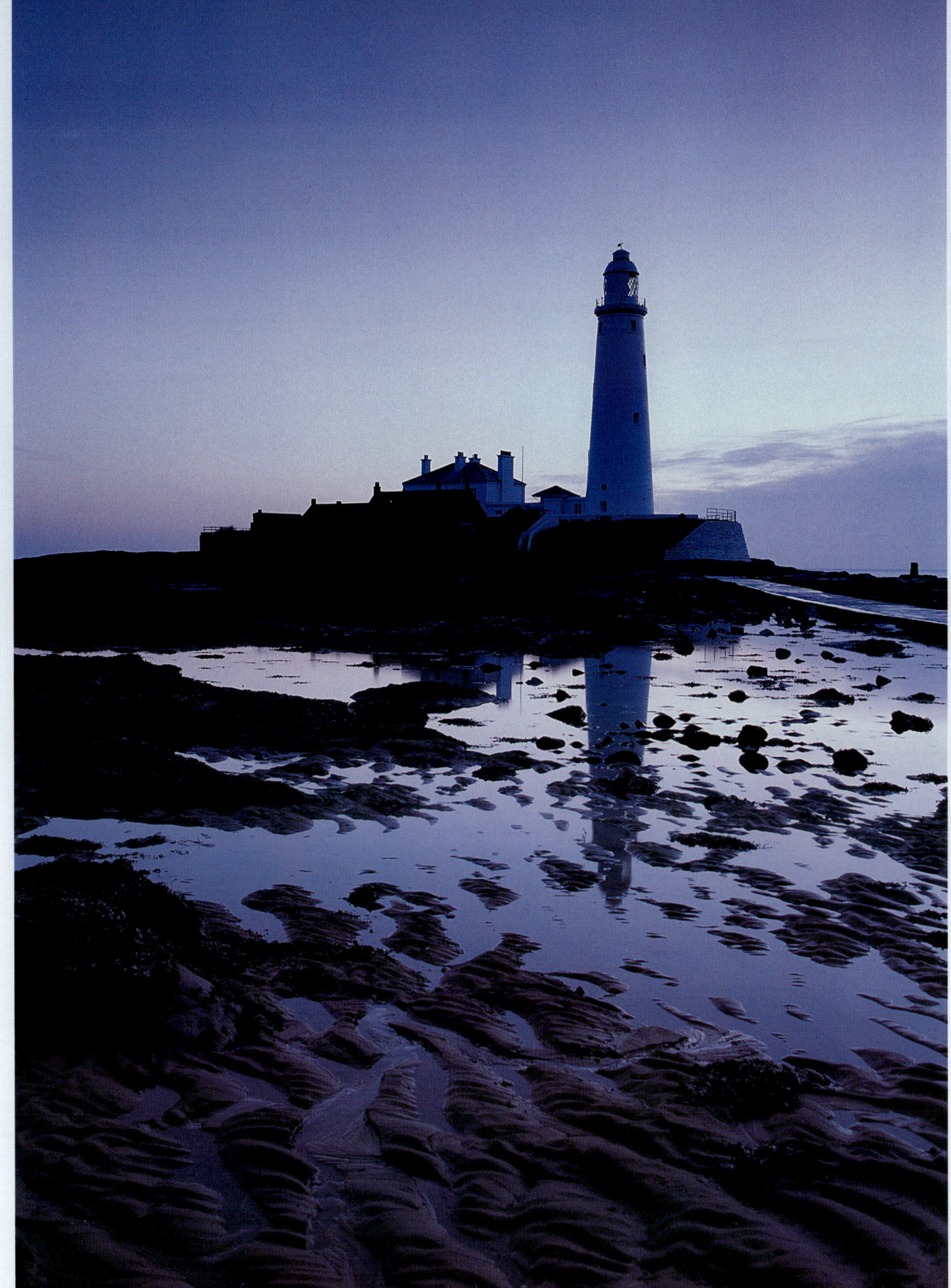

**Blue Dawn,
St Mary's
Lighthouse,
Tyneside**

Before the sun was
over the horizon the
only light on this scene
was the reflected light
from an almost clear
blue sky. Our eyes do
not notice this excess
of blue, but film does.
The blue cast is not
something I would seek
to correct in a scene
like this.

**Mamiya 645sv with
55–110, Velvia 50,
1 second at f/16**

The Colour of Light at Different Times

Sunrise and sunset are not normal daylight in a technical sense. Colour temperature is measured using the Kelvin scale; while normal daylight is about 5,500K, sunsets and sunrises are 2,000–2,500K. When using daylight-balanced film this difference in colour temperature will be apparent as an orangey colour cast. Technically, we could correct the orange cast that will appear on the film by using a pale blue 80-series filter, but who wants technical perfection in these circumstances? Knowing that the film by itself will add an orange cast to the scene does make those orange-sunset filters a little redundant in a real sunset situation. If you do use them, your sunsets can look over the top and false. The only filter you might need for a real sunset is a neutral-density graduated filter to balance the exposure contrast between sky and foreground.

Cooling Off in the Shade

The other place colour temperature varies greatly from normal daylight – 5,500K – is in the shade. In the ordinary shade of cloud there might be a slight blue cast, as the colour temperature rises to around 8,500K. This is why for many traditional landscape subjects, filters in the 81-series are so popular. These filters come in various strengths. There is no real need to know exactly how far from normal the light is, and how far the filter you are using will correct the cast. Overdoing the correction is not a worry either, since if you do, all

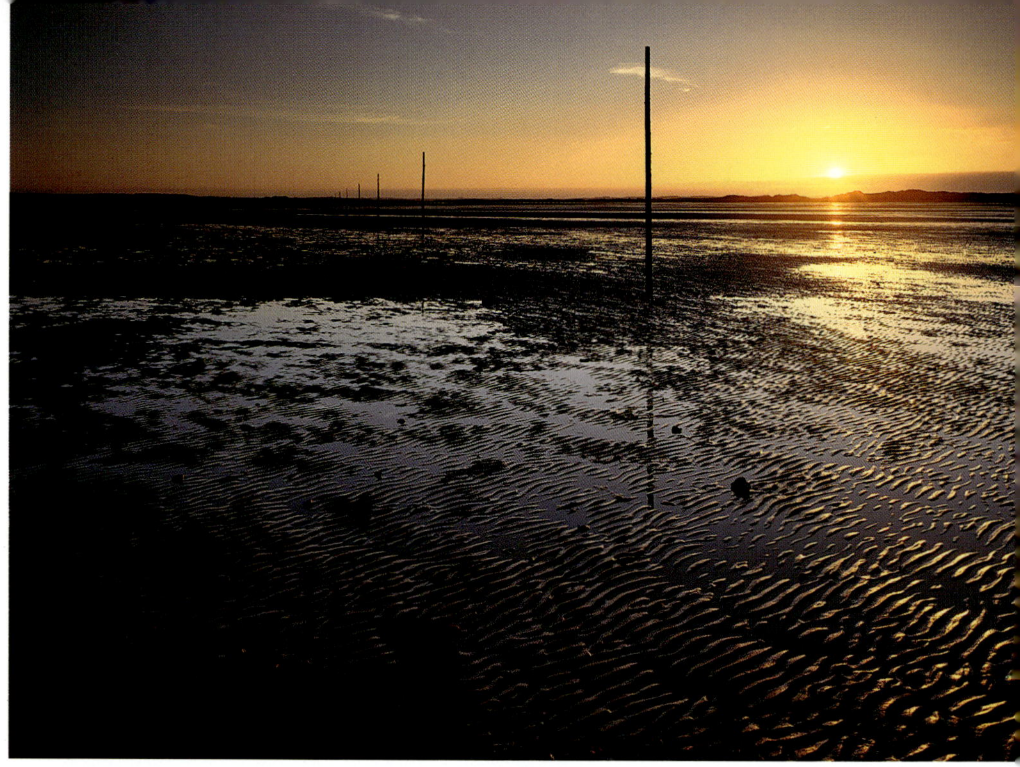

The Causeway, Lindisfarne, Northumberland
The very low sun is casting its orange glow over the beach here. If there were clouds in the sky, that orange glow might have continued after the sun had set, but the sky was almost clear. As soon as the sun vanished all the light was reflected from the pale blue sky and the colour temperature changed dramatically from orange to blue.

Ebony 45s with 90mm lens, Velvia 50, 1 second at f/22, 0.3 ND grad filter

TYPICAL COLOUR TEMPERATURES

Light source	Temperature (°K)
Clear blue sky	10,000–15,000
Shade on sunny day	7,500
Overcast (cloudy) day	6,000–8,000
Noon sunlight	6,500
Average daylight (4 hours before sunset and 4 hours after sunrise)	5,500
Early morning / late afternoon	4,000
1 hour before sunset	3,500
Sunset	2,500

that happens is the colours look slightly warmer than they did, and therefore slightly more attractive. It is a question of taste, of finding the filter that reduces or eliminates the blue cast to a degree that pleases you.

There are times and places where the blue cast in the shade is really strong and the colour temperature might reach 15,000K. This is in the shade under a clear blue sky, before the sun rises or after it has set, or in the shade of a cliff on a bright sunny day. In these circumstances, while our eyes filter the blue out and present us again with the colours we know are there and expect to see, film is balanced for a particular colour temperature so it does not. This is a situation where the blue cast can look as attractive as the orange of sunset, so once again technical perfection gives way to taste. Blue is a very peaceful and cool colour, relaxing to live with and to look at. Some of my favourite prints were taken in shade under clear skies. This is not a time to 'correct' the way film 'sees'; rather, it is a time to be aware and exploit the characteristic of the film you are using.

CORAL FILTERS

I usually carry a Lee Coral No. 1 graduated filter with me. This is slightly warmer and slightly redder than the orange or straw warm-up filters in the 81-series. It removes the blue cast from cool pictures and often tips the scale slightly the other way. I use a graduated filter because I do not like the effect of a warm-up filter on a blue sky.

SEE ALSO:

ND Filters *p 66*

Colour-Correction Filters *p 74*

Kelvin Scale *p 75*

right **Blue Dawn, Black Nab**

To the eye this scene was not so predominately blue as it appears here, but with a total lack of direct sunlight the blue sky is the major source of light in the scene. Film without the 'filter' of the brain just recorded what was there, and I chose to allow that, since the strong blue cast would suit this scene.

Ebony 45s with 90mm lens, Velvia 50, 1/15sec at f/22, 0.6 ND grad filter

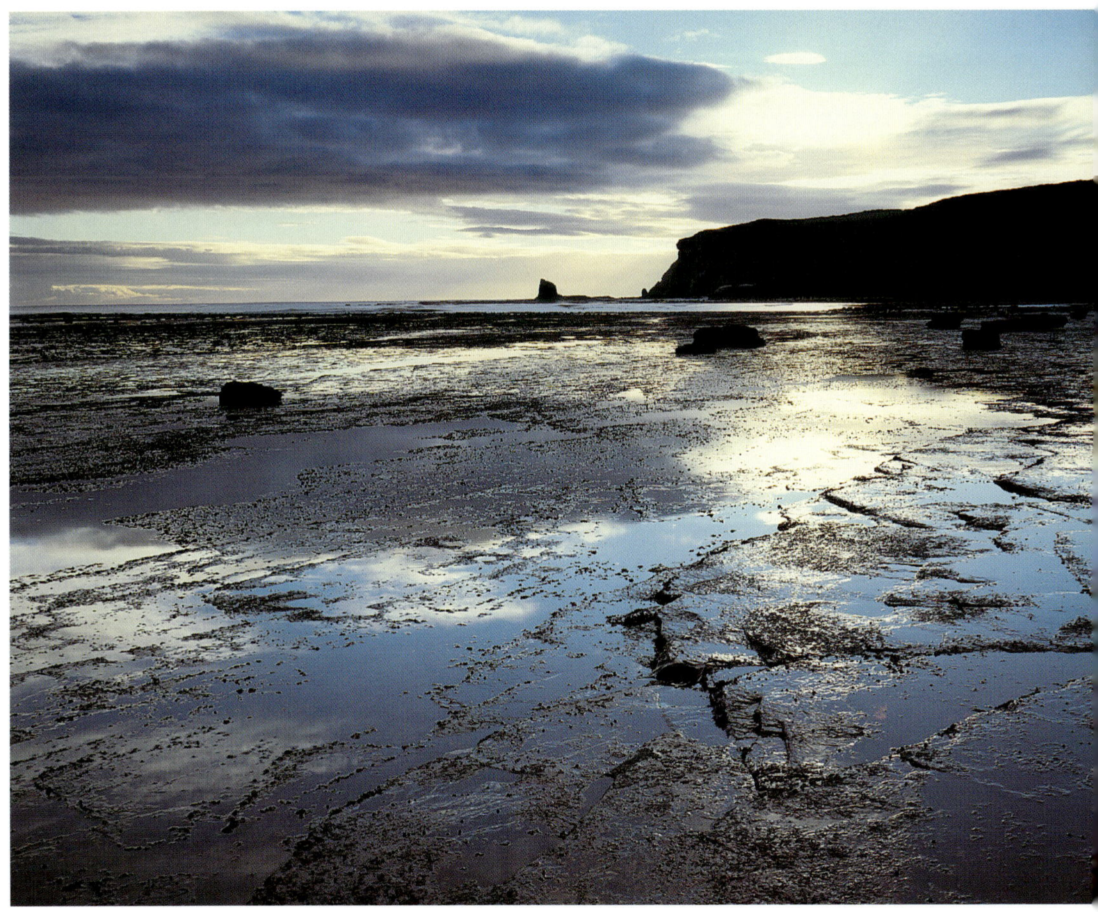

On the North Yorkshire coast just south of the town of Whitby there is a world-class spot for landscape photography that I visit often, especially at dawn in the winter months and at dusk in the summer. It is called Saltwick Bay.

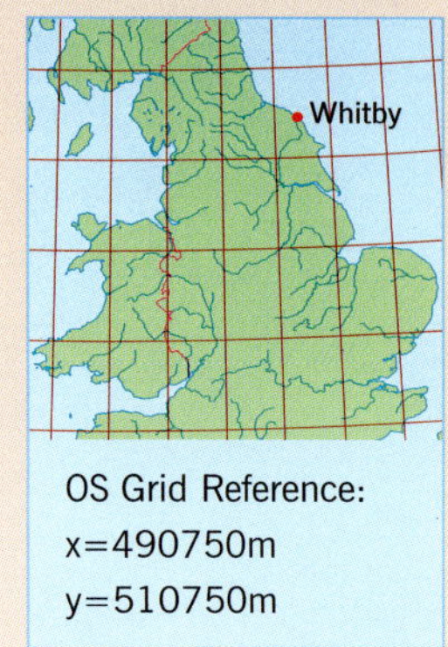

OS Grid Reference:
x=490750m
y=510750m

Saltwick Bay offers the photographer a wave-cut rock platform, an attractive rusting shipwreck and the shapely sea stack of Black Nab. It is also orientated in such a way that all year long the sun rises over the sea and for much of the summer sets over the sea as well.

You have to get to know a place before you can take a really satisfying picture of it. I revisit Saltwick Bay often, especially at dawn in the winter months and at dusk in the summer. I have to ask myself these days what more I can do there, yet it draws me like a magnet and every so often produces another gem. I have the tide tables and know the sunset times. From home I can see how the sky is looking at seven and then be there in good time for a sunset around ten. Being a locally famous landmark and right next to a holiday camp, no matter how wild and remote this spot looks you are never alone here.

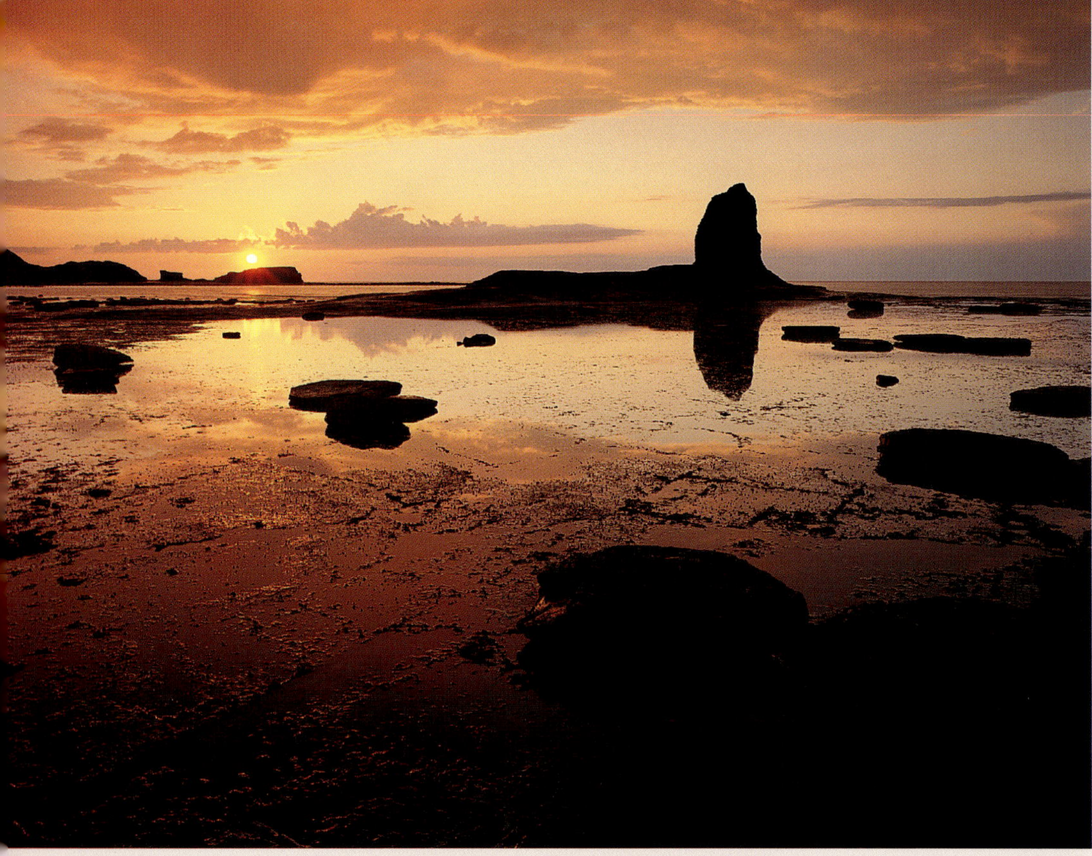

Black Nab, Sunset

This photograph is much more impressive than my memory of the real thing. The film captured the very low direct light casting an orange glow not visible to the naked eye. It is the sort of picture I am delighted to have taken, and it inspires me to get out there and take more.

Ebony 45s with 90mm lens, Velvia 50, 1 second at f/22, 0.3 ND grad filter

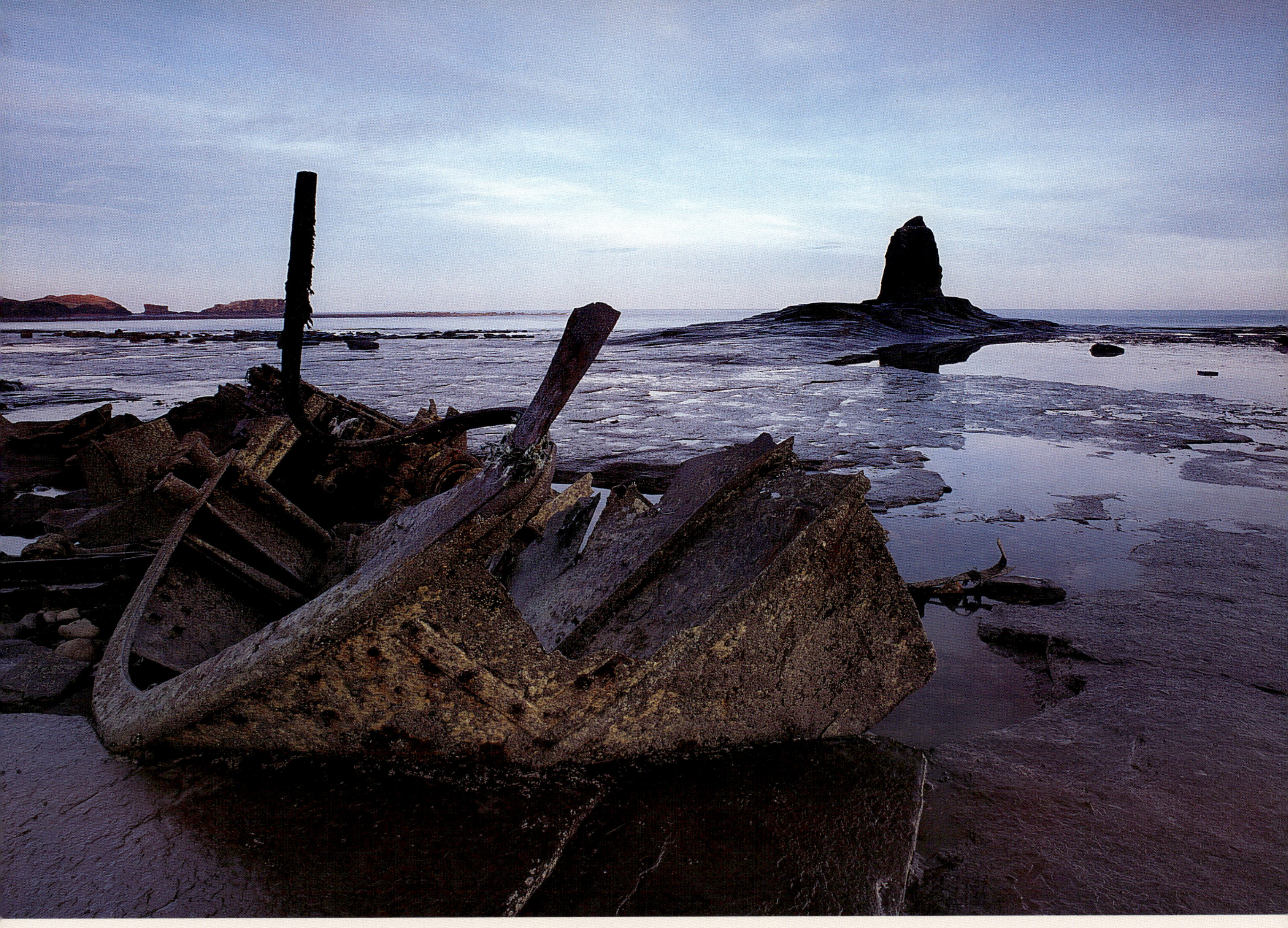

above and following page **Shipwreck, Saltwick Bay and Black Nab**

The cold blue of the picture above has a very different mood to the one overleaf (taken a year later) and a merit of its own. The difference in the colours between the two shots is entirely down to the light.

The rust of the shipwreck overleaf has been warmed by direct, low, early morning sunlight and appears to glow with the same shades as those in the distant cliffs, making it look as though the wreck has become an integral part of the landscape. The use of a 58mm super-wideangle lens for my 5x4 camera meant I could frame the wreck just as I had wanted – close enough to capture all the detail of the texture of the rust and yet at the same time showing the surrounding landscape.

above:
Mamiya 645 camera
with 35mm lens

following page:
Ebony 5x4 camera
with 58mm lens,
6x12 rollfilm back

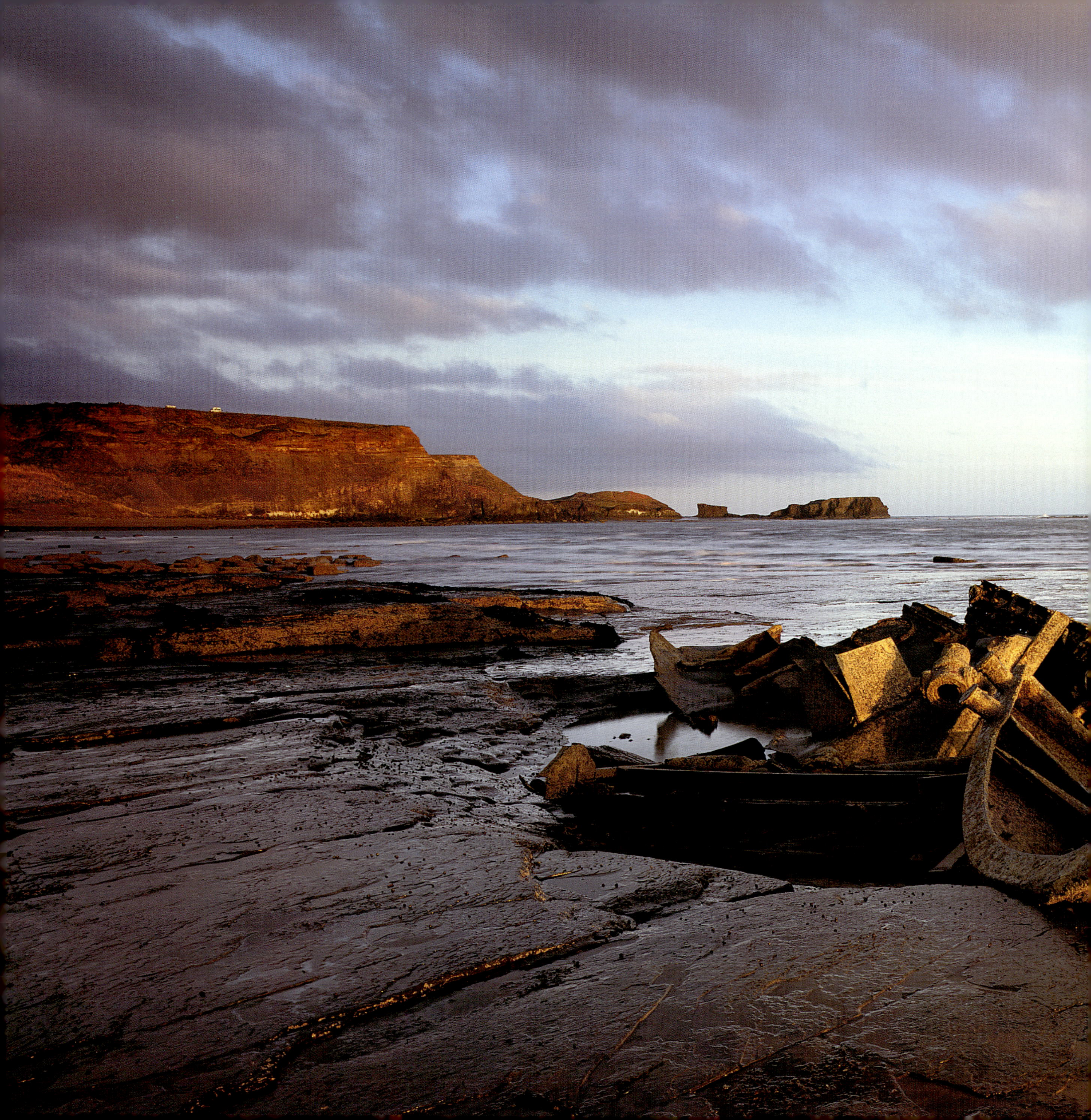

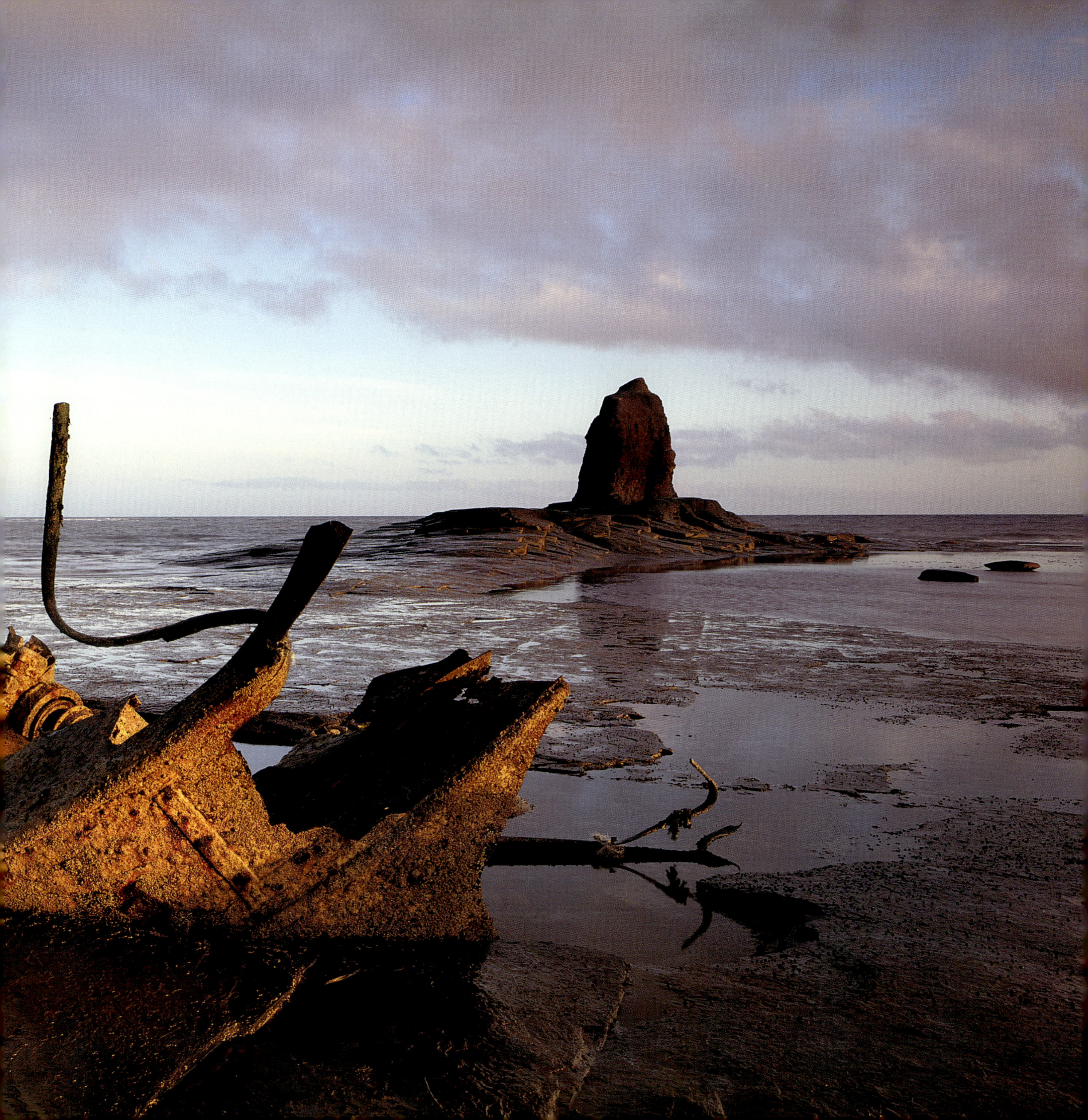

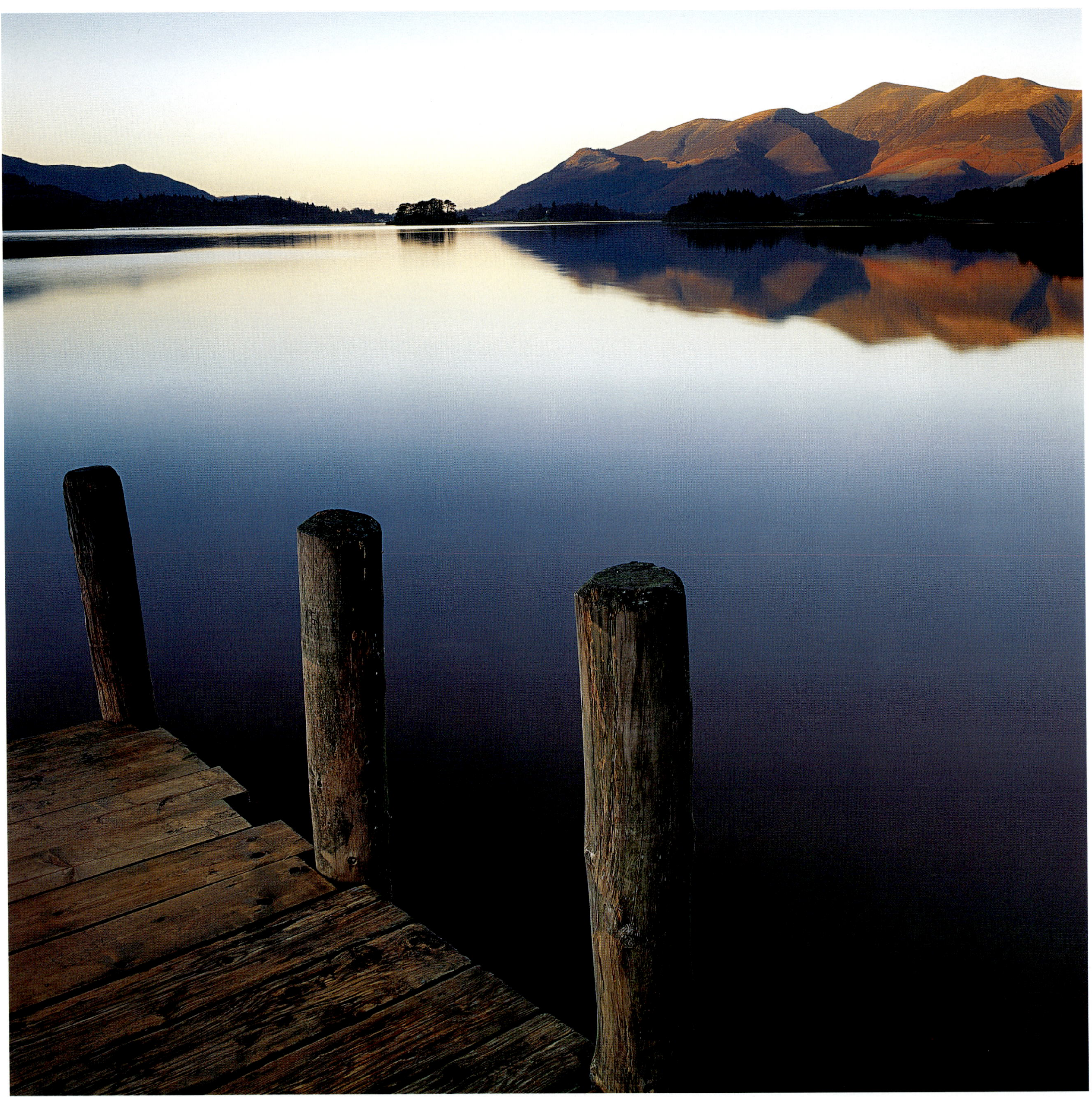

Composition

Composition is the art of selection, of choosing the contents of your photograph. When working in the landscape our primary tools for making this selection are our eyes and legs. Elements of the landscape cannot be moved around to suit our personal taste, so we must move ourselves to find that place from which the view best suits us.

There are some locations where moving to recompose a shot is relatively easy, as the land is laid out in such a way that is perfect for the photographer. These places have often become iconic images of an area – the defining view. They are photographed frequently, and almost always the same with regard to composition. There are other places where you might have to look really carefully to find any pleasing composition at all. It is worth exploring some of these locations, seeking out the unusual view. Finding something from nothing is very rewarding. You can also develop a better eye for detail and the unusual, and then apply your personal vision to those iconic, picturesque areas.

The 'Rules' of Composition

For many photographers, the composition they choose is the signature their work carries. To tie this down, to attempt to write a formula by which a picture, a work of art, can be judged successful or otherwise would seem a ludicrous proposal. For this reason I prefer not to talk about the rules of composition, but rather the tools of composition. Rules are made to be broken, while tools are available to use, or not, as you choose. This distinction is not helped by the fact that the first 'tool' of composition is commonly known as 'the rule of thirds' (see the rule of thirds, opposite).

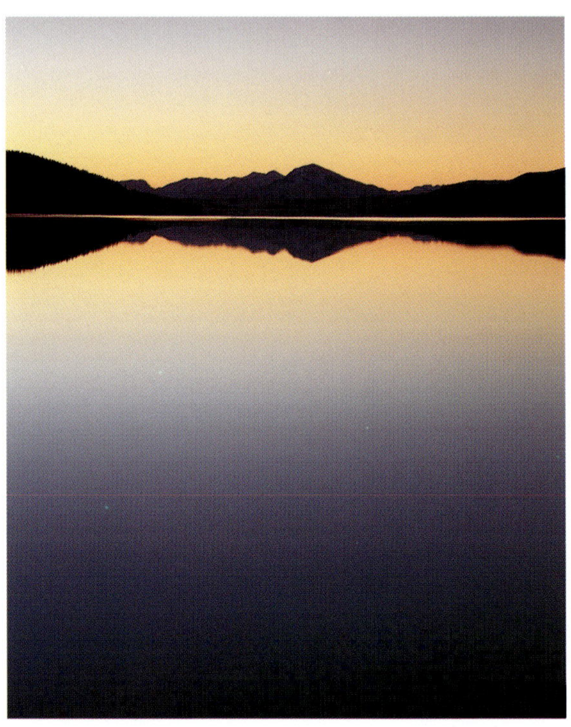

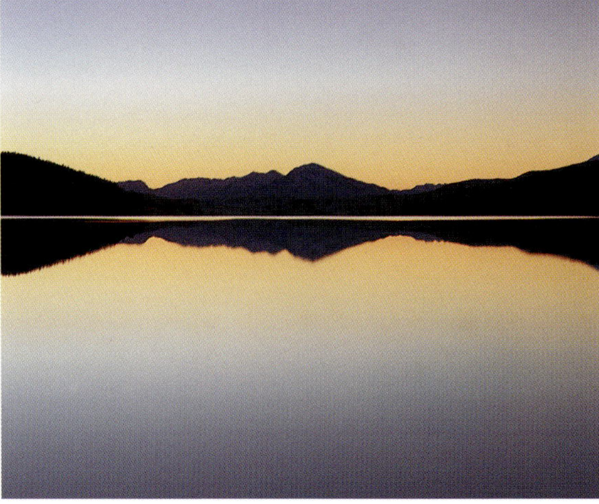

Loch Garry Dusk
Although the majority of this picture is empty, the frame is still filled by the subject. There are no lead-in lines or foreground interest, just a graduation in colour from dark grey to light grey and then orange. The composition is simple yet still pleasing.

For the portrait version I have followed (almost) the rule of thirds by placing the horizon on the line of thirds. For the landscape version I placed the horizon just slightly off-centre. I do not think the off-centre composition would have worked in the portrait version. Orientation affects the whole structure.

Pentax 67 with 135mm lens
Top: 1 second at f/22
Bottom: 3 seconds at f/22

Imagine a grid on your viewfinder made from four lines. Two placed one- and two-thirds into the frame horizontally and the other two one- and then two-thirds into the frame vertically. If you place important elements within your picture on these lines they are often more pleasing to the eye than if the same element was in the centre of the frame.

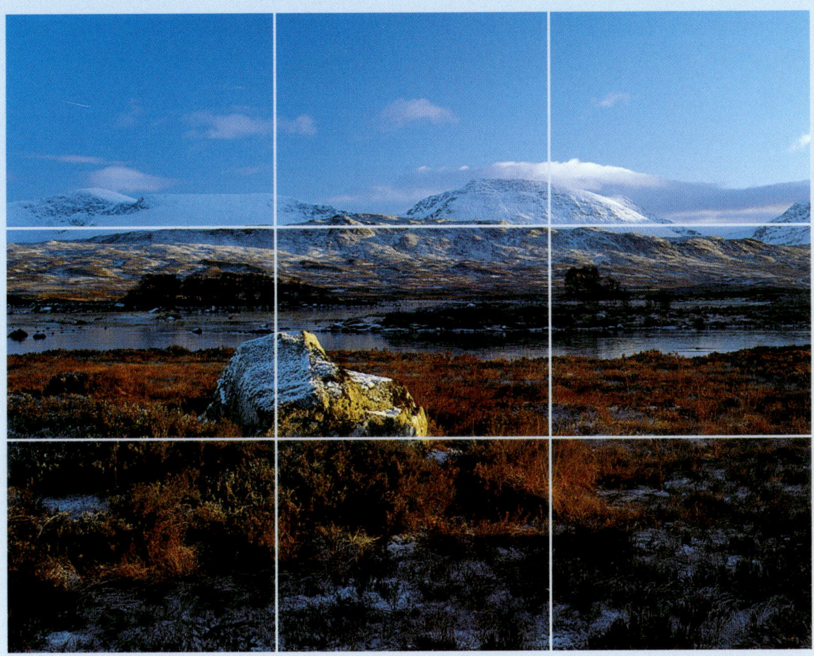

Rannoch Moor

The frost-encrusted rock in the foreground of this scene is lying right on the intersection of two lines of thirds. Had I placed the rock right in the centre of the picture it would have dominated the scene rather than simply adding depth to it. While I do not go out of my way to use the rule of thirds, sometimes it just seems the right thing to do, and then it works a treat.

Pentax 67 with 90mm lens, Velvia 50, 1/2sec at f/22, Coral No. 1 and 0.6 ND filter

While I do tend to avoid the centre of the viewfinder for important elements most of the time, the 'rule of thirds' is a tool I don't often employ. I tend to compose my pictures in a very instinctive way, and am almost afraid to analyse exactly what it is I do. If I take the whole process apart, will I ever be able to get it back together?

Keep It Simple

Antoine de Saint Exupery said, 'Perfection in design is achieved not when there is nothing more to add, but when there is nothing left to take away.' It serves well to remember this quotation when composing your images. Simple designs and ideas are often the best. Think of your compositions in the same way. Adding another element to a picture will seldom improve it, taking one away often will.

following page **Loch Tulla at Dawn**

The first time I saw Loch Tulla I stopped by the side of the road and took a picture of the two pine trees and the loch and the hills. On a later visit I looked at the usual composition and felt that the foreground grasses were looking a little forlorn. I wanted to take something different in any event, but the conditions made it appropriate to do so. I waited at the shore of the loch for the dawn light to strike the snow-dusted peaks. The perfect reflection made this scene. A change in the light or the other conditions in a place can also influence the composition, as was the case here.

Ebony 45s with 90mm lens, 6x12 rollfilm back, Velvia 50, 1 second at f/22, 0.6 ND soft-grad filter

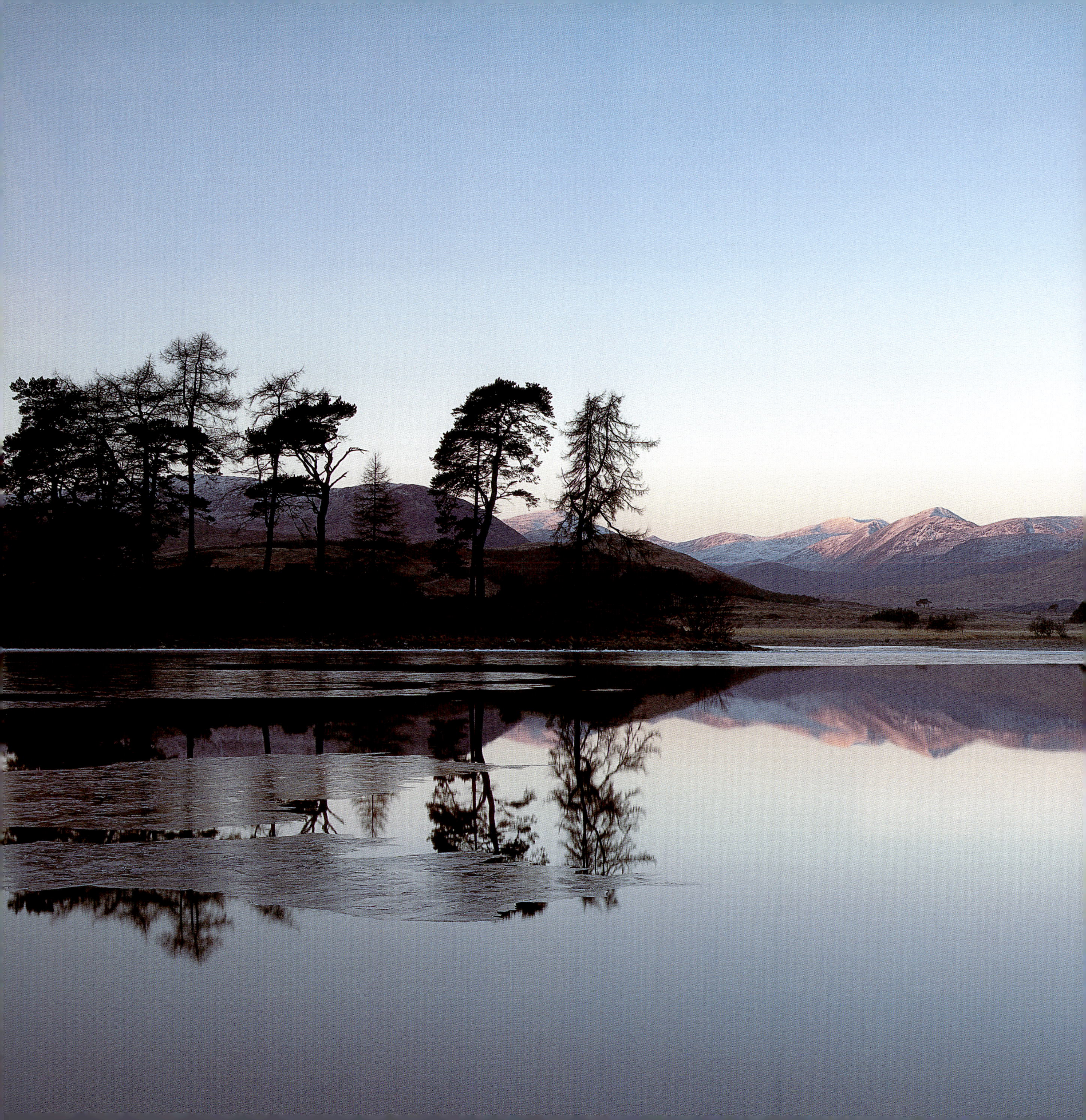

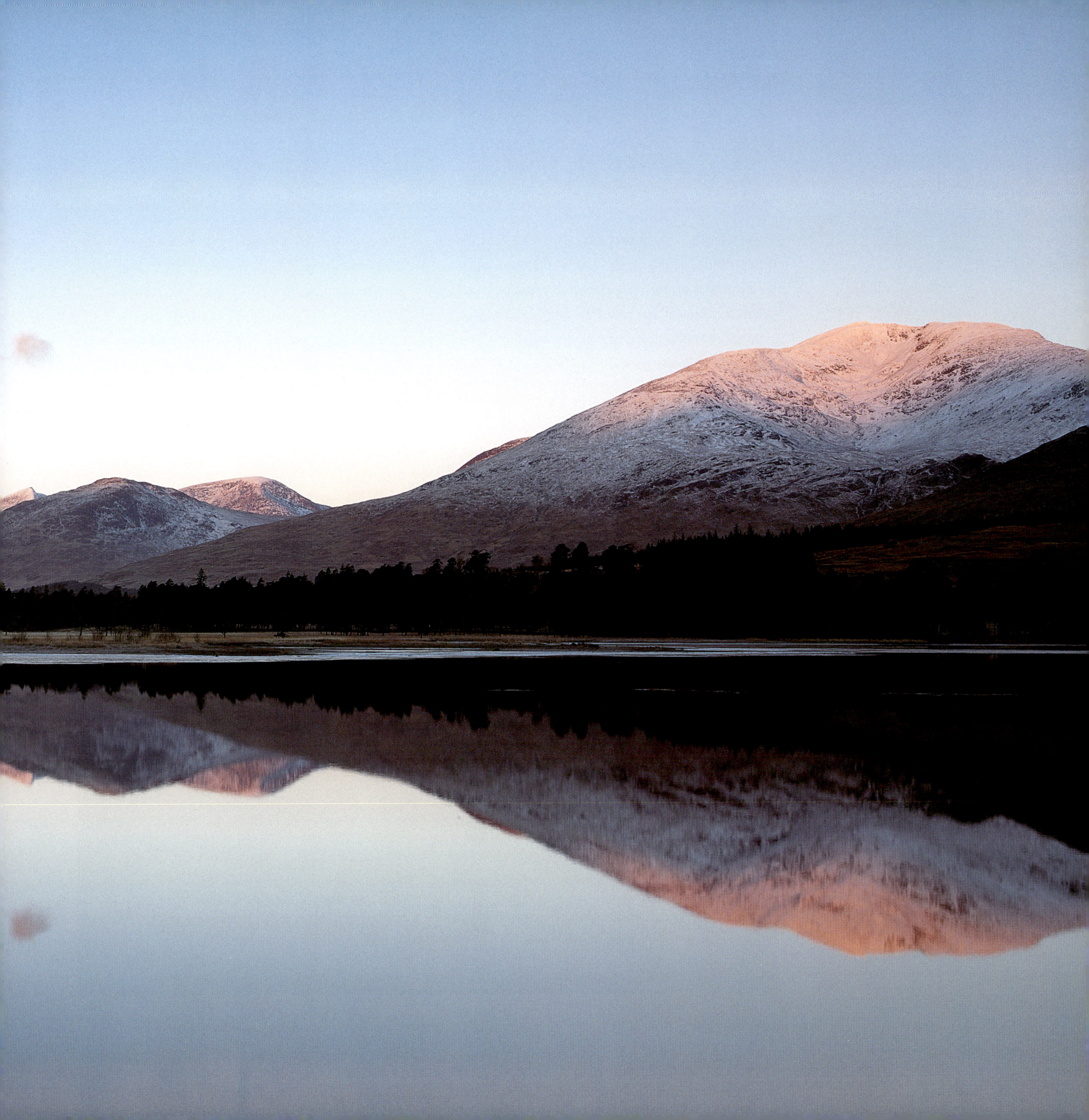

Still Dusk

Three elements: wooden jetty, the lake and the distant hills. Three posts, and a diagonal line for dramatic effect. The contrast between old, grained, rough wood and flat, calm, still water. I consider this picture one of my most successful compositions.

The picture below consists of so very little, yet captures perfectly the stillness and calm that was present at the time. The horizon is roughly one-fifth from the top; the first foreground post supporting the jetty is roughly two-fifths from the right of the picture. Perhaps we should talk about the little-known rule of fifths. The middle of the

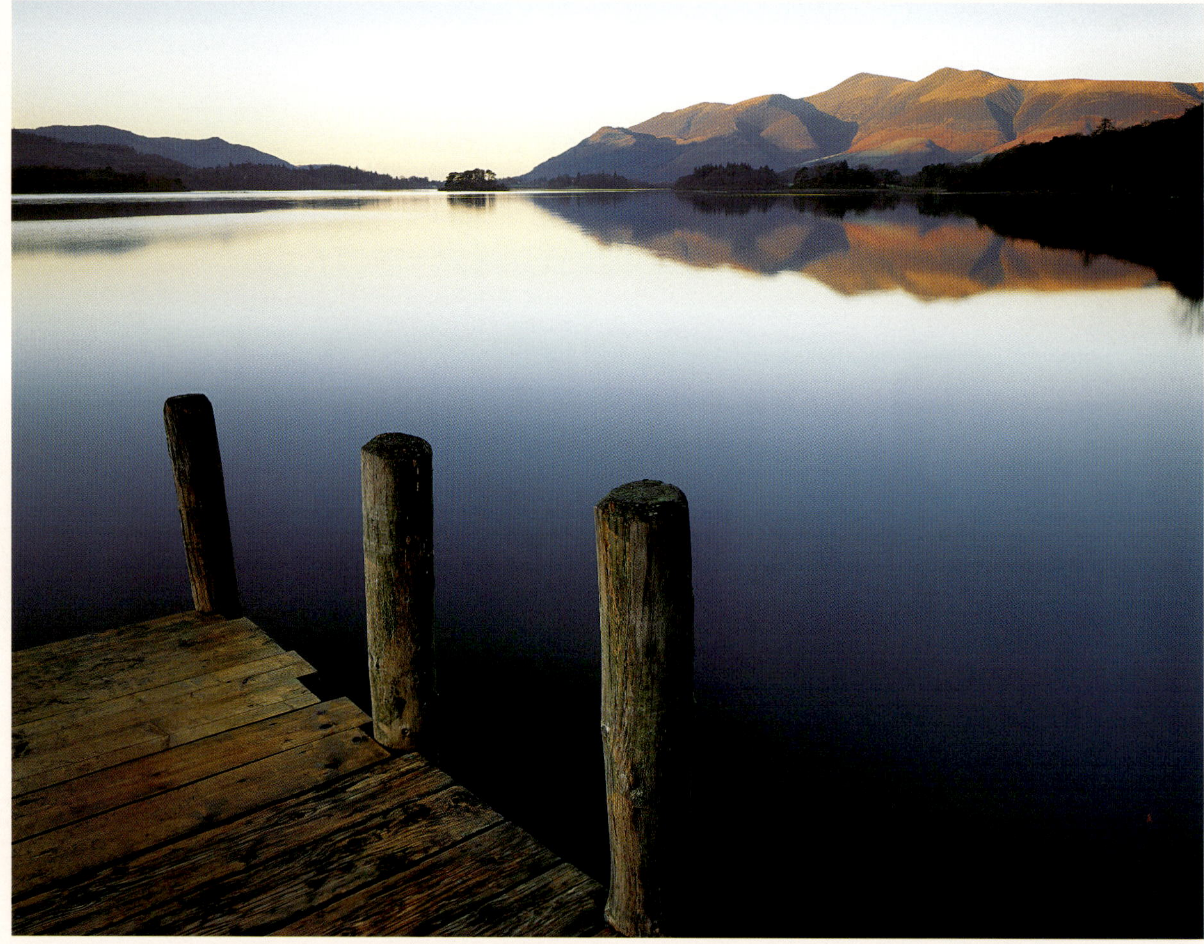

right Ebony 45s
with 90mm lens,
Velvia 50, 1/2sec
at f/22, 0.6 ND
soft-grad filter

three posts is right on the line of thirds. The diagonal line of the jetty gives the scene a little drama. Diagonal lines tend to lead the eye into or around the picture while horizontal or vertical lines divide a picture. It is the near-perfect reflection of the distant hill, Skiddaw, and the warm evening light upon its flanks that create the atmosphere of peace. The majority of the scene is still water. Empty and featureless, it is here that the real tranquillity of the moment was captured. This was one of those rare and magical moments when I could think of nothing that would improve the scene.

As I was setting up the large-format camera, the sun dipped further behind the hills behind me, and the light that had been falling onto the jetty disappeared. I did then pause briefly and wonder if I had missed the best. I soon concluded this was not the case, but that the texture of the wood was being shown in better relief now that it was shaded from the direct rays of the sun. This had been a frustrating day for landscape photography: bright and sunny without a cloud in the sky. Most people would think it a wonderful day, but to the landscape photographer, a sky without cloud is not a welcome sight. In many traditional landscapes a full third of the picture is filled with the sky, and a featureless mass of blue holds no interest.

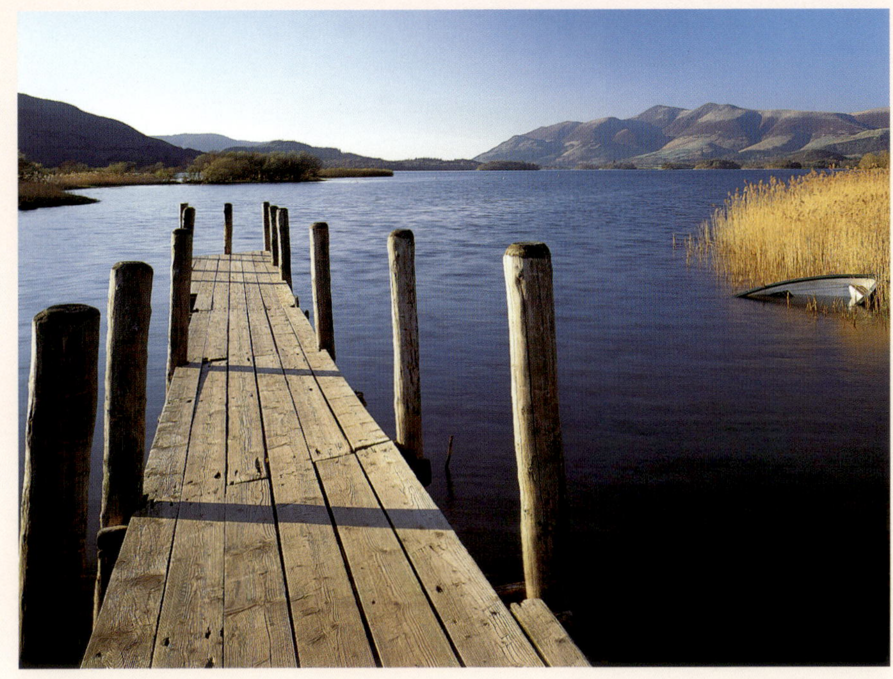

above **Ebony 45s with 90mm lens, Velvia 50, 1/2sec at f/22, polarizing filter**

In many ways the second picture (above) is a more traditional composition than the first image. Looking straight out along the length of the jetty and allowing it to lead the eye into the scene. Once again I was cursed with a near cloudless sky, yet for balance this time I found the rule of thirds worked well. The hills do fill a good proportion of what would otherwise be a plain blue block at the top of the picture. There was no reflection either, and this usually puts me off taking a picture of a lake. This time the scene seemed to work without a reflection, perhaps the reeds and the partly sunken boat made up for it.

The Tools for Composition

Photography is a two-dimensional art form and some of the tools of composition help create the illusion of real depth within an image. Your choice of lens is one of those tools. There may be times when you need to be close to your subject and a wideangle lens is the only way to compose the image you want. There will be other occasions when it might be better to move further away and use a longer lens. As a general rule, however, you should not use a lens as a substitute for being in the right place.

For many years, it has been common practice for professional photographers to use polaroids to give them a better indication of what their final image will look like. These days many use a digital camera instead, which is a much cheaper and simpler alternative. Polaroids and digital cameras are both good aids to composition, but the task of composing the picture still belongs to the photographer.

technique CHANGING YOUR LENS TO CHANGE PERSPECTIVE

Lens selection is about much more than mere content of the viewfinder, it affects the very structure of the image. A wideangle lens will exaggerate perspective and draw attention to the foreground. A telephoto lens does the exact opposite and compresses perspective, foreshortening distance within the scene.

As you move around a subject the most appropriate lens to use might alter. For the first of these photographs of Tangle Creek waterfall in the Canadian Rockies I used a 45mm wideangle lens to emphasize the foreground. Having climbed higher and closer to the top of the falls the 90mm lens was more useful.

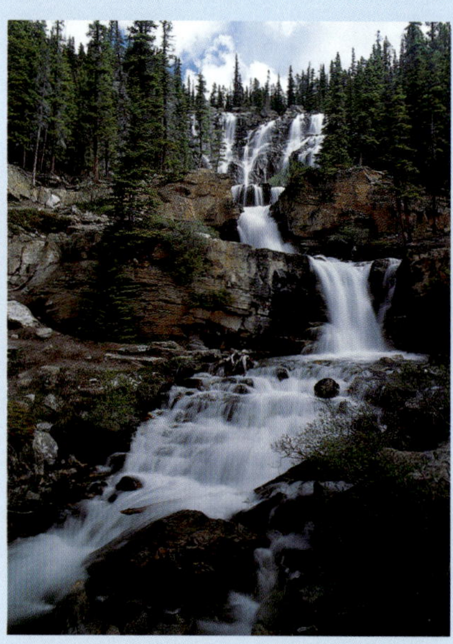

45mm lens

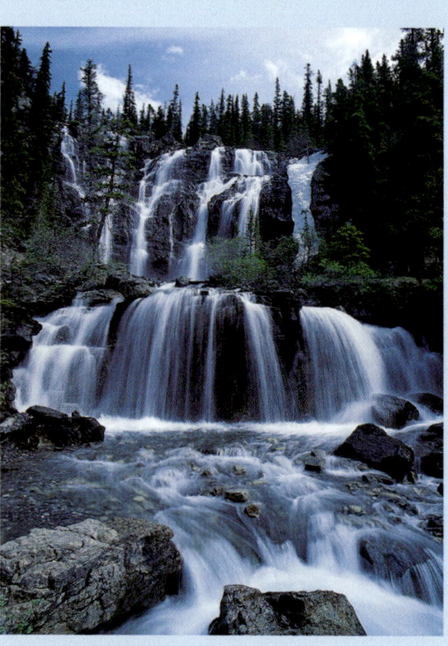

90mm lens

SUPER-WIDEANGLE LENSES

Wideangle lenses are much loved by the landscape photographer because of their great covering power. The grand vista of the landscape looks exciting to the eye, and a wide-enough lens can include almost everything you can see in front of you in the viewfinder, but this often leads to uninspiring photographs. When captured on film the view before you may not look quite as exciting. This is because our eyes dart around the whole scene taking in a part here and another part there, building a montage in our mind's eye. You cannot do this with a photograph. When viewing a photograph you see the whole picture, including those elements that are not so interesting, those that the eyes saw and the mind ignored while building its mental montage. The answer often is to use a longer lens and pick out the elements of the scene that the mind is focusing on and make single images out of these.

right In the height of summer the rivers of the Yorkshire Dales often run shallow, revealing the rocks of the riverbed beneath. For this picture of Wain Wath Falls I have used a 58mm lens on 5x4 (equivalent to 15mm on a 35mm camera). This has caused an exaggerated and stretched foreground, and a picture with plenty of impact. Not only was the exaggerated foreground desirable, it was unavoidable if I wanted to include the pancakes of rock over which the fuller river flows. One step further back and I would have been in the river at a much lower elevation. The super-wideangle lens made possible an interpretation that is closer to my memory of the scene than any other.

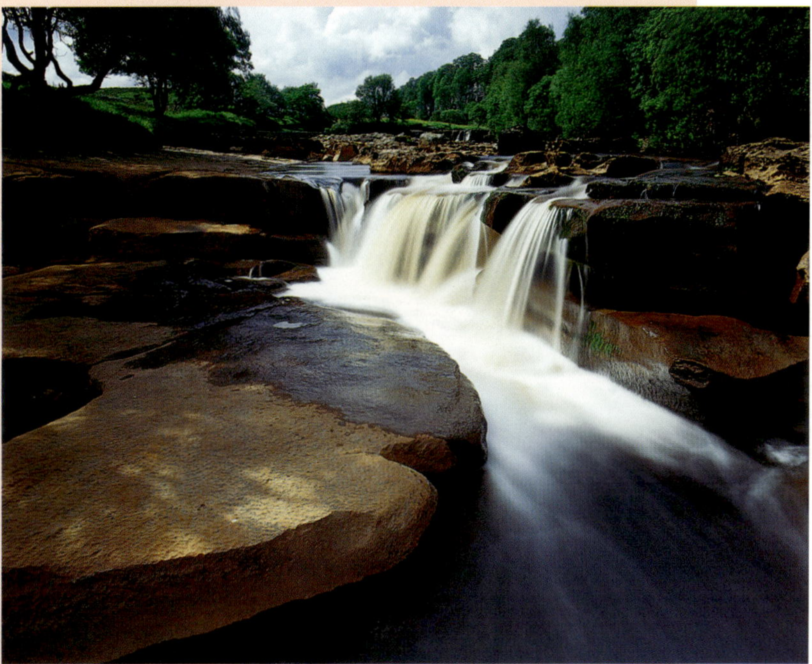

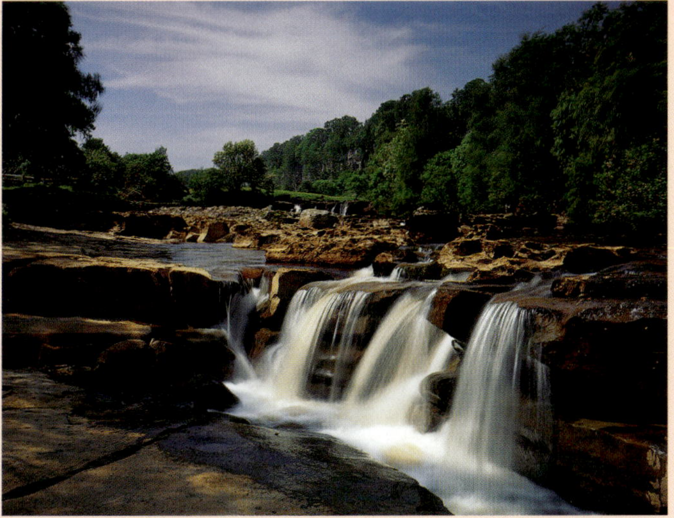

left A 'standard' 50mm lens (150mm on a 5x4 camera) shows the same scene with the natural perspective of the human eye and neither exaggerates nor compresses distance.

The main road that runs from Crianlarich to Fort William traverses some of the wildest-looking countryside Scotland has to offer. It is this wilderness appearance combined with easy access that has led to images of Glencoe becoming iconic.

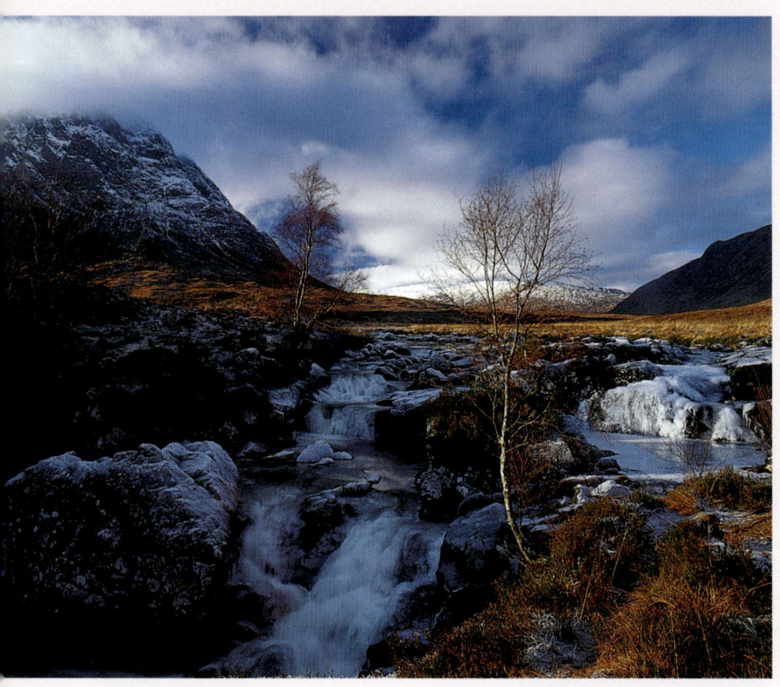

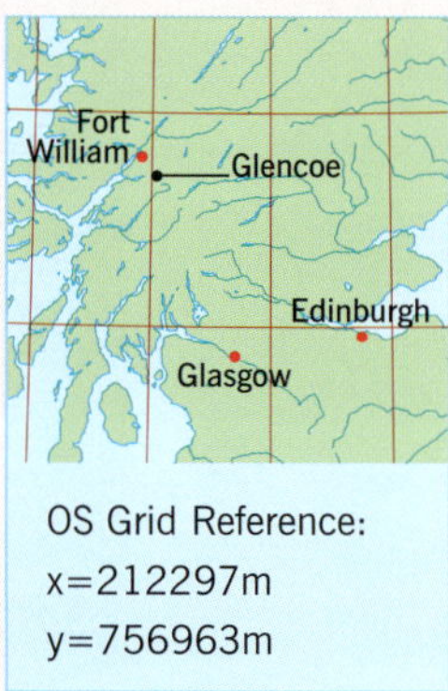

OS Grid Reference:
x=212297m
y=756963m

There is nothing wrong with photographing the well-known views of a place. On Rannoch Moor and in Glencoe it sometimes seems there is little else to do. I can think of few places in Britain that appear as wild and wonderful, and yet have a main road running right through them granting access to all for very little effort. The result is that Rannoch Moor and Glencoe often look like a photographer's convention with tripods gathered all around.

above
Pentax 67 with 90mm lens, Velvia 50, 1/2sec at f/22, polarizing filter

right
Ebony 45s with 90mm lens, Velvia 50, 1/2 sec at f/22, polarizing filter

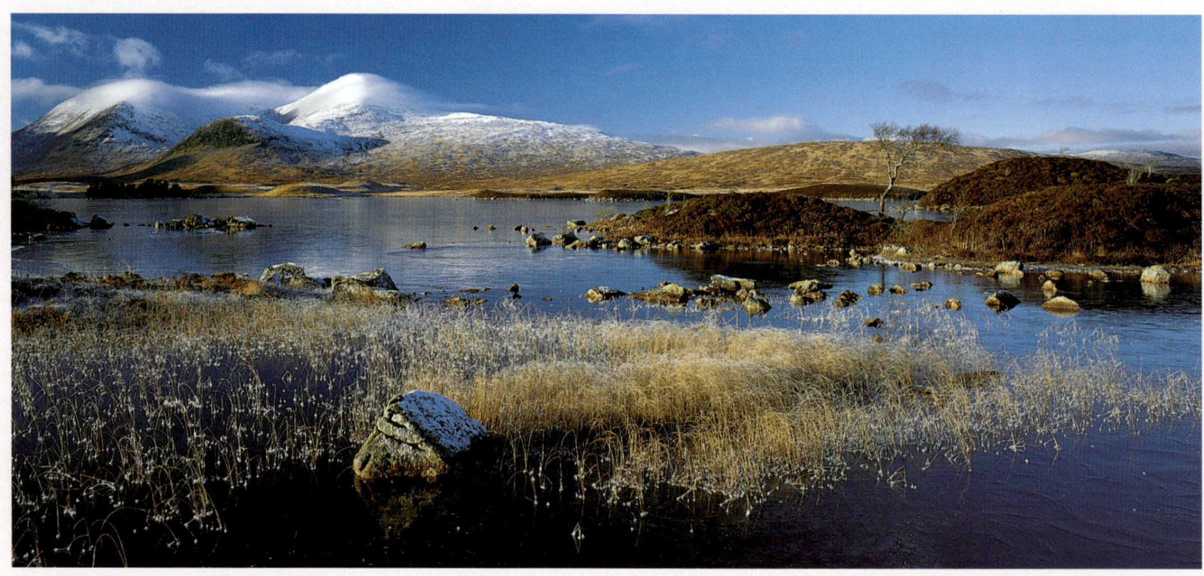

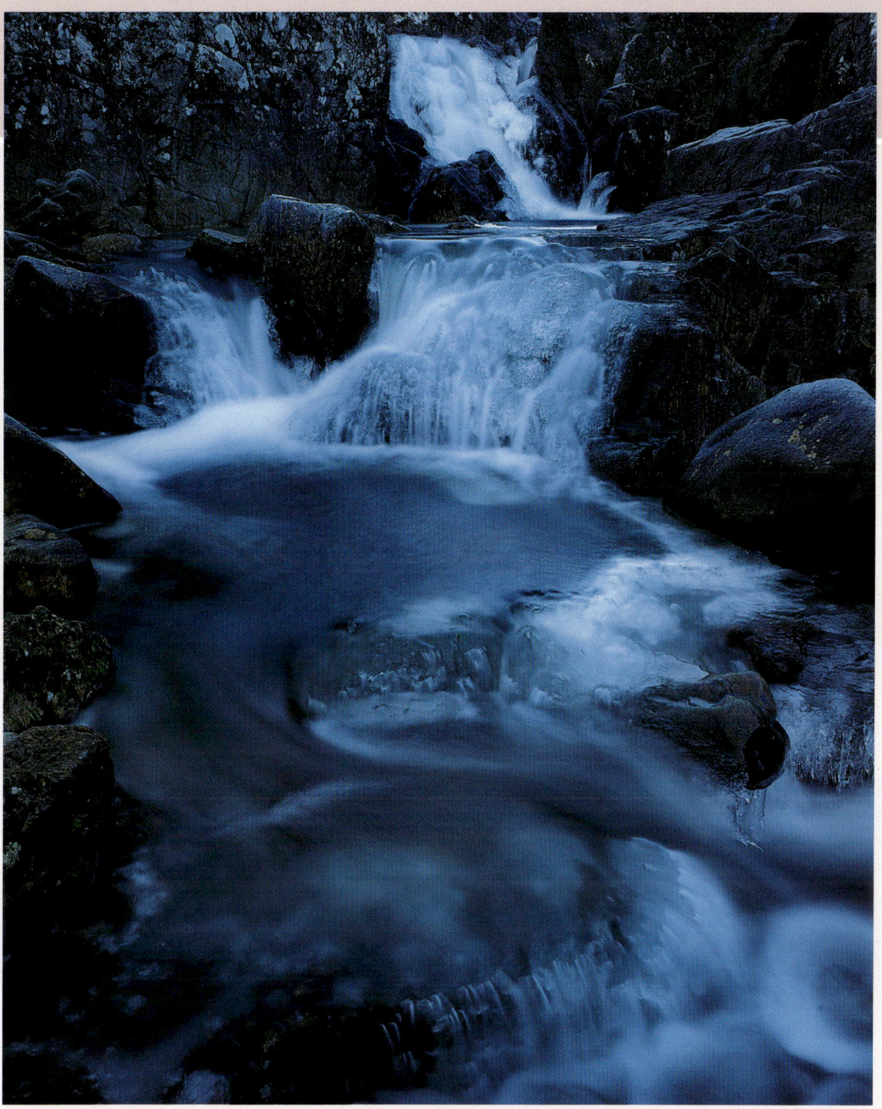

Focusing on the water and ice and allowing the unfiltered light to turn the film blue to emphasize the cold, created the feel I wanted for this study of texture.

Ebony 45s with 150mm lens, Velvia 50, 2 seconds at f/22

Buachaille Etive Mor is the focus for much of this attention. At the north end of Rannoch Moor and the south of Glencoe, this 3353ft (1022m) high pyramid of rock dominates the landscape. There are bare trees, rocks, the white-washed Black Rock Cottage, numerous streams, ponds and the River Etive, all potential foregrounds for another picture of 'The Buckle'.

The sheer grandeur of the scene means it demands to be photographed, but I do sometimes wonder if the world really needs another picture of Buachaille Etive Mor. It is then a short step to thinking that there must be something new there, a view within Glencoe that has not yet been photographed by anyone else, or at least not already photographed by everyone else.

One of the most popular foregrounds is a waterfall just by the side of a minor road that heads into Glen Etive. I have a number of photographs of this waterfall featuring 'The Buckle' as a background. To seek something different, I clambered down into the ravine to look at the waterfall from a different angle, excluding the usual mountain backdrop. The picture above right is one of the results.

on the following page **Frozen River, Glencoe**
This shows another view of Glencoe that I 'found' while clambering around carefully over frost-covered rocks. The warm tones in the rocks contrast with the cold river of ice, and a well-placed stone gives the scene balance.

Ebony 45s with 90mm lens, 6x12 rollfilm back, Velvia 50, 2 seconds at f/22

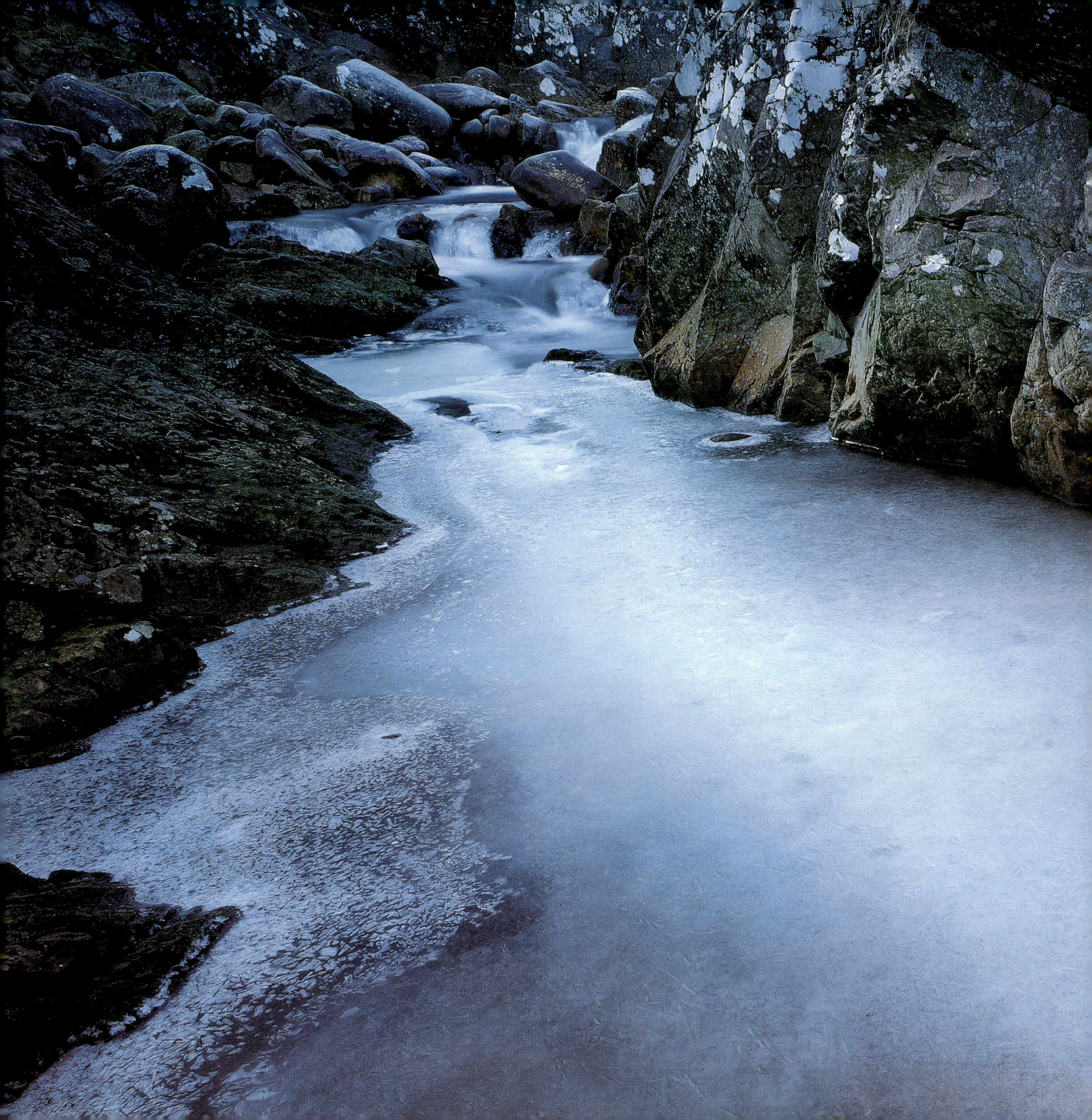

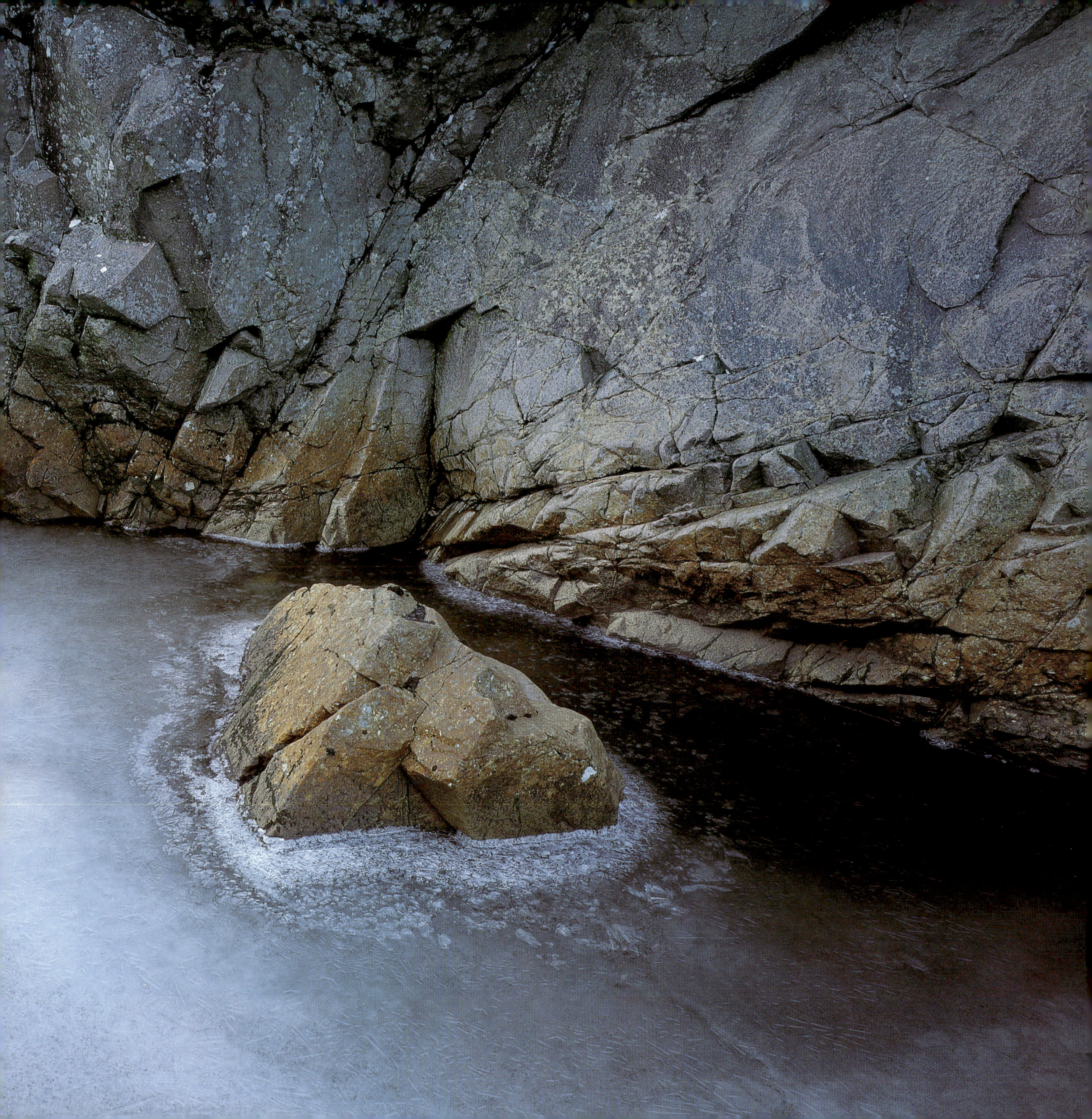

Classic Views of Scotland

Location:
Loch Awe, Scotland

Time of year:
January and April

Camera:
Pentax 67

Lenses:
45mm and 90mm

Film:
Velvia 50

Filter:
Polarizer

Kilchurn Castle is set so perfectly among the mountains on Loch Awe that we can overlook the pylons in the background and the lifebelt on the jetty which would mar a lesser view.

The two images of Kilchurn Castle on this page illustrate a couple of interesting points. Firstly, when the tree is to the left of the castle the picture reads better than when it is to the right of the castle. With the tree on the right, the eye almost stops at this point, cutting the picture effectively in half. This may be a cultural thing. Because we read the written word from left to right we expect to read a picture in the same way. The second point these pictures raise for me is about over-working the composition. Neither are particularly successful images. The tree as an element of foreground interest has not really improved the pictures. Flat light on the background hills and the castle means there is nothing to define and separate one from the other.

This is a good location for landscape photography and, when the conditions are right, Kilchurn Castle is a classic view of Scotland. This January morning it was not working, and that is why I sought some foreground interest rather than simply composing the scene naturally.

Pentax 67 with 45mm lens, Velvia 50, exposure details not recorded

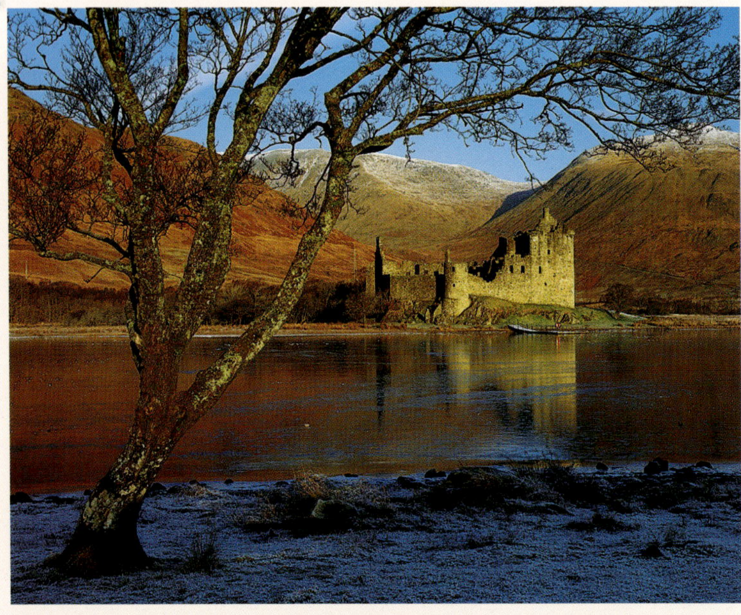

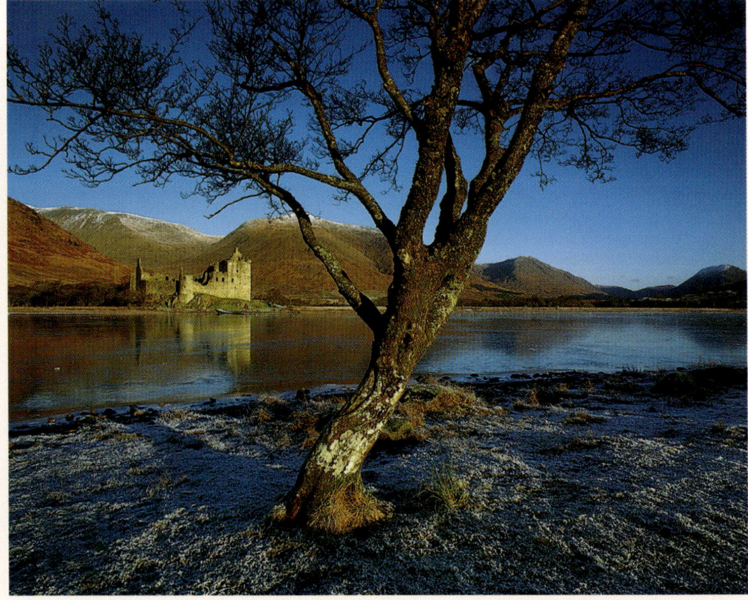

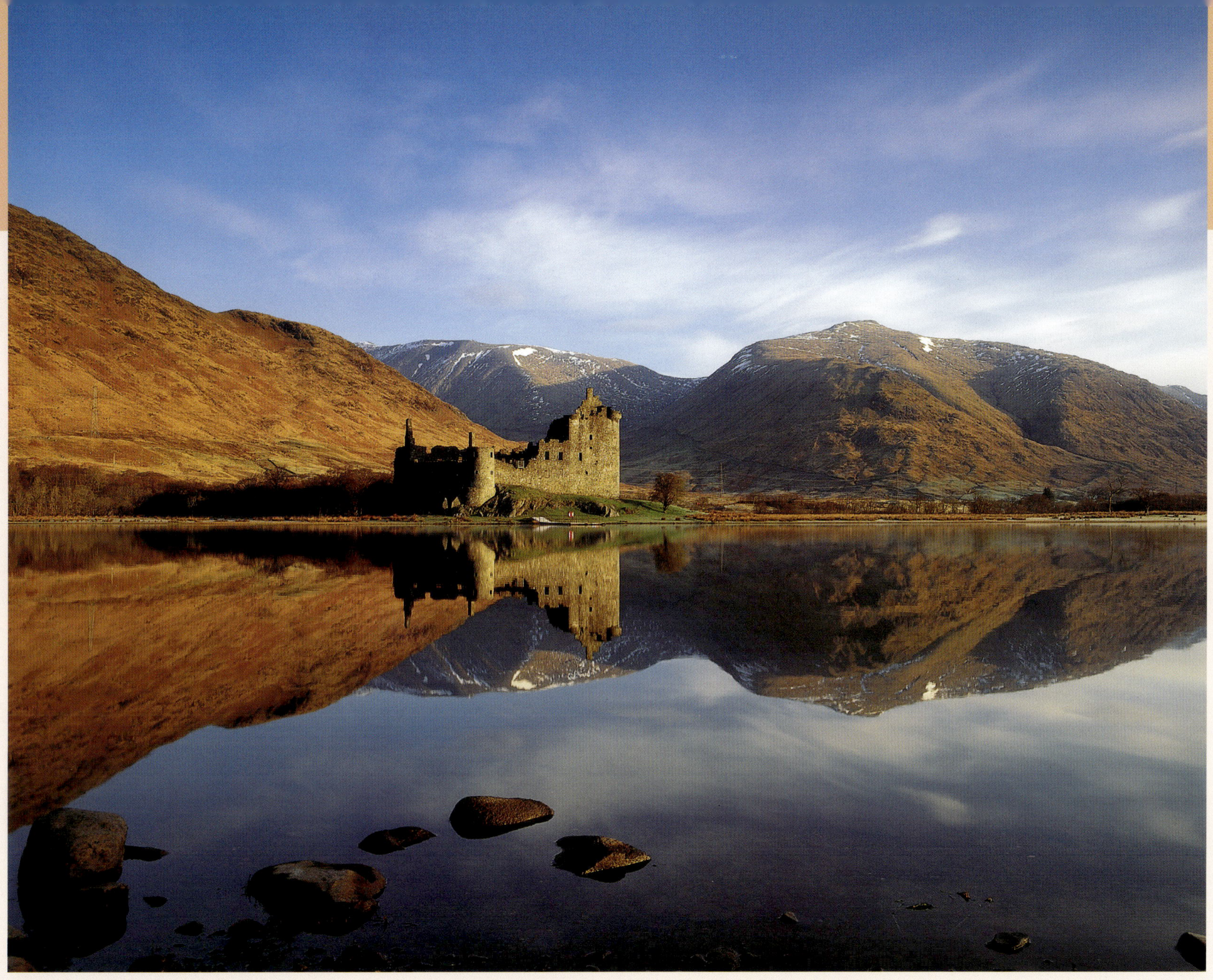

Kilchurn Castle, Loch Awe

On this visit in April the sun was coming from a different angle, and so the hills behind the castle were in shadow. This produced definition between the hills and the sunlit castle. The loch was still and calm, showing a perfect reflection. A few stones on the shore and the line of the reflected hills are enough foreground interest.

Pentax 67 with 45mm lens, Velvia 50, 1/2sec at f/22, polarizing filter

Including Buildings

Buildings are a part of the landscape, not apart from it.

They will always provide a focal point in any landscape

where they appear, so it is important to consider them

in your composition. Some buildings, it has to be said,

seem to blend into the landscape better than others.

Eilean Donan Castle

Always worth a photograph despite its reputation as the most photographed view in Scotland. It is as if this castle simply grew out of the rocks. The contrast of warm light on the castle against dark shade on the mountains makes the building stand out.

Ebony 45s with 240mm lens, Velvia 50, 1/8sec at f/22, Coral No. 1 and 0.6 ND soft-grad filters

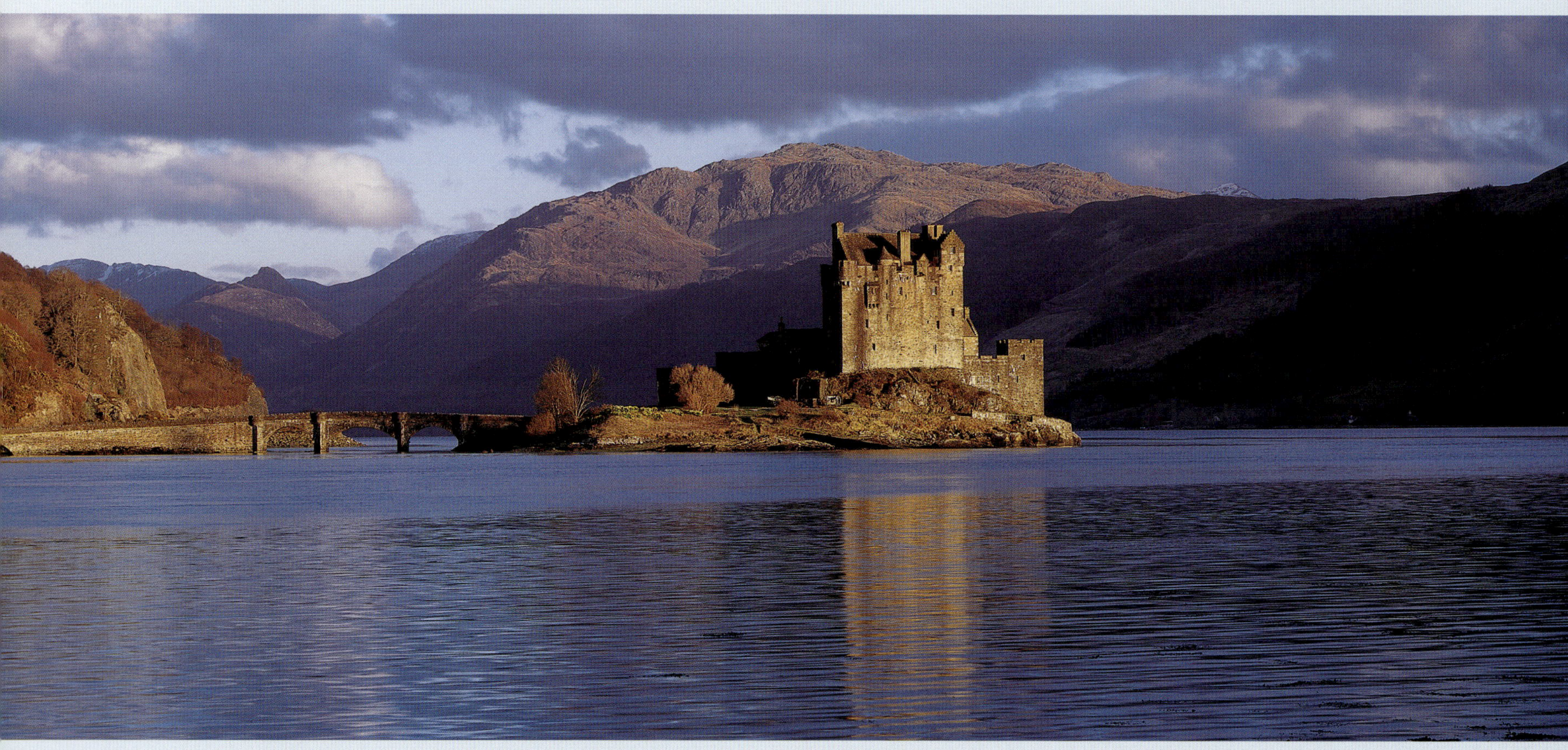

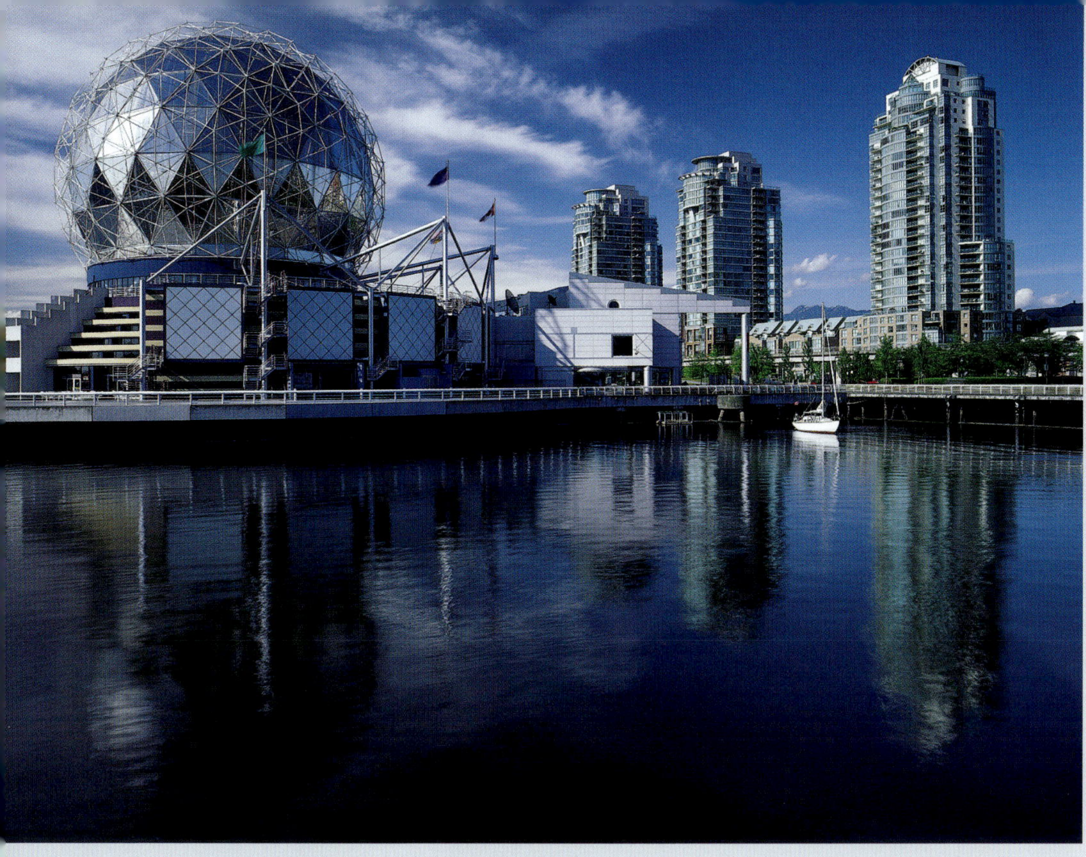

left **Science World, Vancouver, Canada**
What was I saying about some buildings blending in better than others? Still, this space-age structure has great visual appeal.

Ebony 45s with 90mm lens, Velvia 50, 1/2sec at f/22, polarizing filter

right **Dunstanburgh**
Here the building is a tiny element, yet it still draws our eye. The main subject of the photograph is the pool left by the retreating tide. The headland on which the castle stands would have completed the composition on its own, but the truth is that as humans we naturally find buildings interesting.

Pentax 67 with 55mm lens, Velvia 50, 1/2sec at f/22, 0.6 ND grad filter

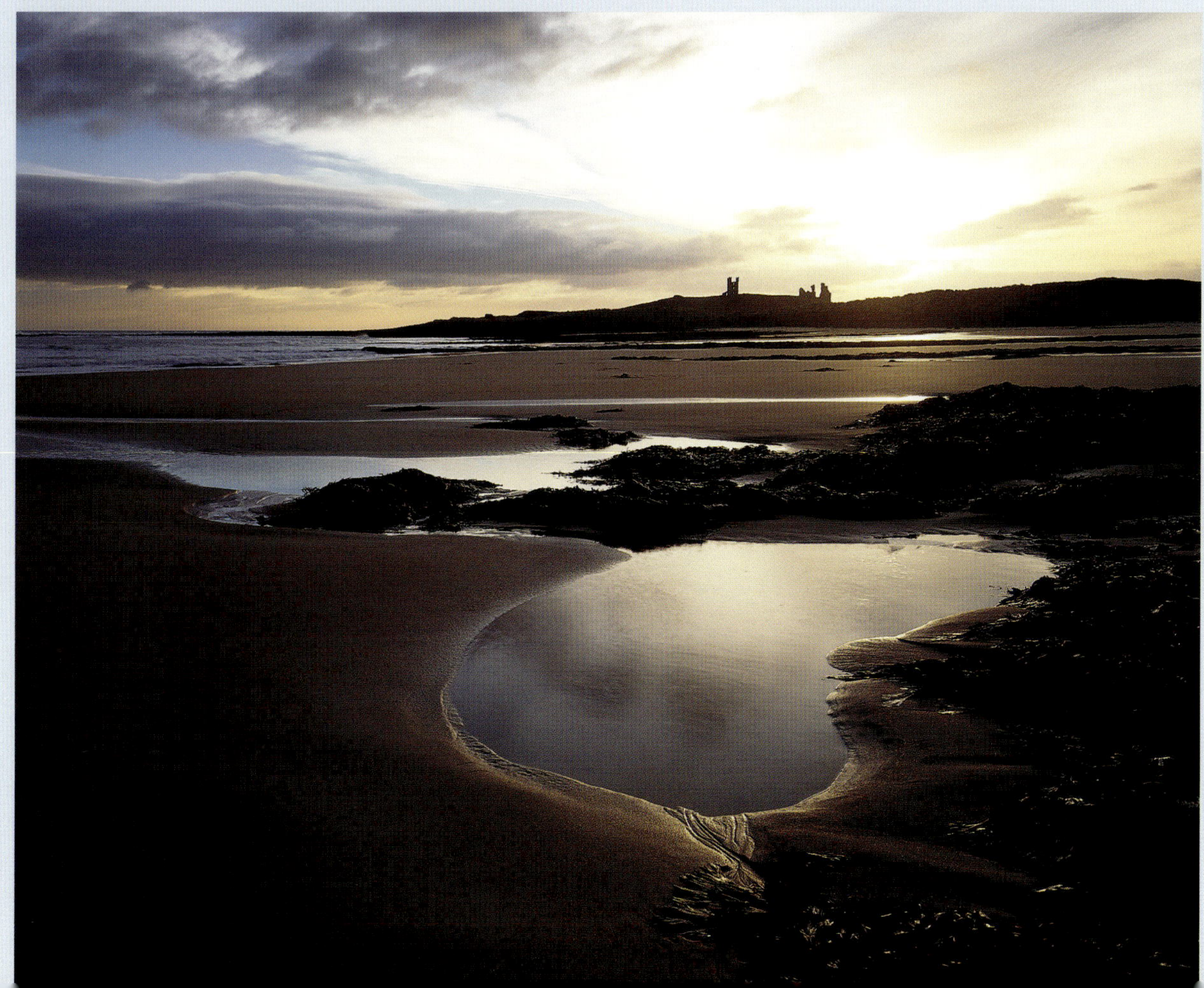

below **Eastbourne Pier, East Sussex**

Piers are wonderful structures that can be used to lead the eye out to sea. These buildings survive against all odds. They must be loved; there is no other explanation.

Ebony 45s with 90mm lens, Velvia 50, exposure not recorded, Coral No. 1 and 0.6 ND grad filters

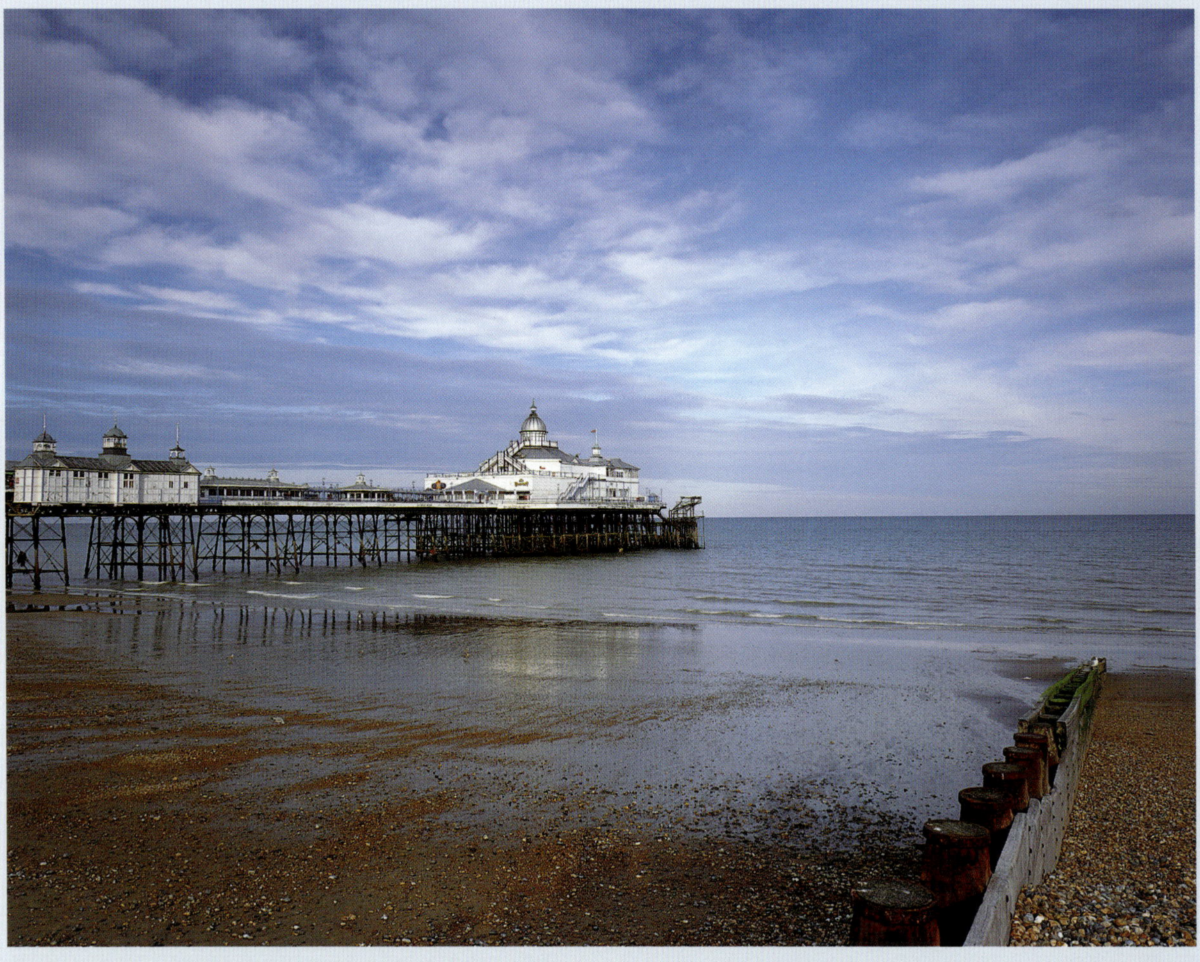

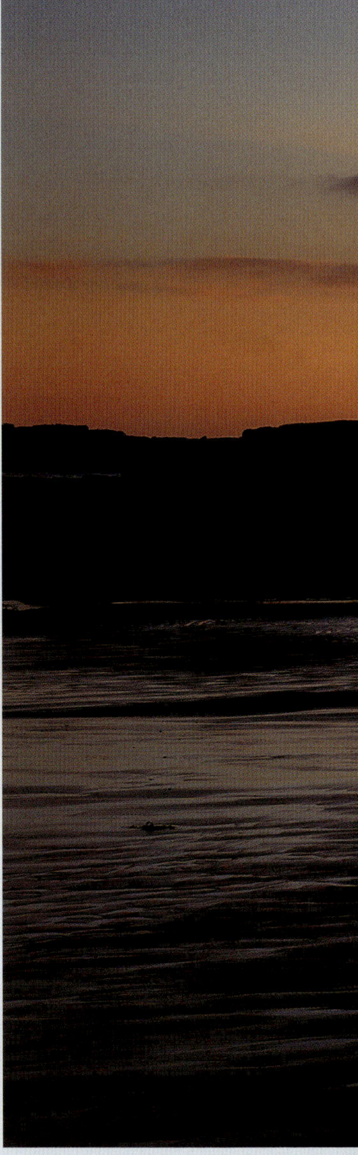

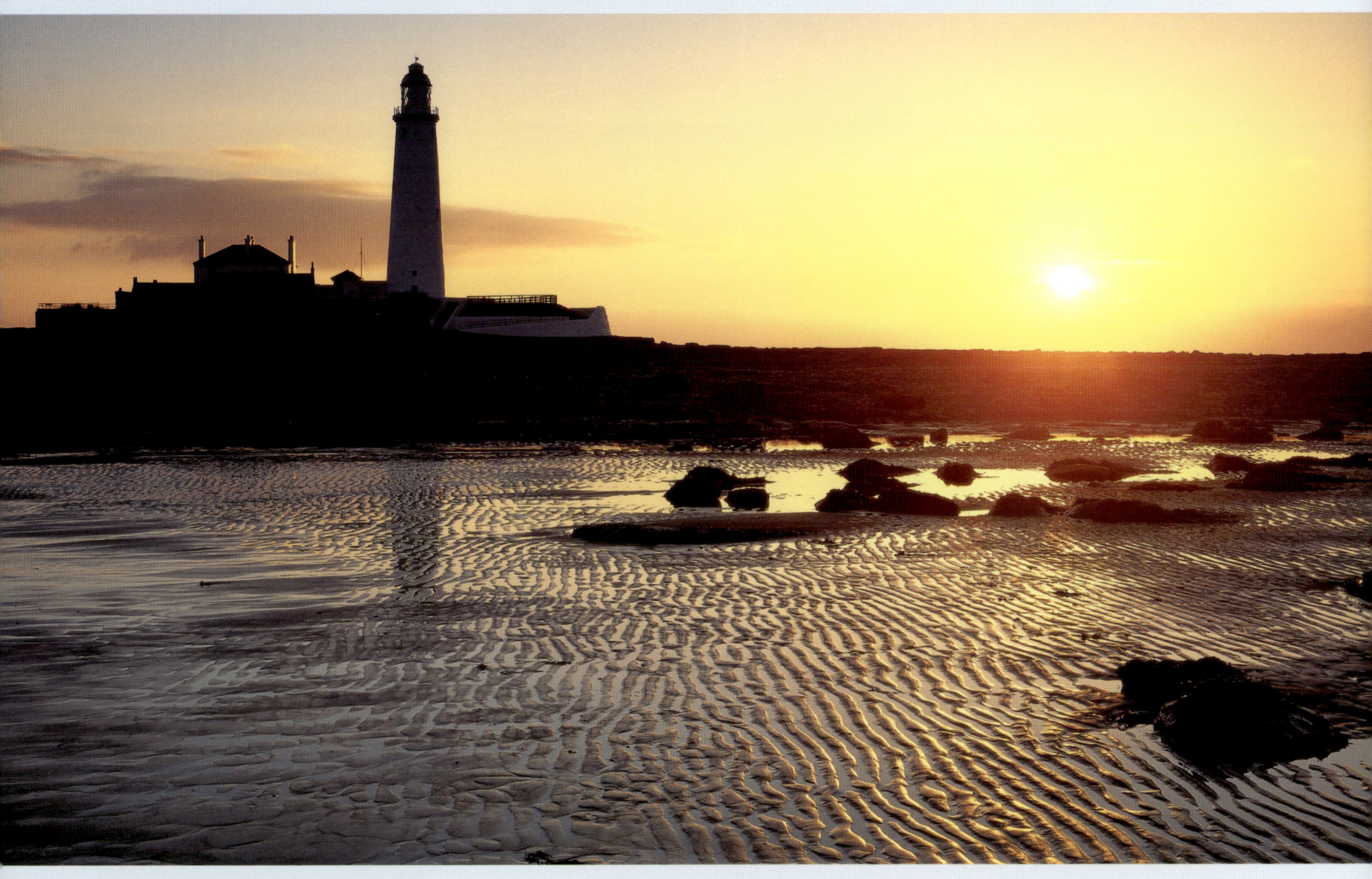

St Mary's Lighthouse, Tyneside

There is no right or wrong way to compose an image. Here I have totally ignored the rule of thirds and placed the lighthouse just off-centre. The ripples left in the sand by the retreating tide act as good lead-in lines heading to the horizon and the lighthouse.

Ebony 45s with 90mm lens, 6x12 rollfilm back, Velvia 50, 1 second at f/22, 0.6 ND grad filter

Foreground Interest

A simple tool for creating depth in your pictures is to add some foreground interest. The inclusion of some foreground is inevitable within a traditional landscape but ensuring that that foreground is interesting is not. While our eyes take in the whole scene in front of us, our mind dwells just on those parts of the scene that we find interesting, such as the distant hills. While with our mind we can ignore acres of monotone green between us and the distant hills, the camera just records everything that is there. Even if we are using a standard lens that has the same perspective as the human eye, without care the foreground can be very boring. The problem is further exaggerated if we use a wideangle lens to emphasize the empty foreground in order to get more of the distant hills in the frame.

Foreground interest is not really an issue separate from the rest of the composition. If you fill the frame with your subject and your subject is interesting, it stands to reason that the foreground will be interesting, too. If it is not, then you are viewing the scene from the wrong place.

Getting it Right

What you should be careful not to do is overwork the situation in order to add some foreground interest. It is not the case that just anything will do. Not every rock or tree is interesting. On the other hand, not every seemingly empty space is boring. If you are using the tool of foreground interest to add an illusion of depth to your photograph then it should not look deliberate or forced. The first thing to consider is 'Am I too far away from the

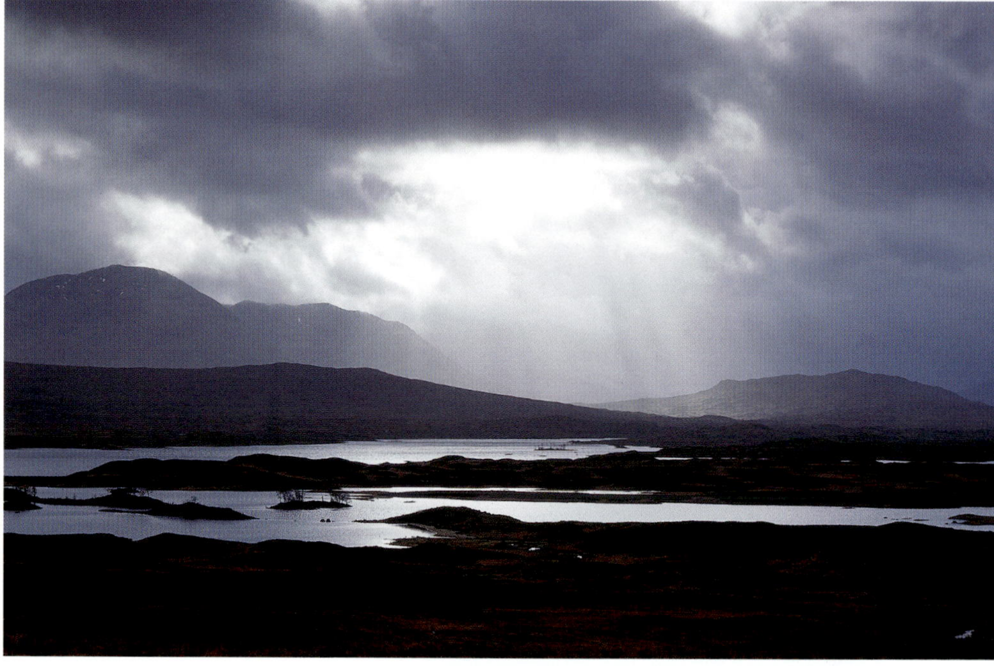

Loch Laidon, Scotland

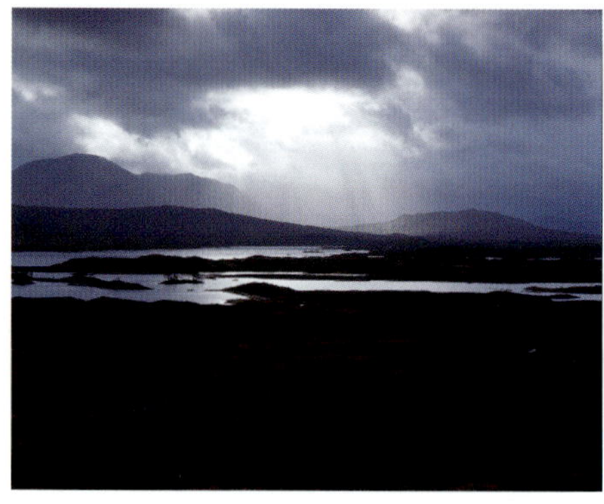

The guidebook describing this walk route said something along the lines of 'save this one for a really nice summer day'. I have seldom been out in weather that was worse, but this photograph captures one of the better moments. Most of the time I was in the teeth of an arctic gale with rain lashing me from seemingly every direction. I would have liked at this point to set up my 5x4 camera and used the 6x12 panoramic back, but in such conditions there was no point – the wind would have caused vibration in the larger camera. So I used my Pentax 67 and the longest lens I had for it – a 135mm lens. It still did not bring me as close to the scene as I wanted to be, but I took this picture anyway, knowing that the dark and uninteresting foreground (seen in the full-frame, smaller version, above right) could be cropped out later (above top).

Pentax 67 with 135mm lens, Velvia 50, 1/15sec at f/22

subject? Should I move closer?' If moving closer is not possible, perhaps a longer lens will remove much of the unwanted, uninteresting foreground. Perhaps a picture that has a boring foreground can be cropped later to remove it.

Panoramic composition is, at its most basic, a standard oblong cropped to remove too much foreground; perhaps this is why the format works so well and has become so popular. If you are viewing a scene that has all the elements of design that make a good photograph, the foreground will already contain enough interest. If it does not, then simply moving so that a rock or a tree can be included in the foreground will not necessarily improve the picture.

Leading the Eye into the Frame

It may be surprising just how little it takes to create foreground interest. A shape, a pattern, a colour, any of these might do the trick. A few stones, some blades of tall grass, the glint of sunlight on water – almost anything that forms a line, straight or curved and especially diagonal, will work. The foreground leads to the rest of the picture, and should, if it is working well, invite the viewer to dwell on the whole image.

Lead–in lines are a part of foreground interest and are useful tools for adding depth to a scene. Curves, zigzags, triangles and crosses act as design elements we all recognize. They lend order to the chaos of the natural world. That we value such devices is evidenced by the way we design our gardens, perhaps angling a path or positioning a flowerbed so that it draws the eye across the garden.

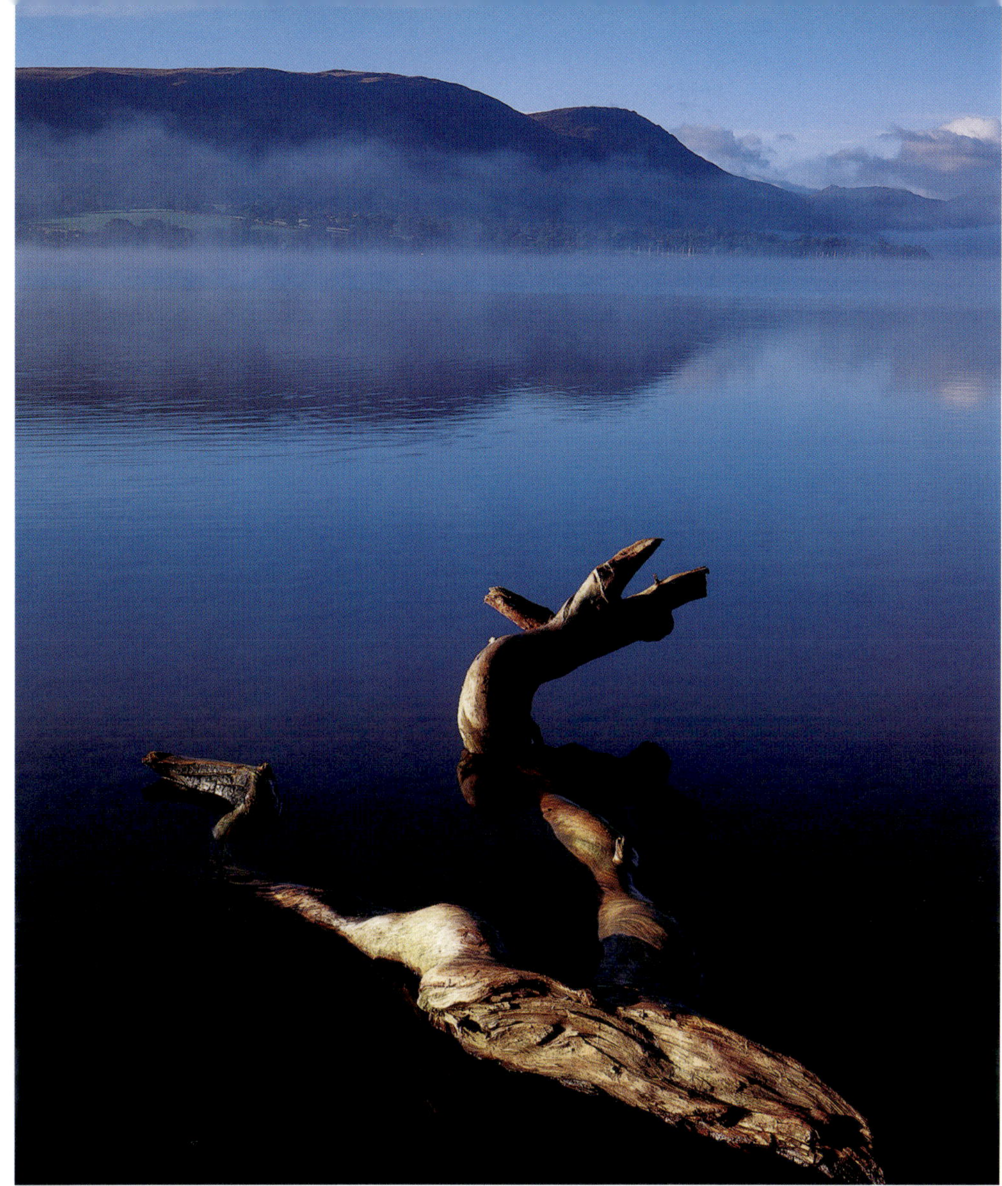

Driftwood in Ullswater

On the lake shore at Ullswater I found this wonderful-looking piece of driftwood, its yellow tones contrasting with the blue reflected sky in the water.

Ebony 45s with 90mm lens, Velvia 50, 1/2sec at f/32, Coral No. 1 and 0.3 ND soft-grad filters

The best way to improve your composition is to think about it more. Just pointing your camera at an attractive scene is not enough to take an attractive photo. You need to be aware of every element in the picture – even those that seem insignificant in the real world can dominate a photograph.

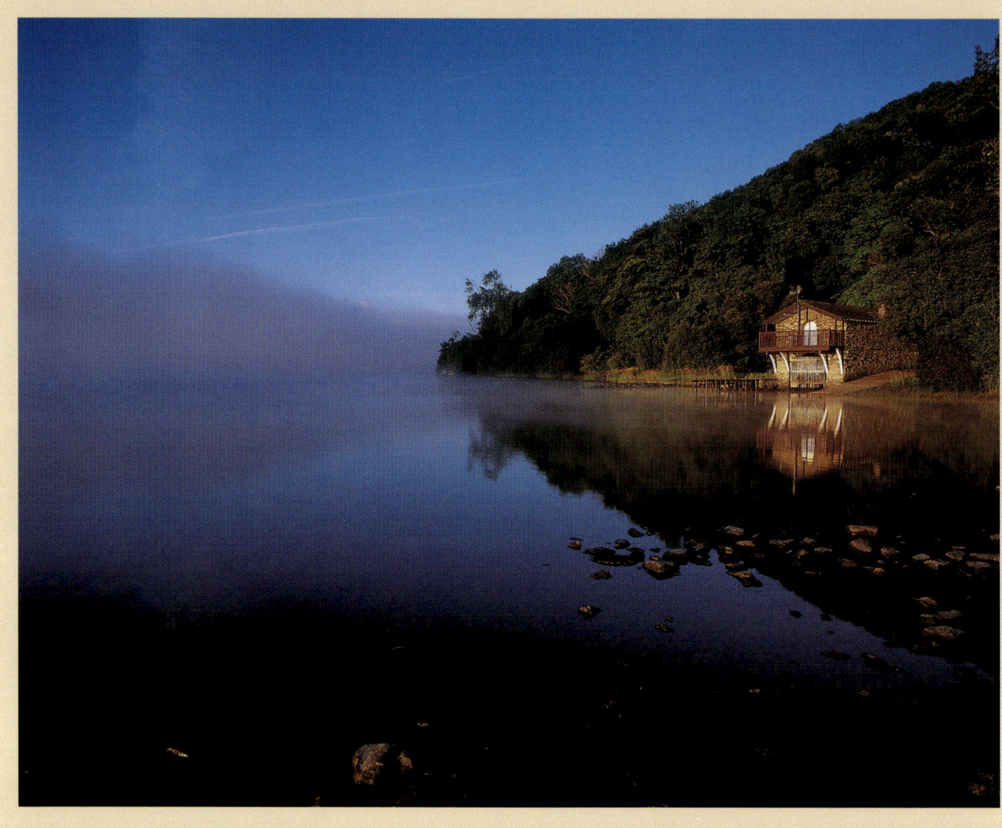

1 KEEP IT SIMPLE

Try not to include too many elements in one image: less is more. If there are several things you want to include and the viewfinder starts to look busy or crowded then it may be time to be more selective. Choose two or three elements at most and find a photograph using just these. You can juxtapose elements that contrast with each other: light with shade, warm colours with cool ones, the softness of water with hard rock. The juxtaposition of elements can produce harmony or tension in a scene. It all depends on how you see it. Ultimately, composition is the art of transferring how you see the world onto film.

2 TAKE A GOOD LOOK

The trick to all compositions is to really look around the viewfinder. Take care to see into the corners of the picture and all the way around the edge of the frame. If you can see with your mind's eye how the finished picture will look before you take it, then you have mastered this part of the art.

above **Boathouse on Ullswater**
In my opinion this photograph would have been far better had there not been aeroplane trails in the sky. This distracting element is something I tend to avoid.

Ebony 45s with 90mm lens, Velvia 50, 1 second at f/32, Coral No.1 and 0.3 ND soft-grad filters

3 **FIND THE RIGHT BALANCE**
There is no reason why you should not have large, seemingly empty areas in your picture. If your subject is a still lake in the early morning or late evening, for example, then a great area of 'nothing' may be just what you are photographing. What might make this more interesting would be colour and texture, or perhaps the juxtaposition of another subject to show how small it looks in the context of such a vast space.

4 **FILL THE FRAME**
Ask yourself, 'What is it I am taking a picture of and why?', and 'How much of my viewfinder is filled with the subject?' The answer to the second question should be 100%. A 'failed' picture is most often caused by the 'subject' making up just a fraction of the overall picture. In short, the photographer was too far away from the subject and did not fill the frame.

right and below **Angel Glacier, Canada**
Adding people to your pictures is a good way of creating foreground interest and adding a sense of scale to the landscape.

Pentax 67 with 45mm lens, 1/2sec at f/22, polarizer

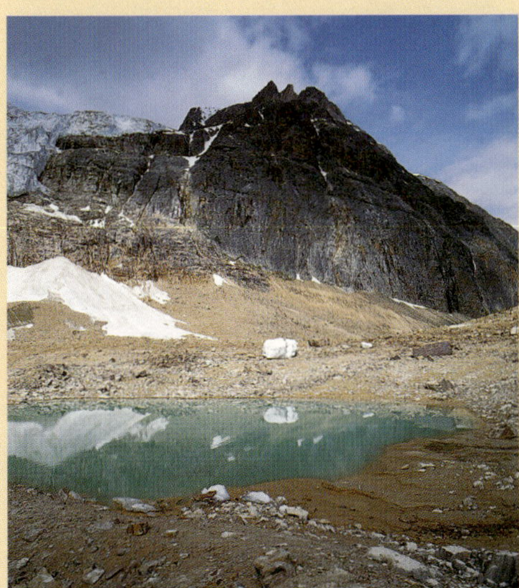

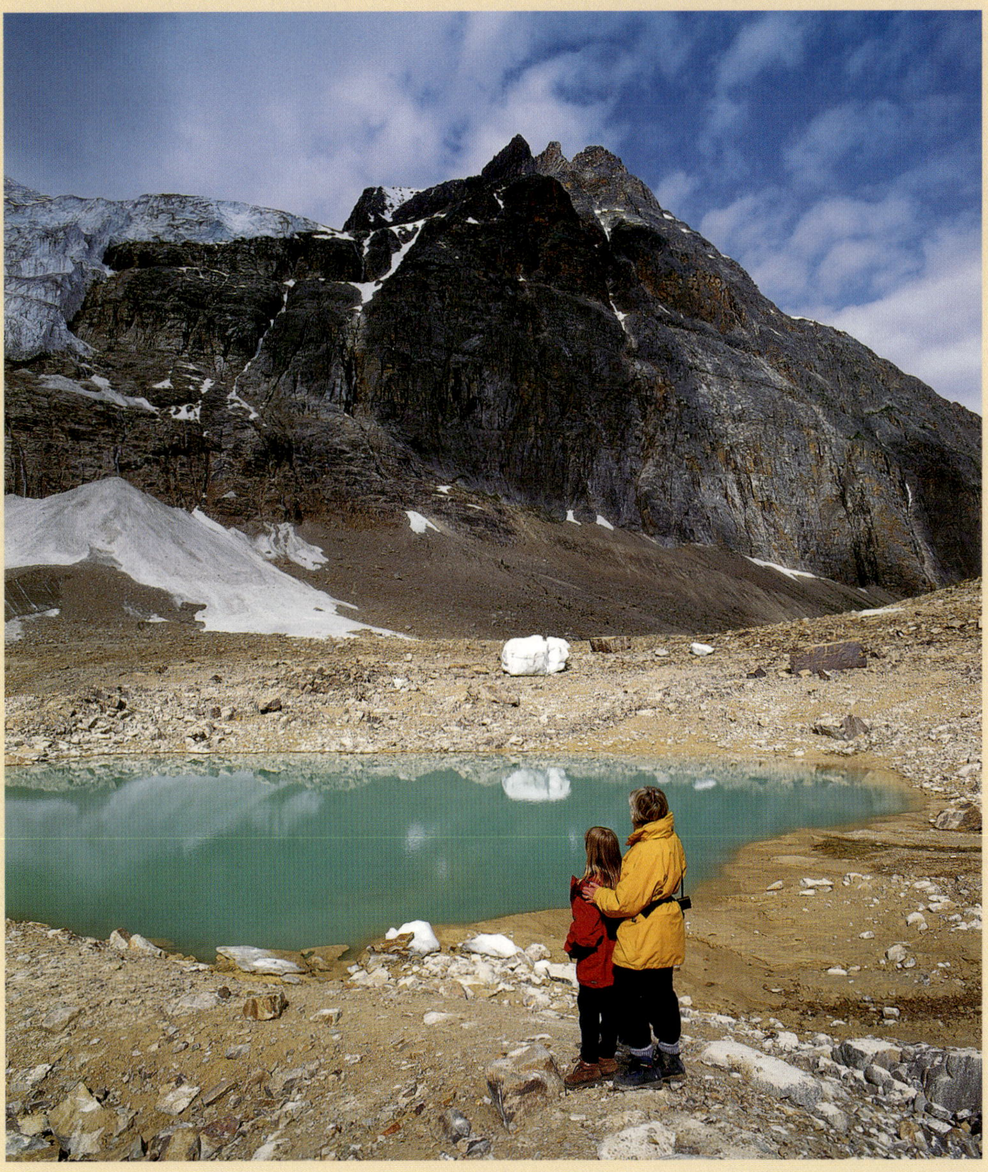

Edges Imposing Order

Whenever water is included in a photograph it forms part of and sometimes all of the composition. It can form the foreground, the background or the middle-distance. It can form lines to lead the viewer into the picture. Water also creates edges within a scene: lake shores, river banks and the coastline, for instance. This is an aid to the photographer trying to capture an image from the chaos of the landscape as a whole. When composing a picture we are trying to create order, we are trying to draw attention to those things in the scene that we found attractive. Edges define shapes and shapes are the primary content of most pictures. Textures and colours fill those shapes defined by any edges in the scene, or by the frame itself if there is no other edge in the composition.

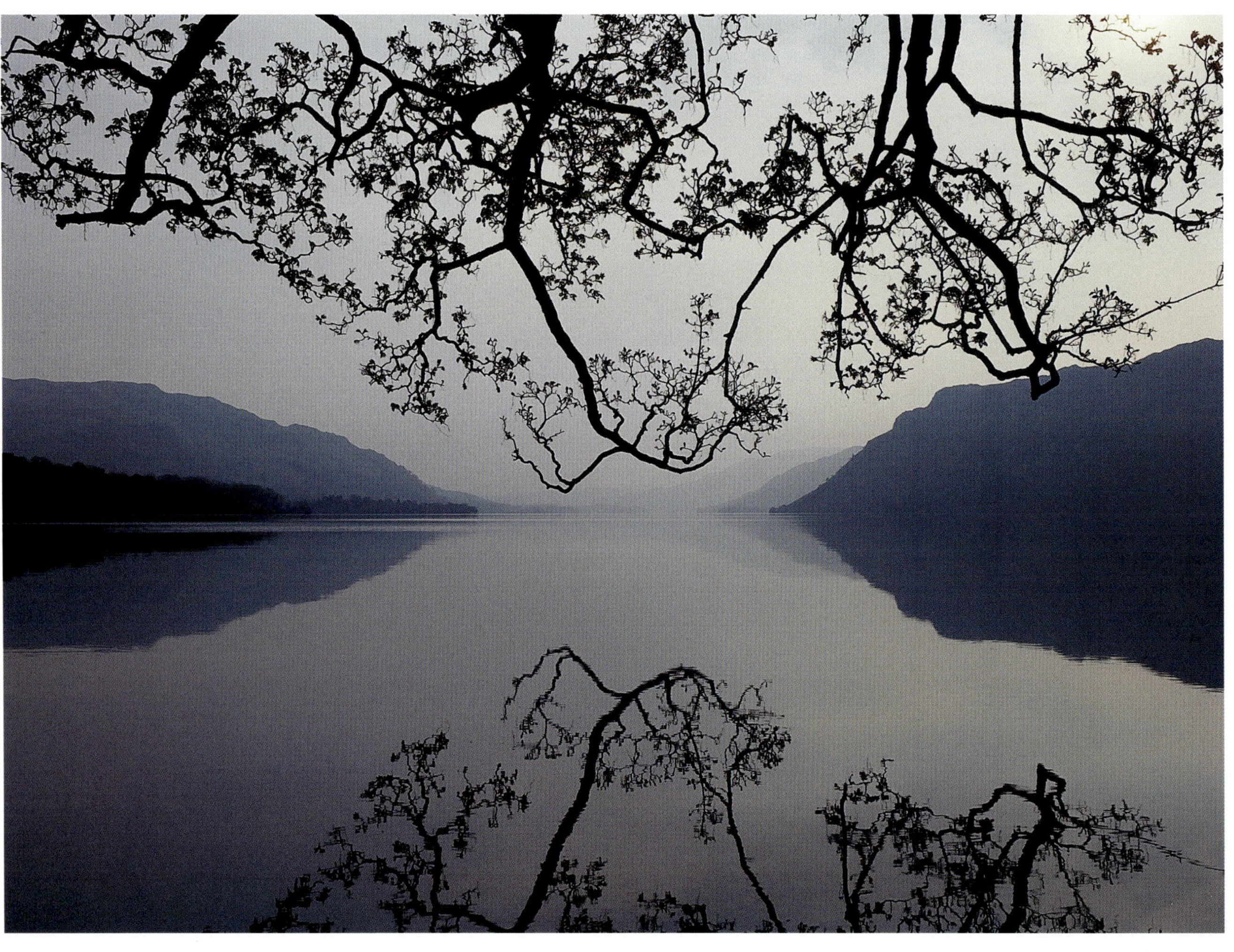

Morning Reflections, Ullswater

An empty sky is not very interesting for the landscape photographer. Most of the time when the sky is clear blue or, as here, clear pale grey, the answer is to avoid the sky and fill the frame with the land. The overhanging branches of this tree gave me another option. By getting down very low with the camera to include the branches and their reflection I was able to fill the frame with this gentle monochrome image.

Mamiya Pro SV 645 with 55–110mm lens at 55mm, Velvia 50, 1/8sec at f/22

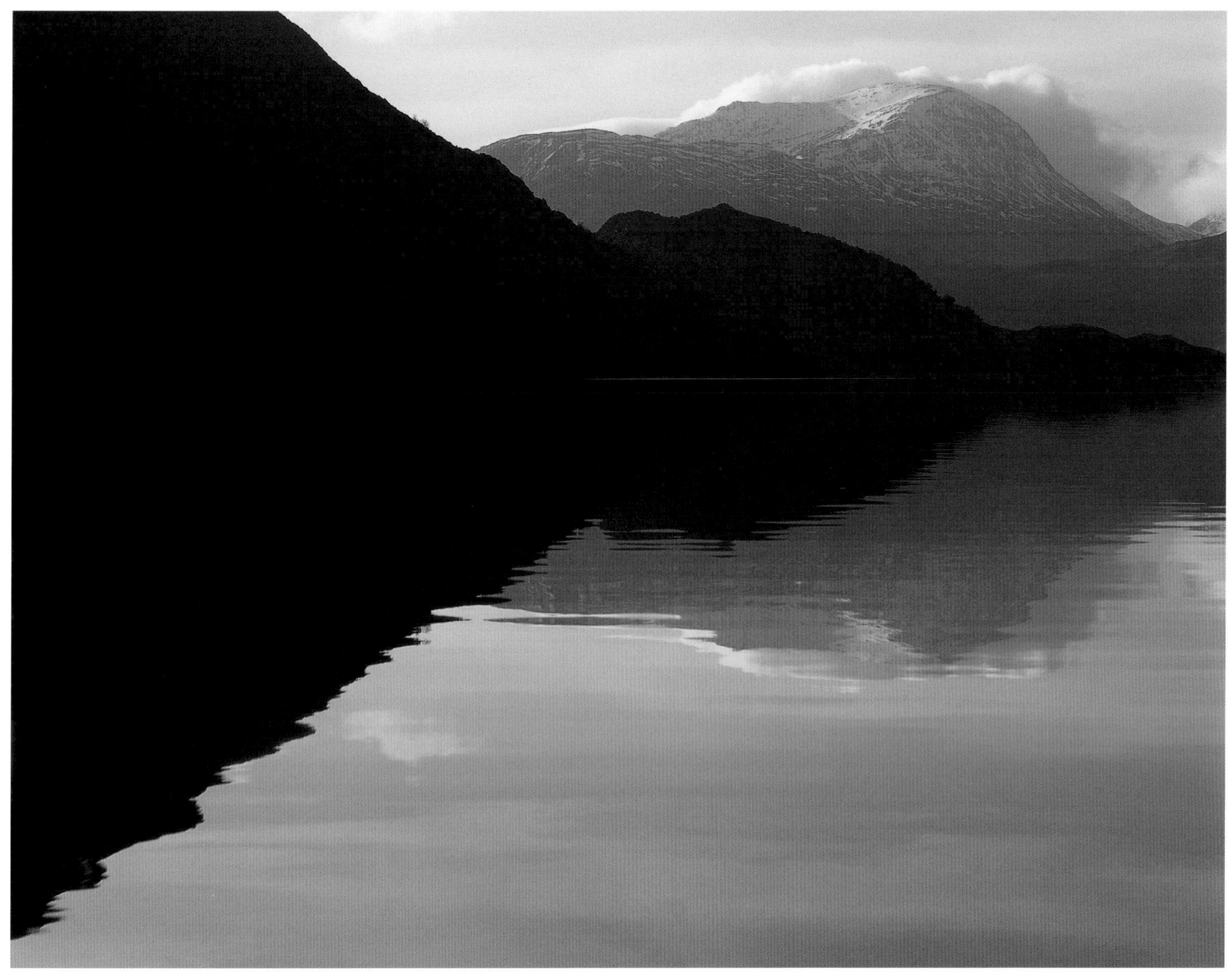

Graphic Monochrome, Ullswater

This picture relies entirely upon the shapes within it for its impact. A strong diagonal line leads the eye into the scene from top and bottom forming a near V-shape. Colour and texture are kept to a minimum. Silhouettes are the ultimate example of a composition made by shapes and edges.

Mamiya RB67 with 180mm lens, Velvia 50, 1/30sec at f/16

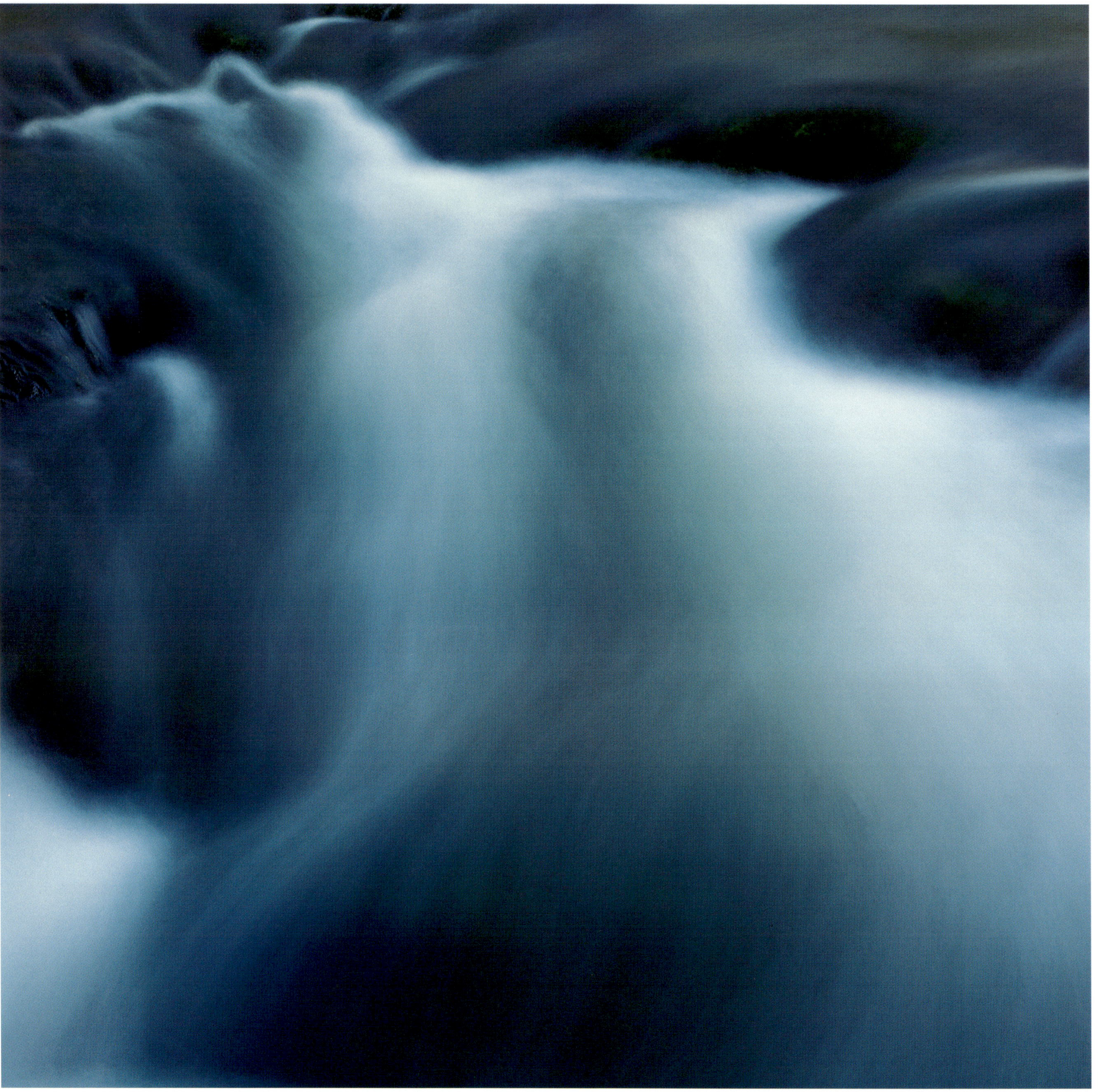

Pushing the Boundaries

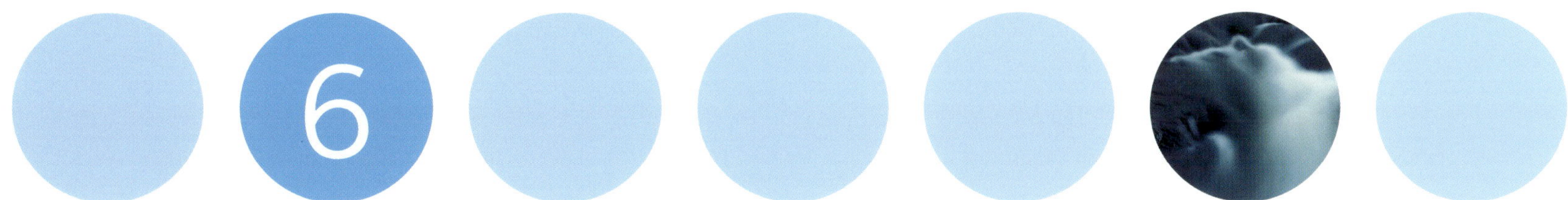

A great deal of landscape photography is about bringing order to the chaos of nature. However, by focusing on the chaotic elements it is possible to capture some very exciting, often abstract, images that are still aesthetically pleasing.

Photography is a fairly recent development, and yet it seems that in less than 120 years the whole world has been photographed. Some of the best-known views, those places where the world is laid out in an appealing composition, have been photographed so often that if photography could erode a place they would be worn away to nothing already. The expression 'there is nothing new under the sun' could have been invented for landscape photography. Yet we all crave artistic originality and seek to create photographs that are uniquely ours. Compositional style and a discerning eye for the right quality of light can make our work recognizable, but that is not the same as unique.

In the search for artistic originality, creative photographic techniques have been developed. Some of these techniques are gentle, some are more aggressive and attention-grabbing. Some have lasted, others are now eschewed in favour of a more natural approach. The ones that do work are soon adopted and reused so often that after a while they become standard practice. Panoramic photography, defocusing the camera or introducing movement blur by deliberately moving the camera during exposure – all of these recent innovations are now well-known techniques. They are special effects and, as such, they should remain special; overuse would defeat the object.

In an effort, then, to create something different without the need to place technique ahead of content, many photographers have moved away from the grand vista to concentrate on scenes of a smaller scale. Photographs that rely for their content on pattern and texture and light, and on a seeing eye to find these things, will never be as commonplace as the more ordinary photographs of a well-known landmark. While pictures of a swirl of water in a river have been taken before, there is a reasonable chance the specific swirl you have framed has not. The well-known vistas are gazed upon and photographed by all who pass that way; a pattern formed in the swirl of a river will be passed by most people without a second glance.

Finding a New Approach

Whenever I visit a place for the first time I will explore it. There is tremendous satisfaction to be derived from the discovery of a new view, one that I have never seen before, either in real life or as a photograph. For a very short time I can pretend I have discovered something new, taking a photograph as a pioneer. If the view is really good it is never long until I find another version of the same picture by another photographer. Shortly thereafter I will discover that there are hundreds of photographs of the same scene published already. But I keep trying.

Romantic Reflections

Location:
West Wycombe Park,
Buckinghamshire,
United Kingdom

Time of year:
August

Camera:
Nikon FM2

Lens:
75–300mm zoom

Film:
Velvia 50

West Wycombe Park is described as having a 'perfectly preserved rococo landscape garden'. The garden was created in the mid-eighteenth century by Sir Francis Dashwood, founder of the Dilettanti Society and the Hellfire Club.

When I went into West Wycombe Park on a dull and overcast day, I was not expecting to take any photographs. My purpose was to plan another visit on a better day, to get to know the best viewpoints in the garden and, by using a compass, determine where the sun would rise and set throughout the year. However, the reflected light in the water lifted the scene before me.

Using minimal depth of field, so that foreground grasses and plants blurred, and by focusing on the reflection, the picture took on a romantic feel that was in keeping with the whole atmosphere of the park. It is an unusual and abstract representation of the place, yet still recognizable. The picture has a painterly feel about it, and I love photographs that look a little like they might have been painted; photography can be too real and harsh at times.

Had I photographed the building itself rather than its reflection it would have been a very straightforward photograph of a building in dull light. Water has acted here as a second light and, in conjunction with the composition, texture, pattern and colour, a good photograph has been made in poor conditions.

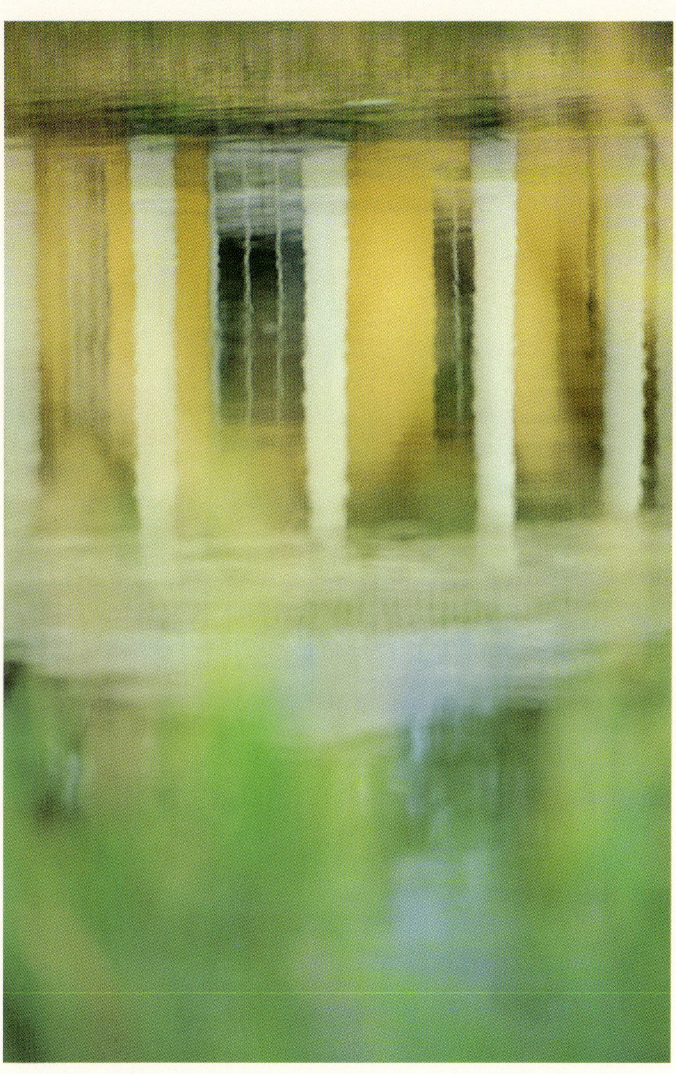

Nikon FM2 with 75–300mm lens, Velvia 50, 1/30sec at f/4.5

Because there are so many landscape images around, if you want your work to be noticed it has to offer something extra. If you want your pictures to linger in the memory of those who have seen them, you need to record more than the contours of a place.

While it is easy to record a scene that will show people what a place looks like, it is far harder to show in a photograph what a place feels like. I remember looking at a fairly competent portrait photograph once and someone described it as a road map of the face. This picture, he said, tells me nothing about the sitter, nothing of his character or personality, you may as well have been photographing a bunch of grapes as a human being. I could see what he meant, and you can get the same effect unless you are careful with a landscape. What you need to do is take your time. Linger at each place you choose to photograph and really get to know it. I have found that it is better to take one good photograph each day than to move quickly from place to place in search of the next image.

I have heard it said that the photographer John Blakemore liked to meditate before taking a picture. When I arrived at this spot on the banks of the River Brathay I very quickly captured the view of Skelwith Bridge. Then I slowed down. I sat still and let my mind wander around the scene for a while. I don't know if you would call that meditation but it did bring me to the realisation that it was not the whole scene that held fascination for me.

On a different day, while out taking photographs for this book, I was following the course of a stream, looking for new shots of flowing water. A few yards ahead of me was a family with a very young child. She too was walking along the centre of the stream in a pair of wellies, stopping and looking at every thing that caught her eye. I realised I was doing exactly the same as this child of no more than two years. Perhaps this is one of the great gifts of photography, it allows you to see the world with the wonder of a child's eyes.

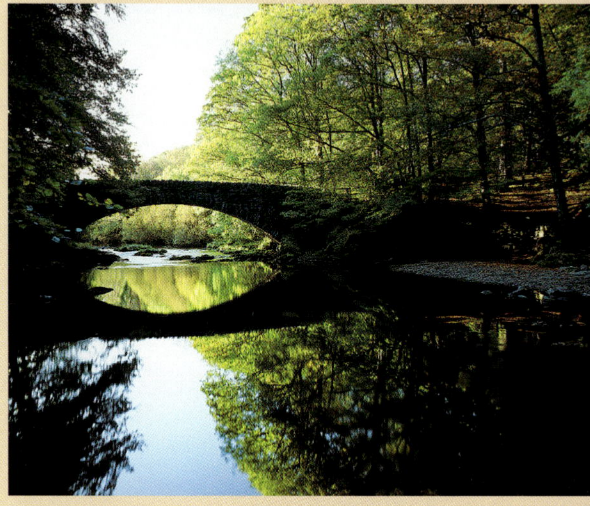

above **Skelwith Bridge, Cumbria**
I initially thought I had caught the mood of this location when I took the picture of this bridge but was not entirely happy.

Ebony 45s with 90mm lens, Velvia 50, 1 second at f/22, 0.9 ND soft-grad and Coral No. 1 filters

facing page **Trees in Watercolour**
Adding a short telephoto lens, I reframed on an area of colourful reflection on the river. I wanted the picture to have an abstract feel, but to contain enough information so that the viewer would still know what it was. This is not a picture of a place. It is not a road map. It is a picture that expresses what it felt like to be there at that time.
Pentax 67 with 135mm lens, Velvia 50, 1 second at f/11 (deliberate overexposure to add to the abstract feel)

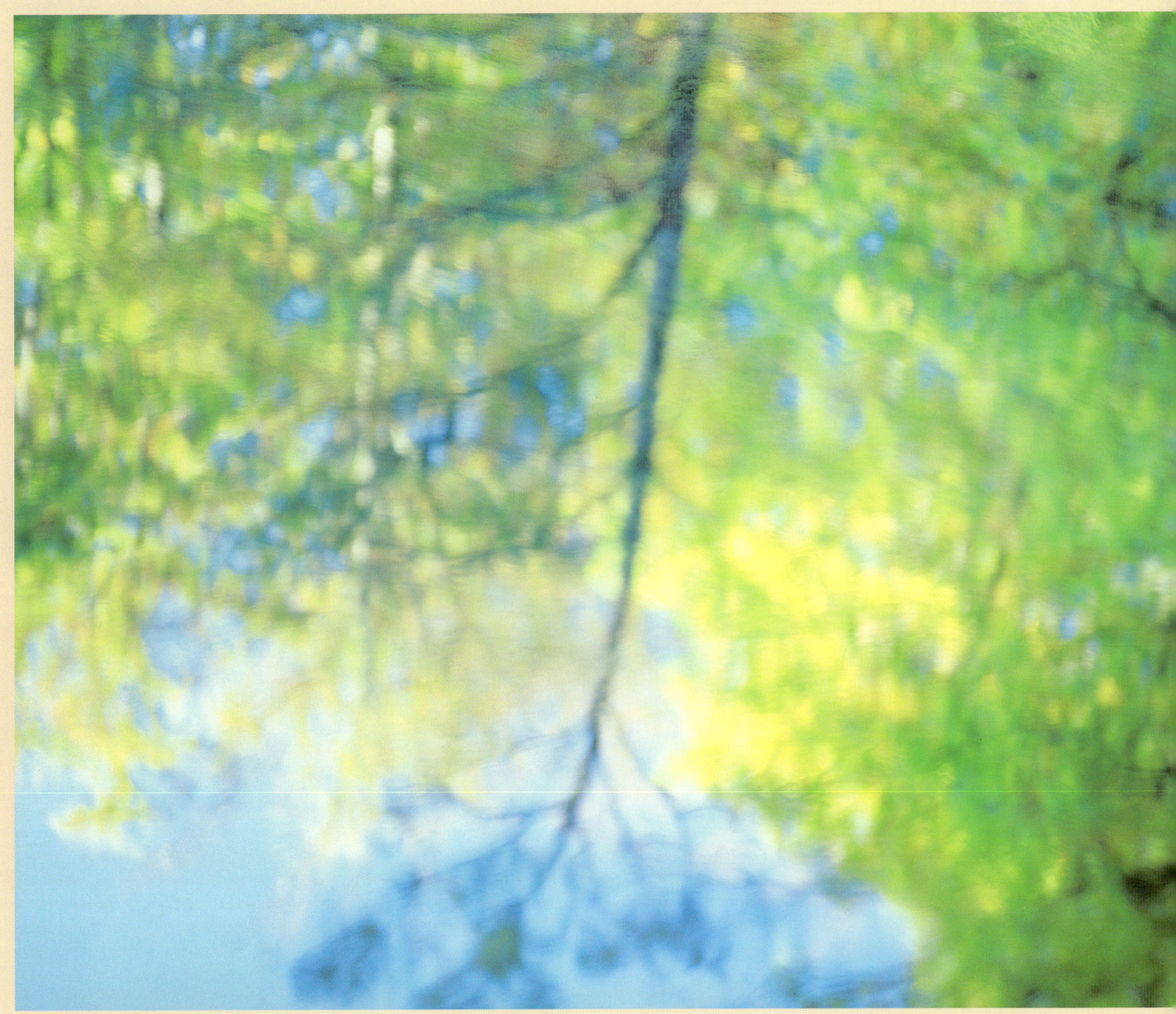

Details and Abstracts

Water is a great subject for detail studies. With movement and reflections you can capture something quite abstract and beautiful. Through careful framing and the use of photographic techniques you can also create harmony out of chaos and beauty from the seemingly mundane. The highest goal of any landscape photographer is surely to produce an image that will cause people to stop and stare in wonder from a scene that they would have passed by without noticing. In the end, the ability to see that which others missed is the highest qualification for any photographer. By comparison, learning to simply record what you see is much easier.

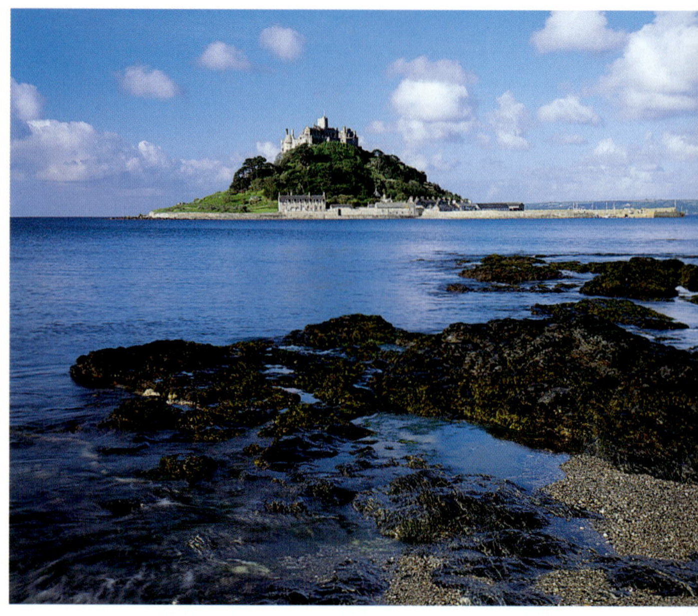

right **St Michael's Mount, Cornwall**
This picture will do for a postcard, calendar or an illustration in a travel guide, but it is not a photograph to excite a photographer; nor is it something I might want to print and hang on the wall with pride.

Ebony 45s with 150mm, Velvia 50, 1/4sec at f/22, polarizing filter

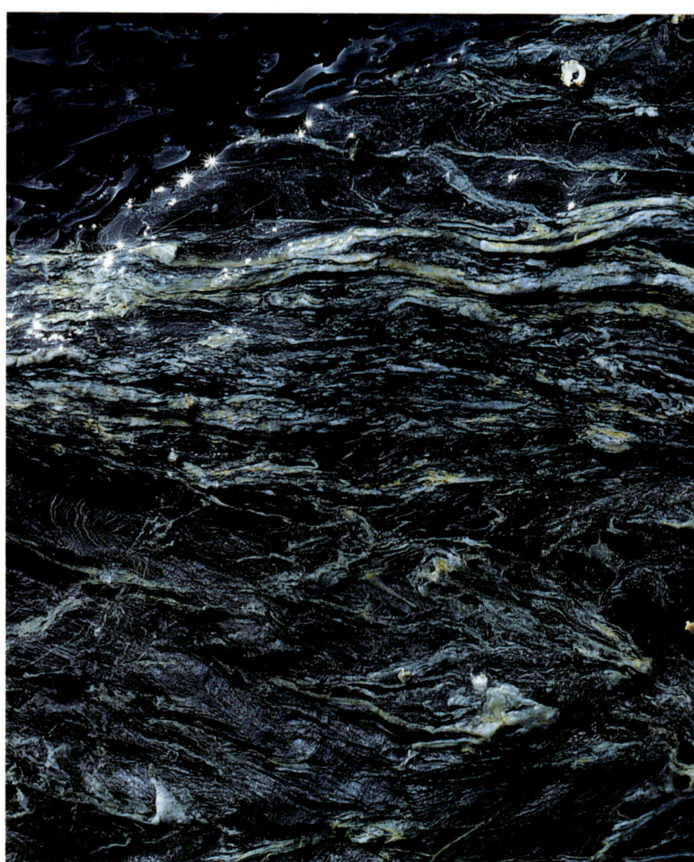

equipment — LENSES FOR DETAILS AND PATTERNS

It might seem obvious that for close details of patterns and reflections in water a long lens will be needed. Certainly, long lenses can be useful for these types of photograph but they are not essential all of the time. Consider all the possibilities, look at all the angles and use whichever lens best captures the detail you are trying to record.
It may well be preferable to move in close with a wideangle lens. There are details and patterns within rivers or lakes that are large enough to fill the frame even with a wideangle lens. The important thing when out in the field is to be open to the possibility. Do not fall into the trap of thinking 'I am after a vista so I need to use a wideangle lens', or 'I am looking for a detail within the scene so I need a telephoto lens'. Keep all options open all of the time.

below **Abstract Wet Rock, St Michael's Mount**

St Michael's Mount is a well-photographed landmark, and I had hoped while staying in the area to catch a really good image of the site. The difficulty was the conditions. When I first arrived at this spot, the tide was high and the area was under water. In addition to this, the sky seemed to be full of aeroplane trails, and so the best early morning light did not yield the picture I was looking for. As the light became ordinary, the sky cleared of trails and the tide fell. As the tide fell it revealed this marbled, near-black rock, looking for all the world like a Jackson Pollock painting, and I knew right away I had my exciting image to capture. The key to the picture's success is the thin film of water over the rock. When dry, the contrast between the light streaks and the darker rock is much less, and what looks black here is a dusty grey.

Ebony 45s with 150mm lens, 6x12 rollfilm back, Velvia 50, 1/15sec at f/22

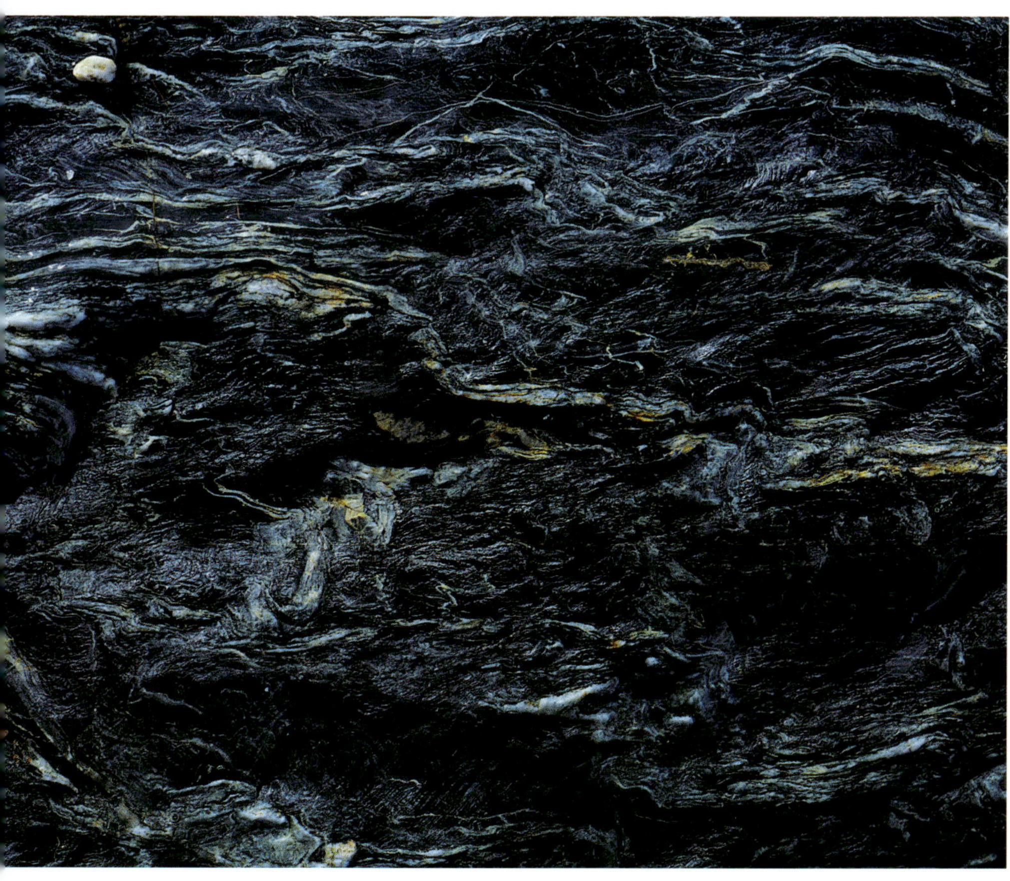

Find Suitable Subjects

I would advise you not to look too hard for these detail pictures. In my experience, they appear to you more readily while you are out looking for other things than when you go off in search of them specifically. Be aware of all your surroundings when you are out hunting for new scenes.

Take a Second Look

Take a little more time to study carefully where you are before continuing your search elsewhere. Just because something is spoiling your view of the distant hills does not mean that there is not a great image right there at your feet. Never assume you have finished with a location just because you have taken some pictures. In any spot where there is a good view there are often two or three more very close by. It really helps to slow the whole picture-taking process down and look carefully at your surroundings with a photographer's eye. I have sometimes spent an hour or two by the river bank trying to frame a scene, and only when I am totally satisfied that there is nothing there to photograph do I move on. I do not consider this as time wasted; on the contrary, it is time very well spent, and the times I do find something make it a worthwhile exercise.

Ice, Mist and Snow

Water comes in other forms than just liquid. If you are photographing water as a subject it might be worth seeing just how far you can stretch the theme without breaking it. Frozen water, in the form of ice or snow, for instance, transforms the landscape to stunning effect.

Moors Sunset and Snow near Castleton

Very obviously, this is a snow scene. Had the same amount of water fallen as rain, the scene would be very ordinary indeed and the water would have quickly drained away. Snow and ice are frozen water, and like water in all of its forms they transform the landscape into a magical place.

This picture was taken at the end of a day's photography. While the pink glow in the sky and on the snow appears slightly warm, I have never been so cold in my life. I had to change films out there as well, so my fingers nearly froze. What you cannot see from this photograph is just how hard the wind was blowing. Back at the car I wrapped my fingers around a cup of coffee from the thermos for about ten minutes before setting off for the drive home.

Pentax 67 with 45mm lens, Velvia 50, 1 second at f/22, 0.6 ND grad and Coral No. 1 filters

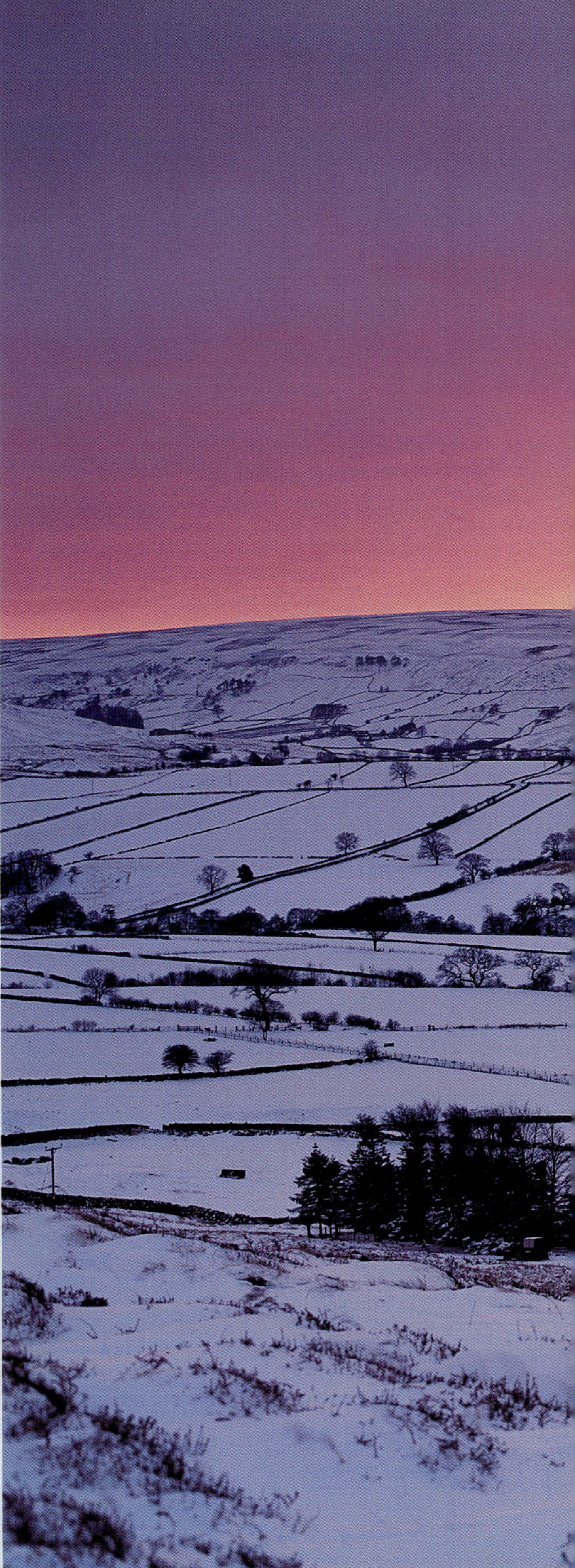

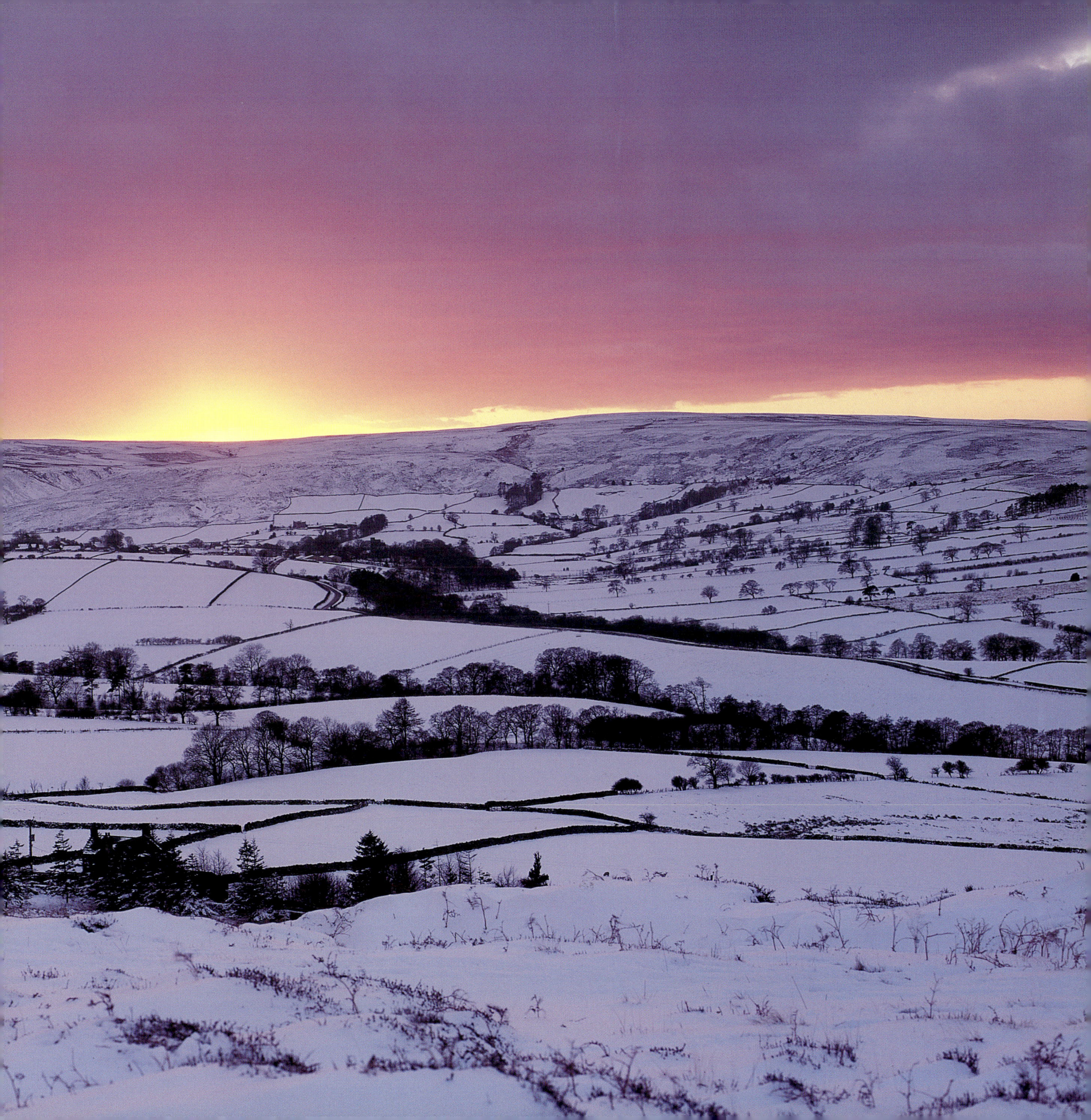

Frozen Stream

I happened upon this shallow stream running into Loch Lubhair in Scotland while I wandered around the shore. Though it was apparent very quickly that the type of photograph I had hoped to take would not be possible, I opted to look around and see if anything else appealed. Landscape photography should be like this, slow and easygoing, no pressure. I took some time considering the best way to capture this stream on film. There were plenty of stretches where the whole stream was frozen and I could fill the frame with ice, but there did not seem to be enough shape there to define an image: the picture needed edges within the frame. This part of the stream, where there is an edge to the ice and free-flowing water on show, gave the scene the structure I wanted. Again, I left the photograph unfiltered and allowed the cold colours of winter to predominate the scene.

Ebony 45s with 150mm lens, 6x12 rollfilm back, 1 second at f/22

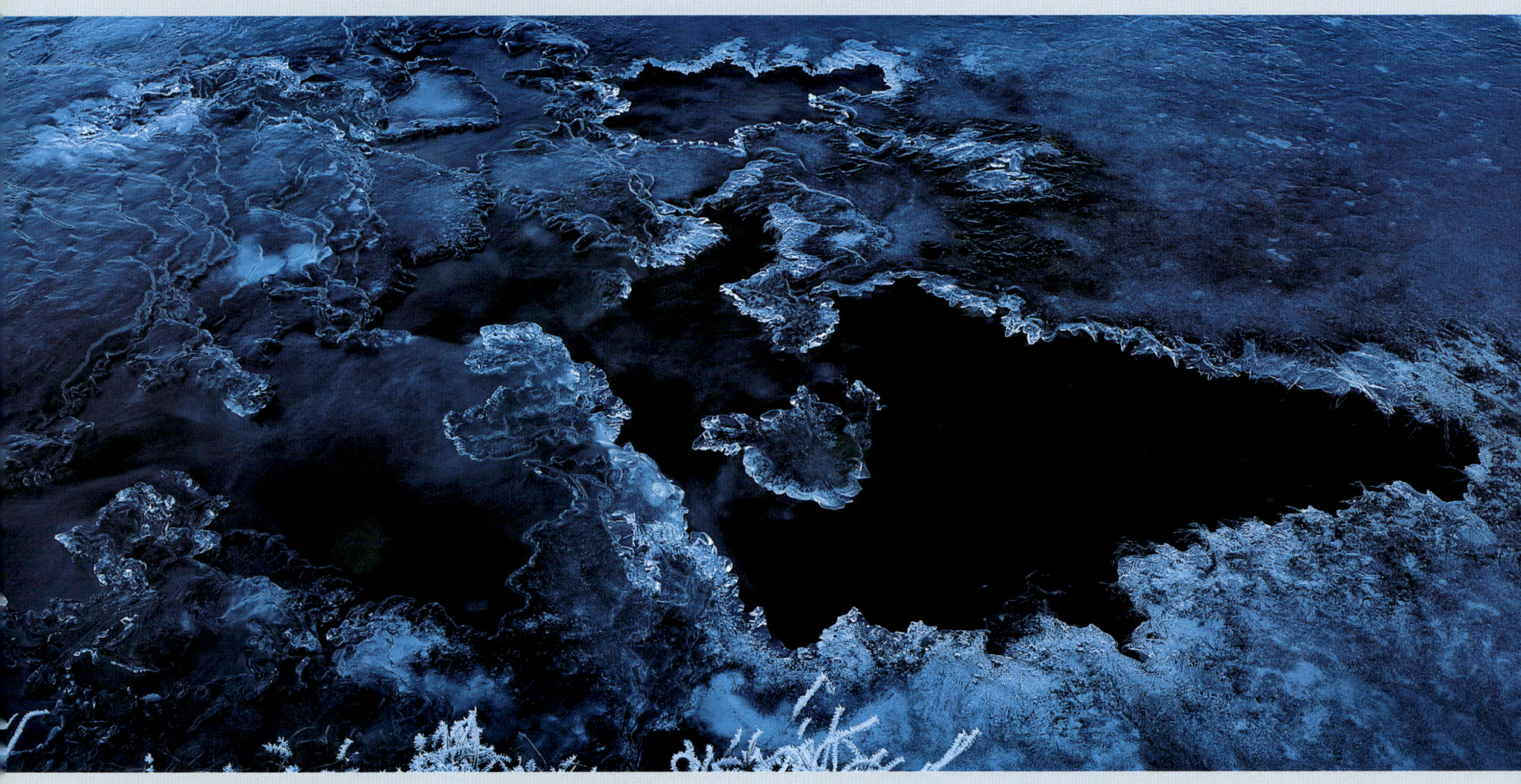

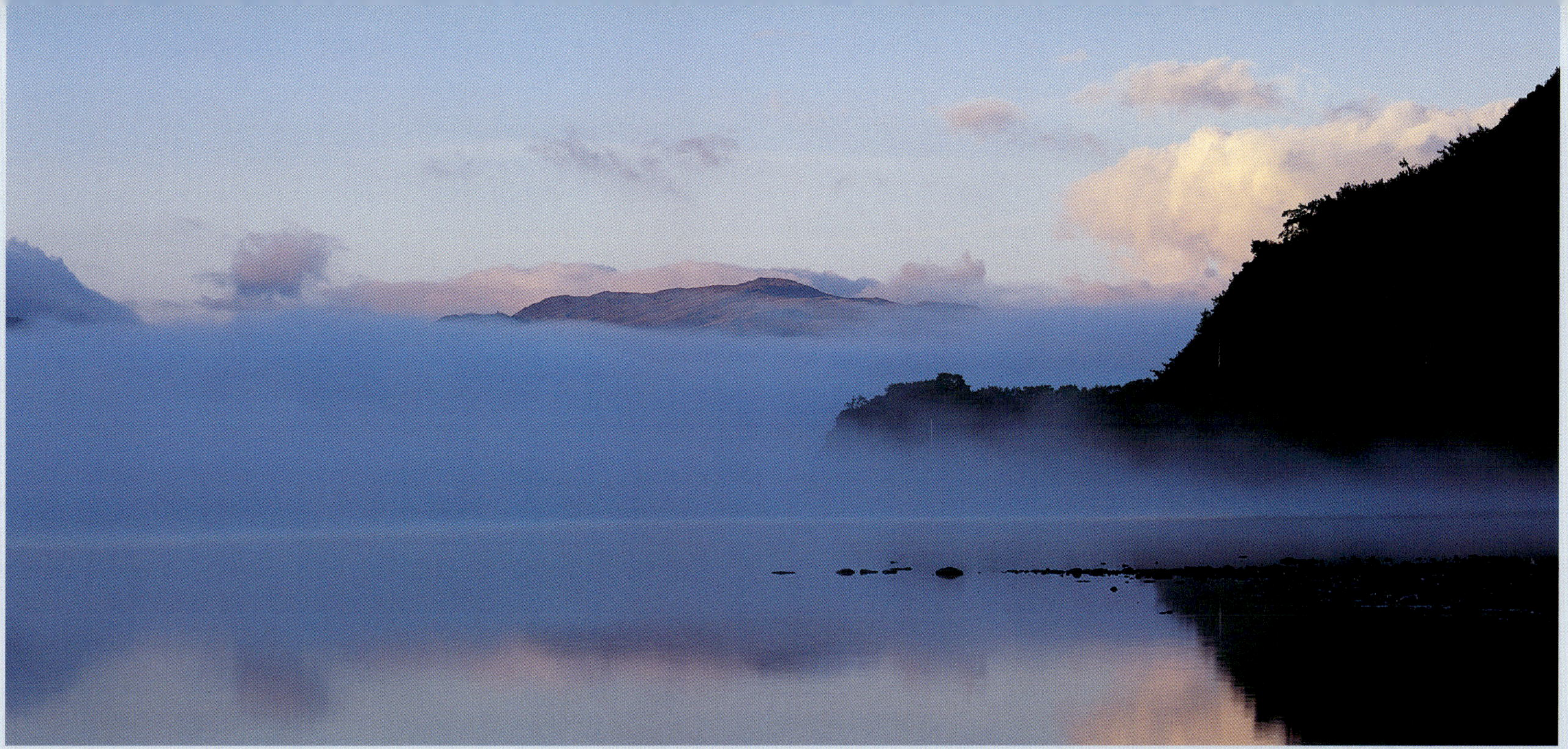

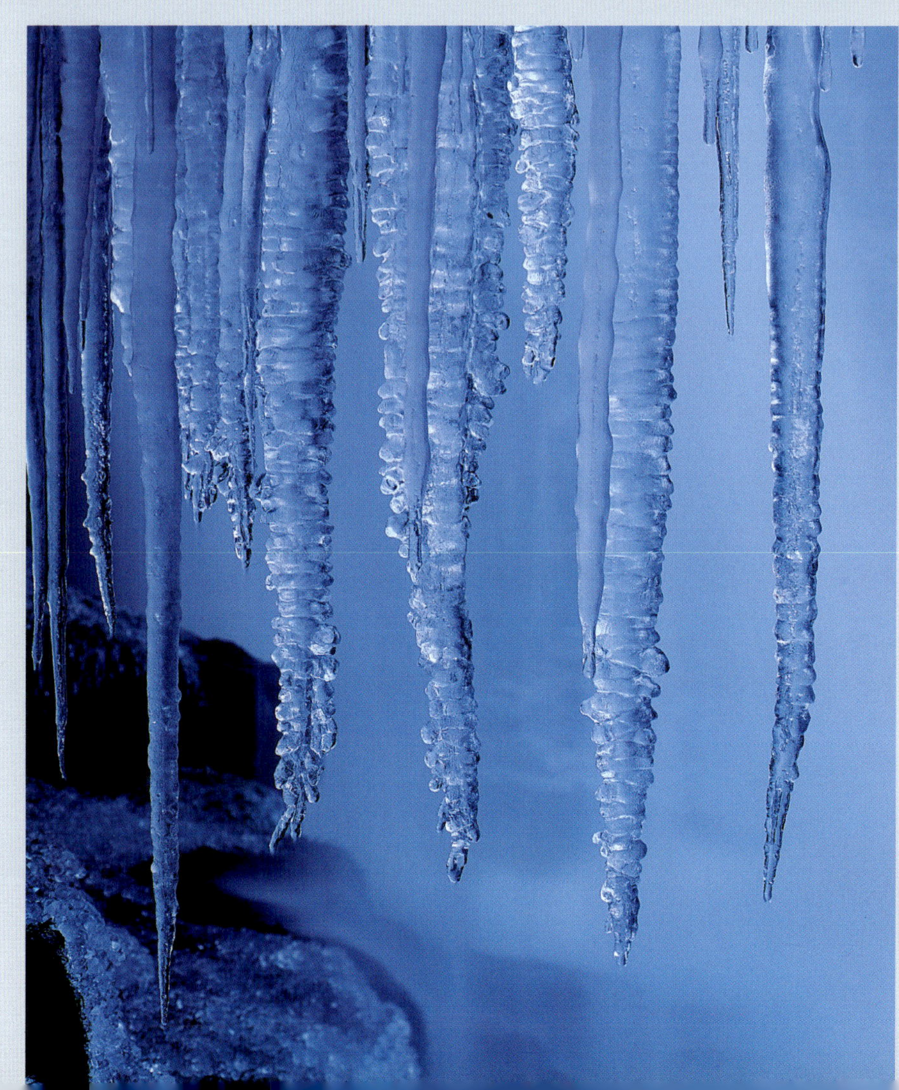

above **Misty Morning, Ullswater**

It is a privilege being a landscape photographer and having a legitimate reason to be up before dawn to see the world looking like this. You need to wait for just the right amount of mist to get the photo to work.

Ebony 45s with 240mm lens, 6x12 rollfilm back, Velvia 50, 1 second at f/22, 0.6 ND grad filter

right **Icicles**

I was delighted to discover these icicles by the side of a waterfall in Yorkshire. I knew right away that if I could resolve all the compositional challenges and find the most appropriate exposure for the delicate details and highlights I would have a very pleasing image.

Ebony 45s with 240mm lens, Velvia 50, 4 seconds at f/22

Morning Mist

Location:
River Brathay,
Lake District

Time of year:
November

Cameras:
Pentax 67 and
Ebony 45s

Lenses:
45mm and 135mm

Film:
Velvia 50

Filter:
0.6 ND soft grad

Photography is fully capable of recording everything in startlingly sharp detail. It can be too literal at times. While the artist with paint and brush can soften nature's sharp edges, the traditional photographer, ever at the mercy of reality, has to wait until nature does that job herself.

On this morning I waited patiently, knowing that if the thick grey mist before me broke there would be a scene of peace and tranquillity. Timing would be everything. The waters of the River Brathay in the Lake District were showing a perfect reflection of any details penetrating the mist. As the sun slowly climbed and began to burn off the mist, I was rewarded for my efforts with this scene – a wonderful moment between impenetrable grey and total clarity.

The wideangle view (below) was the scene I had framed while the mist was thick. As it cleared it seemed more appropriate to change to a longer lens. This picture (right) was composed for balance and harmony. There is nothing in the scene to add tension. The dividing line between image and reflection is almost exactly central again, implying balance. This is a gentle, almost monochrome scene that is very relaxing on the eye.

left Pentax 67 with 45mm lens, 1 second at f/22

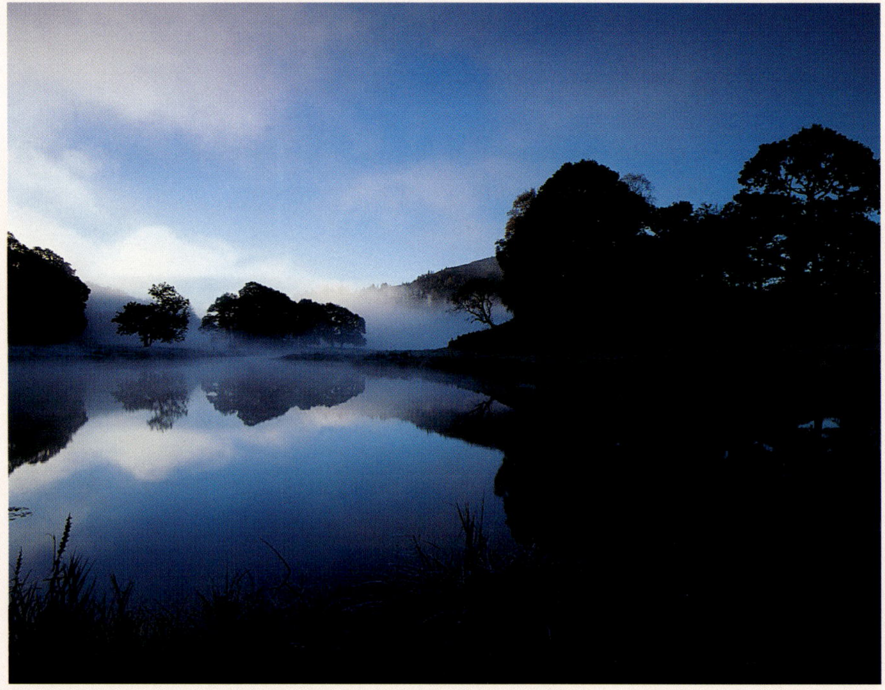

right Pentax 67 with 135mm lens, 1 second at f/22

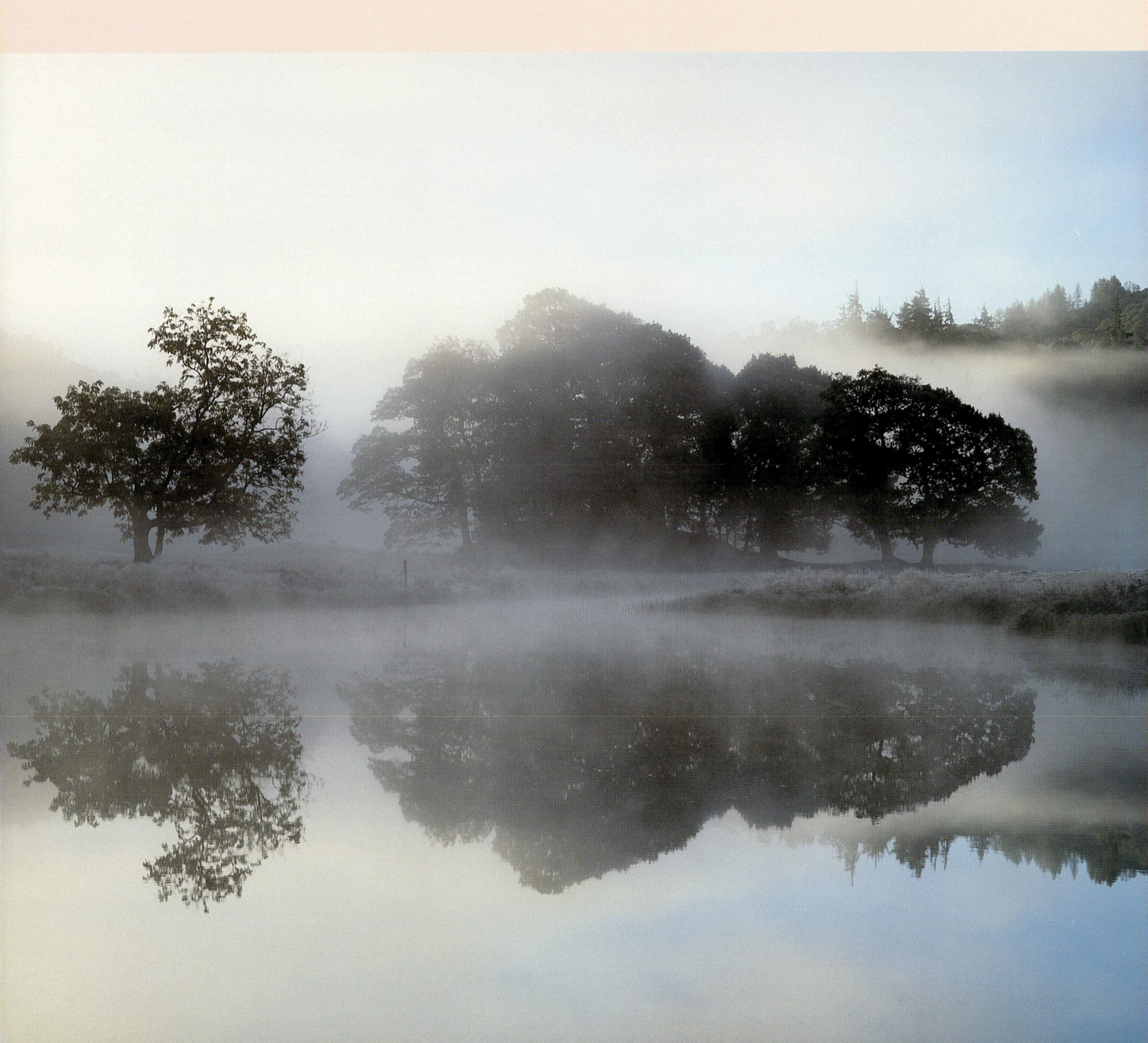

The River Ure begins life as a small stream in Mallerstang in Cumbria and grows as it absorbs other small streams running into it from the valley sides. Glacial deposits have created an open and undulating landscape. Rather than trying to capture the whole scene in a photograph I often get in close and fill the frame.

Though I do not live in the Yorkshire Dales, they are almost on my doorstep and appear in a high percentage of my photographs. Having 'done the dales', captured all the honeypot views in all kinds of weather and at all times of the year, you might think it time to move on and find new locations. The alternative is to look more carefully at the familiar, to seek out those tiny details in the landscape that our eyes dart around and our mind puts together so well to form our impressions of the place as a whole. This is especially relevant if you are not so free to travel the country in search of new pictures whenever you wish.

Having set out early, hoping for some good dawn light and maybe a sunrise, it was soon clear that the conditions were not as I had wished. The location for my early morning shot was not looking as good as when I had last visited. So I decided to walk along the river bank and explore parts of the river I had never seen before. Since the Yorkshire Dales are so familiar, and as I already had a good collection of material, I felt no pressure to produce a new picture if I found nothing that appealed.

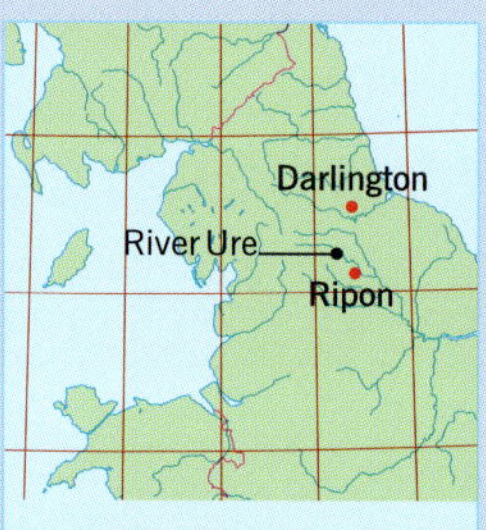

OS Grid Reference:
x= 402100m
y= 488900m

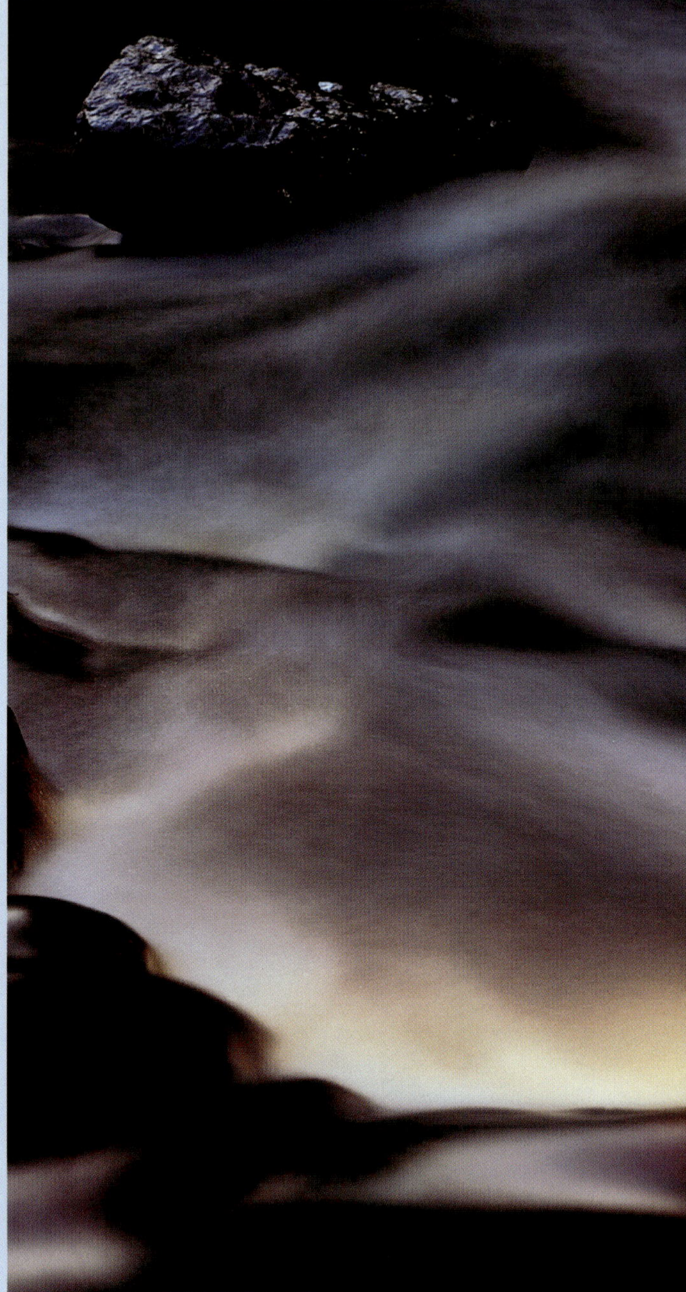

River and Rocks

It is useful when photographing the patterns water forms as it swirls its way along a river to include a few stationary objects, such as rocks, for contrast.

Ebony 45s with 90mm lens, 6x12 rollfilm back, Velvia 50, 4 seconds at f/22, polarizing filter

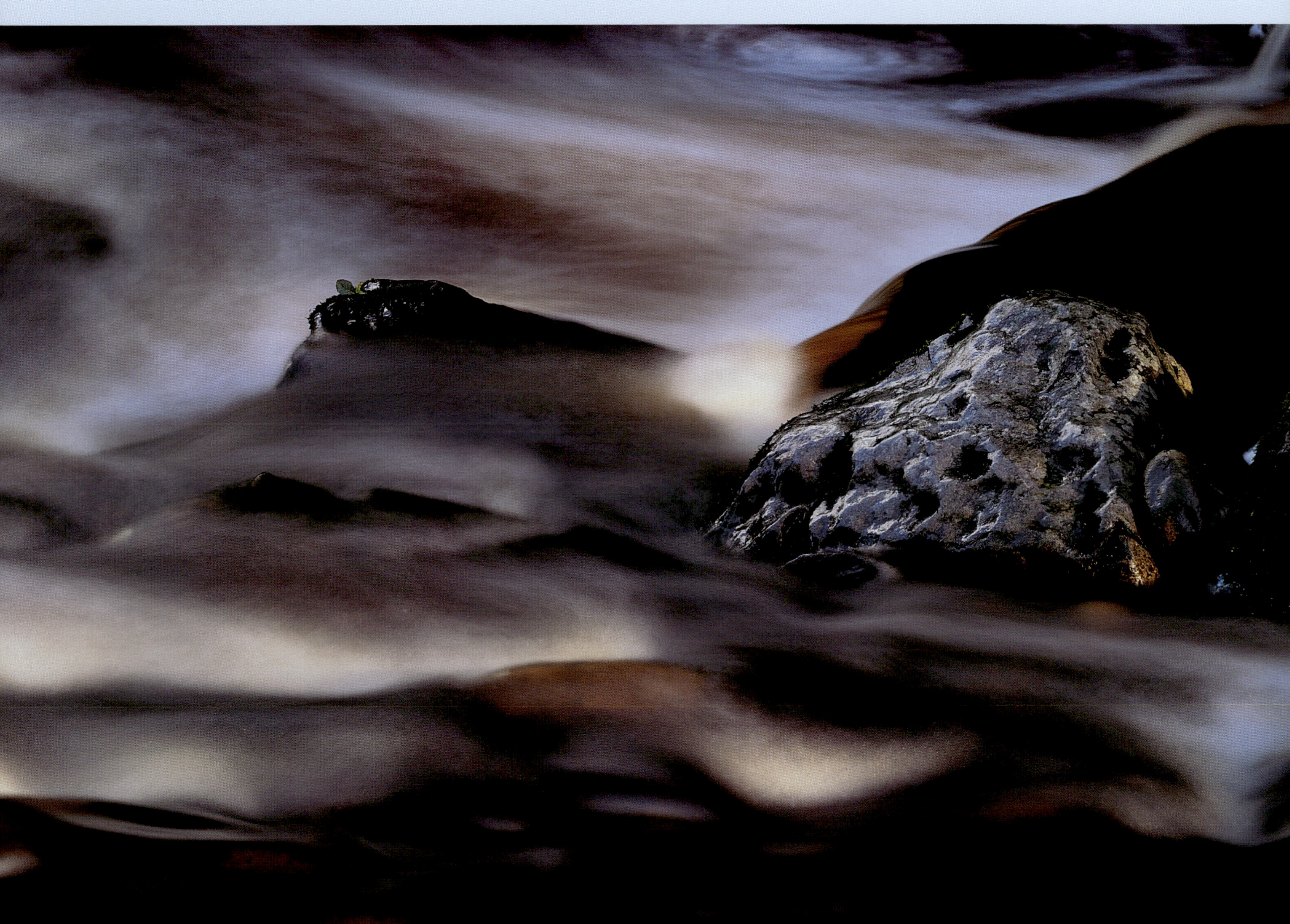

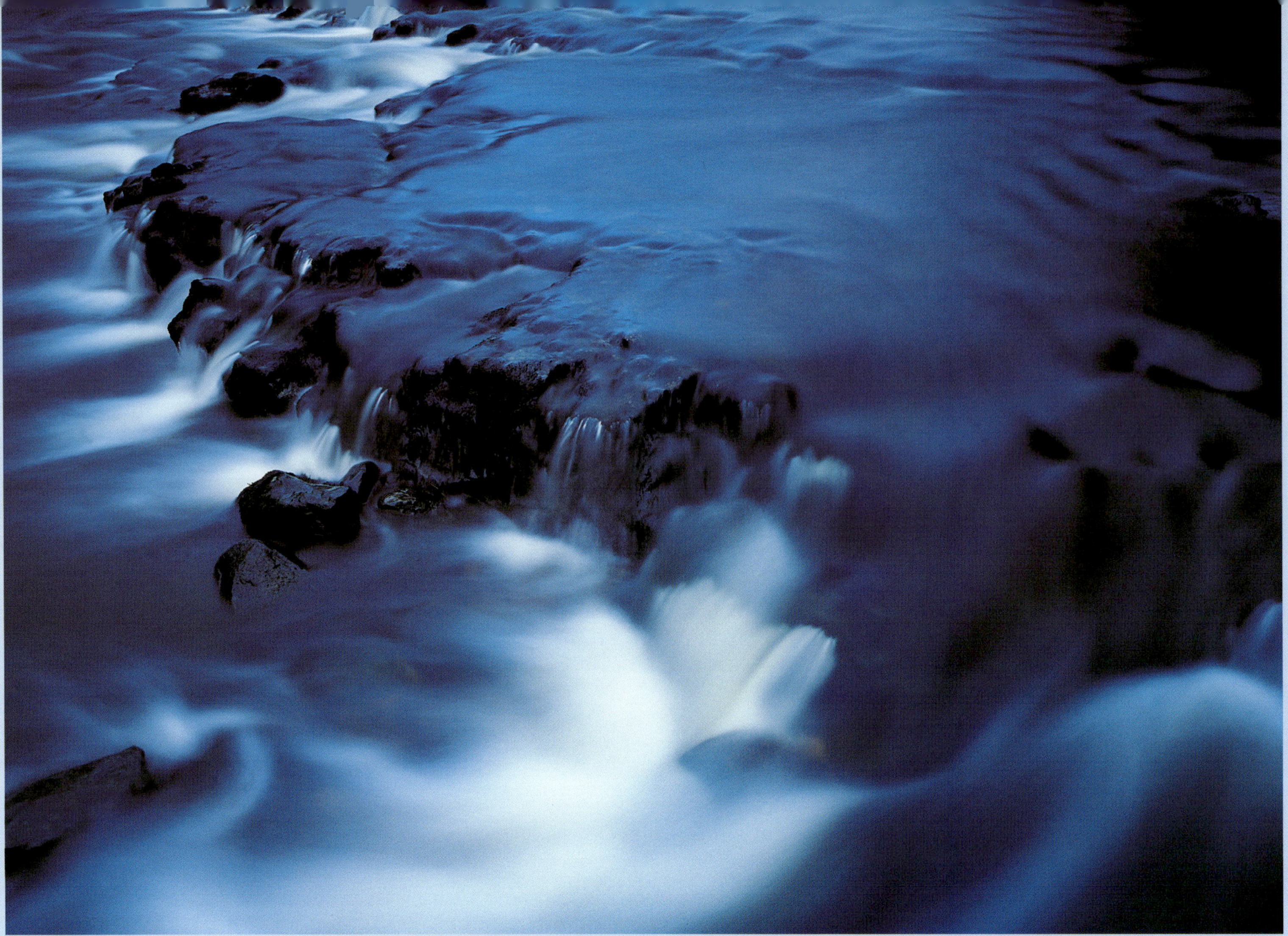

'Rhapsody in Blue'
I used Readyload 54
daylight-balanced film
for this shot and a
neutral-density filter to
emphasize the inky
blue colours.

**Ebony 45s with
90mm lens, Kodak
Readyload 54
E100VS, 8 seconds
at f/22, 0.9 ND filter**

The simple scene for the photograph above caught
my eye right away, but it took a while to find a
way to frame it that would include all the elements
I wanted present. I considered using a much
longer lens for a tighter composition on the area
of the small cascade. I found that the balance of
the cascade and the more gentle undulations on
the surface of the river above told a better story.
Being shaded from direct sunlight and open to the
sky, I knew there would be a strong blue cast in
the final photograph. I did not use any warming
filters to 'correct' this cast as I felt the deep, inky
blue would make a more attractive picture than

the brown colour that the river appeared to my
eyes. To this end as well, I used Kodak Readyload
54 E100VS, a different film than my usual Fuji
Velvia 50. It can be useful to know how different
films will behave in different light.

For this picture to work I had to use a long
shutter speed. At f/22 my lightmeter was telling
me I should use a 1 second exposure. This would
blur the movement but it would not turn the
moving water into the ethereal mist I was aiming
for. A 0.9 (three stops) neutral-density filter meant
I could use an exposure of eight seconds, which
produced the effect I was seeking.

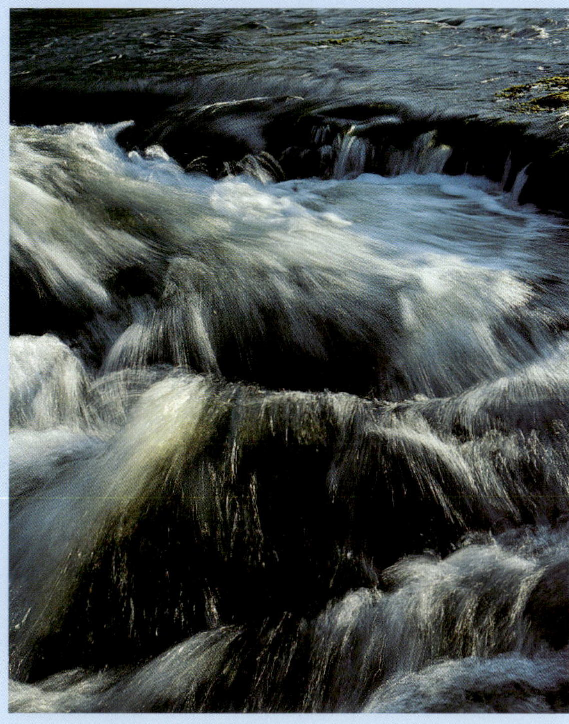

above This picture was taken a few minutes before the one on the right. The sun was out and I wanted to capture the confusion of the water. To record it as it looked to the eye, I used a shutter speed of 1/8sec so that the water was neither frozen nor blurred in an artificial way.

Ebony 45s with 240mm lens, Kodak E100VS, 1/8sec at f/22

right **Pattern in the Flow of the River Ure**

Do you see the bear? It was not visible to the eye while I was taking the picture; it is just one of those happy coincidences. On this occasion I was looking for a stretch of the river with no rocks so that I could fill the frame purely with water. The water level was quite low, so this proved more difficult than I had expected. But that didn't matter to me; I enjoy wandering around the countryside looking for that elusive photograph.

Ebony 45s with 240mm lens, Kodak E100VS, 8 seconds at f/22, 0.9 ND filter

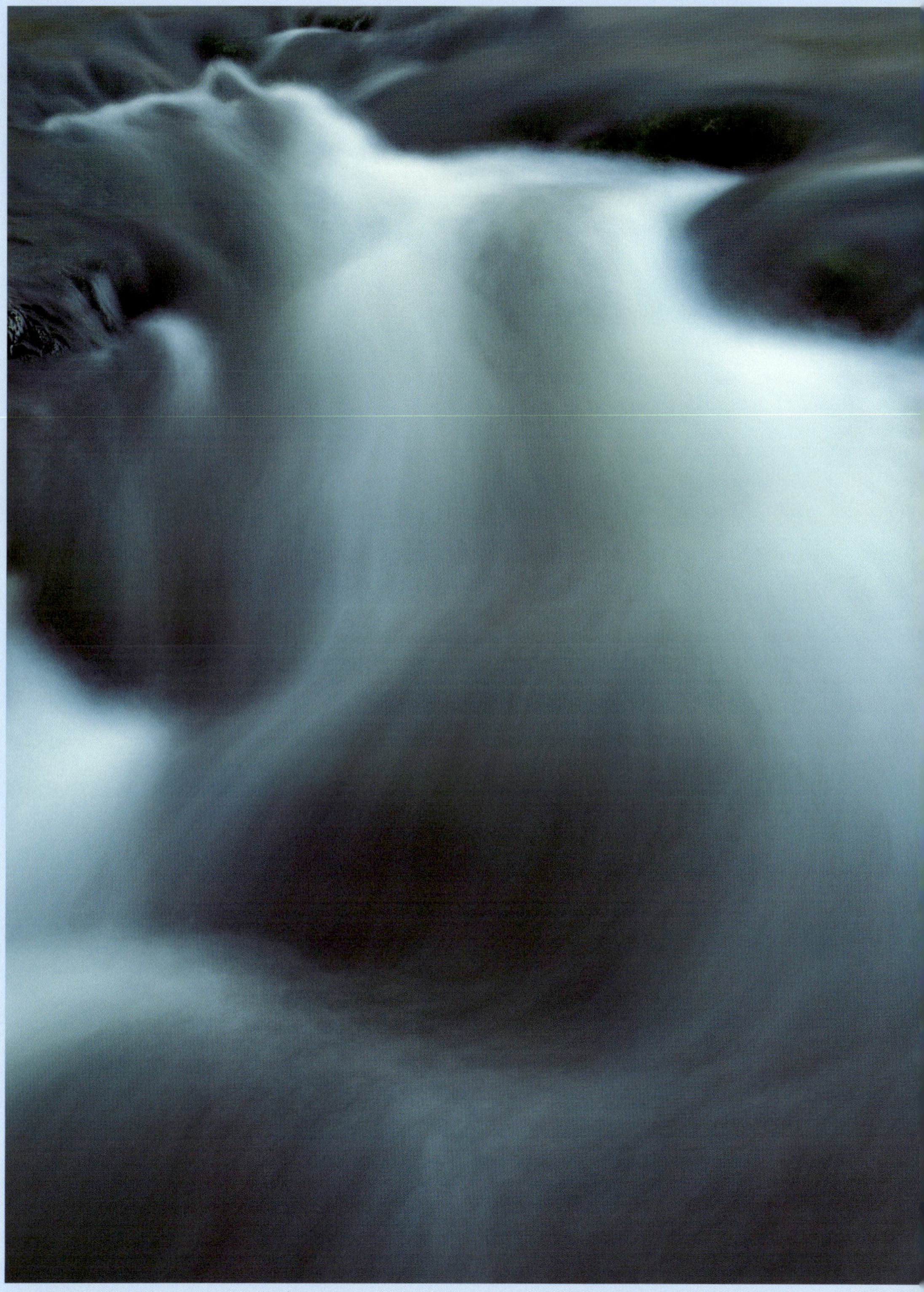

Useful Contacts

Equipment

There are so many manufacturers and retailers of photographic equipment that it would be impossible to list them all here. However, the following is a list of suppliers of the author's equipment.

Ebony – www.ebonycamera.com
Manufacturers of view cameras, including the large-format Ebony 45s that is used within this book.

Fuji – www.fujifilm.com
Manufacturers of film and cameras including Velvia 50, which is used for the majority of images within this book, and the Fuji GSW690 III medium-format camera.

Lee Filters – www.leefilters.com
Manufacturers of filters and filter systems, including the neutral-density graduated, coral and polarizing filters used throughout this book.

Lowepro – www.lowepro.com
Manufacturers of camera bags, including the Super Trekker AW used by the author.

Mamiya – www.mamiya.com
Manufacturers of cameras, including the Mamiya RB67 medium-format camera used in this book.

Nikon – www.nikon.com
Manufacturers of cameras and lenses, including the 35mm SLR Nikon FM2 used within this book.

Pentax – www.pentax.com
Manufacturers of lenses and cameras, including the Pentax 67 medium-format camera and lenses used in this book.

Sekonic – www.sekonic.com
Manufacturers of lightmeters, including that used in this book.

Sigma – www.sigmaphoto.com
Manufacturers of lenses and digital cameras, including the Sigma SD9 digital SLR that was kindly loaned for use in this book.

Maps

It is always a good idea to know where you are going, so maps are an invaluable tool. Make sure that you familiarize yourself with the area beforehand and take note of any particular dangers. Also, let someone know where you are going and when you expect to return. If possible, take a mobile phone with you. Topographic maps and geographical information are available from:

Australian Government, Geoscience Australia, www.ga.gov.au

Canadian Centre for Topographic Information, www.maps.nrcan.gc.ca

New Zealand, Land Information, www.linz.govt.nz

UK Ordnance Survey, www.ordnancesurvey.co.uk

US Geological Survey, www.usgs.gov

Tides

Tides can be dangerous and fast-moving, check locally to see if there are any peculiarities in the local tides. Worldwide tide information and timetables are available from:

The United Kingdom Hydrographic Office – www.ukho.gov.uk

Weather

The weather will affect how water appears in your photographs, what equipment you need to take and where you will be able to go. Check the following websites for weather information:

Australian Bureau of Meteorology, www.bom.gov.au

Canadian Weather Office, www.weatheroffice.ec.gc.ca

New Zealand Met Service, www.metservice.co.nz

UK Met Office, www.met-office.gov.uk

US National Weather Service, www.nws.noaa.gov

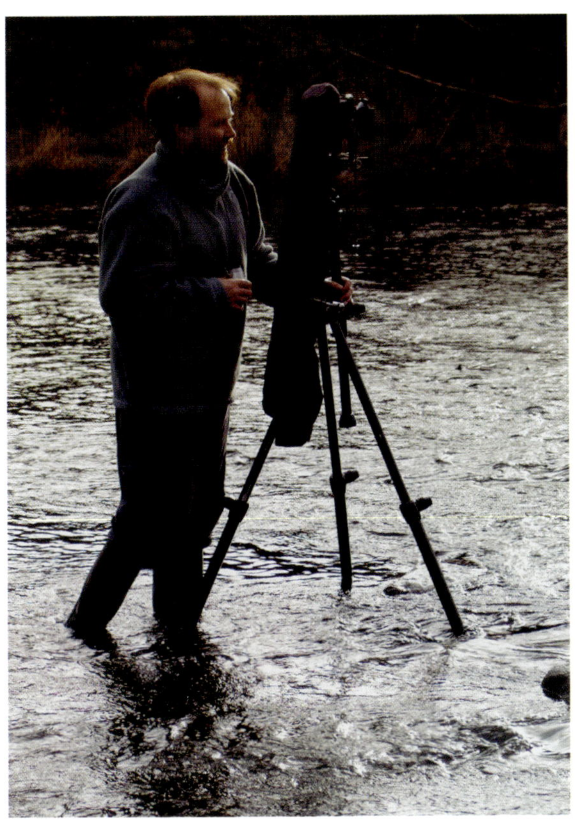

About the Author

David Tarn trained in business and accountancy. He spent a number of years working in financial services selling life assurance and pensions but found he got little fulfilment from it. One day he made the momentous decision to actively work at turning his hobby of landscape photography into his career and he hasn't looked back since. He writes for numerous magazines, gives lectures at photographic societies, holds workshops and has now written this, his first book.

David has always sought moments when the light and land come together to create an unrepeatable, exceptional scene. He believes it is a special harmony that can only be truly appreciated in photography.

Glossary

80-series filters Powerful cool-down filters which correct warm light sources such as tungsten lighting.

81-series filters Also known as warm-up filters. 81-series filters produce a warm colour cast or correct cold colour casts by reducing the level of blue light reaching the film.

82-series filters Also known as cool-down filters. They are less powerful than 80-series filters and are used to either create a cool colour cast or correct a warm colour cast.

Adaptor rings Mounting rings used to adapt filter systems for use with lenses with different filter diameters.

Angle of view The area of a scene that a lens takes in. A wideangle lens has a wide angle of view, while a telephoto lens has a narrow one.

Aperture The hole or opening formed by the leaf diaphragm inside the lens or the opening in a camera lens through which light passes to expose the film. The relative size of the aperture is denoted by f-stops.

Aperture ring A ring, located on the lens barrel, which is linked mechanically to the diaphragm and controls the size of the aperture.

Blower brush A brush with an air bulb attached allowing the user to blow away or suck up dust.

Blur An unsharp image or image area caused by subject or camera movement, or incorrect or selective focusing.

Bracketing The process of exposing a series of frames of the same subject or scene at different exposure settings in order to obtain at least one accurate exposure.

B-setting A shutter-speed setting in which the shutter will stay open as long as the shutter release button remains depressed.

Calibration Determining the accuracy of equipment in order to provide base readings from which accurate measurements can be made.

Cast Abnormal colouring of an image.

CCD (charge-coupled device) A microchip made up of light-sensitive cells and used in digital cameras for recording images.

Cold colours Colours at the blue end of the visible spectrum, paradoxically they have high colour temperatures.

Colour correction filters Filters that are used to correct colour casts.

Colour temperature Description of the colour of a light source expressed in Kelvin (K).

Composition The arrangement of picture elements within the frame.

Cool-down filters Filters that are blue in appearance and have the effect of correcting warm colour casts or introducing cool colour casts.

Compact camera A small camera, normally using 35mm or APS film.

Coral filters A warm-up filter that is slightly redder than the 81-series filters.

Darkslide A slide-in sheet that is used, particularly in medium and large formats, to protect the film from accidental exposure.

Depth of field The amount of the image that is acceptably sharp. This is controlled by the aperture (f-stop) setting: the smaller the aperture, the greater the depth of field. Depth of field extends one-third in front of and two-thirds behind the point of focus.

Depth-of-field preview Some SLR cameras offer the chance to see the available depth of field by stopping down the aperture while the mirror remains in place.

Depth-of-field scale Some lenses have depth of field scales printed around the barrel. These give an indication of the depth of field for any given focusing distance.

Depth of focus The extent to which the focal plane can be moved backwards or forwards without visibly affecting the sharpness of the image.

Digital camera A camera which replaces the chemical process of image capture and storage with an electronic and digital process.

Down-rating Reducing the ISO rating at which a film is used to below the manufacturer's recommended value. The manufacturer's set film speed, measured in ISO, is manually reduced and the film is exposed at a slower film speed so as to increase exposure.

Element The main component of a lens, generally a single piece of glass with two polished and coated surfaces. A combination of elements is used to attain optimum quality.

EV (exposure value) A measurement of light given by an exposure meter that enables exposure settings to be calculated.

Exposure The amount of light that is allowed to act on a photographic material. Alternatively the act of taking a photograph, as in 'making an exposure'.

Exposure compensation A level of adjustment given (generally) to autoexposure settings. Generally used to compensate for known inadequacies in the way a camera takes meter readings.

Exposure latitude The extent to which exposure can be increased or reduced without causing an unacceptable under- or overexposure of the image.

Exposure meter A device either built into the camera or separate with a light-sensitive cell used for measuring light levels, used as an aid for selecting the exposure setting.

Film A light-sensitive product consisting of photographic emulsion coated on a flexible, transparent base that records light.

Film speed The sensitivity of a given film to light, measured as an ISO rating.

Filter A piece of coloured glass, or other transparent material, used over the lens or light source, or between the lens and film to affect the colour or density of the entire scene or certain areas within a scene.

Filter factor The number by which exposure must be multiplied to compensate for the use of filters.

Filter system A collection of compatible filters and accessories, particularly slot-in filters and the relevant adaptor ring.

Flare Non-image-forming light that scatters within the lens system. This can create multicoloured circles or a loss in contrast. It can be reduced by multiple lens coatings, low-dispersion lens elements or the use of a lens hood.

f-numbers A series of numbers on the lens aperture ring and/or the camera's LCD panel which indicate the relative size of the lens aperture.

Focal length The distance, usually given in millimetres, from the optical centre point of a lens element to its focal point.

Focusing The adjustment made to the distance between the lens and the film (and therefore the focal point) in order to bring the focal plane into coincidence with the film plane, i.e. to focus the image on the film.

Focusing screen A surface (traditionally ground glass now normally plastic) mounted on the focal plane, on which the focusing of the image can be checked.

Format The shape and size of a picture. Often used in reference to the size of the frame within the camera.

f-stop A fraction that indicates the actual diameter of the aperture: the 'f' represents the lens focal length.

Graduated neutral-density filter A grey filter that is graduated to allow different amounts of light to pass through the lens at different points. They are used to even up naturally occurring bright and dark tones.

Grey card A grey card that reflects 18% of the light falling on it, representative of a middle-toned subject used for calculating exposure.

Hyperfocal distance The distance between the lens and its hyperfocal point.

Hyperfocal focusing Focusing a lens on its hyperfocal point in order to maximize the available depth of field.

Hyperfocal point When a lens is focused on infinity the hyperfocal point is the point closest to the camera at which the image still appears acceptably sharp.

Infinity The distance at which objects are so far away that light reflected from them reaches the lens as parallel rays.

Kelvin (K) A scale used to measure colour temperature.

Large format A term referring to a negative or transparency with a size of 5 x 4in or larger.

Lens One or more pieces of optical glass, or similar material, designed to collect and focus rays of light to form a sharp image.

Lens hood A device attached to the front of the lens to prevent non-image-forming light from entering the lens barrel and causing flare.

Loupe A magnifying glass used for examining transparencies on a lightbox or for checking the focus of an image on a ground-glass screen on a large- or medium-format camera.

Memory card Removable storage device for digital cameras.

Metering Using a camera or lightmeter to determine the amount of light coming from a scene and calculate the required exposure.

Movements The movement of the standards of a large-format camera in order to affect the coincidence of the focal plane and the film plane.

Negative film A type of film that, once processed, produces negatives.

Neutral-density (ND) filter A filter that reduces the brightness of an image without affecting the colour.

Noise The digital equivalent of graininess in film, caused by stray electrical signals.

Overexposure A condition in which too much light reaches the film or sensor, producing a dense negative or a light print or slide. Detail is lost in the highlights.

Panoramic camera A camera with a frame of which the ratio of width to height is greater than 2:1.

Plate An alternative material to film: a glass plate that is coated in light-sensitive emulsion.

Polarizing filter A filter that transmits light travelling in one plane while absorbing light travelling in other planes. When placed in front of a camera lens, it can eliminate undesirable reflections from a subject such as water, glass, or other objects with a shiny surface except metals. Also used to saturate colours (e.g. to make blue skies darker).

Polaroid film A brand of instant film used to check exposure and composition on medium- and large-format cameras.

Polaroid-film back An interchangeable back designed to enable polaroid film to be used with medium- and large-format cameras.

Prime lens A lens of a fixed focal length.

Pull processing Reducing the development time of a film to reduce its effective speed.

Push processing Increasing the development time of a film to increase its effective speed.

Quickload film A large-format film system designed to be easy to load without the need for darkslides.

Rangefinder A type of viewfinder, or a camera that uses such a viewfinder. Part of the image appears split when out of focus, and continuous when it is in focus.

Reciprocity law A change in one exposure setting can be compensated for by an equal and opposite change in the other. For example, the exposure settings of 1/125sec at f/8 produce exactly the same exposure value as 1/60sec at f/11.

Reciprocity law failure At shutter speeds slower than one second the law of reciprocity begins to fail because the sensitivity of film reduces as exposure increases. This affects different films to different extents.

Rollfilm 120 or 220 film that is supplied on an open spool with paper backing, rather than in a cassette.

Rule of thirds A compositional device that places the key elements of a picture at points along imagined lines that divide the frame into thirds.

Screw-on filters Filters that screw onto the filter thread at the front of most modern lenses.

Sheet-film Film for large-format cameras that is supplied in cut sheets rather than on rolls.

Shutter A curtain, plate, diaphragm, or some other movable cover in a camera that controls the amount of time during which light reaches the film.

Shutter release The button or lever on a camera that causes the shutter to remain open.

Shutter speed The length of time that the shutter is open. Measured in seconds or fractions of a second.

Silhouette An extreme example of a backlit image in which all surface detail is lost.

SLR (single-lens reflex) A type of camera that allows you to see through the camera's lens as you look in the viewfinder.

Spotmeter An exposure meter that allows you to measure the intensity of reflected light from a very small or distant area.

Spotmetering A metering mode that takes a light reading from a very small portion of the scene, often as little as 1°.

Standard The two movable mountings of a large-format camera, the lens being attached to the front standard and the focusing screen to the back standard.

Standard lens A standard lens is one that provides approximately the same field of view as the human eye. This equates to a lens with a focal length approximately equal to the hypotenuse of the frame in use. In 35mm format this approximates to a 50mm lens.

Stepping rings Rings that allow you to attach screw-in filters to lenses with different-sized filter threads.

Stop The alternative name for relative aperture.

Stopping down Changing the lens aperture to a smaller opening, for example from f/8 to f/11. Generally, can be used to refer to any reduction in exposure, either in aperture or shutter speed.

Through-the-lens (TTL) metering A meter built into the camera that determines exposure for the scene by reading light that passes through the lens during picture taking.

Transparency A positive image with correct colour rendition on transparency (or slide) film.

Underexposure A condition in which too little light reaches the film, producing a thin negative, a dark transparency, or a muddy-looking print or digital file. There is too much detail lost in the areas of shadow in the exposure.

UV filter A filter that reduces UV interference in the final image. This is particularly useful for reducing haze in landscape photographs.

View camera Another name for a large-format camera that has a ground-glass focusing screen.

Warm colours Colours at the red end of the visible spectrum. Paradoxically they have low colour temperatures.

Warm-up filters Filters that add a warm colour cast to an image, or correct a cold colour cast.

White balance A function on a digital camera that allows the correct colour balance to be recorded for any given lighting situation.

Wideangle Lenses with a wider angle of view than the human eye. Lenses wider than 60 degrees are wideangle, more than 90 degrees are super-wide.

Zoom lens A lens with a variable focal length that can be altered by the photographer.

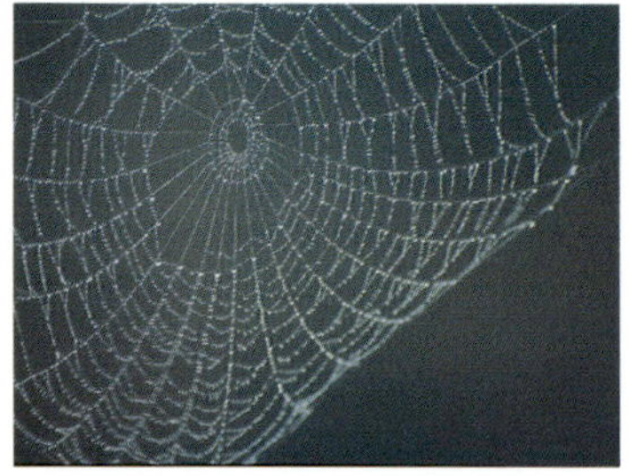

page 8 Cobweb and Dew

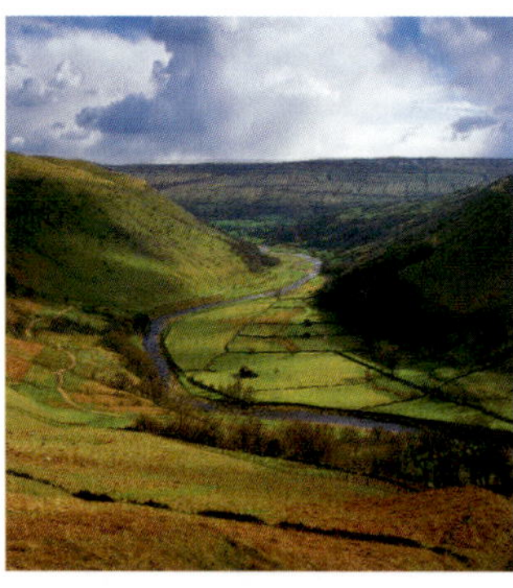

page 9 Swaledale, Yorkshire

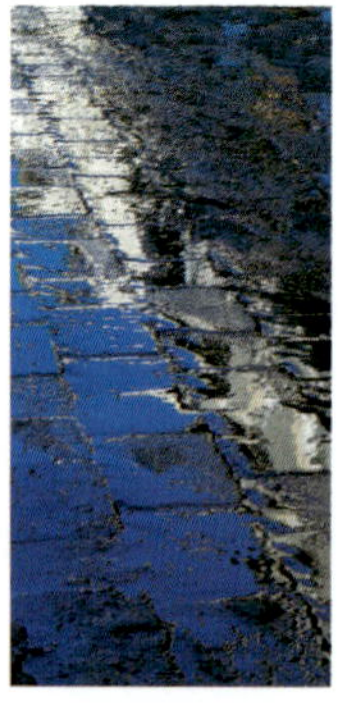

page 9 Finkle St, Richmond

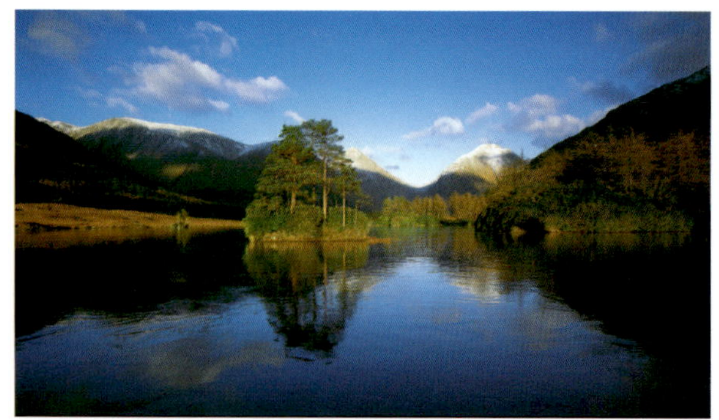

page 12-3 Glen Etive, Scotland

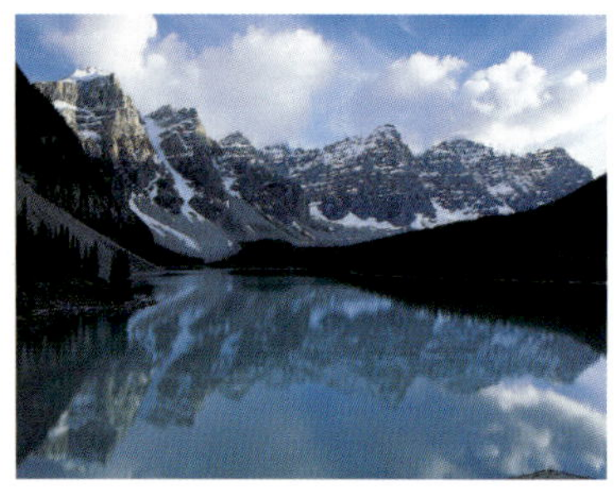

page 10 Ten Peaks Moraine Lake, Canada

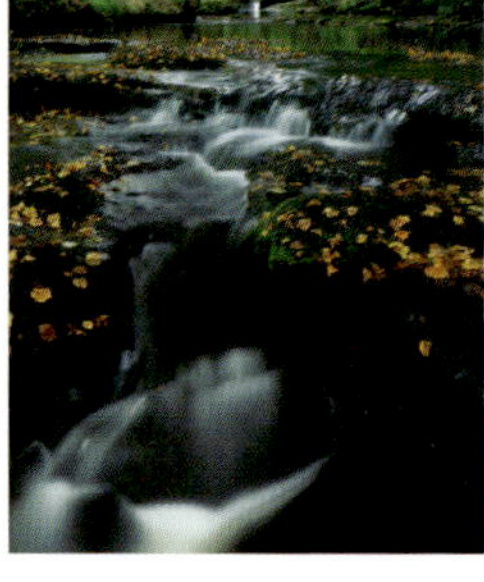

page 11 Thomason's Foss

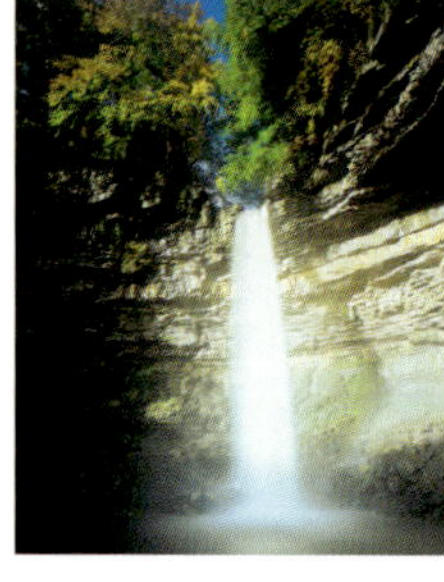

page 17 Hardraw Force Waterfall

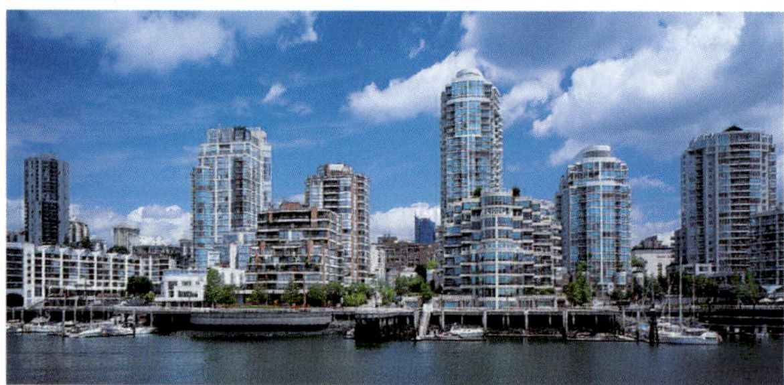

page 21 Vancouver Waterfront

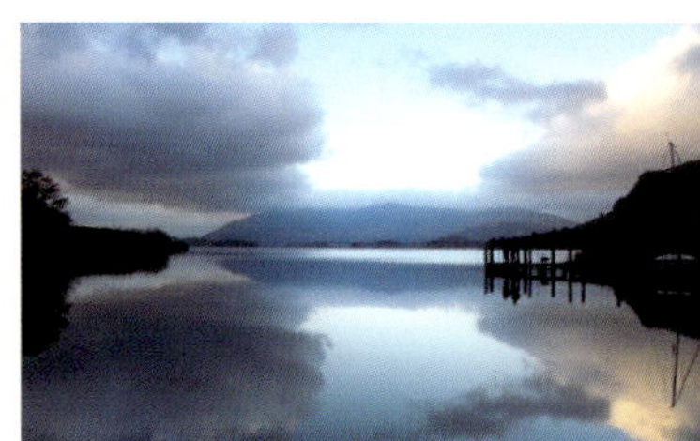

page 23 Derwentwater Dusk

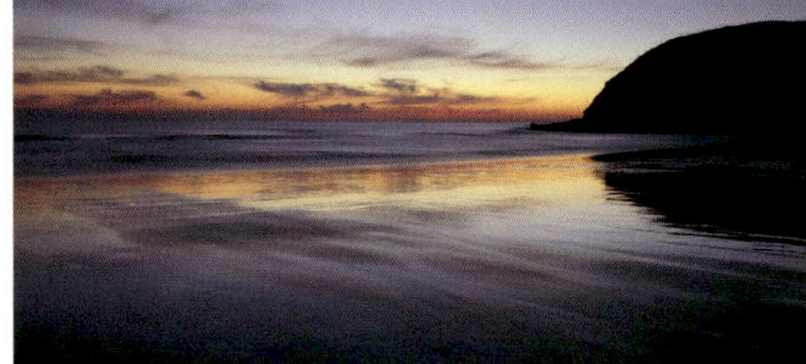

page 27 St Bees at Sunset

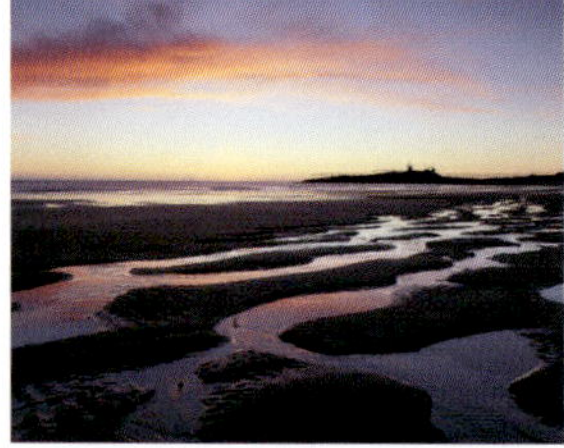

page 36–7 Dunstanburgh Castle, Dawn

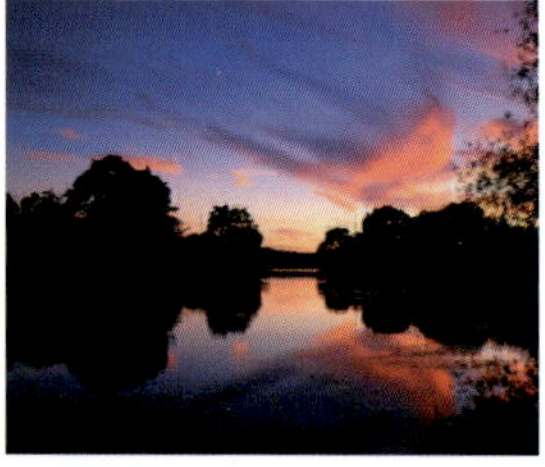

page 38 River Ure at Sunset

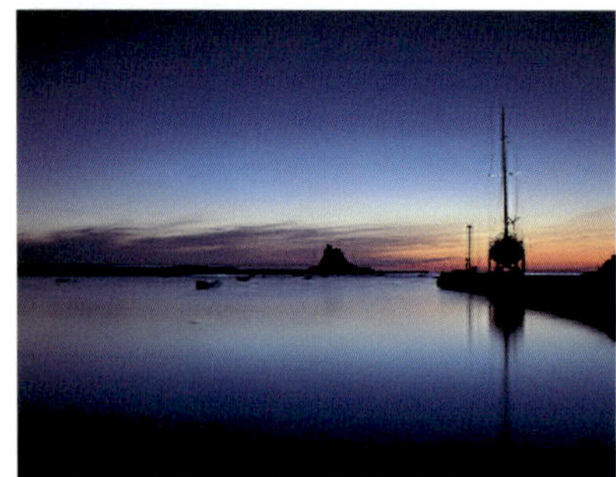

page 39 Lindisfarne Harbour

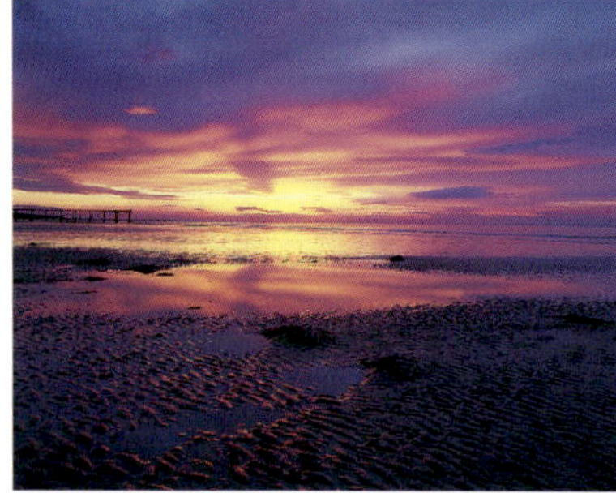

page 39 Saltburn Sunset

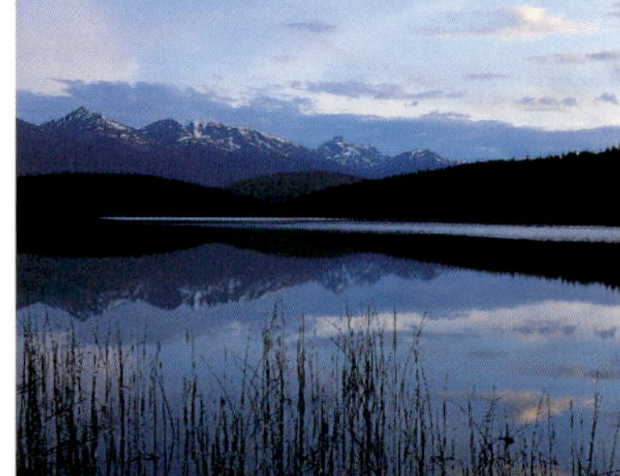

page 41 Patricia Lake, Jasper National Park, Canada

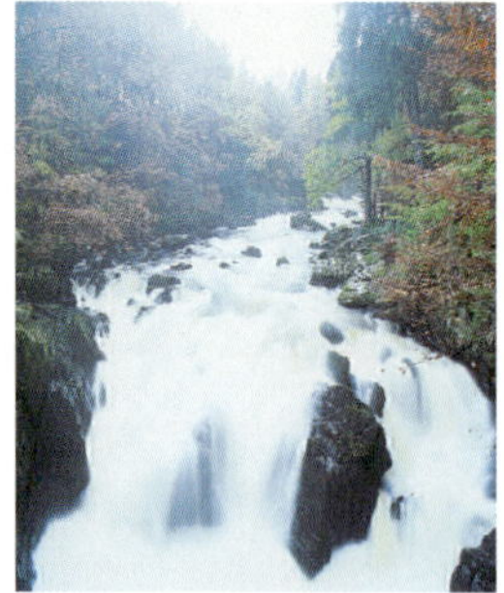

page 49 Waterfall, The Hermitage

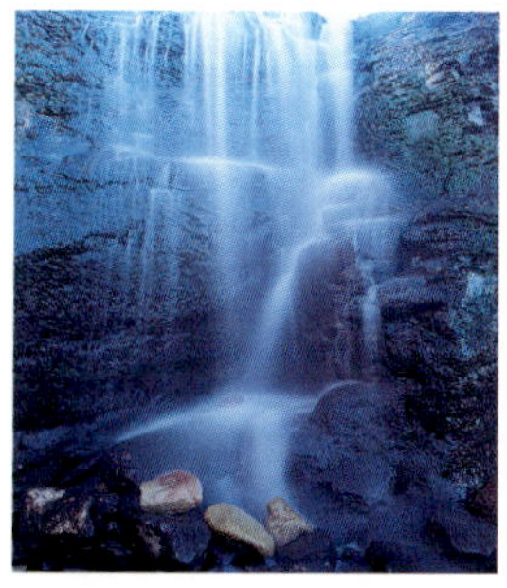

page 50 Waterfall, Saltwick Bay

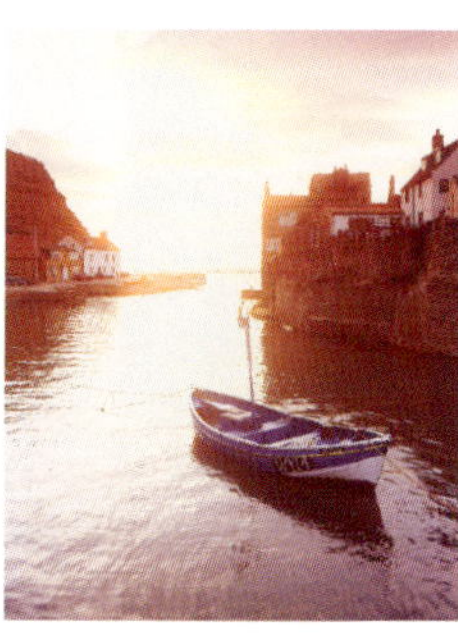

page 53 Staithes Harbour and Boat

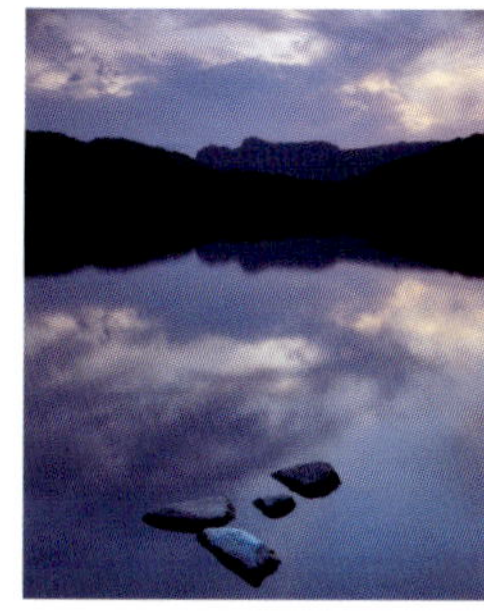

page 55 The Lakes at Dusk

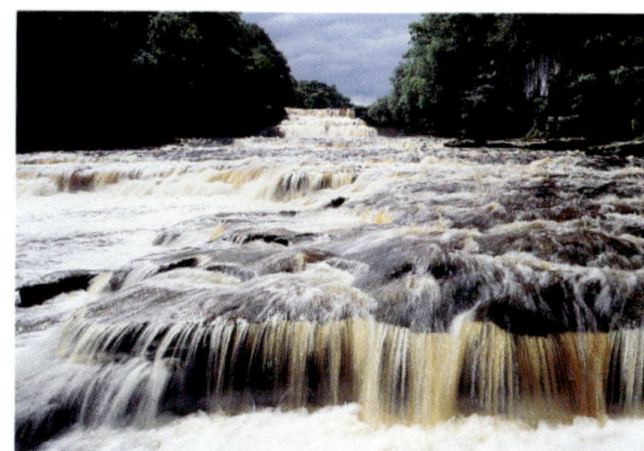

page 58 Aysgarth Falls, Yorkshire Dales

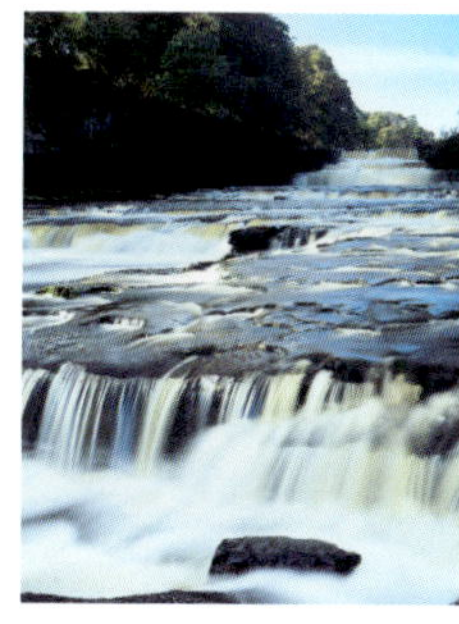

page 59 Aysgarth Falls, Yorkshire Dales

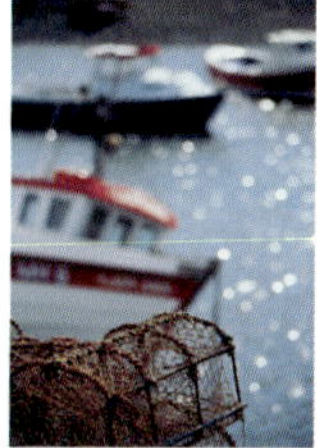

page 61 Lobster Pots and Harbour

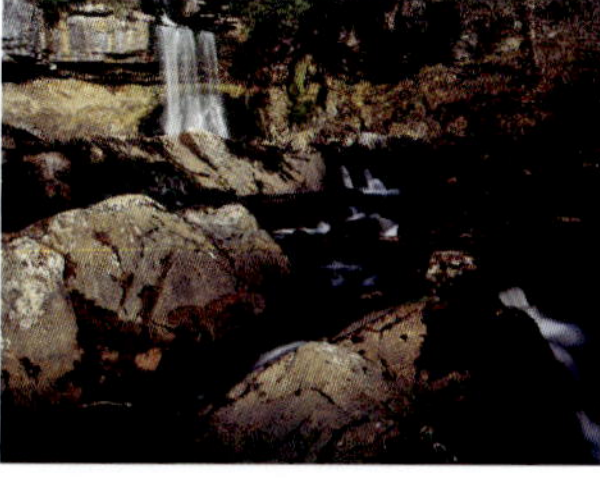

page 61 Thornton Force Waterfall, Yorkshire

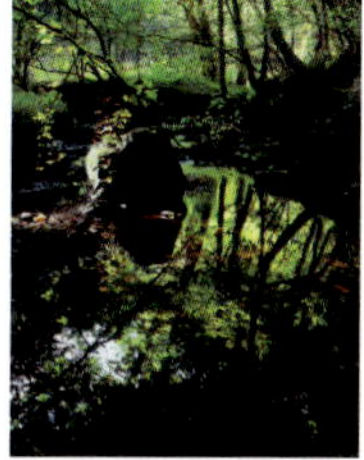

page 70 May Beck

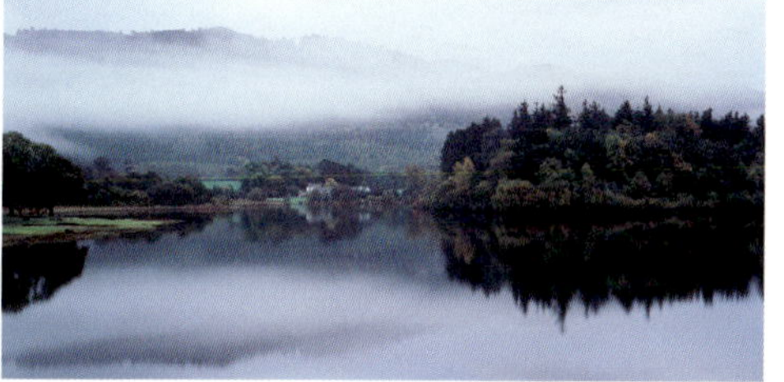

page 71 Misty Morning, Derwentwater

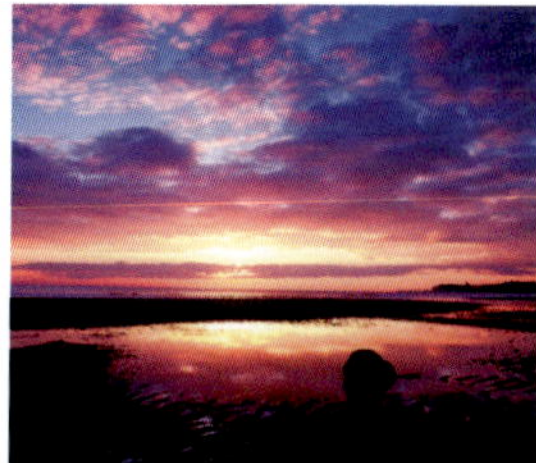

page 71 Whitby

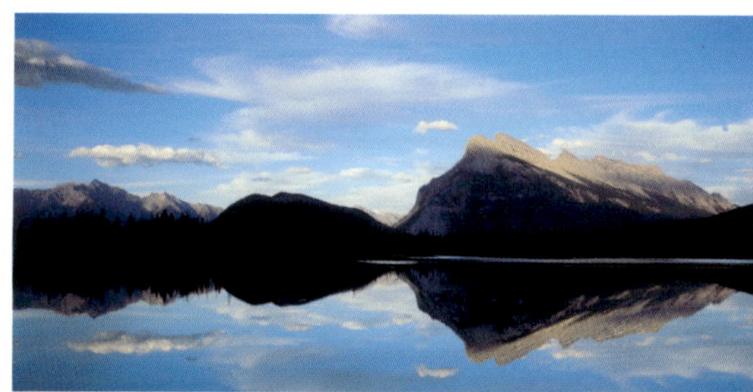

page 72–3 Vermilion Lakes and Mount Rundle

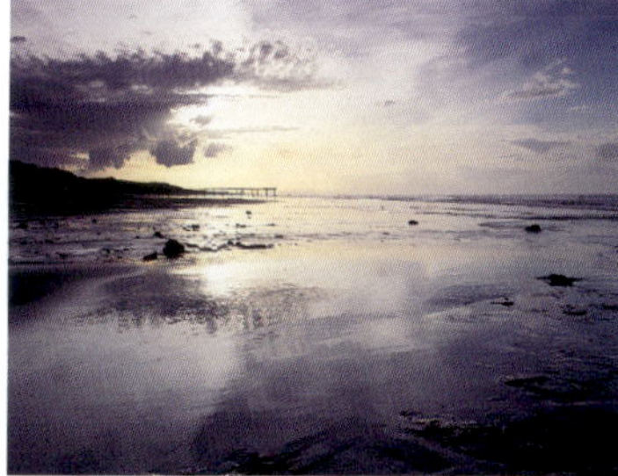

page 74 Saltburn by the Sea

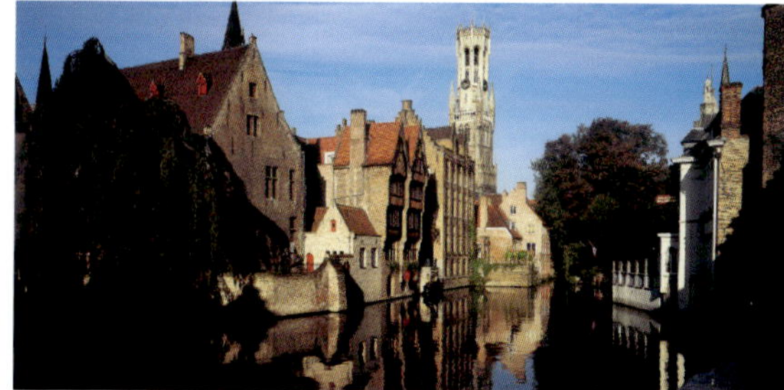

page 78 Bruges, Belgium

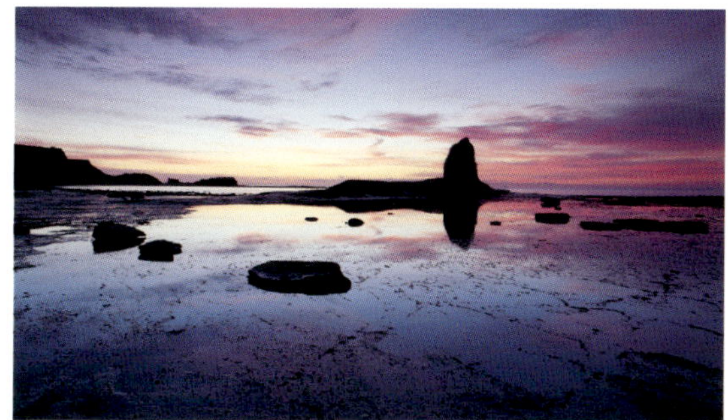

page 79 Black Nab, Saltwick Bay at Sunset

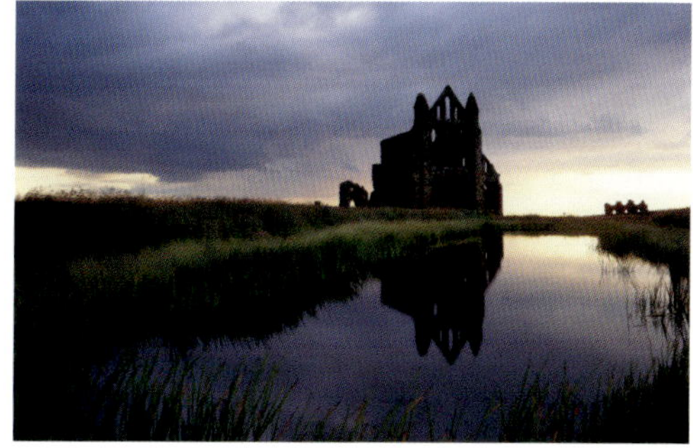

page 80–1 Whitby Abbey

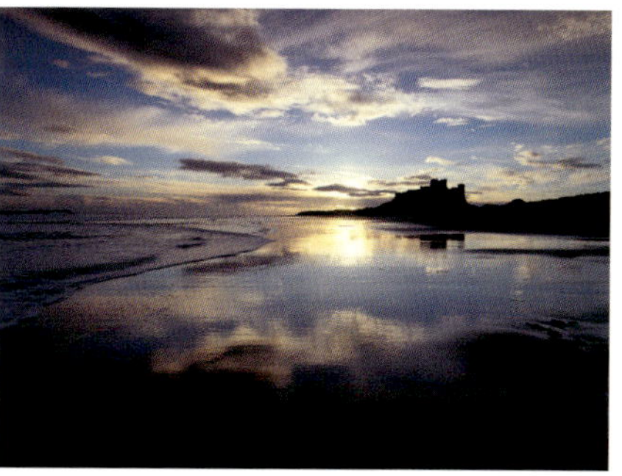

page 82 Bamburgh Castle, Dawn

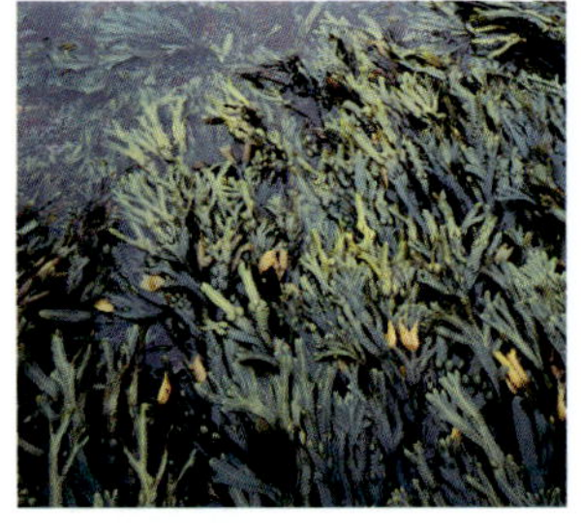

page 83 Seaweed on Bamburgh Beach

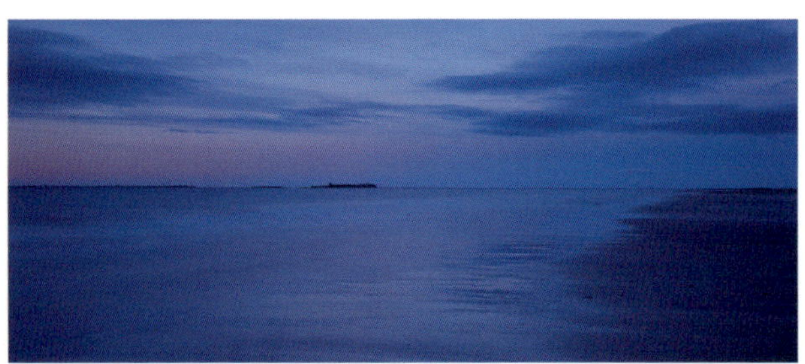

page 83 Farne Islands

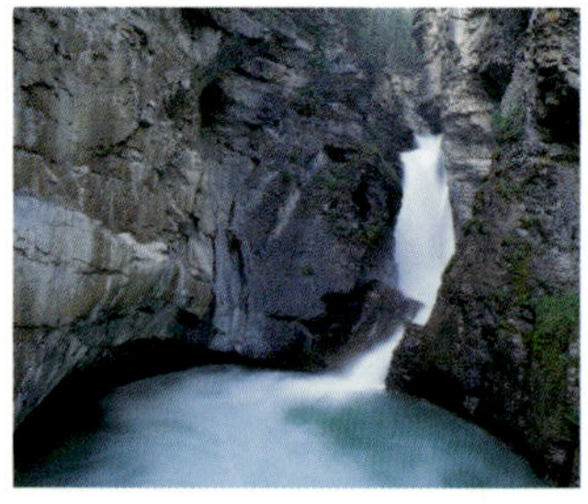

page 85 Johnston Canyon Lower Falls, Alberta, Canada

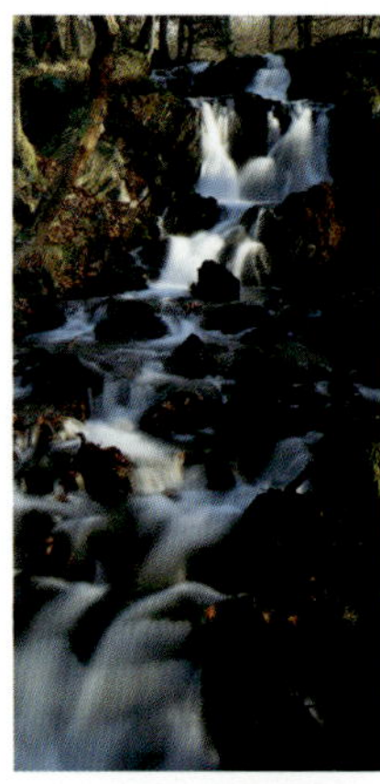

right: page 86 Waterfall, Cumbria

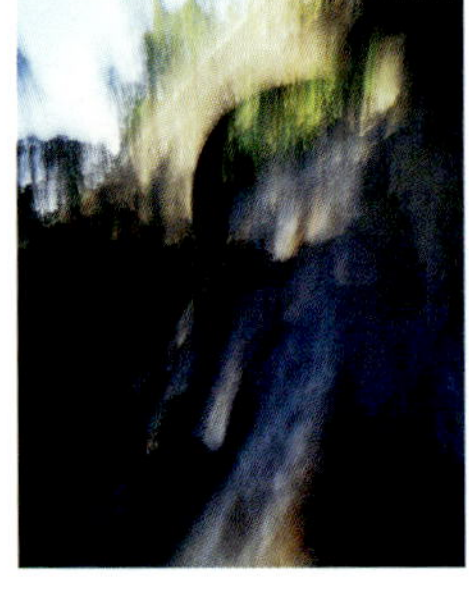

page 87 Breaking the Rules

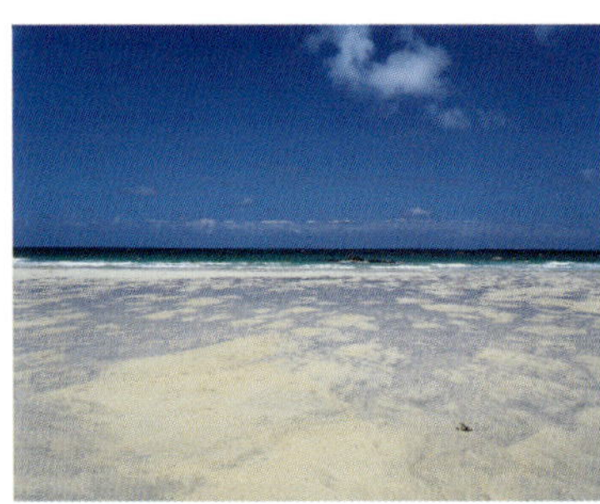

page 89 Beach

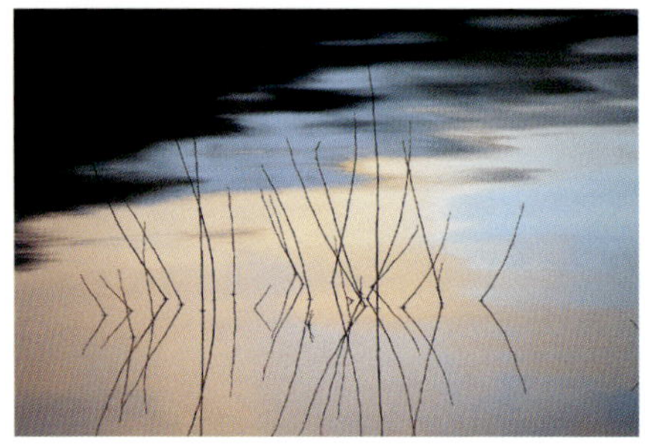

page 90 Thirlmere Detail at Dusk

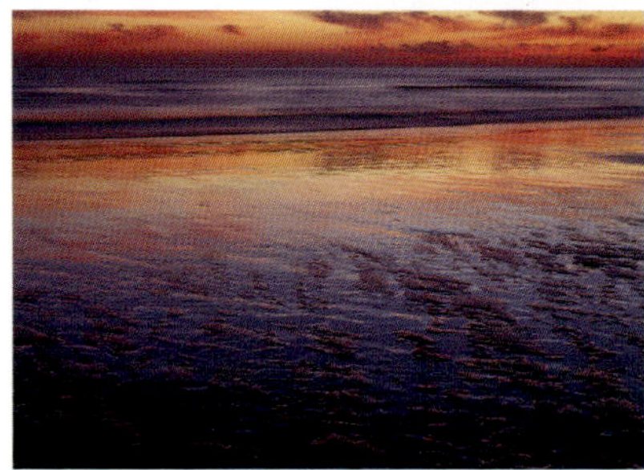

page 90 St Bees Head, Cumbria

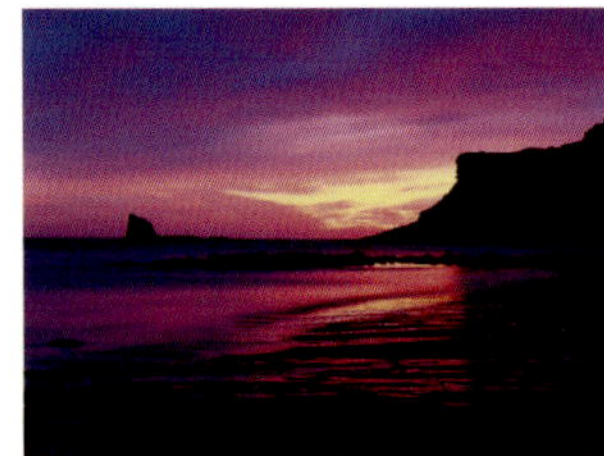

page 91 Saltwick Bay, Sunrise

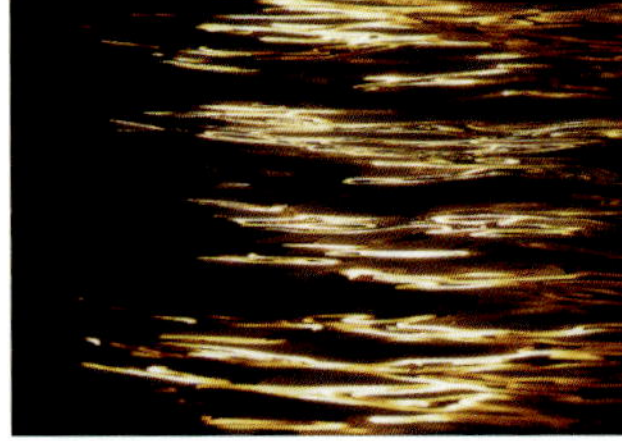

page 91 Golden Water

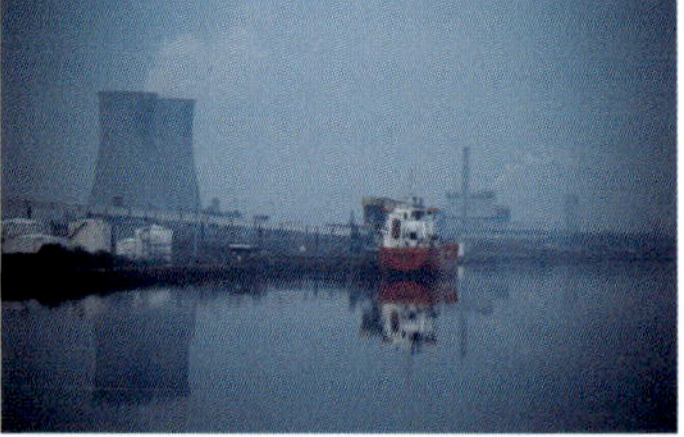

page 95 River Tees, Middlesbrough

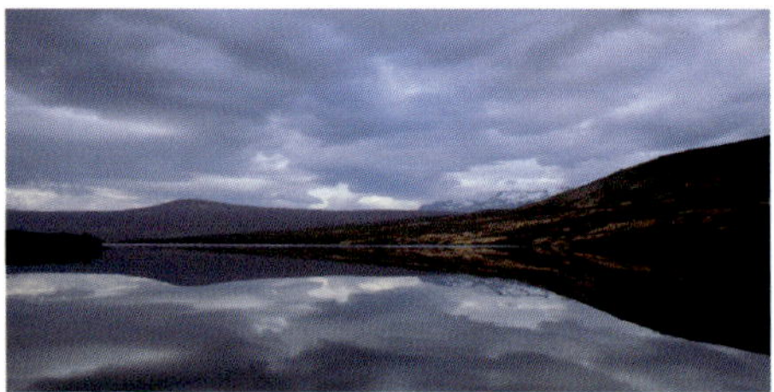

page 96–7 Loch Shin, Sutherland, Scotland

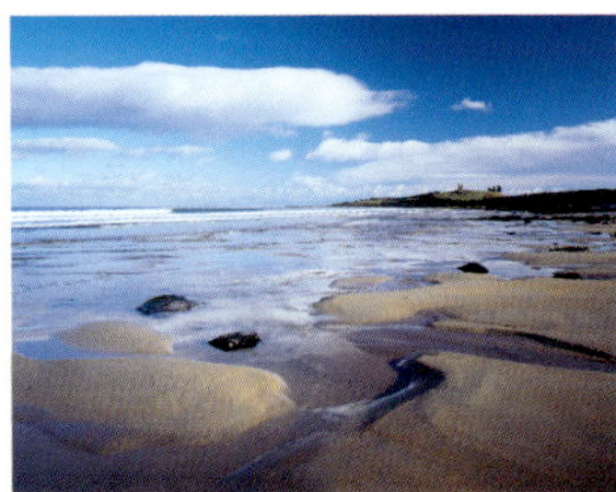

page 98 Dunstanburgh

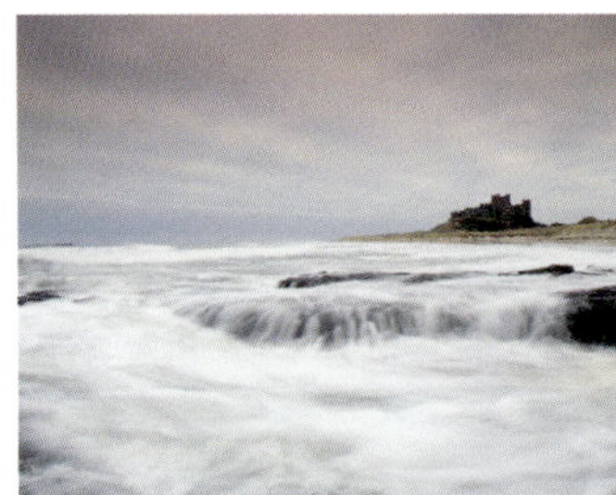

page 99 Bamburgh Castle

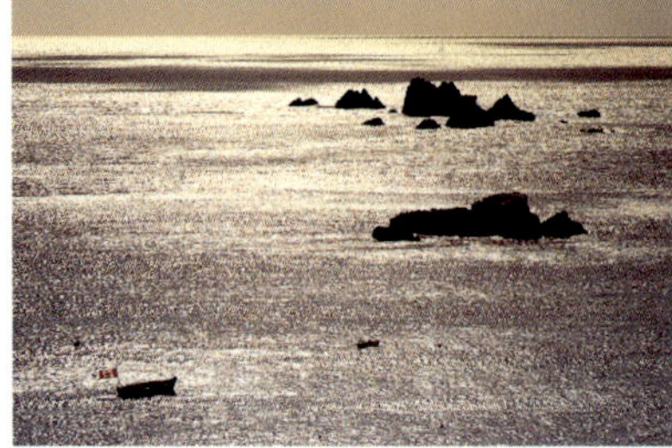

page 100 Sunshine on the Sea, Cornwall

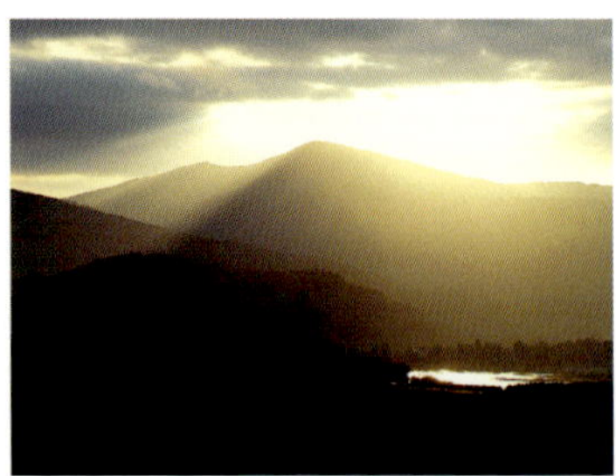

page 101 Dramatic Light over Derwentwater

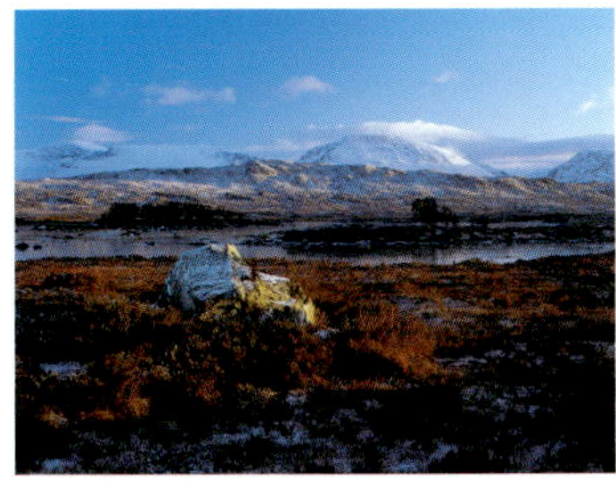

page 101 Rannoch Moor

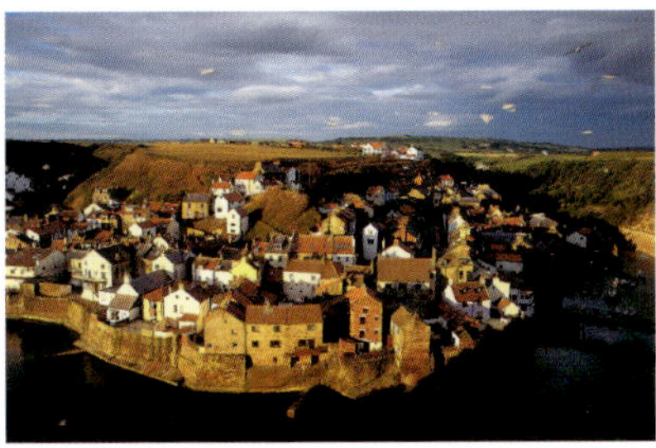

page 101 Staithes from Cowbar

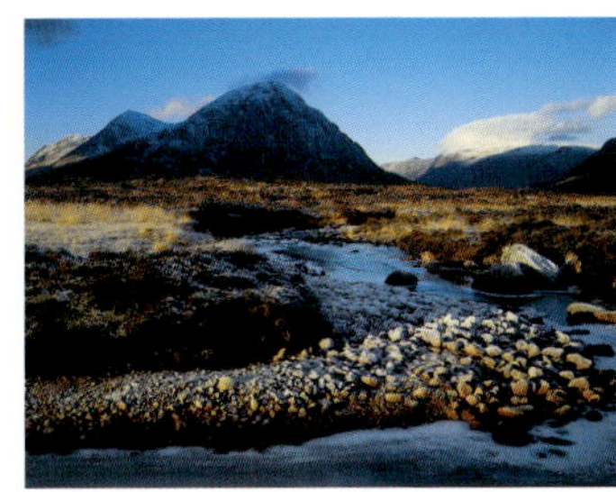

page 102 Glencoe and
Buachaille Etive Mor

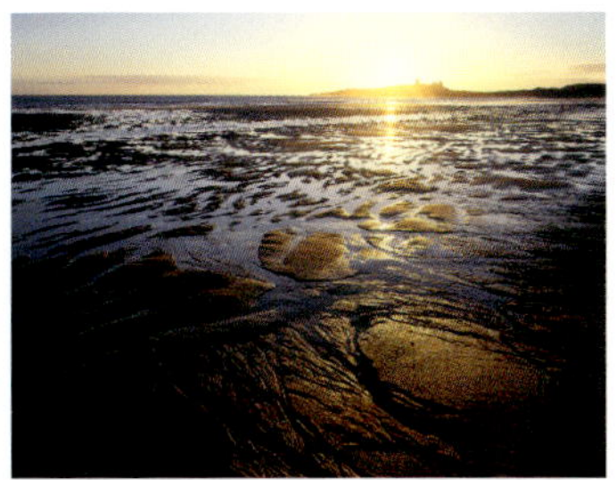

page 103 Embleton Bay
and Dunstanburgh Castle

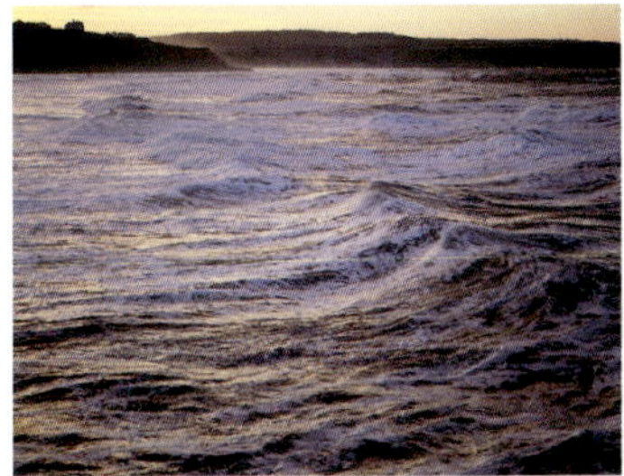

page 103
Rough Sea, Whitby to Sandsend

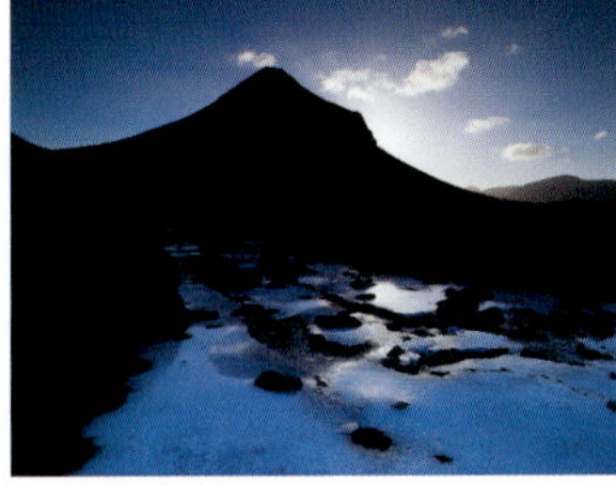

page 104
Cullin Hills, Isle of Skye

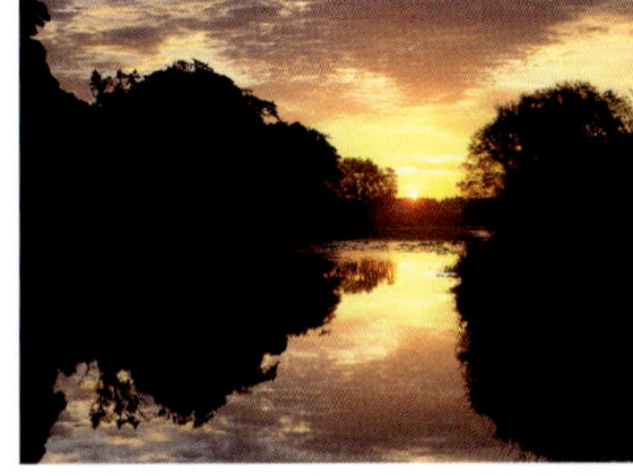

page 105 River Ure

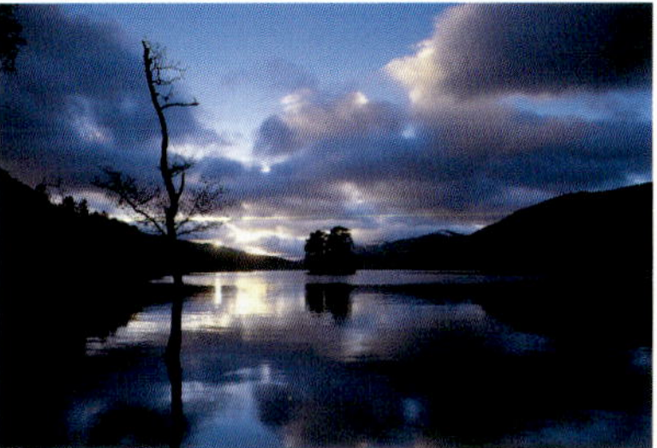

page 105 Loch Tay

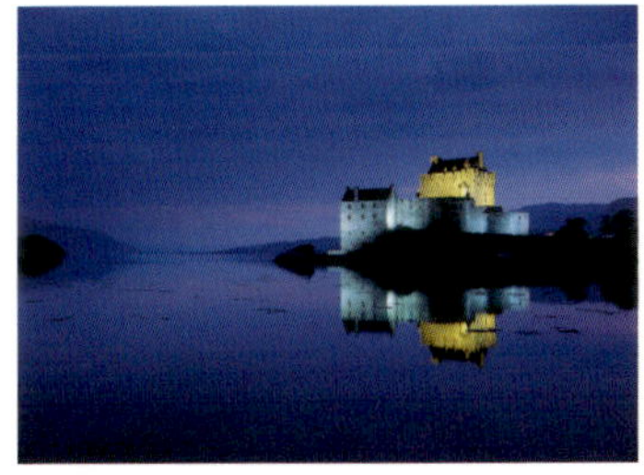

page 106–7
Blue Dusk, Eilean Donan Castle

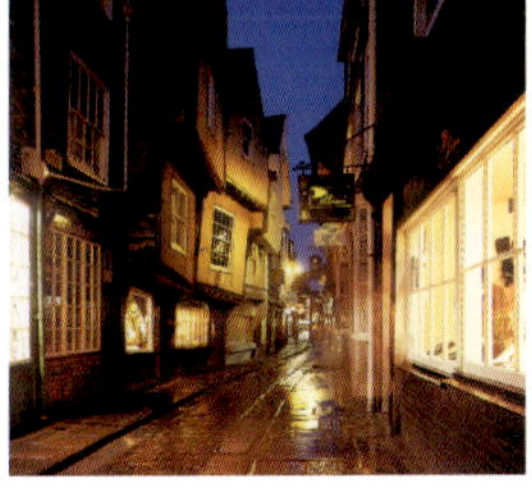

page 108 The Shambles
at Night, York

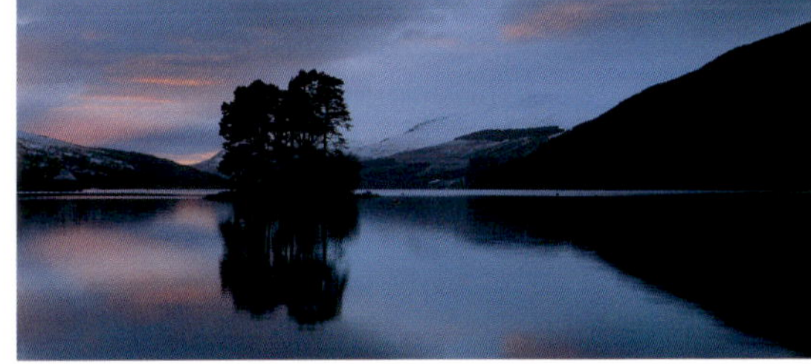

page 108 Loch Tay at Sunset

right: page 109 Blue Dawn,
St Mary's Lighthouse, Tyneside

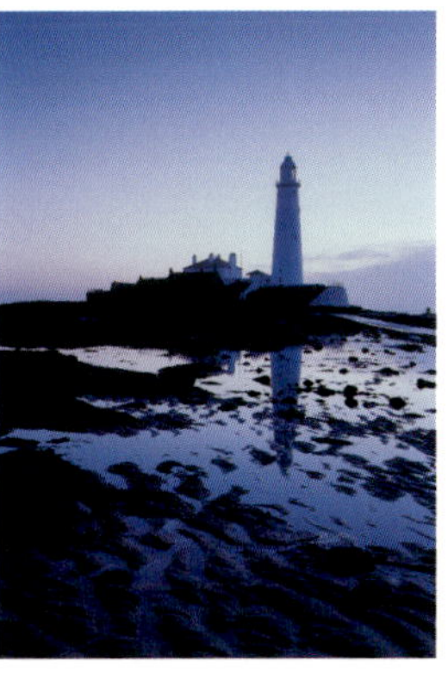

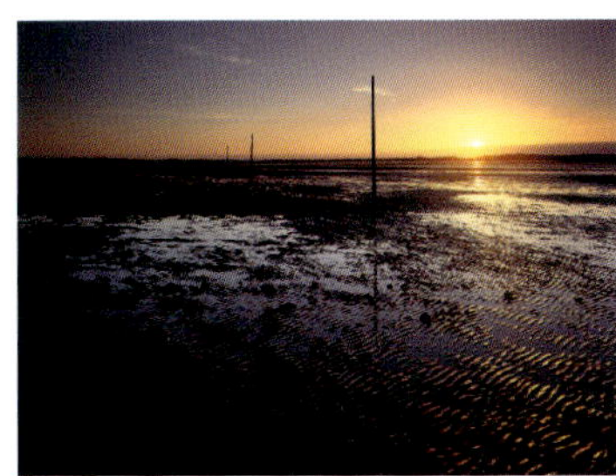

page 110 The Causeway,
Lindisfarne, Northumberland

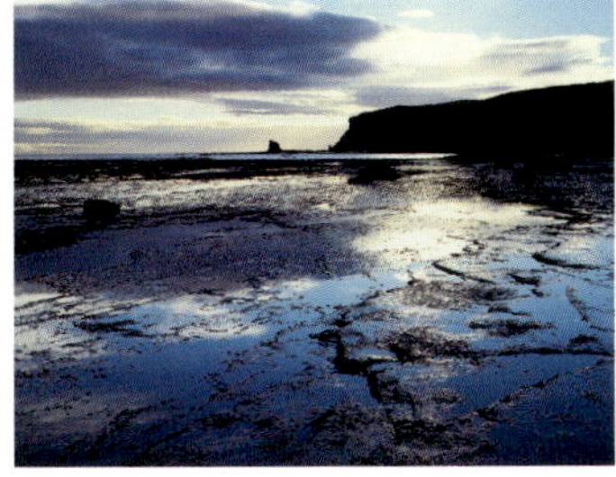

page 111 Blue Dawn, Black
Nab

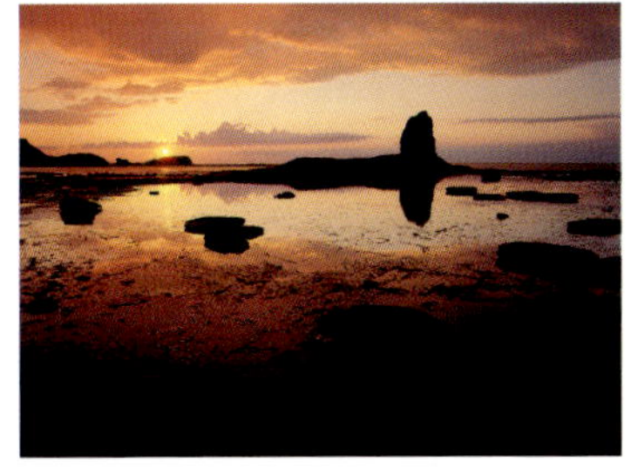

page 112 Black Nab, Sunset

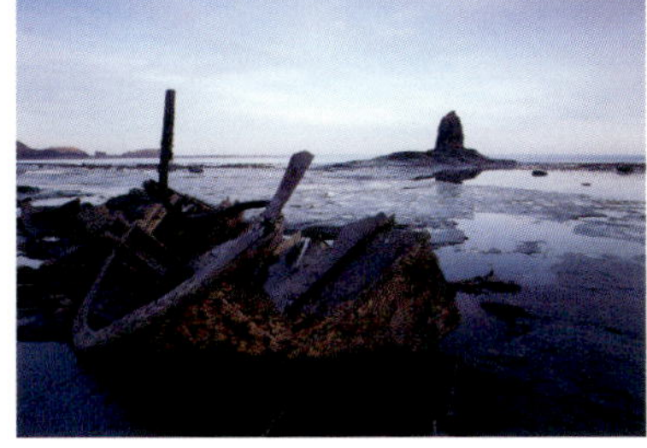

page 113 Shipwreck, Saltwick Bay
and Black Nab

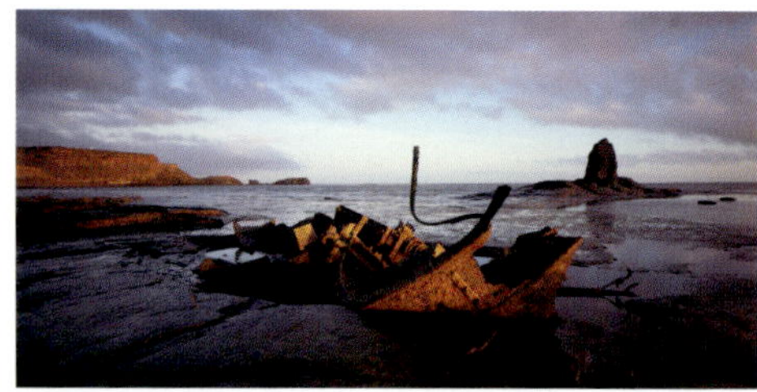

page 114–5
Shipwreck, Saltwick Bay and Black Nab

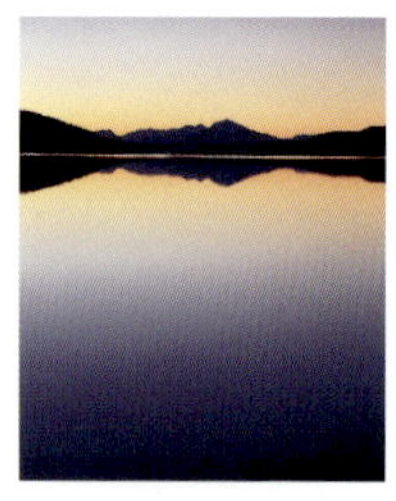

page 118
Loch Garry, Dusk

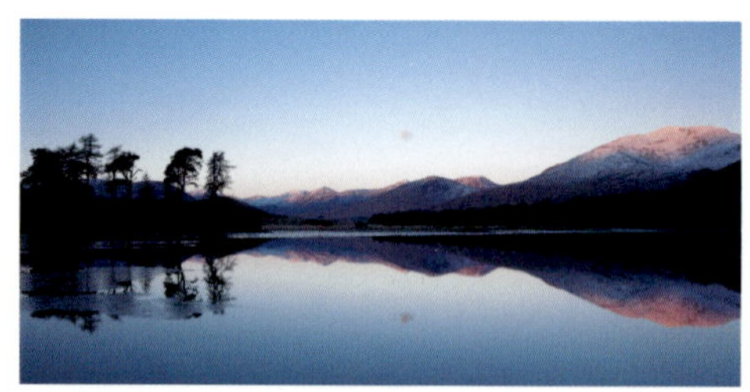 *page 120–1* Loch Tulla at Dawn

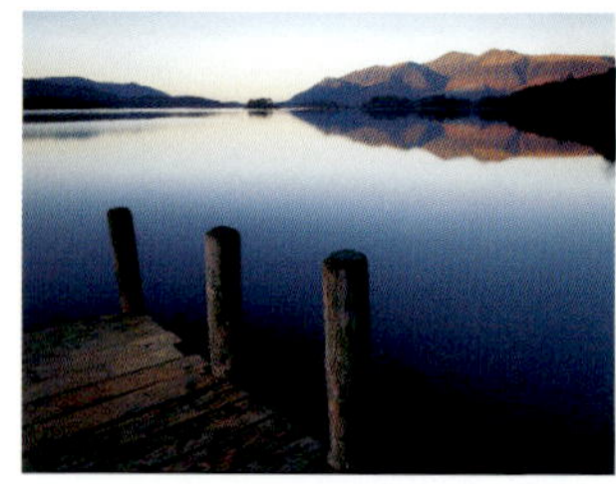 *page 122* Still Dusk

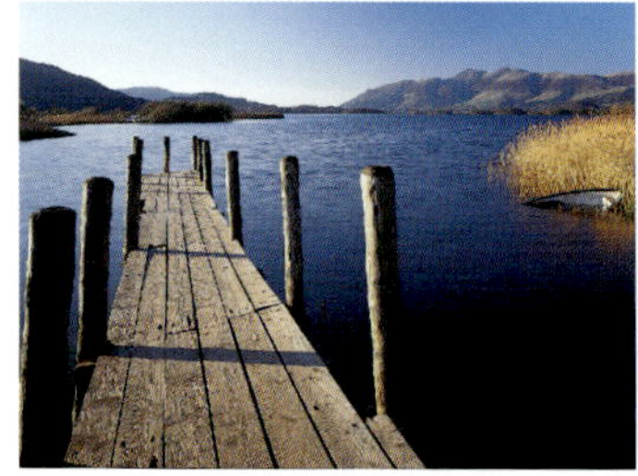

page 123 Still Dusk

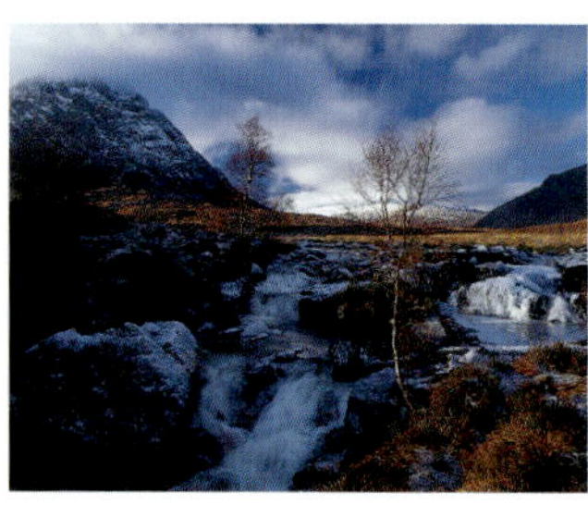

page 126
Glencoe and Rannoch Moor

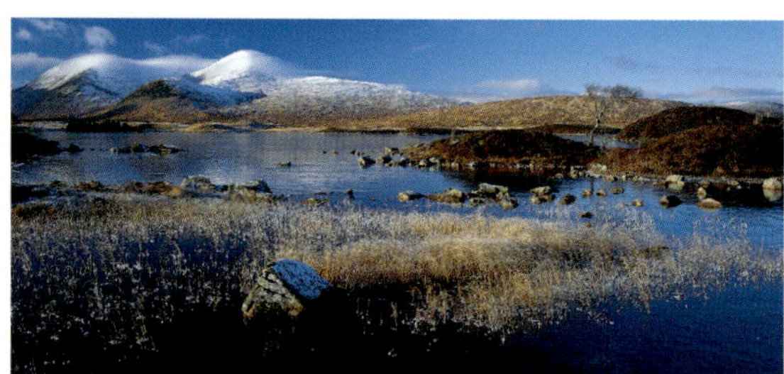 *page 126* Glencoe and Rannoch Moor

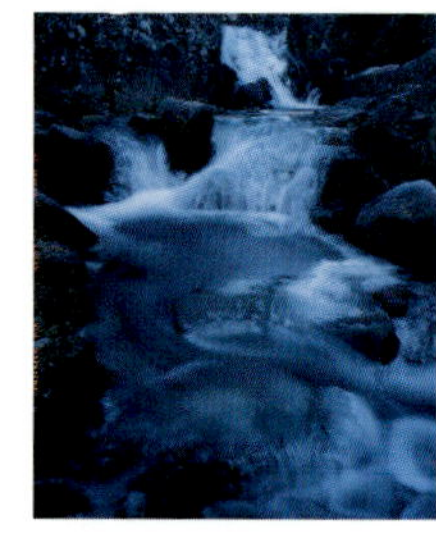

page 127
Frozen Waterfall,
Glencoe

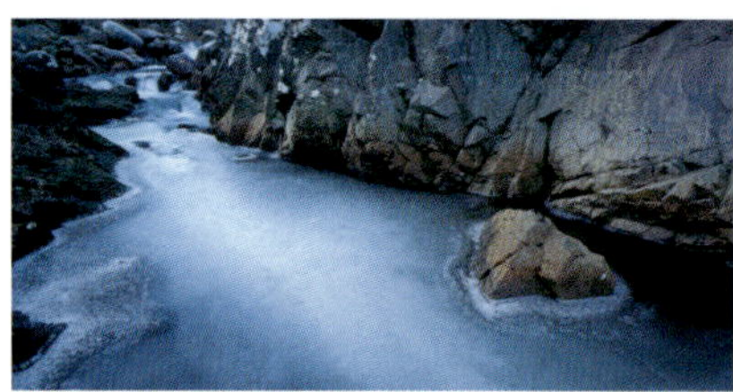

page 128–9 Frozen River, Glencoe

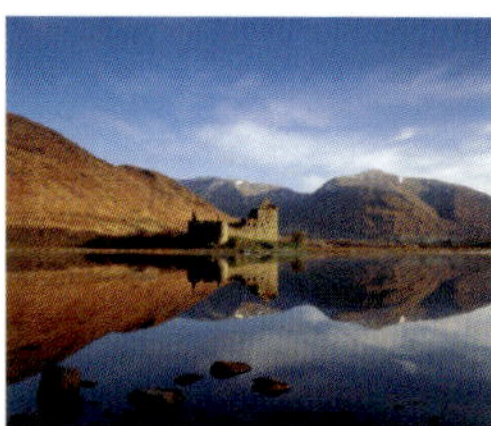

page 131 Kilchurn
Castle, Loch Awe

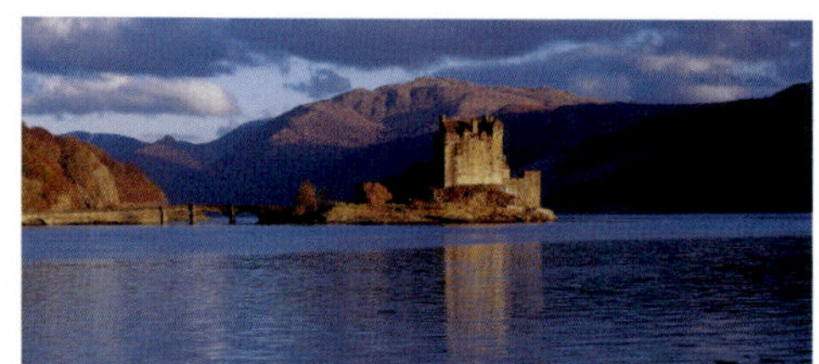

page 132 Eilean Donan Castle

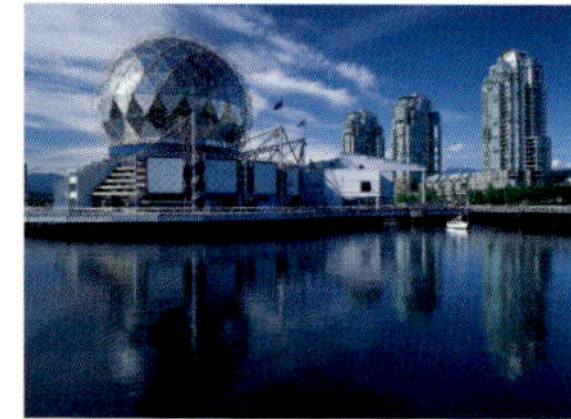

page 133
Science World, Vancouver,
Canada

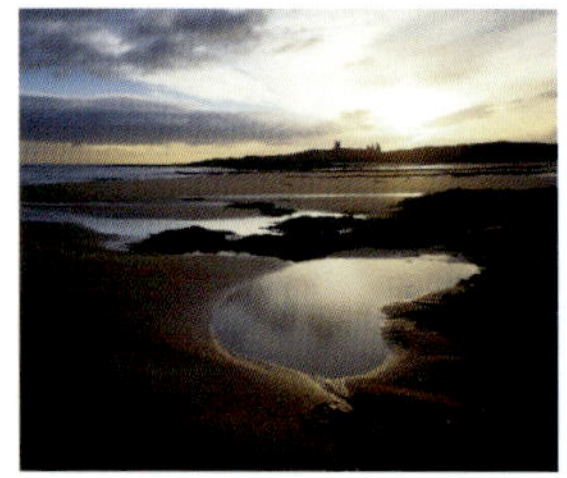

page 133 Dunstanburgh

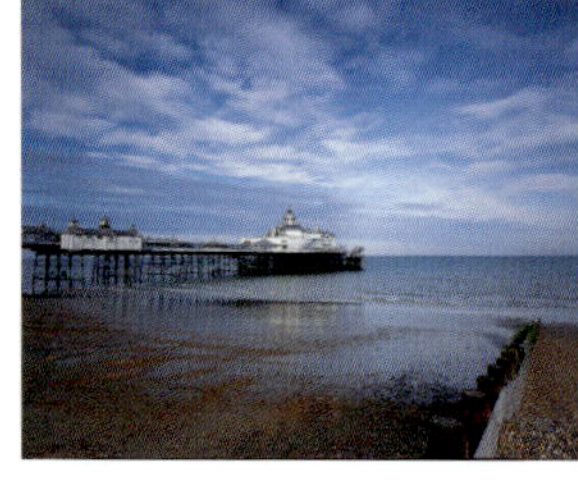

page 134 Eastbourne Pier,
East Sussex

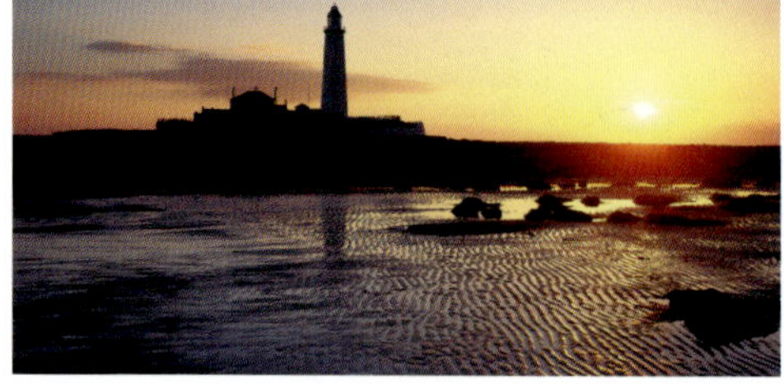

page 134–5 St Mary's Lighthouse, Tyneside

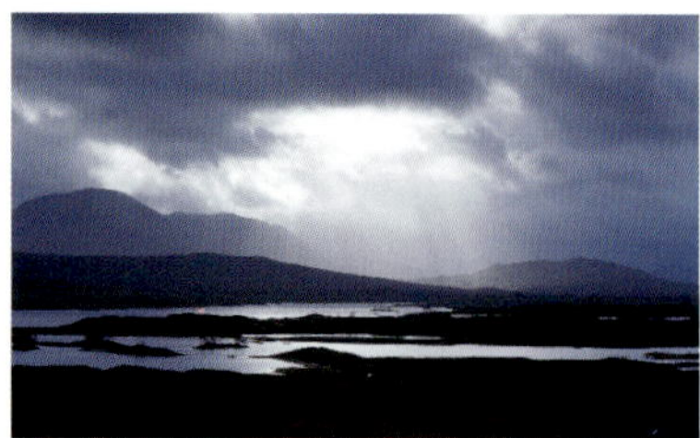

page 136 Loch Laidon, Scotland

 PHOTOGRAPHING WATER IN THE LANDSCAPE

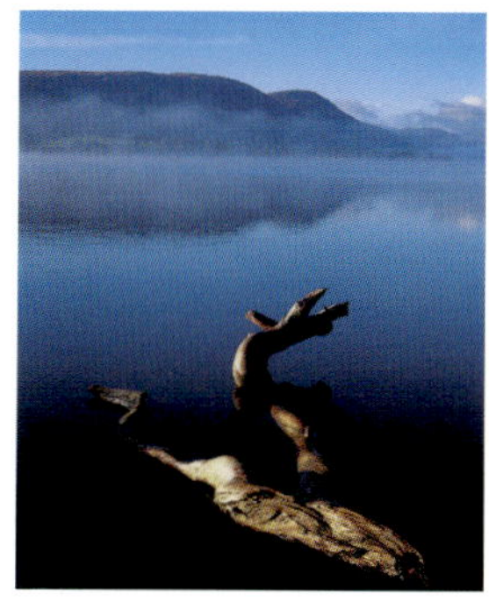

page 137
Driftwood in Ullswater

page 138 Boathouse on Ullswater

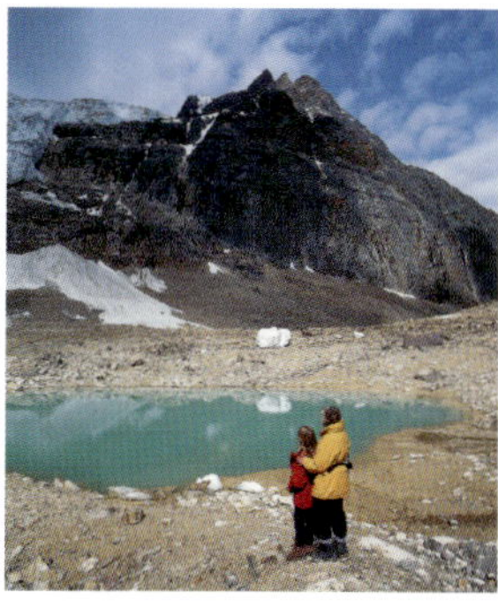

page 139
Angel Glacier, Canada

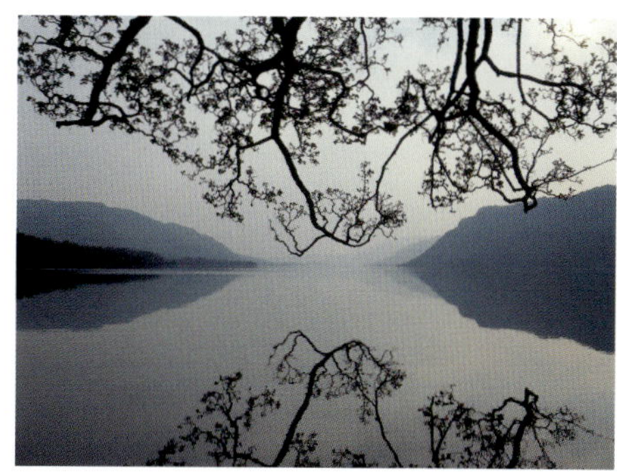

page 140 Morning Reflections, Ullswater

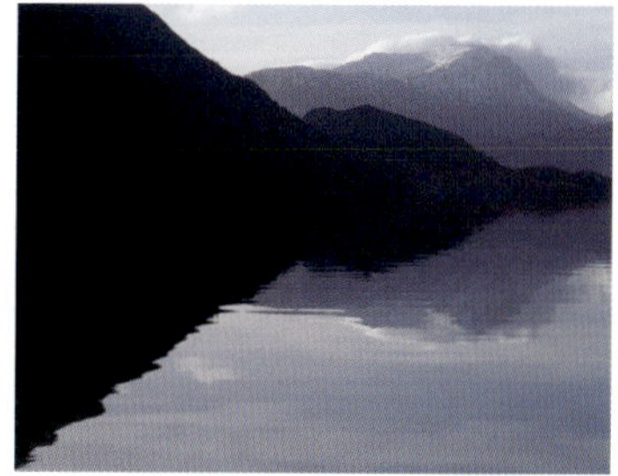

page 141
Graphic Monochrome, Ullswater

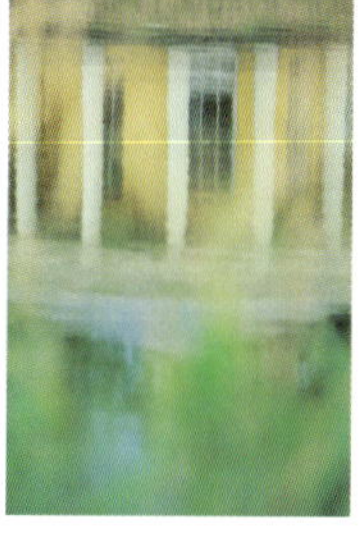

page 145
Romantic
Reflections

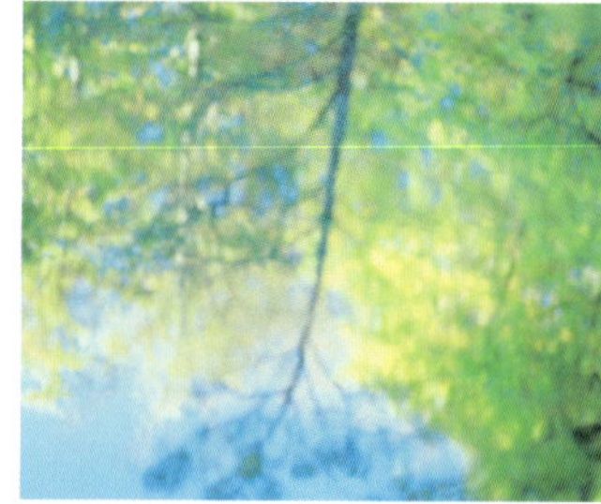

page 147 Trees in Watercolour

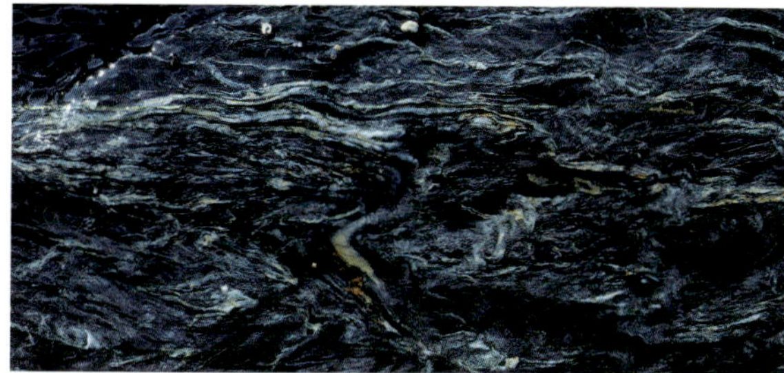

page 148–9 Abstract Wet Rock, St Michael's Mount

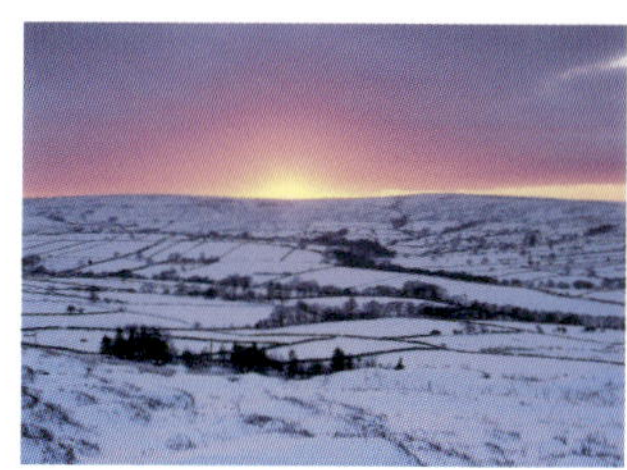

page 150–1 Moors Sunset
and Snow near Castleton

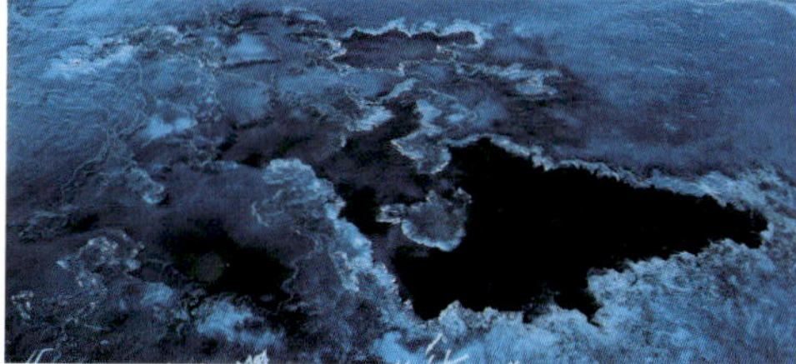

page 152 Frozen Stream

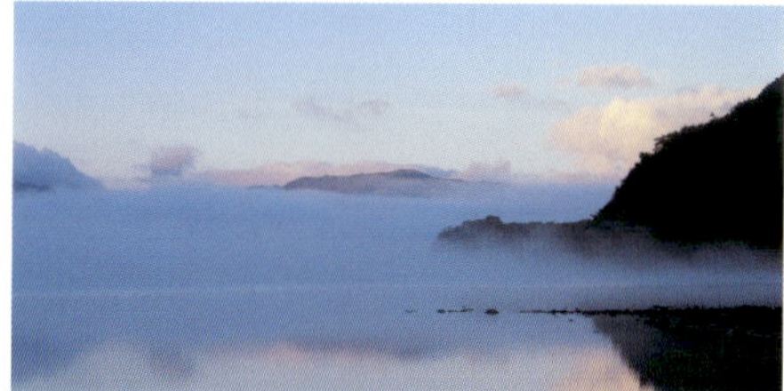

page 153
Misty Morning, Ullswater

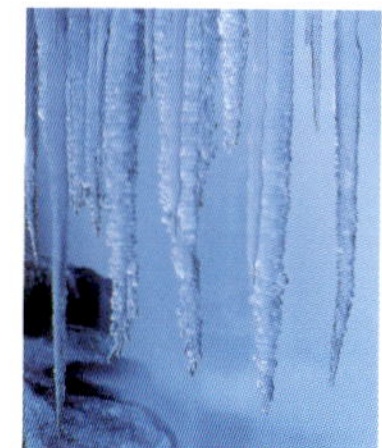

page 153
Icicles

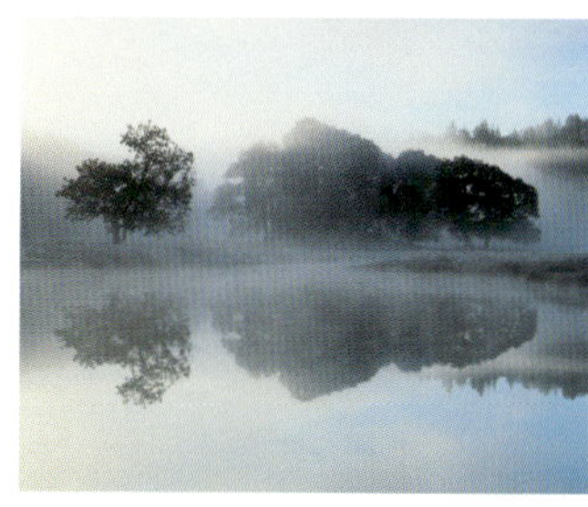

page 155 Morning Mist

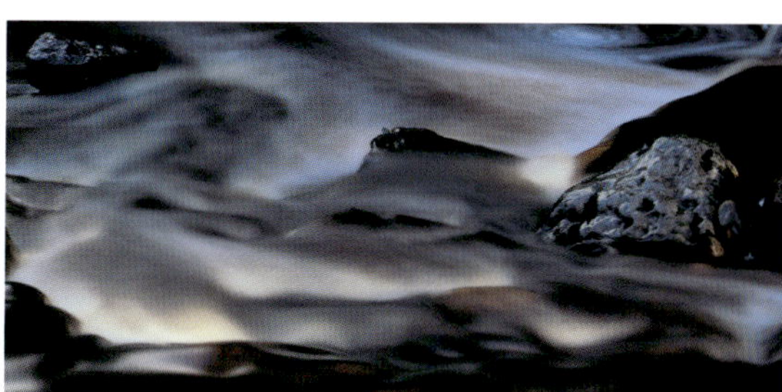

page 156–7 River and Rocks

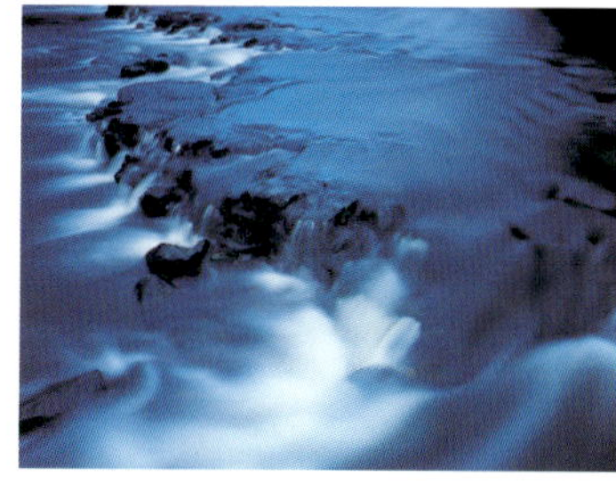

page 158 'Rhapsody in Blue'

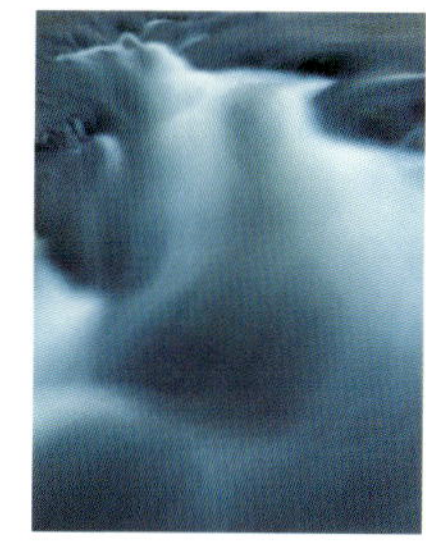

page 159 Pattern
in the Flow of the
River Ure

Index

Rothko, Mark 89

rule of thirds 118–19, 123, 135

rules 87, 118–19, 122–3, 135

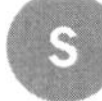

Saltwick Bay 50, 79, 91, 112–115

schools 88

screwdrivers 41

second light 71, 95, 100, 145

second-hand equipment 45, 65

self-timers 40

selling cameras 45

sensor speed 29

shade 110–11

shadow 50, 100, 103, 131

shutter speeds 16, 34, 40–1, 48–50,
    56–8, 66, 87, 91, 159

sidelighting 102–3

silhouettes 82, 100, 104–5, 141

simplicity 119, 138

single-lens-reflex (SLR) cameras
    18, 24, 62

skies 34, 36–9, 54–5, 59, 65, 66–8,
    74–5, 82–3, 90, 96, 98, 100, 104–5,
    110–1, 112–5, 140, 150–1, 158

snow 150

software 29

spirit levels 38, 41

St Bees 26-27, 90

stops 49, 65–6, 68, 100

stopwatches 42, 56

sun-positioning compass 42

super-wideangle lenses 32–4, 86,
    124–5, 136, 148

Sutcliffe, Frank Meadow 80

talks 88

texture 100–3, 111, 123, 127, 139–41,
    144–5

themes 84, 150

through-the-lens (TTL) metering 18,
    35, 51–2

tides 160

tide tables 112

tours 88

tripods 38, 40–1, 56, 80, 94–5,
    103, 126

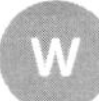

warm-up filters 34, 65, 74–5, 111

waterfalls 17, 49, 50, 86, 98, 124,
    126–7, 153

waterproof sheets 41

weather conditions 82, 85, 94, 98–100,
    136, 150–7, 160

West Wycombe Park 145

white balance (WB) 22, 26, 75

wideangle lenses 30, 124–5, 136, 148
    see also super-wideangle lenses

Williams, Annabel 87

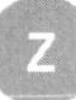

zoom lenses 31

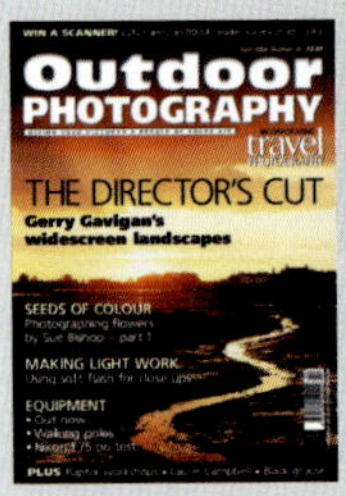

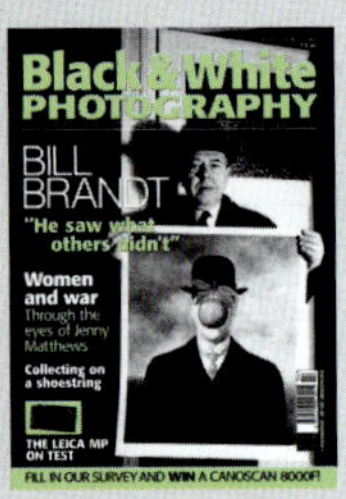

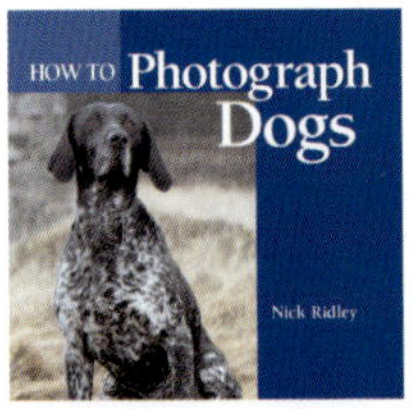

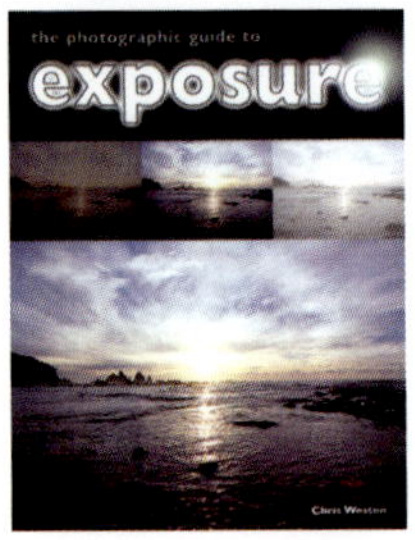

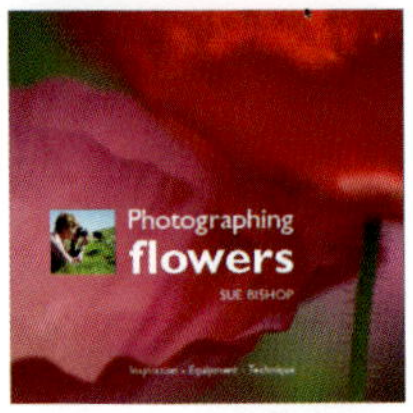

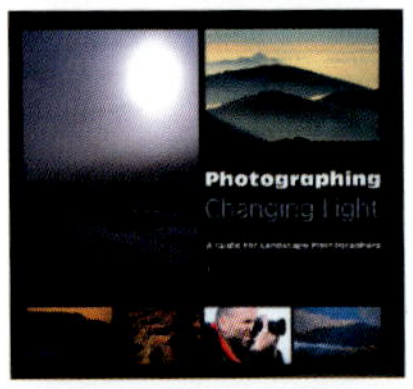

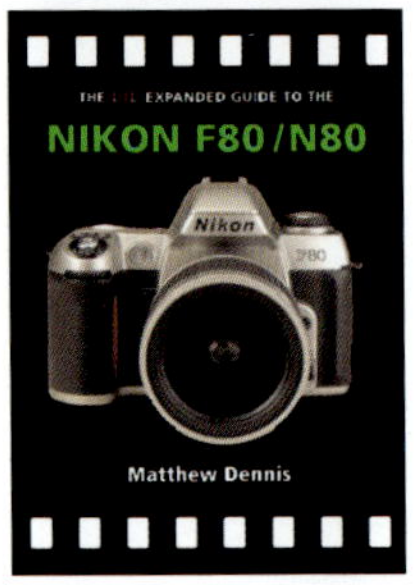

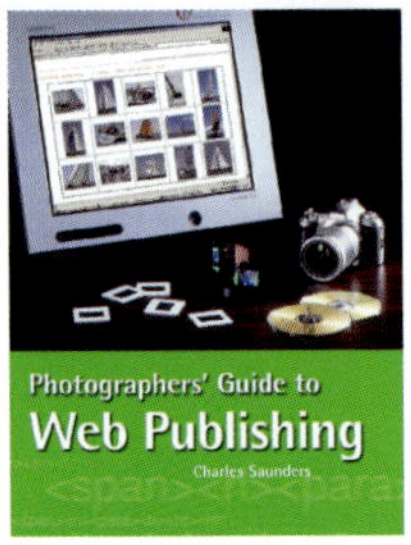